Terror in the Desert

Terror in the Desert
Dark Cinema of the American Southwest

BRAD SYKES

McFarland & Company, Inc., Publishers
Jefferson, North Carolina

LIBRARY OF CONGRESS CATALOGUING-IN-PUBLICATION DATA

Names: Sykes, Brad, 1975– author.
Title: Terror in the desert : dark cinema of the American southwest / Brad Sykes.
Description: Jefferson, North Carolina : McFarland & Company, Inc., Publishers, 2018 | Includes bibliographical references and index.
Identifiers: LCCN 2018005620 | ISBN 9781476672410 (softcover : acid free paper) ♾
Subjects: LCSH: Horror films—History and criticism. | Thrillers (Motion pictures)—History and criticism. | Southwestern States—In motion pictures. | Motion pictures—United States—History.
Classification: LCC PN1995.9.H6 S96 2018 | DDC 791.43/6164—dc23
LC record available at https://lccn.loc.gov/2018005620

BRITISH LIBRARY CATALOGUING DATA ARE AVAILABLE

ISBN (print) 978-1-4766-7241-0
ISBN (ebook) 978-1-4766-3132-5

© 2018 Brad Sykes. All rights reserved

No part of this book may be reproduced or transmitted in any form or by any means, electronic or mechanical, including photocopying or recording, or by any information storage and retrieval system, without permission in writing from the publisher.

Front cover: The mysterious John Ryder (Rutger Hauer) waits for his next victim in *The Hitcher*, 1986 (author's collection)

Printed in the United States of America

*McFarland & Company, Inc., Publishers
Box 611, Jefferson, North Carolina 28640
www.mcfarlandpub.com*

For Josephina
and my parents,
Michael and Linda Sykes

Acknowledgments

This book would not have been possible without the generous support and assistance of the following people:

Thanks to Raul Flores, Brad Heath, Martin Leggett, Sean Lynch, Brian Mattoni, Bryan Moose, Osvaldo Neto and Kris Winters for helping me track down some of the hard-to-find but essential titles for this book. Also, thanks to Tony Nittoli at Eddie Brandt's Saturday Matinee for combing the archive for those all-important stills.

A special thanks to desert terror filmmakers and actors I've had the opportunity to work and socialize with over the years: Larry Brand, Tony Hickox, C. Thomas Howell, Jeff Leroy, Geoffrey Lewis, Peter Locke, Jim Metzler, Mircea Monroe, Ted Newsom, Steve Railsback, Stacy Randall, David Schmoeller, Scott Spiegel, Tim Thomerson, Joe Unger, Duane Whitaker, Jay Woelfel, and, especially, Jeff Burr—for your contributions to the genre and for the inspiration you've given me in my own writing/directing career.

Thanks to script guru Adam Novak for invaluable notes on the first draft of the manuscript, and for the sage advice on how to approach publishers.

Thanks to my parents, Mike and Linda, for instilling a love of books and movies in me from an early age and always being supportive of my creative endeavors over the years.

And, lastly, extra special thanks to Josephina, for encouraging me to embark on such an epic project and for all your creative contributions to *Terror in the Desert*, big and small, throughout the researching, writing, and editing process. I couldn't have done it without you.

Table of Contents

Acknowledgments vi

Introduction: Keep Your Eyes on the Road! 1

1. A Thousand Ways to Kill You — 7
2. A Human Volcano of Unpredictable Terror! — 20
3. California Screaming — 31
4. Highways to Hell Part I: Death Drivers — 78
5. Highways to Hell Part II: Killers on the Road — 99
6. Highways to Hell Part III: Murder Machines — 115
7. The Good, the Bad and the Satanic — 125
8. Gargoyles and Graboids — 158
9. Desert After Dark — 182
10. Franchising Fear — 198
11. Indie Invasion — 226
12. New Blood — 259

Afterword: The Road Ahead 279

Appendix: Filmography 283

Bibliography 294

Index 295

Introduction:
Keep Your Eyes on the Road!

"People out here in the desert just go bonkers for some damn reason."—
Ed, *U-Turn*

For over half a century, desert terror movies have been scaring audiences at drive-ins, multiplexes, and television screens across America—and all over the world. Distinguished primarily by their atmospheric Southwestern locations, shocking storylines and bizarre characters, these idiosyncratic films branch out in a multitude of directions, often mixing elements from multiple genres (horror, film noir, road movie) into one-of-a-kind cinematic oddities. Over the years, desert terror films have embraced a wide range of subjects and styles, including cult horror films (*The Hills Have Eyes*, *The Hitcher*), crowd-pleasing franchises (*Tremors*, *From Dusk Till Dawn*), and quirky auteur fare (*Natural Born Killers*, *Lost Highway*); as a result, many of these films have escaped both proper classification and subsequent critical analysis. But the sheer number of desert terrors in existence (hundreds have been produced since the mid–1960s), as well as their cultural and historical significance, demands that desert terror be recognized as a separate genre with its own distinctive archetypes, themes, imagery and subcategories. *Terror in the Desert* is an attempt to unite, for the first time, all of the many desert terror films that have appeared over the years, from the very first desert terror movie, 1963's low budget, black-and-white thriller *The Sadist*, to recent releases like *Bone Tomahawk* and *Nocturnal Animals*.

My own personal love of desert terror films began in the mid–1980s, when I first caught *The Hitcher* on cable television. A dark, relentless story of a young motorist tormented (for no apparent reason) by a murderous yet enigmatic hitchhiker, *The Hitcher* had a greater psychological depth than any horror film I'd seen up till that point, and it was more disturbing than a simple thriller. It also possessed a unique and memorable setting: an ominous yet beautiful landscape of empty highways and desert vistas which helped the film stick in the mind long after the end credits had rolled. Soon afterward, I bought a VHS of *The Hills Have Eyes* from the music store in our local mall. Another essential desert terror film, *Hills*' intense, brutal tale of a "nice" American family besieged by a clan of cannibals in the middle of the Nevada desert lacked *Hitcher*'s slickness, but in its own way, the film's down-and-dirty, documentary style approach was equally effective in conveying sheer terror. Perhaps even more than *Hitcher*, the film derived much of its impact from its openly hostile, and often physically dangerous, desert setting of rocky peaks and desolate stretches of arid wasteland populated by venomous wildlife.

John Ryder (Rutger Hauer) stalks his prey in *The Hitcher* (1986).

After the one-two punch of *Hitcher* and *Hills*, I found myself increasingly drawn to weird, disturbing, violent movies set in the Southwest; *White of the Eye, Sonny Boy, Ghost Town, Near Dark, Far from Home* and *Highway to Hell* all helped develop my taste for desert terror. Not only was I increasingly aware how much these films stood apart from other horror or even accepted cult films, I also began noticing various thematic similarities between them. In the early '90s, around the same time I began studying film production at Boston University, desert terror exploded into the mainstream. The serial killer/road movie *Kalifornia* hit theatres a few months into my freshman year, followed by the even wilder *Natural Born Killers* the following summer. I saw *NBK* four times during its theatrical run, along with *From Dusk Till Dawn, Breakdown, Lost Highway, U-Turn* and a plethora of direct-to-video, noirish psychothrillers (*Eye of the Storm, Ultraviolet, Nature of the Beast*), all of which further cemented my commitment to desert terror.

After graduation, I embarked on my own Westward journey (minus the cannibals or killer hitchhikers) to Los Angeles, where I gained exposure to older desert terrors (*Hex, Barn of the Naked Dead, The Velvet Vampire*) at midnight shows or on bootleg videotapes before occasionally decamping to Mojave to write and direct a few of my own contributions to the genre. Wherever I went, desert terror seemed to follow me. I met my future wife on the set of a horror western; years later, she and I made a film starring *Hitcher* star C. Thomas Howell. All the while, desert terrors continued appearing in every form imaginable, from microbudget thrillers (*Hell's Highway*) to slicker indies (*Reeker, The Canyon*) to big-budget studio remakes of *Hitcher* and *Hills*—the two films that got me hooked in the first place.

Despite my nearly thirty-year obsession with desert terror, it was not until recently that I took the decision to write this book. From the start, my three main goals were: 1) to identify desert terror as a specific genre and explore its unique qualities, 2) examine its cinematic, historical and sociological origins, various themes, and development, and 3) categorize and critique every desert terror film ever made in one comprehensive volume. As with any large-scale creative undertaking, the depth and scale of the project soon outgrew its original ambitions. My initial list of films to cover nearly tripled as I discovered a wealth of obscurities, including (but not limited to): regional exploitation (*Blood Shack, Werewolves on Wheels*), made-for-TV terror (*Dying Room Only, The China Lake Murders*), shot-on-video epics (*High Desert, Ghost Gunfighter*), VHS-only horrors (*Blood Frenzy, The Oasis*) and legendary "lost" movies like *The Brave* (which I first rented as a bootleg tape from the sadly now-defunct Jerry's Video Rerun in Los Feliz) and *Dark Blood*. Many of these were hard to track down but most were well worth the effort, filling in crucial gaps in an ever-expanding filmography. In the process of researching the genre's roots, I also discovered dozens of significant "precursor" films—silents, early horror westerns, noirs, and sci-fi B-movies—that preceded and eventually led to the production of the first spate of desert terror films in the '60s and early '70s.

Pluto (Michael Berryman) is just one of the cannibalistic clan in *The Hills Have Eyes* (1977).

Armed with dozens of newly unearthed titles, I traced the growth of desert terror over five decades, a process which challenged and often redefined my preconceived ideas about the genre. The term "desert terror" refers to a film's primary setting and subject matter, but it rarely summarizes the full depth or detail of its creative content. Even the most technically inept or crassly commercial of these films grapple with uniquely American themes and conflicts—such as self-reinvention, the romance of the road (and its counterpart, the nightmare of being stranded in "the middle of nowhere"), the dissociative effects of rural isolation, environmental concerns, Native American issues, and deconstruction of western myths—in personal, idiosyncratic ways. Like the westerns and film noirs that contributed to its development, desert terror is a genre that could only have been conceived in America—and deserves the same consideration as its cinematic forebears. Desert terrors tend to be more artistically and thematically progressive than their straight horror and thriller contemporaries, with unexpected detours off the usual genre paths that make them fascinating and unpredictable. Appropriately for a genre based in road mythology, in desert terror films it's often the journey, not the destination, that's important.

In charting the development of the desert terror genre, I have developed a structure

Grace (Jennifer Lopez) seduces Bobby (Sean Penn) in Oliver Stone's postmodern noir *U-Turn* (1997).

that is both chronological and thematic. The book's main structure follows a chronological order, beginning with the earliest examples of the genre (*Greed*) and ending with recent releases like *Nocturnal Animals*. Each chapter, however, bears a theme that illustrates the variations within desert terror and demonstrates how the genre has evolved over the years due to social, economic, and political changes as well as stylistic and technical transitions within the movie industry. The first chapter discusses those films that precede *The Sadist* (horror westerns, 1950s sci-fi, film noir), while *The Sadist* itself (the original desert terror film) warrants its own separate chapter. The seven chapters that follow examine those desert terrors made between 1963 and 1999. The first of these, "California Screaming," focuses on land-locked "stranded scenarios," often set within the borders of a small town or the desert itself. "Highways to Hell" covers road thrillers and encompasses three separate sub-groups (death drivers, hitcher-killers, and murder machines), each of which receives its own chapter. Western and Native American–themed horror films concern the fifth chapter, while the next focuses on more fantasy-oriented "creature features." The seventh chapter specifically concerns desert-set vampire films. The final three chapters of the book, which examine twenty-first century desert terrors (from 2000 through 2016), are divided between studio and independent releases. For easier reading, and to better chart the development of each category, the films in each chapter are ordered sequentially, from oldest to most recent.

Master vampire Jan Valek (Thomas Ian Griffith) rises from a desert grave in *Vampires* (1998).

Throughout this volume, my primary intention is not to critique so much as to shed light on a wide swath of movies that have been neglected or dismissed over the years. Many of my favorite movies are desert terrors, and I honestly believe that most of the films profiled in these pages—flaws and all—have something to offer the viewer. Most judgments are based on a film's success within the desert terror genre (i.e., how well setting is incorporated into the narrative, if the story offers any new twists on familiar themes, etc.), with additional focus given to production circumstances, shooting locations, connections to other desert terror films, etc. It was a pleasure to visit (or revisit, in many cases) all these films, and hopefully that enthusiasm can be felt in the text.

I'm sure my final selections will inspire debate, but throughout the process, I've preferred to overstuff my trunk rather than leave a stray title by the roadside. Some of the desert terrors examined here will be familiar to the well-read horror or cult movie fan, while many others have yet to be written about at all, especially in the present context or with this degree of attention. Due to desert terrors' U.S.-based locations and themes, I have elected to focus only on films that are American-financed and shot on location in the United States. Occasional exceptions apply (*Sonny Boy*, for example, is Italian-financed, but was filmed entirely in New Mexico with an American writer, director, and cast), with special leniency granted to sequels or remakes (the *From Dusk Till Dawn* sequels or the *Hills* remake, for example), which have roots in U.S.-produced originals. Within the realm of domestic productions, I have also omitted the majority of post-apocalyptic flicks made in the '80s (which would mostly be categorized as sci-fi/action films and have received ample coverage elsewhere), the desert-set action thrillers of the '90s (most of which lack any overtly shocking or terrifying content) and rural horror flicks featuring off-the-beaten path scenarios (such as *The Texas Chainsaw Massacre* or *Tourist Trap*), which lack the appropriate desert topography necessary for inclusion in this book.

Now, it's time to journey through over sixty years of cinematic craziness with this book—written in bloodstains, gunpowder, and burnt rubber—as your guide. So, buckle up, put on your shades, and, as Tommy Howell wrote on my *Hitcher* poster, "Keep your eyes on the road!"

It's going to be a hell of a ride.

1

A Thousand Ways to Kill You

"It's alive, and waiting for you. Ready to kill you if you go too far. The sun will get you, the cold at night. A thousand ways the desert can kill."—John Putnam, *It Came from Outer Space*

Since the early days of American cinema, the deserts of the Southwest have fascinated both filmmakers and audiences alike. Photographically, the desert offers an impressive array of natural imagery—awe-inspiring canyons that descend deep into the earth, striking rock formations, rippling sand dunes, and seemingly infinite salt flats—more visually impressive than any other part of the country. Historically, the desert is also a constant reminder of our bloody, not so distant frontier past, as long-abandoned ghost towns (some of which now function as tourist attractions) and Native American pictographs still haunt the dusty valleys of the West. The more unpopulated of these wild, rugged landscapes reach even further back in time to invoke a prehistoric era, as well as a possible apocalyptic future. Exotic foreign lands, alien planets, or even internalized dreamscapes have all been depicted on film by the desert's unique topography.

Alongside its breathtaking beauty, the desert has always carried a strong element of real-life danger and death. It is a harsh, unforgiving world of physical extremes, with broiling days followed by frigid nights. Its indigenous life forms are lethal predators: wolves, tarantulas, rattlesnakes. The minimal human population consists mostly of tough-minded, individualistic locals and urban expatriates with colorful pasts, each with his or her personal reasons for rejecting civilization. Tales of murder, disappearances, or travelers simply expiring after getting "lost" without proper supplies are not uncommon, and have plagued the desert since the time of the first settlers and continue today. Despite its proximity to the cities, the desert is a world apart from civilization, equally frightening and intriguing to curious visitors. In many ways, it's a refreshing escape from of an overdeveloped, homogenized, increasingly tech-reliant America, but one that should be approached with a degree of caution.

Desert terror films have traded on these traditions of fear—along with inventing plenty of new, even more horrific scenarios—for over fifty years. Within the genre, several major subcategories exist. Contemporary tales of small town insanity and road thrillers derive their inspiration from true crime cases published in books and newspapers, while supernatural westerns and stories of Native American vengeance draw from historical accounts or tribal legends. Other desert terrors incorporate sci-fi and fantasy elements—aliens, vampires, and even werewolves—into their Southwestern landscapes. Despite a tremendous amount of diversity within the genre, all these films feature disturbing content and rugged, otherworldly desert settings. The best desert terrors merge narrative and location so well that it is impossible to separate the two; lesser entries use the desert backdrop to lend visual appeal to an otherwise pedestrian storyline.

Although the desert terror genre didn't emerge fully formed until the early 1960s, its cinematic roots date back nearly a hundred years, to the silent era. During the motion picture industry's early days, filmmakers were quick to capitalize on Southern California's naturally arid and rocky landscapes, particularly those found in the San Fernando Valley and its immediate environs. Most of these early desert-set films were westerns, an enormously popular genre whose narratives were based on relatively recent history. Dozens of "movie ranches" were constructed throughout the Valley and later, in other Southwestern states such as Arizona; many still function today. Southern California's deserts and dunes also stood in for more exotic locales like North Africa and the Middle East in romantic dramas like *The Sheik* (1921) and *The Son of the Sheik* (1926), and Biblical epics like Cecil B. DeMille's *The Ten Commandments* (1923), fragments of whose massive sets lie buried beneath northern California's Guadalupe Dunes. All these films, regardless of genre or setting, focused almost exclusively on the desert's ravishing pictorial qualities.

Erich Von Stroheim's silent epic *Greed* (1924) was the first feature film to use the desert in a more realistic and transgressive way. Based on Frank Norris' 1899 novel *McTeague*, Von Stroheim's masterpiece (which was infamously cut from eight to under two hours by its studio prior to release) tells the cautionary tale of two friends, McTeague (Gibson Gowland) and Marcus (Jean Hersholt), undone by a fateful lottery win, which results in a chain of tragic events. The film's climactic sequence depicts Marcus' pursuit of his former friend through the infernal flatlands of Death Valley, where the two eventually have their final confrontation. One can almost hear flesh sizzling as the exhausted, sunburned McTeague leads his horse over the cracked earth, avoiding attacks from rattlesnakes and Gila monsters as the sun blazes overhead. By the time the equally weary Marcus finally catches his prey, both men's horses have succumbed to the desert, and a dwindling water supply insures certain death for both men, as well. In a weakened, desperate struggle, the older man overpowers the younger, but it's an empty victory. The existential final shots show McTeague handcuffed to the dying Marcus, the two of them bound together by their own obsessions in the middle of an infinite desert plain.

Spanning just twenty minutes, *Greed*'s Death Valley sequence represents the cinematic debut of the type of material that would eventually be termed "desert terror." Von Stroheim's insistence on location shooting was highly unorthodox for the time, but resulted in some truly hellish visuals and a queasily believable pair of performances (indeed, Hersholt was reportedly hospitalized for internal bleeding during the Death Valley shoot). Death Valley is expertly captured, achieving a savage beauty in the film's final five minutes, especially in the oft-referenced wide shots of the two men framed by an endless horizon. While the novel is technically set in the previous century, the film (particularly the final sequence) achieves a contemporary, if not timeless, feel thanks to Von Stroheim's accent on realistic performances and documentary-style visuals. Both men's loss of humanity, exacerbated by the harsh, spare setting, is profoundly felt, and would become one of the central themes of the desert terror genre.

As the sound era began, sinister images and darker themes began to infiltrate some of the studios' more conventional releases, beginning with the western genre. The early John Wayne–starrer *Haunted Gold* (1932) is generally considered the first horror western,

The friendship between Marcus (Jean Hersholt, standing left) and McTeague (Gibson Gowland, seated center) begins to sour in front of dinner guests (uncredited) in Erich Von Stroheim's silent masterpiece *Greed* (1924).

even though its "scary" elements are mostly played for laughs. Clichéd horror imagery (spooky lights in a cemetery, howling wolves) abounds as rancher John Mason (Wayne) rides into a nearly-deserted "ghost town" to claim ownership of an abandoned gold mine. Standing in his way are rival businessman Joe Ryan (Harry Woods) and a hooded "phantom," who supplies the film with many of its more overtly spooky scenes before being unmasked in a predictable, and decidedly non-supernatural, conclusion. A remake of the "lost" silent western *The Phantom City* (1928), *Haunted Gold* relies more on horseback pursuits and broad humor than spooky atmospherics, with a *Scooby Doo*–like plot that would be recycled in future efforts like *Phantom of the Range* (1936) and *Haunted Ranch* (1943). The film's biggest asset is its moody lensing by Nicholas Musuraca, who would go on to contribute his talents to essential film noirs like *Out of the Past* (1947) and desert terror prototype *The Hitch-Hiker*.

Released the same year as *Haunted Gold*, *Tombstone Canyon* (1932) features a "phantom killer" whose costume appears borrowed from one of the creepy leads of Universal's contemporary horror pictures. Doomed by the wooden performance of lead Ken Maynard, the film lacks even *Haunted Gold*'s occasional attempts at scariness, yet images of the black-clad killer creeping about the blindingly white rocks of the canyon occasionally achieve a strange, almost surreal poetry. The crudely made *The Rawhide Terror* (1934) also attempts to shock with its titular "raving maniac," a cave-dwelling strangler who lacks the quasi-supernatural origins or stylish wardrobe of either of the previous Euro-influenced Phantoms. The film is technically shoddy and schizophrenically plotted, but its killer's rugged appearance and deranged behavior (in one sequence, the titular villain converses with a poisonous lizard) point ahead to the outsider serial killer "stars" of future desert terror films.

The best of all these early efforts is *The Riders of the Whistling Skull* (1937), which moves further away from gothic traditions by drawing its storyline more directly from Southwestern ethnography and environments. During an expedition to find a legendary "lost city," several members of the party turn up dead or simply disappear before reaching the "whistling skull," a large, cranium-shaped cave inhabited by a cult of killer Indians. Directed by *Haunted Gold*'s Mack Wright, the film's horror elements are both less obvious and more effective than anything previously seen in horror westerns, such as when a roomful of Indian mummies unexpectedly spring to life. The Native American presence, if depressingly racist, lends the film a certain verisimilitude, as do the rocky desert locations that function as more than just a backdrop to the various action scenes. The Whistling Skull canyon itself (augmented by memorably creepy sound effects) achieves a careful balance between scenic beauty and foreboding atmosphere that would become the trademark of many future desert terrors.

Boasting the initial appearance of a vampire in an old west setting, Universal's *Curse of the Undead* (1959), is generally considered the first "official" horror western. The deaths of several young girls in a small frontier town coincide with the arrival of the black-clad, heavily accented Drake Robey (Michael Pate), a mysterious stranger who charms his way into the life of pretty heiress Dolores (Kathleen Crowley). Local preacher (and Dolores' would-be suitor) Dan (Eric Fleming) unearths the macabre truth about Robey, whose real name is Drago Robles (in a nod to Southwestern history, he was a Spanish landowner) and became a vampire after killing his brother years ago. After a series of spooky confrontations (a sequence where Robey stalks Dan at night is particularly suspenseful), Dan finally destroys his rival with a bullet imbued with a tiny wooden cross.

Universal's groundbreaking western/horror hybrid *Curse of the Undead* (1959), starring Kathleen Crowley (left), Eric Fleming (right) and Michael Pate (bottom), has yet to be released on any digital format.

Curse treats its supernatural elements more seriously than previous horror westerns, but overall the film is easily more western than horror, with the film's "programmer" origins felt in its limited setting, talky script, and straightforward visual style that lacks the sense of scope and on-location charm of earlier entries like *Whistling Skull* or *Tombstone Canyon*. Perhaps in an effort to downplay the horror elements as much as possible (the word "vampire" is uttered only once during the film), the filmmakers diverge from classic notions of vampirism; Robey walks in direct sunlight, resists baring fangs, and exhibits a world-weariness ("The dead don't bother me. It's the living that give me trouble," he groans) common to many of the post-modern vampires in future desert terrors. The result is a film that is both old-fashioned and progressive in equal measure.

While horror westerns were first to influence the development of desert terror, they were not the only style of films to play a role in the genre's creation. In the early fifties, a number of science fiction/horror "B-movies" invaded cinema screens across America, and some of the more memorable entries—like *It Came from Outer Space* and *Them!*—place their stories in the deserts of the Southwest. Though still trading in thrills and chills, these sci-fi/horror outings differed considerably from their period-set, less serious western counterparts, with present-day storylines driven by post–World War II anxieties about the consequences of atomic testing (which were mostly conducted in the deserts of Nevada), along with present-day fears of America's possible invasion by Communists. Owing to more modern filmmaking technology and studio backing, these productions

John Putnam (Richard Carlson) and Ellen Fields (Barbara Rush) search for extraterrestrial invaders in *It Came from Outer Space* (1953).

were technically superior and benefited from location shooting—much of it outdoors during the daylight—that focused extensively on the otherworldly qualities of the desert. Sci-fi/horrors were also the first films to directly comment on the desert and its distance from civilization, not only topographically but socially, which would become one of the key themes of the desert terror genre. To illustrate their points about how alien and deadly the desert could be, native species often feature in or, in some cases, even drive their storylines.

Universal's *It Came from Outer Space* (1953) was the first SF/horror film to take place entirely within a desert environment, and remains one of the best. After amateur astronomer John Putnam (Richard Carlson) witnesses a "meteor" crashing in a nearby mine, his exploration of the resulting crater turns up the remains of a spacecraft and its (mostly unseen) inhabitant before a landslide buries everything under a mound of rocks. Though his girlfriend Ellen (Barbara Rush) believes Putnam's strange account, no one else in the town is convinced. To facilitate the rebuilding of their spacecraft, the aliens (who are rarely glimpsed) begin abducting the townspeople (including Ellen) and assuming their forms. In a tense climax, Putnam is caught between the body-snatching aliens and an angry mob of locals as the "visitors" try and depart Earth.

Working from a story by Ray Bradbury, director Jack Arnold (*Creature from the Black Lagoon*) uses the potentially gimmicky 3-D process to bring the desert's unique landscape and its various features to life. In one sequence, Ellen is briefly scared by a spiny, twisted Joshua tree, which she mistakes for an alien. On a deeper level, the film explores the type of "outsider" who would choose to live in such an openly hostile, isolated environment. Putnam is described by residents of the nearby town as "individual and lonely," and his refusal to "settle down" with Ellen, along with his discredited theories about the spacecraft, further identify him as the classic desert terror anti-hero. Frustrated by the ignorance of the townspeople, Putnam declares: "The reason I came out here to the desert was to try and get away from that kind of thinking." Both visually and thematically, *It Came* remains one of the most intelligent, and well-crafted, desert terror influences.

Due to its use by the army for atomic testing (a period which would be revisited by the desert terror genre, time and again), the desert was also the also the ideal setting for a group of "giant creature" films, the first of which was the Warner Brothers release *Them!* (1954). The memorably eerie opening finds a little girl wandering alone in the desert, carrying a broken doll. Two cops accompany her to her trailer home, which has been torn apart by some terrible force; later, they find the local general store in shambles, its owner's body buried by the rubble. High-pitched chirping signals the arrival of "them"—giant ants created by "lingering radiation from the first atomic bomb." Atmospheric location photography, complimented by a spare soundtrack that highlights the howling desert wind, adds tremendously to the effectiveness of these early scenes. The film's action gradually expands beyond the desert to the sewers of Los Angeles, where the military finally destroy their *ant-versaries* in a fiery finale. The larger-than-life ant puppets are hard to take seriously, yet the closing coda sums up public concerns of the time: "When man entered the atomic age, he opened a door into a new world. What we eventually find in that world, nobody can predict."

One could have easily foreseen, however, the rash of similar films made in the wake of *Them*'s success, many of which were variations on its successful formula of gigantic beasties running (or, more likely, crawling) rampant over a desert backdrop. Universal's

Universal's *Tarantula* (1955) pits John Agar and Maria Corday against a giant arachnid.

Tarantula (1955), again helmed by Jack Arnold, was one of the first follow-ups, opening with a brief but striking shot of a hideously deformed man staggering through the desert before collapsing. The victim is traced to a scientist living alone in the desert whose experiments with radioactive isotopes have resulted in, among other abominations, an oversized, constantly growing tarantula. Instead of the puppetry of *Them*, *Tarantula* uses matte-style photographic effects, which range from semi-successful to blatantly phony. The film lacks the more consistently bleak desert atmosphere of earlier efforts, but still manages a few standout moments. During a romantic desert excursion, Dr. Matt Hastings (John Agar) and his female companion Stephanie (Maria Corday) marvel at the beauty of the environment before stopping at a large rock formation, described by Matt as "something from another life, serene, quiet, yet strangely evil." When Stephanie tries to figure out the cause of a sudden rockslide, Matt cuts her off, insisting, "You can't second guess the desert." Over the next few years, more desert-set SF/horrors played drive-ins to varying degrees of success, including Universal's final swipe at the form, the turgid killer rock flick *The Monolith Monsters* (1957), American-Independent's atomic-testing opuses *The Amazing Colossal Man* (1957), its sequel *War of the Colossal Beast* (1958), and, last but probably least, *The Beast of Yucca Flats* (1961), starring Ed Wood's favorite wrestler-turned-actor, Tor Johnson.

Both horror westerns and SF/horror contributed thematic and aesthetic elements to desert terror, but film noir was the most significant influence on the genre's eventual style, tone, and subject matter. A curious blending of German Expressionist visuals and Americans' emerging concerns over the dangers of city life, noir traditionally deals with urban environments and subject matter. A few crucial anomalies, however, managed to break through the usual boundaries to the rougher world of desert-based crime and suspense. Unlike horror westerns and SF/horror, which were largely derived from fictional sources, these desert noirs dispensed with escapist fantasy to tell violent, true-life stories that were often ripped from the headlines. Along with their tougher subject matter, desert noirs were often produced outside the traditional studio system, on smaller budgets and reduced schedules. Due to their content and production circumstances, these films attained a sense of realism that would have a profound effect on desert terror films to come.

Adapted from Robert Emmet Sherwood's popular stage play, *The Petrified Forest* (1936) opens with charming but self-destructive novelist Alan Squier (Leslie Howard) trudging alone through a barren desert landscape before arriving at the middle-of-nowhere Black Mesa Café, described as "miserable little service station in the middle of nowhere" by its principal employee, Gabby Maple (Bette Davis). Abandoned by a French mother who "couldn't live here" and controlled by a doltish father and old-time "pioneer" Gramp (whose main claim to fame is having once been shot at by Billy the Kid), "desert rat" Gabby longs to leave her humdrum life behind and indulge her artistic aspirations in her Gallic birth country. Sensitive intellectual Alan is in many ways her opposite; unencumbered by responsibility (or money), he drifts from one place to another without apparent purpose. Their budding attraction is interrupted by the sudden arrival of bank robber Duke Mantee (Humphrey Bogart), on the lam from a recent bank robbery. Mantee's choice of the café as a rendezvous point proves problematic, as a gathering sandstorm traps him there with a handful of clients as the authorities gradually close in. Alan, who sympathizes with the rough Mantee as "the last great apostle of rugged individualism," makes a bargain with the killer, which finally gives his life meaning and allows Gabby to pursue her dream.

Gabby (Bette Davis) and Alan (Leslie Howard) are alarmed by criminal Duke Mantee (Humphrey Bogart) in *The Petrified Forest* (1936).

Forest is primarily an interior piece, with the desert material limited to a sprinkling of exterior shots, but director Archie Mayo nevertheless sums up an authentic atmosphere throughout, lending the café a convincingly bleak ambience while mostly eschewing a musical score for the low drone of wind outside. Bogart's performance as Mantee (based on John Dillinger, and widely considered his breakthrough film role) is effective, but he doesn't show up until nearly halfway through the film, and even after he does, the script's tensions continue to have less to do with his threats against the various patrons than their own individual frustrations. In many ways, the film uses its hostage drama setup to comment on America's transition from the previous century's lawless ways to the more civilized yet emasculating contemporary era. Former college quarterback Boze frets over failing to make All-American, Gabby's father "plays soldier" as part of a laughable vigilante group, and frontier romantic Gramp welcomes "real old-time desperado" Duke's arrival, excited to "see some real killing." The climactic shootout provides some rat-a-tat action, but the film's bittersweet, unsettling finale focuses on self-sacrifice and broken dreams. Predating the noir boom by several years, *The Petrified Forest* is a significant work in the desert terror genre's formation, setting forth many of the character types (locals desperate to escape, self-destructive protagonists), themes (Squier's insistence on "survival of the fittest"), plot structures and conflicts which would come to define many ensuing desert terror films.

Marked Men (1940), a PRC programmer that is also known under its (more appropriate) television title, *Desert Escape*, is a more traditional, and simplistic, noir. Wrongfully accused Bill Carver (Warren Hull) escapes from prison and breaks free of the gangster who set him up, Joe Mellon (Paul Bryar), before traveling West to Arizona, where he camps in the desert before settling in nearby Tempe. Using an alias, Bill quickly joins the community and begins a burgeoning romance with his employer's daughter Linda (Isabel Jewell). Bill's past catches up to him, however, with the sudden appearance of Mellon's gang, whose botched bank robbery ends with a retreat to the surrounding desert. There, Bill must outsmart his former nemesis and clear his name while surviving broiling temperatures and inhospitable terrain. Overly talky and stiffly directed, *Marked Men* is chiefly distinguished by its opening and closing desert sequences, which were shot on location and contain the film's most memorable moments. Particularly compelling is the final act, which applies noirish twists and turns to *Greed*'s "survival struggle" climax. Interestingly, the film demonstrates a distinct ambivalence about its setting, as the desert becomes (at various times) both the perfect getaway and hell on earth. Bill's personal "desert escape" is largely one of self-reinvention, a theme that would recur in many subsequent desert terror films.

Another poverty row production of the era, Edgar G. Ulmer's minimalist masterpiece *Detour* (1945) is both a road movie and (as its title implies) a deviation from the form. Hitchhiking west to Los Angeles (a route which would be revisited in many subsequent desert terror films), down-at-heel piano player Al (Tom Neal) accepts a ride from Haskell, a bookie who drops dead of natural causes soon afterward. Worried about possible criminal implications, Al hides the body, assumes the dead man's identity, and continues his westward journey. Further complications ensue after he picks up Vera (the appropriately named Ann Savage) a tart-tongued hellcat of a femme fatale who knew Haskell, recognizes Al as a fake and gradually draws him further

Detour (1945) stars Ann Savage and Tom Neal as a pair of ill-fated travelers whose chance meeting leads to murder.

into her web of deceit. Despite rear-projection backgrounds that assure us we're in Hollywood, *Detour* is really a travelogue through one man's fevered memories, which ends not on the West coast, but in a world constructed and controlled by Vera, whose hateful yet somehow pitiable ghost haunts Al even after the credits roll.

Shot on the cheap (allegedly in one week!) by director Ulmer, *Detour* is the first proto-desert terror film since *Greed* to visualize the psychological possibilities of the desert. While Von Stroheim strove for (and achieved) documentary-style perfection, the cash-strapped Ulmer uses an even more interesting blend of stark realism (mostly for exteriors of Mojave gas stations and diners) and studio-based stylization (for most of the interior scenes). The resulting mix of styles works surprisingly well, and was subsequently adopted by many desert terrors, which often begin in reality, but find the characters lured off their original route by a "detour" that forces them into an alternate reality of physical and mental extremes. The film's nightmarish story structure also contains many story elements and themes—among them the perils of hitchhiking (and, conversely, offering rides to strangers), individual need for reinvention/rebirth, the promise of the West Coast—which would drive many desert terrors. Many films in the genre also adopted *Detour*'s narrative structure, which begins and ends on the road and comprises a closed loop existing outside of everyday experience. Ironically, the budgetary factors which Ulmer undoubtedly found limiting forced the filmmaker to create a new vocabulary of imagery and tone which would prove immensely popular, if not in noir, then certainly in desert terror.

The Devil Thumbs a Ride (1947), while not quite living up to its provocative title, offers a blunter, more realist take on *Detour*'s "hitchhiking horror" scenario. After robbing a bank in San Diego, wanted criminal Steve Morgan (Lawrence Tierney) grabs a ride with Los Angeles–bound traveling salesman Jimmy Ferguson (Ted North). While traveling up the coast, Morgan invites a female travelers Carol (Nan Leslie) and Agnes (Betty Lawford) to their group; the quartet eventually winds up in Laguna Beach, where an all-night party ends in several deaths. *Devil*'s slightly increased budget allows for more location shooting, yet the overly straightforward direction of Felix Feist (who previously teamed with Tierney for the true-crime pic *Dillinger*) lacks *Detour*'s psychological depth and doom-laden atmosphere. It's still a nasty little number, however, and features plenty of elements that would figure into many desert terror films; the narrative, which begins and ends on the road and adopts a roughly twenty-four hour timeframe, would become typical of many scripts, while Hollywood-bound Carol's "ambitions for pictures" lend the film an element of showbiz commentary that would also reappear in many subsequent desert terror films. Most significantly of all, its charming yet murderous "hitcher killer" antagonist would become one of the most popular character types in the desert terror genre.

The realist aesthetic pioneered by previous desert noirs—and, to a certain extent, sci-fi/horror, was pushed to another level by Ida Lupino's thumb-tripping terror tale *The Hitch-Hiker* (1953), whose strong, spare visuals and three-hander premise would have enduring impact on desert terror films. An opening card ensures the veracity of the events portrayed in the film: "This is the true story of a man and a gun and a car. The gun belonged to the man. The car might have been yours…. What you will see in the next seventy minutes could have happened to you. For the facts are actual." A montage of dead bodies and newspaper headlines sets up the film's unseen "hitchhiker murderer" before the film arrives on two traveling buddies, educated family man Gil (Frank Lovejoy) and bachelor Roy (Edmond O'Brien), on their way to a fishing trip in Mexico. Their trip is permanently altered after picking up Emmett Myers (William Talman), a hair-trigger felon on the run from police ("Yesterday the devil thumbed another ride," squawks a radio broadcast) and eager to cross the border. After various close calls and confrontations, the sadistic Myers is captured by authorities in Mexico thanks to clues left behind by the resourceful Gil.

Unlike previous desert noirs, *The Hitch-Hiker* is directly inspired by real-life events, in this case, the cross-country "killing spree" of Billy Cook, who claimed six lives over three weeks in 1950–51. The events of Cook's last few weeks—his kidnapping of two men, a border crossing, and his eventual capture and arrest—are presented with a fair amount of accuracy in Lupino's film. Character and place names are altered, but, for the most part, the film hews closely to the facts, to the extent of giving Myers a lazy eye, just like Cook. The result is a new level of realism in desert noir, with much of the action acquiring a "real time" quality that increases the level of tension. At the same time, Lupino emphasizes character at least as much as suspense; Gil and Roy are quickly developed with small but significant details, while Myers' dim world view is symbolized by a brief speech toward the end: "Nobody ever gave me anything, so I don't owe nobody. Folks were tough, don't need 'em … got what I wanted my own way." *The Hitch-Hiker*'s uncommon attention to character—and especially its (occasional) humanization of its villain—allows

In Ida Lupino's *The Hitch-Hiker* (1953), killer Emmett Myers (William Talman, standing left) takes vacationing friends Roy (Edmond O'Brien, middle) and Gil (Frank Lovejoy) on a deadly journey as a civilian (uncredited) looks on.

it to stand apart from many other noirs, and would be repeated by many desert terror films.

The Hitch-Hiker also contains some of the most evocative desert photography of any desert terror precursor film. From its first foreboding shots of Gil's car winding through the desert at night, the film ventures far beyond *Marked Men*'s solid location work to establish an unshakable atmosphere of isolation and abandonment key to the success of its twisting plotline. Daytime scenes achieve a harsh, almost existential, quality, as the three men travel a lonely, hostile path littered with deadly-looking rock formations. While Universal's SF/horror entries were first to take advantage of the cinematic power of such landscapes, *Hitch-Hiker*'s director of photography Nicholas Musuraca differs from the polished look of those films by imbuing breathtaking views with a gritty, high contrast texture that brings the audience closer to the "desert experience" than ever before. Despite its determinedly contemporary plotline, the film smartly addresses the desert's past, too, in sequences set in Spanish-speaking border towns and around an abandoned, old west–like mineshaft. Such historical references would play a significant role in future desert terror films, as well.

Equally important as its subject matter and forward-thinking approach is *The Hitch-Hiker*'s independent production circumstances. In a time when studios (both big and small) dominated the landscape, Lupino (best known as a studio actress) and her husband produced *The Hitch-Hiker* through their own company, Filmmakers Inc. (the film was released by studio RKO). The film earns further distinction as the first noir directed by a woman after its original director became sick, forcing Lupino to step in and direct the film herself. *The Hitch-Hiker*'s "outsider" status and progressive filmmaking approach predates the next decade's rise of independent and regional production, which would allow the desert terror genre to flourish.

Despite these advances, Lupino's film remains a product of censors of the time (who forced the filmmakers to shorten the number of murders shown in the film) and its own recalcitrance. Myers is more bark than bite; despite his threats ("You guys are gonna die—it's just a question of when"), he only strikes Roy a few times, and we never see him shoot anyone. Repeated TV-style cutaways to police tightening the net on Myers (which also spoil *The Devil Thumbs a Ride*) also disrupt the tension, and Myers' capture by the police feels a shade too easy after such a rough ride. For the early '50s (the movies were still seven years away from *Psycho*), however, *The Hitch-Hiker* is intense stuff, and a strong indicator of what kind of dark and twisted routes desert noir could take in the future.

Over three decades and a variety of superficially dissimilar films, the horror western, sci-fi/horror and film noir genres contributed equally to laying down the visual, stylistic, and thematic ground rules for what would eventually become known as desert terror. All three formative genres contributed distinct elements: horror westerns leant their historical perspective and explored new, edgier ways to present a darker take on old west–themed material, sci-fi horrors focused on the visual possibilities of the desert terrain and its inhabitants while commenting on current events in the region, and noir brought more contemporary, hard-edged stories told with greater attention to realism and with character. Ten years after *The Hitch-Hiker*, the first "official" desert terror film to see release was much more than the sum of all these influences, with several new twists to this formula—more adult content, stronger violence, heightened atmosphere, unpredictable plotting, social commentary and—most importantly—a genuine sense of shock and terror.

2

A Human Volcano of Unpredictable Terror!

"I'm givin' you fifteen more minutes to live, mister. If you don't want it, I'll blow your head off!"—Charlie Tibbs, Jr., *The Sadist*

In the decade since *The Hitch-Hiker*, seismic shifts had occurred within the American film industry. For years, cinema attendance had been down due to the increased popularity of television, and the studios' response—old-fashioned westerns, musicals, and costume dramas in Cinemascope—failed to connect with an increasingly younger, hipper audience. Independent mini-majors like American International or Allied Artists took advantage of this generational shift and achieved major success by producing cheaper, livelier pictures aimed at the teenage drive-in crowd. Most of these films, while still conservative in nature, were at least topical and represented an alternative to the studios' bloated epics.

The success of drive-in market resulted in the rise of a third group of films, the "regional independents," which would often fill out double or triple bills at rural drive-ins or urban grindhouses. Made far from the industry centers of New York or Los Angeles, these movies were often rougher around the edges, but what they lacked in dollars they made up for in quirkiness, a willingness to experiment and a fresh point of view. Characterized by an emphasis on location shooting, employment of local talent, and neophyte, envelope-pushing directors, these films often achieved a strong sense of realism, dealing with taboo subjects that neither the studios, nor the mini-majors, would touch. Many regional independents, such as *Carnival of Souls* (1962, Utah), *Blood Feast* (1963, Florida), and *Night of the Living Dead* (1968, Pennsylvania) went on to become certified cult classics.

Made on a $33,000 budget over two weeks in the small rural town of Newhall, California (about an hour north of Los Angeles), *The Sadist* (1963) was another significant regional independent of the era. The first outright horror picture from its makers, there was nothing in its credentials to suggest potential greatness. Producer Arch Hall, Sr., was a former B-Western bit player turned independent producer/distributor whose previous low-budget movies *The Choppers* (1961), *Eegah* (1962) and *Wild Guitar* (1962) had gone mostly unnoticed by audiences. Writer/director James Landis' resume was similarly undistinguished, consisting of a handful of unmemorable war films and westerns. The film's twenty-year-old star, Arch Hall, Jr., was more comfortable performing with his band The Archers than acting, with his screen contributions limited to playing crooner heartthrobs in his father's offbeat musical dramas. None of *The Sadist*'s participants, let alone audiences, could have suspected that this modest black and white thriller made on the deserts outside Hollywood would eventually be known as the very first desert terror film.

While previous horror westerns, sci-fi horrors, and noirs had explored the dangers of desert life, *The Sadist* was the first to combine (and elevate) aspects of all three "precursor" genres while adding new visual and thematic elements that would become quintessential aspects of modern desert terror. More than any previous desert thriller, *The Sadist* uses its isolated, dusty setting to make some startling observations about humanity. The film's societal commentary, which explores the troublingly short distance between civilization and savagery along the forgotten back roads of America, emerges fully developed for the first time and would be adopted by many future entries in the genre. The film's unapologetic focus on its amoral yet endlessly watchable "thrill killer" antagonists, whose outsider status and brutally transgressive acts set them far apart from the decidedly non-threatening Phantoms and supersized spiders of the past, was also prescient. The film's graphic levels of violence, sexual suggestiveness, unpredictable plotting, and postmodern sense of irony all went far beyond the safer, more traditional storylines of previous desert-based chillers. Visually, *The Sadist* also distinguished itself by creating an all-encompassing alternative world out of its desert-bound location, which dictates the story as much as any of the characters and operates on both a physical and psychological level. The result was the first entry in a genre which goes beyond the usual horror or thriller clichés into a shockingly believable world poised somewhere between nightmare and reality—a twisted soulscape which would become the exclusive province of desert terror.

Landis' film gets off to a confrontational start as an expressionistically-lit pair of eyes stare out of the darkness while a croaking voice-over (an uncredited Hall Sr.) threatens: "I have been hurt by others. And I will hurt them. I will make them suffer like I have suffered." As if shaking off a bad dream, the film quickly fades up on an innocuous daytime shot of a car driving along an isolated mountain road. It's sunny, arid, and deceptively calm; the same type of shot opens both *Night of the Living Dead* and *Carnival of Souls* before abject terror commences. Palpable tension sets in as the vehicle pulls into a dusty salvage yard full of rotting car bodies and rusty tool sheds. The occupants are a trio of high school teachers from the desert community of Lancaster, California—strapping Army vet Ed (Richard Alden), his middle-aged colleague Carl (Don Russell), and prudish Doris (Helen Hovey, actually a cousin of Hall Jr.)—headed for a Dodgers game and waylaid by a broken fuel pump. They're clean cut and overly formal with one another, especially Doris, who wears a virginal white dress and is careful to call Ed "Mr. Styles." Though contemporary, the abandoned junkyard gives off the ghost town vibe of previous horror westerns, with dust blowing continuously and low wind whistling on the soundtrack. "This back highway's good for time, but have car trouble and you got problems," says Ed, referencing the type of ill-advised shortcut, which would doom so many desert terror protagonists over the years.

As Ed and Carl fruitlessly search for the owner of the yard, commenting on their relatively good fortune ("We're lucky ... another few minutes and we'd have been in the desert"), the camera stalks them, often creatively framed through chains, pipes, or even broken glass, adopting the point of view of an off-screen menace. Most one-location films eventually become monotonous and stifling, but Landis and Hungarian émigré director of photography Vilmos Zsigmond (credited as "William Zsigmond" in his first American feature credit) work wonders with the salvage yard, picking out menacing details and off-kilter angles that create a strong sense of atmosphere and effectively make the location as much a character as Tibbs or his victims. The desert's indigenous (and deadly) wildlife makes an appearance as Doris jumps at the sight of a snakeskin, saying, "I can't stand snakes." Entering the main house on the property, Carl finds a table set for four, with two plates untouched. By the time he has informed the others of his discovery, it's too late for all of them.

A gun slowly rises into the foreground, aimed at the stranded motorists and encouraging the audience to identify with the (unseen) killer. Landis only reveals his villain's face after reaction shots from Ed, Carl, and Doris, then closes the deal with a menacing, low angle dolly toward Charlie Tibbs (Arch Hall, Jr.), who is accompanied his girlfriend, Judy (Marilyn Manning, who had previously appeared alongside Hall, Jr., in *Eegah*). With his jean jacket and greaser hairstyle, and her "tobacco road" floozy fashion, these two are instantly iconic, like the tawdry cover of a 1950s pulp novel suddenly come to life, with acting styles to match. Hall Jr.'s performance as Tibbs is the one the film ultimately hangs on, and it's one of a kind, propelling the film from one insane act after another till its crazed conclusion. A shocking about-face from his previous lightweight singing roles, Hall, Jr., abandons his guitar for a gun to effectively channel the stunted man-child at the heart of every mass murderer, one who "gets his kicks from hurting people." Landis' script refuses to investigate Tibbs' past in an even rudimentary fashion, expecting us to assume (based on the opening voice over?) that Tibbs was irreparably damaged by some unspecified childhood abuse and is now taking it out on others as an adult. With little motivation or backstory, Hall, Jr., relies on sheer force of will and personality to fashion the character into one of the vilest, craziest, most unpredictable screen heavies of the '60s—and the original desert terror "anti-hero."

The mentally underdeveloped, deaf-mute Judy registers equally as strongly as her boyfriend, despite virtually no dialog and less screen time. The news that their hostages are high school teachers manages to dredge up a bit of her troubled backstory. "We don't like schoolteachers, do we, Judy?" Tibbs teases as he rifles through Carl's wallet. "Teachers used to call Judy dumb … make fun of her … send her home crying." Tibbs strikes Carl, shattering his glasses and bloodying his face. It's the first act of violence in a film that is full of such moments that keep coming, even after you think the worst is over. As the senior member of the group, and the first to assert his profession, Carl represents not only education, but authority, making him the perfect target for Tibbs' frustrations. Clearly as sociopathic as Tibbs, Judy spends much of her screen time giggling at murder, stealing from the dead, and exhibiting a noticeable jealousy (and at times, emulation) of her closest competition, "nice girl" Doris. Without uttering a single word, Manning's coolly effective portrayal is equally as powerful as Hall, Jr.'s wild-eyed, manic posturing. Together, the psychotic pair set the standard for decades of larger than life yet horribly human desert terror villains.

"Remember reading last week about those brutal killings in Arizona?" Ed says, alluding to the couple's real-life inspiration. Like *The Hitch-Hiker*, *The Sadist* is based on the exploits of real-life criminals, in this case Charles Starkweather and his teenage girlfriend Caril Ann Fugate, who committed eleven murders during a two-month, cross-country crime spree between December 1957 and January 1958. Landis' approach to his murderous twosome, however, couldn't be more different than Lupino's; despite its title, *Hitch-Hiker*

2. A Human Volcano of Unpredictable Terror!   23

Charlie Tibbs (Arch Hall, Jr.) and his main squeeze Judy (Marilyn Manning) watch over their captives in *The Sadist* (1963).

clearly places its focus on Myers' hostages, but *The Sadist* enthusiastically makes Tibbs and Judy the primary focus of the film. A couple of truly marginalized, uneducated outsiders, they lack even the rudimentary polish or faux sophistication of Duke Mantee or Steve Morgan. Their darker, dirtier look (Tibbs has a tanned, almost Native American complexion, Judy has dark hair) automatically sets them apart from their blonde, Caucasian captives, and makes them more "at home" in the dusty salvage yard, even if they are the real intruders.

The film continues to push the boundaries of acceptability as Tibbs accompanies Doris to a water pump, where he launches into a litany of insults ("You think you're so much better than me. You called me inhuman. You called me an animal."), while suggestively stroking his knife as Doris wets a rag for Carl's wound. "How does it feel to be touched by dirt? Eat it, eat the dirt!" Tibbs yells as he presses Doris' face to the ground, rips her earrings from her ears, and tears at her dress. It's as close as *The Sadist* comes to a rape scene, and, without showing any nudity, is far more transgressive than any previous desert noir. The following shot, with Doris staggering through the salvage yard, dress ripped and dangling off one shoulder, face smudged and hair tousled, feels like the aftermath of a violation. Few words are exchanged after this incident, but the sexual tension between the "dirty" (and, like Clyde Barrow, likely impotent) Tibbs and frigid, virginal Doris continues to build until the very end of the film.

Tibbs presents Judy with the stolen earrings like a hunting trophy as a battered Doris rejoins the men. Finally losing his cool, Ed calls Tibbs by name for the first time and questioning his masculinity. After firing at Ed (and purposely missing), Tibbs forces the wounded Carl to his knees, gun aimed at his head. Tibbs proposes an infantile game where, upon finishing his bottle of soda pop, Carl's life will be over. Ed and Doris' plead with Tibbs to stop, citing his and Judy's families. "Her old man's dead and her old lady's a drunk" is Tibbs' typically nihilistic response as he gulps his soda. *The Hitch-Hiker* contains several scenes like this, yet ultimately shies away from the ugly outcome; *The Sadist* does not. In an unflinchingly graphic composition, Tibbs makes good on his threat, emptying his weapon point blank into Carl's bloodied face, smoke erupting from the barrel.

It's fitting that Carl should be the first of Tibbs' victims, as *The Sadist* is a study of not only generational divide, but, like many desert terrors to follow, class conflict. The three teachers are immediately presented as being socially and economically "superior" to people like Tibbs and his girlfriend (when Doris complains about how the yard is "greasy and dirty," Ed replies, "Not everyone can be white-collar workers."). It's a thoughtful response, but the point is made: these (upper) middle class characters have entered a blue-collar world where they do not belong, even before Tibbs makes his appearance. Carl is also described by Doris as having a "nice home, a lovely wife, two handsome children." Tibbs rips a photo of Carl's family to shreds before killing the man and leaving him dead in the dirt. With Carl's death, the film essentially kills off the '50s postwar "per-

Ed (Richard Alden) plans his next move during the climactic showdown of *The Sadist* (1963).

fect family" ideal that was already wearing thin by the '60s, and would implode completely just a few years after *The Sadist*'s release.

Famished after killing Carl, Tibbs asks Judy to get him another soda "and a pie, too." Now fully aware of what Tibbs is capable of, Ed and Doris stall for time while trying to facilitate an escape plan while Tibbs casually mentions how he and Judy have been getting around: by hitching rides and murdering the drivers. "Somebody'll pick us up. They always have," he laughs while pointing the gun directly at the camera. When two motorcycle cops (played by real LAPD officers) arrive at the yard, it appears Ed and Doris' ordeal may finally be over. A tense sequence crosscuts between Tibbs chatting with the cops, Ed trapped in the trunk of a car, and Judy holding Doris at knifepoint. Surprisingly, it's Doris who fights off her captor and screams for help, attracting the attention of the police but—as with many heroic actions in the film—it only results in further violence. The Sadist quickly shoots down both cops, adding them to his list of victims.

"How does it feel when you're about to die?" laughs Tibbs, waving the gun at his helpless captives as Ed replaces the fuel pump. The Sadist seems almost flattered when the police radio mentions an APB on him, while the car radio comments ironically on Ed and Doris's plight ("It's a beautiful day for a ball game!") as they try and devise yet another strategy, In a last-ditch effort to survive, Ed sprays gas from a pump directly in Tibbs' eyes. Tibbs falls back, blinded (shot from the killer's point of view, with the frame blurred), and in the confusion, accidentally (and ironically) shoots Judy, mistaking her for one of their captives. Realizing what he has done, Tibbs screams like a wounded animal.

The genre's horror western roots are felt once more as the yard becomes an elaborate maze, with Tibbs on the hunt for Ed and Doris. Compositions echo the opening, with every corner a possible killer's hiding place, and every tool a deadly weapon. Extreme close-ups of Tibbs' eyes (again, echoing the opening titles) alternate with tense shots of Ed lying in wait and Doris stumbling upon the owners' dead bodies inside a chicken coop. After she literally runs for the hills, Tibbs chases after Ed, whose luck runs out as he reaches a dead-end. Our hopes are briefly raised (again) as Tibbs runs out of ammunition, but Ed's attempt to rush him is cut short when The Sadist unexpectedly produces a second pistol and pumps several slugs into Ed's chest. Virile, cool-headed Ed, who we pegged as the hero from the outset, is reduced to yet another notch on Tibbs' belt. But The Sadist isn't satisfied until he's emptied the chamber into Ed's dead body. After this shock, the film's biggest so far, we can only imagine what's in store for Doris.

Tibbs' final pursuit of Doris expands the film's action beyond the salvage yard, transporting us into the dusty ruins of the surrounding desert environment. Zsigmond abandons the careful framing and smooth dollies of earlier scenes, adopting a handheld technique to capture Doris' flight with documentary-style urgency. The crazed Tibbs, now behind the wheel of Ed's car, pursues Doris through the surrounding desert with grim determination. When the car engine dies, Tibbs gives chase her on foot, firing madly at her. After running out of bullets, he unsheathes his knife. Charlie Tibbs' implacable need to destroy, by any means necessary, elevates his character to a nearly superhuman level. Ultimately, though, Tibbs' overwhelming need to kill also seals his own fate. After stalking Doris through the ruins of an old farmhouse, Tibbs falls into a literal snake pit crawling with vipers. In these moments, thanks to Hall's believably terrified performance (entirely understandable given the circumstances) and Zsigmond's unnervingly intimate camerawork, we see Tibbs, finally, as just another victim—this time, of the desert itself.

As Tibbs is repeatedly bitten, the scene acquires a truly surreal, bizarre dimension that supersedes its convenience to the plot and fixes it in the mind as the film's final act of violence, one which outdoes all the others and plays, on some unconscious level, as an act of self-annihilation—and one which would be mimicked by countless desert terror films.

Unlike the heroes in most thrillers, Doris has no hand in Tibbs' demise; she doesn't toughen up or outsmart him. Like the audience, she can only watch, too exhausted to be elated as Tibbs lets out a terrible scream and—in his final onscreen shot—his hands loosen and drop into the hole. Tibbs' death scene effectively sums up the film's tough-minded approach to human life (and death). No one is ever really in control of their own fate, not even The Sadist himself. The ragged handheld camera follows Doris as she staggers over to the car, its radio cheerfully announcing, "It's a home run!" The visual elements are essentially the same as the film's opening shot—a car, a mountain road—but the film's perspective has changed completely. Like the catatonic pseudo-heroines of *Night of the Living Dead* and *Carnival of Souls* (and perhaps mirroring the audience), a stunned Doris staggers forward into an uncertain future.

Distinguished by Landis' shockingly intelligent script, Zsigmond's dynamic lensing, and Hall Jr.'s inimitable performance, *The Sadist* stands worlds apart from other horror films or suspense thrillers of the time, and for the most part delivers the "most terrifying ninety minutes ever made" promised by its lurid trailer. Released just three years after the groundbreaking *Psycho* (1960), the film taps into the rural madness and random violence of Hitchcock's film in a much more relatable and disturbing way—too disturbing, in fact, for its intended audience. *The Sadist*'s action takes place far from the stylized gothic trappings of the Bates Motel (which is essentially a contemporary update of the classic "old dark houses" of the '30s and '40s), in a queasily recognizable everyday America populated by believably flawed killers committing brutal murder in the cold light of day. The main character, Tibbs, is as much protagonist as antagonist; there are no "heroes," only a sole survivor, and the discomfiting ending is far from *Psycho*'s belabored denouement. More than just a simple suspense story, the film is an all-out assault on American values, as institutions from middle-class family life to baseball and Coca-Cola are perverted or annihilated by its salt-of-the earth murderers.

In many aspects, *The Sadist* presaged a shift in cinematic tastes toward realism and irony which would bloom fully later in the decade, in groundbreaking works like *Night of the Living Dead* and Peter Bogdanovich's self-reflexive *Targets* (1968), both of which redefined modern cinematic horror. But in the early '60s, *The Sadist*'s potent cocktail of "torn from the front pages" content and tough-minded aesthetic went too far for the censors of the time, causing the film to be severely edited when shown on late-night television and retitled (to the less-threatening *Profile of Terror*) in the UK. In 1971, *The Sadist* was re-released by infamous exploitation distributor Jerry Gross (*I Spit on Your Grave*), who retitled the film *Sweet Baby Charlie*. By then, a new mass murderer named "Charles" was enjoying media attention, but the film again failed to make much of an impression in the grindhouse/drive-in circuit. *The Sadist* would not be truly recognized until the late '80s, when a 1988 home video release shepherded by exploitation curator Johnny Legend made the film more accessible to movie fiends who gradually elevated it to "cult movie" status.

The Sadist was the first and last outright horror picture produced by Hall Sr., although he continued to contribute (often uncredited or under pseudonyms) to the burgeoning Las Vegas–like exploitation scene, producing *The Thrill Killers* (1964) for exploitation maven Ray Dennis Steckler (who directed the Hall Jr., vehicle *Wild Guitar*

Johnny Legend's 2008 DVD release of *The Sadist* (1963) utilizes a new print (supposedly provided by Joe Dante) and includes an interview with Arch Hall, Jr.

and would go on to direct *Blood Shack*, one of the first desert terror films to follow in *The Sadist*'s wake) and penning Ted V. Mikels' legendary *The Corpse Grinders* (1971). Writer/director Landis helmed two more films for the Halls before leaving the film business altogether in the late '60s. *The Sadist*'s unlikely star followed a similar pattern, abandoning both film and music for a career in aviation. Zsigmond, whose endlessly inventive and adaptable photography places the film closer to European New Wave classics like *Breathless* (1960) and *Knife in the Water* (1962) than the cruder stylings of its regional contemporaries, easily achieved the most success of all the *Sadist* alumni. He continued shooting various exploitation films (including Steckler's fabulously-titled *The Incredibly Strange Creatures Who Stopped Living and Became Mixed Up Zombies*, 1964) until landing his big break on Robert Altman's revisionist western *McCabe and Mrs. Miller* (1971). He would go on to photograph a string of major movies (*Deliverance*, *The Deer Hunter*) before winning the Oscar for Best Cinematography for his work on Steven Spielberg's desert-set sci-fi opus *Close Encounters of the Third Kind* (1979). Zsigmond would attain several more Oscar nods over the course of his long career.

The Sadist's most important accomplishment, however, was its ability to transcend its humble origins along with drawing from thirty years of desert-bound horror westerns, sci-fi/horrors, and film noir influences to emerge as the first "official" desert terror movie. With its edgy, noir-influenced storyline that borrows equally from *The Petrified Forest* and *The Hitch-Hiker*, a "ghost town" junkyard setting familiar from *Haunted Gold*, and realistic use of the desert's deadly wildlife, Landis' film simultaneously references these earlier, formative genres in numerous ways while updating and synthesizing their characteristics with its own unique contributions. While hundreds of desert terror films of varying styles and budgets have been released in the decades following *The Sadist*, the majority bear its distinctive tonal and aesthetic imprint, along with a tendency to mimic and recycle the 1963 film's locations, time frame, script structure, characters, situations, themes, and production circumstances.

The Sadist's contemporary time frame and deceptively sunny California setting were adopted by many films in the desert terror genre, which also utilize the desert environments of neighboring Southwestern states, specifically: Arizona (which comes in second to California as the most popular desert terror destination), New Mexico, Nevada, and Utah. Like Landis' compressed scenario, stories often revolve around one primary location that is isolated from civilization, with *The Sadist*'s desolate salvage yard proving particularly influential on the junk-strewn landscapes of *Sonny Boy*, *The Brave*, *Dark Blood*, *Hurt*, and *Mojave*. Other common desert terror locations—old motels, trailer parks, and dilapidated roadside attractions—exude a similarly disconnected, neglected vibe. Within such settings, conventional civilization is replaced by intricate, self-created worlds that mirror the warped minds of their creators/residents, as in *The Barn of the Naked Dead*, *South of Reno*, and *Eye of the Storm*. An additional group of even more extreme desert terror films, including *Savages*, *The Hills Have Eyes*, *Fleshburn*, *The Oasis* and *The Canyon*, abandon any trace of civilization altogether and set their narratives within the open desert itself. Those desert terrors set in the past, such as *Into the Badlands* or *Silent Tongue*, are almost exclusively Western-themed, and their rundown locations (ghost towns, lonely frontier dwellings) tend to mimic those of contemporary tales. Regardless of specific location or period, setting comes first in desert terror films, with the accompanying dark mood and atmosphere defining and often taking precedence over plot details.

Desert terror narratives also imitate *The Sadist*'s minimalist, action-driven storyline, with stories that usually revolve around no more than a handful of characters, and take place over a limited time span of a few days or less. Many films in the genre adopt Landis' "stranded" set-up, with characters stuck in the middle of nowhere pitted against a Tibbs-like antagonist(s), each other, or simply the forces of nature. These land-locked tales tend to be more melodramatic and psychological, focusing on small desert communities and the madness caused by societal withdrawal, as in *When You Comin' Back, Red Ryder?*, *White of the Eye*, and *Far from Home*. An equally significant strain of desert terrors take their inspiration from *The Sadist*'s car-based opening and climax to tell tales which begin and end "on the road," with little use for the events of the past. Plots tend to emphasize action over dialogue and often revolve around situations relating to desert road travel, such as the perils of picking up hitchhikers (*The Hitcher*), accepting a ride from the wrong person (*Breakdown*), or vehicles as instruments of terror (*Duel*). Like their predecessor, both strains of desert terrors emphasize irony, psychological and physical violence that can explode out of nowhere at any time. Recurring themes include class conflict, modern man's troubled relationship with nature, self-destruction/rebirth, and unsettled issues from a character's past returning to plague the present. Like the haunting final shots of *The Sadist*, desert terror endings tend to be ambiguous and downbeat.

Desert terror characterizations are also strongly influenced by *The Sadist*'s warped, animalistic killer couple and their more civilized adversaries. Characters are painted with broad strokes and defined by their present actions rather than treated with complex backstories. The main character is often a psychologically disturbed societal outcast, an "antihero" whose deranged actions set the story in motion. Charlie Tibbs' larger-than-life imprint can be found on the otherworldly leads of *The Hitcher* or *Blood River*, who, like Tibbs, exhibit almost superhuman qualities at times. Main characters can also appear as Tibbs and Judy–inspired couples (*Kalifornia*, *Natural Born Killers*) and even expand to entire killer pseudo-families (*The Road Killers*, *The Devil's Rejects*). Authority figures, such as police or local officials, are either ineffectual (*Dying Room Only*), untrustworthy (*The China Lake Murders*, *U-Turn*) or nonexistent. The nominal heroes are usually average people who are suddenly thrown into life-or-death circumstances and must summon their baser instincts to survive. Those that live exact a grim victory over their tormentors, and are, like Doris, forever marked by the experience.

Along with all these stylistic, thematic, and narrative influences, *The Sadist*'s scrappy production circumstances also cast a long shadow over future entries in the genre. Most desert terrors would be independent films, made on lower budgets by small production companies and first-time filmmakers. Even those made on bigger budgets and starring name actors, like *The Kingdom of the Spiders* or *Raw Courage*, were shot on location, using local cast and crew. As a result, many of these movies tend to exhibit a stronger atmosphere and quirkier storylines than comparative studio-produced entertainment. Even the safer, more conventional desert terror films that fell into the horror, fantasy and sci-fi genres, like *Near Dark* and *Tremors*, often introduce new, unexpected desert-oriented twists into their otherwise straightforward storylines. Nearly all these films, regardless of budget or tone, manage to preserve the careful balance of nightmarish atmosphere and searing, realistic horror familiar from *The Sadist*.

The Sadist initiated the desert terror genre, but its release did not immediately spawn a rash of similar movies. For years, desert terror remained dormant, consisting of a single semi-obscure film. But as the '60s wound down, a series of cultural and political shifts allowed independent filmmakers to gradually infiltrate the studio system. The first of these "New Hollywood" films was Dennis Hopper's critically acclaimed, game-changing biker epic *Easy Rider* (1969). Photographed across a variety of iconic Southwestern desert sites (Death Valley, Monument Valley) by Vilmos Zsigmond's colleague Laszlo Kovacs, Hopper's film shared many of *The Sadist*'s defining attributes—atmospheric location shooting, contemporary social commentary, and shocking bursts of sex and violence—while achieving major box office success. *Easy Rider*'s massive popularity hastened the demise of old-fashioned studio entertainment and ushered in a wave of movie brats, like Francis Ford Coppola and Martin Scorsese, who would use the techniques and viewpoints pioneered by Landis' landmark film to create a series of politically charged, formally challenging films that would permanently alter the cinematic landscape. In the free-wheeling early '70s, experimentalism was not only encouraged, it was the norm; anything and everything was possible. It was the perfect moment for the first wave of desert terror films to arrive.

3

California Screaming

"This is our territory out here. You folks come here ... this is my place. You have something I want, I take it, see."—Tom, *Dying Room Only*

As if making up for time lost since *The Sadist*'s debut, the early '70s witnessed a sudden explosion of desert terror films, including such varied titles as *Blood Shack*, *Werewolves on Wheels*, *The Velvet Vampire*, *Hex*, *Barn of the Naked Dead*, and *Phase IV*, along with made-for-TV movies *Duel*, *Black Noon*, *Gargoyles* and *Dying Room Only*. This eclectic group of films, which encompasses witchy westerns, bisexual bloodsuckers, lycanthropic motorcycle gangs, and a killer-ant apocalypse, gives a fair representation of how many different directions the genre could stretch while still building a unified cinematic identity.

The most memorable examples from the first wave of desert terrors, however, were stranded scenarios: land-locked tales which drew directly from *The Sadist*'s real-time plot structure and restricted setting, as well as its psychosexual underpinnings. Just as that movie's ill-fated trio of outsiders made the fatal mistake of pulling into a vacant salvage yard, the characters in these films are similarly waylaid, either by engine trouble, taking ill-advised shortcuts, or both. The upper-middle class couple in *Dying Room Only* and the trio of Vegas-bound starlets in *Barn of the Naked Dead* couldn't be more different, but both end up stuck in "middle of nowhere" crumbling desert oases run by Tibbs-like psychotics. *Savages* reverses the accepted roles by making city folk the interlopers, while *The Hills Have Eyes* raises the stakes further, stranding its nice suburban family smack in the middle of the barren desert, far from the most rudimentary vestiges of civilization and under constant attack from an inbred clan of cannibals. *Hills*' influential "survival horror" themes and bracing, kill-or-be-killed storyline would dominate desert terror films throughout the late '70s and into the '80s, in the form of more action-flavored outings like *The Oasis* and the first desert terror sequel, *The Hills Have Eyes Part II*.

An equally effective group of stranded scenarios adopt more dramatic methods for their storytelling, shifting their point of view (and, in some cases, their sympathies) from naïve, suburbanite outsiders to the psychologically stifled inhabitants of such forgotten, out of the way Southwestern towns. Having spent their lives enduring the harsh desert lifestyle while watching others pass through on their way to (presumably) better lives, these tortured souls often retreat into self-created worlds which gradually degenerate into madness and murder. The first of this group, *When You Comin' Back, Red Ryder?* introduces new layers of sociological complexity to the traditional hostage drama, paving the way for existential thrillers like *South of Reno*, *White of the Eye* and *Far from Home*, all of which are fueled by frustrated sexuality that explodes into violence. Later examples of the form, like the slick and stylized neo-noirs *Eye of the Storm*, *Lost Highway* and *U-Turn*, adopt a more postmodern tone, focusing on both victims and victimizers equally while deliberately quoting *The Sadist*'s twisted true-crime elements, and even at times, the entire noir genre itself.

Aside from borrowing from *The Sadist*'s scenario, many stranded scenarios reference California in a multitude of general and specific ways. It's appropriate, given that the "Golden State" is both the setting (though the exact locale is never named, references to Los Angeles abound) and real-life filming location of *The Sadist*, and, indeed, many stranded scenarios were produced in or around the Los Angeles area. From a narrative perspective, the state assumes various roles, as both the characters' home/point of departure (*Savages, Naked Dead, Red Ryder, Survival Run, Hills Part II, Leatherface: Texas Chainsaw Massacre III, Lost Highway*) or their intended destination (*Dying Room Only, The Hills Have Eyes, White of the Eye, Far from Home, U-Turn*). Repeated mentions of California, Hollywood and L.A., expressed more as a state of mind or a dream of a better life than an actual place, abound. The concept of California as a goal or utopian ideal would recur in other, more road-based desert terrors such as *The Hitcher* and *Kalifornia*, but never with the level of forcefulness expressed in these small-town narratives, in which the journey to or from the West Coast is interrupted by a life-threatening breakdown that tests the mettle of both locals and visitors alike.

The stranded scenario category got off to a strong start with *Dying Room Only* (1973), in which a short stopover for lunch has deadly consequences. Passing through the Arizona desert and hours behind their scheduled arrival in Los Angeles, married couple Bob (Dabney Coleman) and Jean Mitchell (an excellent Cloris Leachman) elect to stop for refreshments at the Arroyo Motel, a rundown property consisting of a diner and a few rotting bungalows. The only other people in the café, cook/head waiter Jim (Ross Martin) and his beer-swilling pal Tom (Ned Beatty) are indifferent, if not downright hostile to the "city folks," prompting Jean to insist they leave. Bob holds his ground, but not for long, as Jean discovers her husband missing after her short visit to the washroom. Her attempts to locate him, or enlist the help of the increasingly surly Jim and sleazy Tom, are unsuccessful, even after the local sheriff (Dana Elcar) arrives to assess the situation. Stranded at the café and surrounded by suspicious locals, the determined Jean conducts her own investigation to uncover the dark truth about Bob's disappearance.

Written by Richard Matheson (author of road-rage classic *Duel*), *Dying Room* packs an impressive amount of tension, paranoia and violence into its seventy-three minutes. Though it starts off talky (the café-set first act, dominated by a *Duel*-style diner scene, resembles a stage production), the film gradually unfolds in more disturbing directions. Driven primarily by Bob's mysterious disappearance, the film really catches fire after Jean solves the mystery, igniting a series of savage acts and violent double-crosses. As with many 70s TV terrors, *Dying Room*'s reduced cast and limited locations work in its favor, with a distinctly grimy, down-at-heel atmosphere conjured by the empty diner and dusty bungalows. Leachman carries the film with a committed, sympathetic performance that perfectly conveys the growing hopelessness of the situation, but the supporting cast is equally adept at creating a convincingly desperate group of lowlifes, particularly Beatty, whose sweaty, sexist Tom emerges as the unexpected ringleader. His scenes with Jean have a particularly unsavory quality, from one of his first descriptions of her ("She's some kinda jackrabbit, ain't she?") to their final ride together ("Only thing I'm gonna regret, lady, is I don't have ten minutes to spend alone with you before I kill you").

Smaller-scale and less celebrated than Matheson's "other" desert terror film, *Dying Room* is in many ways the more troubling of the two works. As in *Duel*, mild marital discord gradually takes the backseat to a more urgent, life-threatening situation. *Dying Room*'s gang of bumbling killers, while lacking the instantly iconic quality of *Duel*'s driverless truck, are inarguably, and troublingly, more human in nature. Despite Tom's troubling assertion that "killing don't mean nothin'," he and the other criminals who populate the bleak landscape are far from calculating monsters; rather, they seem to be making up their increasingly lunatic schemes up as they go along. Lacking the otherworldly or exotic qualities of the usual desert terror antagonists, the film's would-be murderers are as common as their generic names—and all the scarier because of it. If a bit too neatly resolved in the end, for the most part *Dying Room Only* works as a nicely scaled-down treatment of the "city versus rural" conflict at the heart of many desert terror films.

Another made-for-television effort, the survival thriller *Savages* (1974), is even more stripped down than *Dying Room*, with its cat-and-mouse narrative driven by a pair of opponents. Based on Robb White's 1972 young adult novel *Deathwatch*, the film takes place in the Mojave Desert, where big-shot lawyer Horton Madec (Andy Griffith) hires young tracker Ben (Sam Bottoms) to help him hunt bighorn sheep. Age is the least of their differences, as nature-lover Ben takes an immediate dislike to the arrogant, overeager Madec. After accidentally shooting a grizzled old prospector, Madec implicates Ben as a possible suspect by firing several rounds from the young man's rifle into the corpse. Not leaving anything to chance, the cold-blooded Madec forces Ben to strip to his shorts at gunpoint while concocting an eerily plausible scenario: "We were hunting, became separated. By the time I found you, you were dead from exposure and dehydration. Apparently, you went crazy. Happens all the time in the desert."

Over an excruciating forty-eight hours, Ben is forced to trek through inhospitable terrain and endure scorching temperatures while Madec stalks him from afar. Hunted like an animal, the sunburnt, weakened Ben manages to stay a few paces ahead of his tormentor, using his knowledge of the land to combat Madec's superior mobility and firepower. Armed only with a slingshot, Ben makes the fateful decision to stop running and eventually confront his pursuer. Back in civilization (easily the film's weakest section), Madec once again reframes the ordeal in his favor, convincing the authorities of his innocence and playing off local suspicions of Ben as an "emotionally unstable" outsider who even his friends consider "a little strange." Madec's getaway is spoiled, however, by a thirteen-hour *deus ex machina* that proves Ben's innocence once and for all.

If not as masterful as *Duel* or *Dying Room Only*, the no-frills *Savages* nevertheless adds a few new layers to the small-screen stranded scenario. The first two-thirds of the film are easily the best, as veteran TV director Lee H. Katzin (who would go on to helm the post-apocalyptic desert flick *World Gone Wild*) skillfully balances physical action and suspense with psychological depth. The rugged beauty of California's Red Rock State Canyon Park functions as the perfect backdrop to the film's two-hander storyline, and Griffith and Bottoms successfully flesh out a pair of characters who, taken together, offer an unexpected inversion of the genre's established "city versus rural" stereotypes. Unlike *The Sadist* or *Dying Room Only*'s upstanding city folk, Madec is a smiling sociopath who can calmly sip a martini while watching his quarry die of thirst. Contrasted with such a predator, eccentric local loner Ben, a man more comfortable around vultures than people, emerges as an unlikely hero. The film echoes *It Came from Outer Space* in its clear sympathy for desert-dwelling "outcasts" like Ben or the murdered prospector. When Ben

Robb White's young adult novel *Deathwatch* was the basis for both *Savages* (1974) and *Beyond the Reach* (2015).

sums up the old man by saying, "Everyone thought he was crazy, but he wasn't. Just lived the way he wanted to," he could just as easily be talking about himself.

Savages' unconventional characters and authentically treacherous-looking action scenes are nearly undone by a turgid final act, which strands the characters in series of a plodding, dialogue-heavy interrogations which are not only dull, but ultimately unbelievable. If dry and static compared to the preceding material, these scenes still make a few interesting observations about its pair of "Savages" and the biases inherent in even the smallest desert community. "Just because someone's different, doesn't mean he's guilty," Ben insists as the local eagerly embrace the outright lies of the more outwardly "normal" Madec. Ben and Madec's final exchange is even more telling: "I'm a hunter, Ben." "And I'm your trophy." One gets the sense that whoever wins, the deadly game between the two adversaries is far from over. In this scene, and many others throughout the film, *Savages* feels like a clear precursor of future desert terror classic, *The Hitcher*.

Barn of the Naked Dead (1974), an early directorial credit for future Robert Altman protégé/arthouse auteur Alan Rudolph (*Choose Me, Mrs. Parker and the Vicious Circle*), relocates the stranded scenario from the small screen to the drive-in. *Barn*'s rambling narrative centers on Andre (an excellent Andrew Prine), a psychopathic momma's boy living in the middle of the Nevada desert, surrounded by the rotting remnants of his father's fledgling circus operation. When a trio of showgirls driving from Los Angeles to a Las Vegas gig suffers a breakdown, Andre is all too eager to offer a helping hand. While exploring his compound, the girls stumble onto the titular barn, which houses five or six female prisoners clad in rags, nearly catatonic and chained like animals to posts in the ground. "We're his toys, his pets, his animals," moans one of the captives; the three new arrivals soon join her as part of Andre's human circus.

As the girls' agent, Derek (Chuck Niles), searches for his clients, "ringmaster" Andre finds myriad ways to abuse his captives. In one sequence, the women encircle a tower while Andre cracks a whip over their bodies, later bringing them a pail of slop while calling out "dinner time!" When one woman nearly escapes, she's lashed to near death by Andre; the next day, he takes an "untrainable animal" (i.e., a girl who fails to obey his orders) outside, where he paints her clothes with calves' blood before releasing her into the desert. The girl escapes Andre's pet cougar only to be mutilated by an unseen, subhuman thing that lives in a shack on the border of the property. A more psychological dimension is introduced as Andre fixates on showgirl Simone (Manuela Thiess), who he confuses with his long-lost mother ("Father had an accident. I do everything now!"). In the gory finale, Simone's escape attempt is interrupted by Andre's father (Gerald Cormier, who also produced), a homicidal freak hideously mutated by H-Bomb radiation who attacks Andre's menagerie in an orgy of screams and bloodletting. An ironic coda—which finds the sole survivor driven mad by the experience while the grotesque father slinks away unseen by clueless lawmen—is even more downbeat than *The Sadist*'s.

Less sadistic or exploitative than one might expect given its outrageous title, *Barn* (also known as *Terror Circus* and *Nightmare Circus*) nevertheless wallows in an unpleasant psychosexual atmosphere. What ultimately saves the film from sinking into a morass of misogyny is Prine, who consistently finds ways to humanize his character. Lines which a lesser actor might have played as high camp ("I'm your trainer! You obey me and you'll be part of the greatest animal menagerie in history. But if you disobey me, you will suffer!") become, in his hands, genuinely disturbing, while the quieter scenes with Simone play with surprising tenderness. To be fair, the script at least provides adequate motivation for Andre's behavior, as well as explaining his love/hate mother fixation. Equally as important in contributing to Andre's mental disintegration is the circus compound itself which, with its tattered circus posters and neglected cages, is one of the most powerful examples of rural isolation ever presented in a desert terror film. Despite his sadistic behavior, Andre never actually kills anyone; that dirty work is left to his father, another misunderstood monster hidden from view until the film's downbeat ending. Just as Andre was victimized by his parents, the father is a casualty of atomic testing in the area. These themes, which feel like a more adult-oriented update of atomic-age flicks like *Them!*, would be further developed by *The Hills Have Eyes* a few years later.

On the down side, *Barn*'s female characters are woefully underwritten; of the three new arrivals, only Simone registers, and mainly through her tenuous association with Andre's past. The film also stumbles a bit during its numerous cutaways to the girls' agent on the phone, talking to the cops, etc., which threaten to destroy the considerable atmosphere worked up by the decaying circus and other surrounding environs. An interesting, if undeveloped, commentary on the entertainment industry lingers over the entire enterprise, as just about all the characters—from former animal trainer Andre to the young hopefuls he pulls into his lethal orbit—share a showbiz background. Despite these missteps, the relative novice Rudolph (who was, according to Prine, the *third* director on the project) manages to combine the film's stronger elements—a stark environment bordering just on the edge of reality, charismatic anti-hero, and random acts of increasing brutality—to form one of the more atmospheric stranded scenarios of the '70s.

Equally exploitative, if not as well executed, is *Trip with the Teacher* (1975), which strands a school bus full of attractive teenage girls in the middle of the open desert. On their way to see "ghost towns, Indian ruins, junk like that," four Los Angeles–like classmates and their chaperone Ms. Tenny (Brenda Fogarty) stop to refuel at a gas station where they run into with biker brothers Pete (Robert Porter) and Al (future *Red Shoe Diaries* auteur Zalman King, here resembling a hungover Sean Penn) and their new pal, clean-cut Jay (Robert Gribbin). As cheeky blonde Julie (Cathy Worthington) flirts with Jay, sociopathic weirdo Al crushes the garage's mechanic underneath a car. Things get progressively worse once the girls' bus breaks down "right smack dab in the middle of nowhere," with the bikers their only option for help. After towing the bus to an empty clapboard house, Al suggests that Ms. Tenny "trade" Bobbie (Dina Ousley), the "loosest" of the girls, for his further assistance ("You'd be surprised what a piece of ass would do for my disposition."), leading to a scuffle with the bus driver, who Al runs down with his bike.

From this point on, *Trip* descends into a sleazier (and slower-paced) version of *The Sadist*'s hostage drama, as Al violently rapes Ms. Tenny while laughing like a madman. Shades of that film's sexually charged water pump scene permeate the film's most grim sequence, as virginal Tina (Jill Voight) tries to escape. When Al finally catches up to her, he shoves her face into the dirt, his face contorting orgasmically as she suffocates. Ms. Tenny and the remaining girls eventually get the upper hand on the bikers, but not in a particularly believable or satisfying way, and the artificially upbeat ending, in which no one seems to acknowledge the previous day's events, is ludicrous. Producer/director Earl Barton is better known as a choreographer on musicals like *Rock Around the Clock*, but this, his sole directing credit, demonstrates little feel for movement of actors or the camera; the flat visual style makes only perfunctory use of its desert setting. King's over the top histrionics and a few choice moments of grindhouse grittiness keep things watchable,

Sexy admat for Earl Barton's *Trip with the Teacher* (1975).

but overall the film lacks the atmosphere, suspense, or character development of previous stranded scenarios.

At the other end of the spectrum, *The Hills Have Eyes* (1977) summons a queasily uncomfortable atmosphere from the first frame, as credits roll over silhouetted rocky peaks while dissonant music rumbles in the background. Wes Craven's belated sophomore film after the landmark *Last House on the Left* (1972) shares many things with its predecessor, namely a narrative based around savage, life-or-death conflict between rival "families" and a willingness to pull out all the stops to shock and disturb its audience. But at the same time, it is a huge leap forward artistically and technically, and finds its

Doug (Martin Speer) searches the desert for his infant daughter in *The Hills Have Eyes* (1977).

creator successfully working on a larger scale while embracing a truly distinctive setting. By rooting Hills' action in the barren, rocky deserts of the Southwest (the film was lensed in Victorville, California), Craven lends his film a truly alien, threatening backdrop, in addition to tapping into years of road-travel urban legends that had been haunting Americans for years. The resulting film is not only one of the most enduring horror films of the '70s and Craven's finest work, but easily ranks among the best desert terror movies ever made.

Harsh winds blow dust over Fred's Oasis, a dilapidated gas station situated off an isolated desert road, as the crusty old owner (John Steadman) packs his belongings into a pickup truck. Fred's hasty departure is interrupted by the sudden appearance of Ruby (Janus Blythe), a feral-looking young woman whose look is somewhere between prehistoric and post-apocalyptic. Their unexpected encounter is interrupted as the Carters, driving cross-country from Ohio to Los Angeles (fabled land of "movie stars and fancy cars")—arrive to gas up their station wagon, which tows a large trailer. While patriarch/retired detective "Big Bob" Carter (Russ Grieve) seems more worldly, the rest of his clan are oblivious to the inherent dangers of the desert. Naively cheerful wife Ethel (Virginia Vincent) prattles on about a silver mine they're looking for, while All-American teens Bobby (Robert Houston) and Brenda (Susan Lanier) wonder how far it is "to the nearest cheeseburger." Also along for the ride are the Carters' older daughter, starry-eyed Lynne (Dee Wallace), her laid-back husband Doug (Martin Speer), and their newborn daughter

Katy. Craven sets up the family dynamics quickly and believably as the characters verbally spar with each other and comment on the strange environment. As Fred warns Big Bob to "stay on the main road," the family's twin German shepherds, Beauty and Beast, sense a presence on the ramshackle property. Soon after the Carters drive away, Fred's truck explodes, trapping him there.

The Carters become similarly waylaid after an accident leads Big Bob to crash the station wagon. Stuck deep in the desert with a snapped axle, Big Bob elects to head back several miles to the gas station, taking a gun with him for protection.

Ruby (Janus Blythe) proves an unlikely ally to the Carters in *The Hills Have Eyes* (1977).

Doug walks in the opposite direction looking for a military installation, leaving Bobby to guard the women. As the family joins in a communal prayer, off-camera voices reveal they are being watched from a distance, by more than one person. Brenda jokes about their fate as "human french fries" while Beauty takes off toward the rocky hills. After Bobby locates the animal's gutted corpse, Craven springs the film's first big scare on us as someone—or something—leaps roaring out of a bush, scaring Bobby back to the makeshift camp.

By nightfall, the characters' discomfort—their creeping fears, exhaustion, and chill of the nighttime desert climate—is deeply felt and all too believable. At the oasis, Big Bob finds Fred, whose tragic tale about his "monster kid," who eventually became old enough to "raise a passel of wild kids" in the desert hills is interrupted by the bearlike Papa Jupiter (James Whitworth) himself, who overpowers Big Bob before sending his sons—grungy Mars (Lance Gordon) and bald Pluto (Michael Berryman)—to invade the Carters' camp. The invasion of the trailer, set off by Big Bob's crucifixion to a burning Joshua Tree—is truly horrifying, and ends with Lynne dead, Ethel clinging to life, Brenda raped, and baby Katy stolen. As in *Last House*'s infamous rape sequences, the violence feels sickeningly real, but here, Craven's skillful framing and editing creates suspense as well as revulsion. Heretofore relegated to the background, sensitive Doug is forced into heroics, as he cries out in the darkness, "Why are you doing this? What do you want?" Craven's camera pulls back as wide as it can, showing how small and defenseless Doug seems against the cannibal family—and the desert itself.

"We gotta get out of this ourselves," Bobby rightly says, precipitating a series of confrontations the following day: Bobby and Brenda take on Jupiter, Beast attacks Pluto, and Doug gets a surprise assist from Ruby while he rescuing Katy from the murderous Mars.

Spanish poster for *The Hills Have Eyes* (1977).

Linked through skillful montage, all three sequences have their unforgettably brutal moments; Brenda and Bobby dispatch the hulking Jupiter with axe blows and bullets, proving that these two kids aren't going to become french fries anytime soon. Craven saves the most memorable image for last, as nice-guy Doug drives a knife again and again into the snakebitten Mars' chest. The scene achieves its impact through quick cutting rather than bloodletting, the excellent performances of all involved, and Craven's decision to explore, rather than glorify, violence. The final image of Doug, breathless and horrified at his own victory over Mars, freezes before (appropriately) fading to red. The appearance of "The End" on screen is hardly comforting, or suggestive of any real closure (a wisely excised denouement, available on DVD and Blu releases of the film, finds Brenda and Ruby joining hands before literally walking into the sunset together). The few survivors will be changed forever by the past twenty-four hours of kill-or-be-killed savagery. Audiences, too, will find what they have just witnessed impossible to shake off.

In the nearly four decades since its release, *Hills* has become one of Craven's most-analyzed films, with most discussions focusing on the differences and similarities of its two rival families while examining the thoughtful, intricate script, which incorporates both literary and cultural allusions (*Beauty and the Beast*) and historically documented events (the cannibal family was inspired by incidents which took place in 15th Century Scotland). Few of these writings, however, focus on the film's consistently inspired use of its desert setting, which not only showcases but drives the action. Like all great desert terror films, *Hills*' storyline grows organically out of its desert location. Possibly inspired by East Coast native Craven's cross-country pilgrimage to Los Angeles (he was, by the time of the film's production, ensconced in Hollywood) and exposure to Southern California's more isolated outskirts, the boulder-strewn landscape of *Hills* reflects its writer/director's own fears of being stranded in such a place as much as the characters' (or, in turn, the viewers'). From the first shots of Fred's Oasis, Eric Saarinen's bleak but vivid cinematography achieves a documentary-style look without sacrificing style (the film was shot in 16mm but blown up to 35mm, which lends it a grainy look which only serves the rugged, you-are-there ambience). Craven uses the desert to create formidable tension long before the cannibal family arrives, as a jackrabbit causes the fateful car crash, Brenda complains about the broiling heat, and Lynne is spooked by a tarantula inside the trailer. Scenes of Bobby ascending the boulder-strewn hills feel treacherous, as if one false step could ensure certain death, and one can almost feel the chill as the temperature drops after dark. The hills may have eyes, but the desert could kill the Carters all by itself, the film suggests.

It's also hard to imagine the film's life-and-death struggles, and the subsequent dehumanization of the Carters, occurring anywhere else. Together with talented art director Robert Burns (whose excellent work also graces *The Texas Chainsaw Massacre* and *Tourist Trap*), Craven creates a true alternate reality in the desert that is expressed in the cannibal clan's cavelike home and individual looks, fashioned from military surplus and human remains, which have since become iconic (Berryman in full junk-punk regalia remains one of the most indelible horror characters of the '70s). In many ways, Jupiter's inbred clan is as indigenous to the desert environment as rattlesnakes and jackrabbits—and equally as primitive. Their instincts, skills, and worldview are completely formed by a profound isolation from society, and they act accordingly. Stranded on an alien planet just a few miles off the "main road," the Carters must learn to adapt to the new environment, and to the behavior of their tormentors, if they are to survive; hence Bobby's callous but ingenious use of Ethel's still-warm corpse (unimaginable under any other circumstances) as bait for a trap. The desert, ever indifferent, even assists the Carters in some situations, as when a rattlesnake that could have easily killed Doug gives him a decisive edge over Mars, after Ruby uses it against her brother.

While the desert setting may be *Hills*' most obvious asset, there are many other elements that contribute to its success. The cast of talented unknowns, while the result of budgetary constraints, gives the film an unpredictable edge. Also, Craven's talents as a film editor are evident throughout, as he creates numerous jarring and surprising moments during the action/suspense scenes. Like *Chainsaw*, *Hills* is not an especially bloody film, but one that creates the impression of violence and gore through skillful editing and well-chosen sound effects. The stark terror of the middle-of-the night trailer attack (a "home invasion" which never gets any easier to watch) is eroded slightly by some of the later scenes, as Jupiter and his brood lose some of their nightmarish mystique when viewed in the daylight. But this is a minor quibble, and for much of its ninety-minute running time, Hills creates a palpable atmosphere of terror and suspense unmatched by most horror films of the '70s. It's easily one of the best stranded scenarios, and one of the most important achievements of the desert terror genre's first active decade.

The lackluster *Survival Run* (1979) recycles *Hills*' stranded-in-the-desert narrative while trading Craven's shocking violence and insightful commentary for goofy humor and lame action sequences. The film begins about as far from desert terror as one can imagine, introducing its attractive cast of Valley girls (and guys) via a series of high school hijinks that wouldn't be out of place in a Crown International release of the period. "Headed for some California fun … running in the California sun," blares a grating theme song as a trio of good-looking couples leaves sunny suburban Tarzana for an illicit weekend campout in the surrounding deserts. The opening credits have scarcely finished when disaster strikes, as wisecracking Sal (Cosie Costa) accidentally crashes their van while off-roading in the desert. Despite a few angry outbursts ("What the hell are we gonna do now? We're out here in the middle of the desert, a million miles from nowhere!"), most of the teens are surprisingly sanguine about their situation, settling down for a night of campfire sing-alongs before pairing off for sleeping-bag sex.

While apparently heading in the direction of many slasher films of the period (the desert terror genre wouldn't fully embrace the form until 1982's *Death Valley*), *Survival Run* swerves abruptly into action movie territory as the foursome, on foot and in search of help, stumble onto a makeshift camp run by Kandaris (Peter Graves) and the sinister Professor (Ray Milland), a pair of "prospectors" whose actual purpose is far more sinister. Despite Diane's (Randi Meryl) assurances that the Professor is "a beautiful man," the others aren't so sure, especially after Brian (Robby Weaver) stumbles onto of a cache of weapons in the prospectors' truck. Before the group has a chance to flee, flirtatious Steph (Susan Pratt O'Hanlon) is raped and Sal murdered by two of Kandaris' crew. The five survivors, led by Chip (Vincent Van Patten) escape the camp, pursued by Kandaris and the Professor across the desert in a series of bullet-riddle skirmishes and motorcycle chases that find the "goddamn kids" matching wits and, eventually, firepower with their more experienced, better-armed opponents.

Survival Run's disparate mix of survival horror and rat-a-tat action is not an unwelcome combination, but unfortunately, writer-director Larry Spiegel fails to deliver on either count, let alone merge the two genres into an entertaining whole. Early sequences focusing on the teens' desert trek feel rushed and lack the appropriate air of desperation, while later action sequences deliver only a modicum of suspense or thrills. The middle section is the most disappointing, as Spiegel bungles the growing tension between the two groups and soft-pedals the potentially devastating one-two punch of Steph's rape and Sal's murder. Like much of the film, these two defining moments are clumsily dramatized, with an almost embarrassed air to the proceedings that rob them of any emotional

The theatrical poster for *Survival Run* (1979) emphasizes the film's action sequences.

content. This was never going to be *Straw Dogs* in the desert, but the filmmakers' indifferent approach consistently consigns *Survival Run* to the lesser tier of drive-in programmers.

A U.S./Mexico co-production filmed in Lancaster, California, and Baja, Mexico, *Survival Run* is not only first desert terror film to shoot partially south of the border, it's also the first to include Latino characters in its storytelling. Steph's rapists are sweaty, brutish caricatures, but good-hearted senior member Paco (Pedro Armendariz, Jr.) emerges as one of the film's more well-developed characters, especially in the few scenes he shares with Chicana teen Angela (Marianne Sauvage). The film also differs from other stranded scenarios in its characters' origins: none of the principals are actually from the desert, leaving the Mexicans to serve (more or less by default) as the film's "indigenous" desert people, by manner of their introduction (we meet all the other characters elsewhere) and grungier appearance and behavior. Again, this extends to Angela, who is later revealed to originally hail from Arizona, a state with more rural connotations than California. The closest the film comes to dealing with the cultural divide between the two groups, however, is disappointingly simple-minded, as "gringa" Steph gyrates suggestively in front of a group of Mexican locals.

These tensions are accompanied by a loosely presented generational conflict, as the older, white (and corrupt) establishment clash with the youth, whose fun-seeking quest for sex, drugs, and rock n' roll ultimately lands them in trouble. Once again, the film does little with this concept, instead keeping characterizations of both parties as one-dimensional as possible. None of this would matter much if the action sequences had more vigor, but as such, they are serviceable at best, with director of photography Alex Philips, Jr.'s tendency toward zooms and aerial shots that create more distance than scope. Even the few inspired moments of drive-in madness ("You still find me sexy, senorita?" cackles a rapist before a vengeful Steph machine-guns him) are somehow rendered limp by the filmmakers' consistent inability to understand, or even properly exploit, the potentially vivid horrors of their own hybrid concept. Alternatively known as *Spree* and *Nightmare*, by any title the film is a missed opportunity.

In a reverse of the prevailing trends toward physical action and increasingly graphic violence, the intensely dramatic *When You Comin' Back, Red Ryder?* (1979) derives its impact from psychological plotting and complex characterizations. Adapted by playwright/screenwriter Mark Medoff from his own 1973 play, noted theatre director Milton Katselas' movie updates *The Sadist*'s real-time structure with an intriguing combination of contemporary politics and overt sexuality. The 1968-set story begins with a south-of-the-border desert opening that riffs on *Easy Rider*, as charmingly deranged Vietnam vet Teddy (Marjoe Gortner) rips off a pair of Mexican drug smugglers before making love to his hippie girlfriend Cheryl (Candy Clark). As Teddy and Cheryl carve a crime-ridden path to the U.S., the film bounces between a middle-of-nowhere town in New Mexico, where diner waitress Angel (Stephanie Faracy) is desired by crippled motel owner Lyle (Pat Hingle), but carries a torch for closeted Stephen "Red" Ryder (Peter Firth), who can't wait to "get the hell out of this lousy little town," and road-tripping couple Clarisse and Richard Ethridge (Lee Grant and Hal Linden), who stop at Lyle's motel on the way to violinist Clarisse's engagement in New Orleans. All these characters are marked by frustration of one kind or another, as Lyle makes awkward advances on Angel while the Ethridges' tearful coupling unfolds to B.B. King's "The Thrill Is Gone."

The various dysfunctional threads coalesce at Benton's Diner the following Sunday morning, as Teddy and Cheryl (described by Stephen as "a coupla weirdos") join the others for steak and eggs. Despite his disadvantaged status (broken down van, no money), Teddy quickly assumes control of the group, convincing Lyle to obtain a new generator and psychoanalyzing the other patrons ("Living off the little woman's residuals, are you?" he quips to Richard) while keeping his own background intentionally vague (despite his vehicle's California plates, Teddy is from "Istanbul."). Angel falls for his dubious charms, but Teddy is more intrigued by Stephen, especially after he learns of his serial-invoking nickname. Teddy's theatrical blustering— "Ain't room enough in this town for the both of us, Red Ryder!" he shouts while miming a *High Noon* style shootout—hides a dark edge that becomes more pronounced as the day wears on.

Cheryl (Candy Clark) and her outlaw boyfriend Teddy (Marjoe Gortner) are "the disaffected youth of America" in *When You Comin' Back, Red Ryder?* (1979).

The first action against Teddy is not taken by Red (who, despite his tough guy demeanor and "Born Dead" tattoo, remains an impotent bystander throughout much of the film), but by suburbanite Richard, whose attempt to leave results in a literal shot in the arm. Teddy sends the armed Cheryl to make sure Lyle fixes their van while continuing to harass his now-captive audience. Teddy indulges in bitter war reminisces ("I know a lot of good ol' boys who became somebody by getting their good ol' asses shot off.") before descending deeper into cinematic fantasy as he "directs" the patrons in a self-made reconstruction of a *Red Ryder* serial from the '40s, assigning roles to Stephen (who, naturally, plays "Red Ryder") and Angel while Clarisse provides background music with forks and spoons.

Cheryl and Lyle's return, and the news that the van is fixed, fails to extract Teddy from his psychic cocoon. Despite protesting "I'm not one of them—I'm with you!," Cheryl gives in to Teddy's demands, relinquishing the pistol to him before participating in a bizarre last dance, which finds the exhausted, terrified victims paired up and shuffling slowly to Tammy Wynette's achingly melancholy "Kiss Away." The fragile peace is shattered when Teddy's molesting of the frigid Clarisse prompts yet another (unsuccessful) attack from Richard, followed swiftly by Teddy's decision to tie up and gag the others, using Stephen as his accomplice ("one last gesture for the old west"). Stephen's clumsy attempt to attack Teddy fails, and he soon finds himself bound up like the others. Instead of engineering a series of *In Cold Blood*–like executions, Teddy simply ducks out, leaving a traumatized Cheryl behind to wander amidst the trussed-up hostages.

The film's western themes return to the forefront during the climax, which finds "Red Ryder" pursuing Teddy into a surreal landscape of wind-swept dunes. Armed

Psychotic drifter Teddy (Marjoe Gortner) threatens Clarisse Ethridge (Lee Grant) as her husband (Hal Linden) watches in the background in *When You Comin' Back, Red Ryder?* (1979).

with a shotgun, Stephen finds Teddy sitting in a meditative pose, asking, "You want to kill me, don't you, Stevie? I'm going to give you the opportunity to try." While clearly meant to invoke classic westerns (as well as its revisionist contemporaries), the final confrontation between the two men plays out on a more existential level; Teddy neatly orchestrates his own death, once again directing the action ("You'd better use that shotgun.") towards its inevitable outcome. The result provides freedom for both men: Teddy is finally released from his own psychological prison, while Stephen acquires the car he needs to leave the town behind ("Price goes down if you're a hero."). *Red Ryder*'s ending is uncharacteristically promising for the genre, as Stephen and Angel ride away together into the sunset.

An indispensable title in the genre's development, *Red Ryder* is at once a back-to-basics return to the rough minimalism of early stranded scenarios like *The Petrified Forest* (with which it bears a remarkable number of similarities and themes) and *The Sadist* and a precursor to the more psychologically complex desert terror films to come in the '80s and '90s. The film's killer couple, stranded travelers, and wind-blown, sun-parched setting are by now staples of the genre, but, in this case, also serve to reflect how much the model had changed in the last fifteen years. Troubled Teddy and naïve flower child Cheryl (self-described as "disaffected youth of the United States of America") owe less to brutish '50s thrill killers like Charles Starkweather and more to the more educated, politically motivated dropouts of the late–'60s. And unlike more recent model Charlie Tibbs, Teddy is highly intelligent, often funny, and brutally accurate when judging his companions; Cheryl also differs from her most obvious predecessor, less a psycho sidekick than a dazed onlooker goaded into participating in Teddy's criminal acts. The "normal" folks, too, are just as unsettled as their antagonists: Richard and Clarisse's upper-class suburbanites are no happier than the sexually frustrated townsfolk who congregate around the diner every morning and bury their dreams in plates full of home fries.

In a notable departure from past stranded scenarios, *Red Ryder*'s characters are all equally stuck in the small town, each with his or her own reasons. Residents Angel and Stephen are trapped by their own lack of ambition; Lyle by his handicap. Teddy and Cheryl have an automotive breakdown, while the Ethridges are waylaid by Teddy's scheming. Rather than the brute violence familiar to the genre by this point, Teddy manipulates his companions through a variety of techniques, including flattery (Angel), casual insults (Lyle), masculine challenges (Richard, Stephen) and sexual harassment (Clarisse). Even more insidiously, Teddy drives them against each other, teasing out long-standing resentments and conflicts until they explode. Actual physical conflict or graphic violence is not only rare, it takes a backseat to the characters' devastating personal realizations about themselves or their significant other. Many of the most searing emotional exchanges in the film (such as a heated bout between Clarisse and Richard) don't directly involve Teddy at all, giving the film the added distinction as one of the most intense, yet largely bloodless, desert terrors of the '70s.

Unlike the last decade's worth of desert terror degenerates, Teddy acts as more of as instigator rather than antagonist; his imprisonment and terrorization of the group, while clearly indebted to his own psychosis, arguably gives his captives a psychoanalytic "safe space" in which to directly address their private and interpersonal issues. The Ethridges finally express their true feelings about one another, while Angel is directly confronted with the possibilities she has let pass her by. None of the characters, however, benefits more from their encounter with Teddy than Stephen, who finds himself the chief target of the Nam vet's jibes from the beginning. Their first mocking exchange (Teddy: "How are you, kid?" Stephen: "Okay, Dad.") suggests an unspoken bond that deepens as Teddy focuses relentlessly on the young man, veering between bullying ("How'd you rate yourself on a 'guts' scale?") and sage advice ("What's going on in your mind, boy? Don't let it touch you. You do and it's liable to eat you alive."). Teddy's decision to let Stephen—and the others—live suggests not so much mercy as a self-destructive complicity in his own demise. The connection between the two lends the film a character depth—and a fleeting homoerotic charge—previously unseen in the genre; this type of fractured but fascinating male bond would reappear in many subsequent desert terrors including *The Hitcher*, *The China Lake Murders*, and *Nature of the Beast*.

Teddy and Stephen's shared obsession with the western-themed comic books and serials of the '40s and '50s—the final decades of America's innocence—allows the film to comment on the genre's western roots in a more direct way than any other non-supernatural desert terror film thus far. Stephen insists on being called "Red," after a once-popular cowboy character, but Teddy is completely besotted with western pop culture, borrowing shooting tricks from "The Gunfighter, Gregory Peck," calling "Hi, ho!" after robbing a Mexican cafe and pondering the disappearance of The Durango Kid and Lash LaRue ("those boys had guts") while Ennio Morricone's iconic theme from *The Good, the Bad and the Ugly* wails on the jukebox. Aside from providing a common connection between Teddy and Stephen, the consistent references to the cowboy heroes of the past pits the simplistic straightforward pleasures of those innocent past entertainments (and, the film infers, wars) against the desperation of modern-day life in New Mexico, as well as the muddied politics of Vietnam. Even these more topical remarks are often coached in old west metaphor, as Teddy jokes that World War II was "the one John Wayne won for us," and longs for "how it used to be ... all the old rider knew was that he got sealed orders to go away, so he was a'goin.'" In the film's final scenes, both Teddy and Stephen get their wish, as they enact a cowboy-movie fantasy that ends with the "black hat" dead and Stephen finally getting to prove his manliness.

Though revolutionary in many aspects, *Red Ryder* suffers from a jumbled first act, as the film struggles to expand its scope without losing the basic essence of the stage play. The first forty-five minutes are spent setting up, and contrasting, various characters and locations (some of which add little to the narrative) without establishing a connective thread or creating enough forward momentum. Once the story settles into the diner, however, it finds its groove, particularly after Teddy and Cheryl's arrival. While the performances are excellent across the board, the film is chiefly driven by Gortner's live-wire portrayal of Teddy. Alternately bemused, obnoxious, charming, and dangerous, Gortner commands the screen like few desert terror villains before or since. Though undeniably spellbinding (one actually believes he could hold the group in his thrall, despite a lack of weaponry) and at times truly terrifying, Teddy's most memorable moments come during his brief moments of self-awareness and regret. While tying up Clarisse, he says, "I'm sorry." "Are you?" she asks plaintively. "No, but I wish I was," is his studied response. Such flashes of humanity make Teddy all the more frightening, and point ahead to the more psychologically complicated criminals of *Natural Born Killers*, *Kalifornia*, and *The Road Killers*.

Visually, the film is more dynamic and expansive than one might expect for a stage adaptation, with Katselas and director of photography Jules Brenner (*Return of the Living Dead*) finding many creative ways to frame the largely confined action. Exterior sequences, particularly those centered on Lyle's motel and filling station, are equally well-handled, opening up the film while preserving a nicely down-at-heel ambience. The film also gains an extra visual (and story) dimension from its closing scenes on the dunes (shot in Las Cruces, New Mexico), which easily contain is finest location photography. Underappreciated composer Jack Nitzche (*Hardcore*, *Cruising*) also adds to the disturbing atmosphere, contrasting gritty, warbling soundscapes with a series of dead-on perfect tunes emanating from the jukebox. Perhaps it's legal issues over its eclectic soundtrack (which include songs by The Doors and others) that have insured the film such spotty video releases over the years ... when you comin' to DVD, *Red Ryder*?

The ultimate stranded scenario of being marooned in the open desert, so far dramatized to varied effect in *The Hills Have Eyes* and *Survival Run*, finds its purest, most grueling expression in *The Oasis* (1984), which redefines the term "survival horror" in new and frightening ways. An ear-splitting explosion rocks the soundtrack, followed by an apocalyptic tracking shot surveying the flaming wreckage of a downed plane, the pilot's head bloodily smashed through the windshield while bodies of dead passengers litter the ground. Wailing fills the smoky air as quick flashbacks reveal the former lives of the few survivors. Among them are physician Jake (Scott Hylands), married fitness–nut lawyers Alex (Rick Podell) and Anna (Anne Lockhart), brothers Matt (Chris Makepeace) and Paul (Richard Cox), New Yorker Jill (Dori Brenner) and cute blonde Jennifer (Suzanne Snyder). Stranded somewhere in the Mexican desert with minimal provisions, this ragged group struggles against the harsh environment, a lack of supplies, and, eventually, each other. Along the way, *The Oasis* (released on video as *A Savage Hunger*) makes some startling observations about human nature.

Initially, many of the surviving Angelenos are slow to abandon their old routines. The film pokes fun at la-la land clichés as vegetarian Anna turns down caviar, fitness nut Alex insists on doing his daily run and vain Jennifer fusses over her hair and makeup. The surviving co-pilot "blacked out" and has no idea where they are, but insists there's a settlement "just over the mountains." Once it's discovered that the transmitter battery is dead, serious questions arise about how long they can survive on the dwindling food and water supply. The selfishness of self-preservation is invoked for the first time as Matt's badly injured father dies while Jake and the others neglect him in favor of signaling a passing plane. Coldly logical Jake assumes control of the situation, espousing his "survival of the fittest" position to Paul. He considers human beings "just another species, a kind of animal." When Paul argues that people have thoughts and feelings, Jake responds coldly, "You know what counts out here? Food. Air. Water. And putting one foot in front of the other." Alpha males Jake and Paul continue to clash throughout the film, as they struggle to retain control of the group.

Jake's tough-minded Darwinist viewpoint is proven correct, though, as the weaker members of their party start to die off during an extended trek into the mountains to find help. With food gone and water scarce, overweight Louis insists on being left behind, and the zombified co-pilot collapses after hallucinating and gulping mouthfuls of sand. After Anna finds Alex drinking his own urine, she steals all the group's water and the two of them disappear in the night. When Jake and Paul discover an old well, it seems like the answer to their prayers, but ends up leading them all to a new level of Hell, surrendering to the "savage hunger" alluded to in the film's alternate title. Jill's death triggers a fight between Paul, who has concealed her corpse, and Jake, who insists "she's food." Jake strangles Paul to death while Matt, dazed and deep into a heated, animalistic relationship of sorts with Jennifer, idly stands by. Desperate with hunger, Jake drags Paul's body to his cave-like dwelling and cuts into his leg. The next shot reveals chunks of meat cooking over a fire. Famished, Jennifer quickly switches sides, moving from Matt's campsite to Jake's cave. She brings "meat" to Matt, pleading, "You gotta eat, or you'll die." Matt chooses to leave, only to find the dried-out corpses of Alex and Anna. He returns to face off against Jake, who he finally finishes off with Jennifer's help. Fortified after consuming Jake's body, the two survivors again set off to find help. The pessimistic ending suggests that Paul and Jennifer are doomed to die in the desert, despite all they have endured, as they head toward a new, illusory "oasis."

The Oasis is an uncompromising story of survival, with its frank, disturbing tone maintained from first frame to last. The script by Tom Klassen (*The Last Horror Film*) is utterly unpredictable, with the character-driven narrative constantly shifting as the situation worsens. The ensemble cast's performances are naturalistic and unaffected, never lapsing into melodrama despite the extreme situations which occur on an almost minute-by-minute basis. Instead, director Sparky Greene focuses on private moments of desperation, even gallows humor at times (at one point Anna quips: "Boy, you never know how a vacation's gonna turn out," in another scene Louis jokes about his "crash diet"). The film's violence—including the potentially exploitative or graphic scenes of cannibalism—is handled in a similarly underplayed, matter-of-fact manner; more unnerving than any act of savagery is the relentless atmosphere of death that hangs over the entire enterprise. What little hope we have of the situation improving is dashed early on; instead, the question becomes, "How much worse are things going to get?"

Unlike most films in the desert terror genre, *The Oasis* does not rely on an iconic *Sadist/Hitcher*-like villain or a deranged clan of *Hills Have Eyes*-like killers to propel the action along. Instead, human nature itself, pushed to the breaking point by extreme circumstances, drives the characters to acts of murder and worse in the interest of self-preservation. The film's final section is especially dark and best illustrates the film's theme of dehumanization, as the three remaining survivors devolve into prehistoric archetypes. Jake and Matt become rival hunter-gatherers, with Jennifer the sexual "mate" caught between them. Unexpectedly, Jennifer displays the strongest survival instincts, as her loyalties shift between the two men, depending on her momentary needs. "I didn't mean to hurt you, but he's feeding me," she tells Matt after moving in with Jake. Later, after they've killed Jake together (and devoured him), Matt asks Jennifer why she took his side. "He would've killed me when he was done with you," she answers coolly before casually adding, "Besides, there's more of him." The answer would almost be funny if it wasn't so brutally honest.

While some of the uniformly excellent cast have gone on to bigger things (Snyder had a strong cult horror run in the late '80s with roles in *Killer Klowns from Outer Space* and *Return of the Living Dead Part 2*), neither director Greene nor scripter Klassen ever made another film. Given its unpleasant subject matter, lack of obvious genre affiliation, and low-profile video release (like *Red Ryder*, the film has yet to make the leap to any digital format), *The Oasis*' rarity isn't totally surprising. But it's precisely those stubbornly individualistic qualities, along with some excellent Death Valley location lensing by Alexander Gruszynski (who went on to photograph *Tremors*, one of the most successful desert terror movies of all time), that make it worthy of attention. Not only does it completely immerse the viewer in another world for its ninety-odd minutes, it leaves one with plenty to chew on (sorry) afterward. Provocative and immersive, *The Oasis* easily ranks as one of the most unrelenting desert terror films ever made.

Despite *The Hills Have Eyes*' considerable box office success, it took seven years for a belated sequel, *The Hills Have Eyes Part II* (1984) to finally arrive in theatres. Even a casual comparison of the two films shows how much the horror genre had changed in the interim, as *Hills II* drops the first film's focus on environmental perils and interfamily dynamics in favor of a more simplistic slasher-style scenario, as a group of young people are slaughtered one by one by a pair of monosyllabic boogeymen. The straightforward tone is set early on as composer Harry Manfredini's score, sounding like recycled cues from his trademark themes for *Friday the 13th*, plays over the opening credits. After a lengthy series of flashbacks to the first film, the present-day story finds a group of professional motorbike racers led by Roy (Kevin Blair) heading out of L.A. to a competition in the desert, where they plan to test a new superfuel developed by Bobby (returning *Hills* cast member Robert Houston, who appears in a throwaway role, never to be seen again). Aside from trusty German shepherd "Beast," the bikers and their girlfriends are also accompanied by chaperone Rachel (Janus Blythe), who reacts badly when biker Harry jokes that their route takes them past the place where "the hills have eyes."

After taking an ill-advised shortcut and suffering a punctured gas tank, the group's bus stops at a sprawling, dilapidated ranch in the middle of the desert. While wandering around the property, Rachel is attacked by Pluto (Michael Berryman), who quickly retreats after the others come to her aid. "Rachel" admits that she is actually Ruby, formerly

Pluto (Michael Berryman) is one of the few original characters to return for Wes Craven's sequel *The Hills Have Eyes Part II* (1984).

part of the original film's cannibal family, now integrated into society. Soon afterward, Pluto steals one of the group's bikes, leading Harry and Roy deep into the hills, where Harry is crushed by a giant rock and Roy is knocked unconscious by a towering maniac known as The Reaper (John Bloom). As night falls on the ranch, everyone splits up to chitchat, shower, or make love. The Reaper, described by Ruby as "Papa Jupe's big brother" who "took over" after Jupiter died, does most of the killing, crushing his victims to death in bone-breaking bear hugs or hurling them through windows until only Roy's blind girlfriend Cass is left alive.

Hills II is considered by many fans to be one of the worst horror sequels ever made, with Beast's infamous canine flashback its biggest cinematic innovation. There's no denying that it pales in comparison with the original, but if taken on its own merits, the film is certainly no worse than most of its slasher contemporaries. Craven's script feels forced, as he struggles to merge characters and images from *Hills* with a new group of generic teen victims who—in typical slasher fashion—are aware of the bloody atrocities committed in the area, but venture forth anyway. While some of the new group deviate from the standards of the time (African American characters were a rare find in '80s slashers, and blind Cass is an unusual heroine), they often conform to contemporary standards of stupidity, wandering off alone to take open-air showers or playing complicated pranks on each other. The script's most intriguing idea—Ruby's reinvention as Rachel—suggests a return to themes explored in the first film, but again, it's downplayed in favor of recycled, dimly lit kill scenes.

The vast ranch property, with its dusty sheds and network of underground tunnels, is a production designer's dream, but never succeeds in provoking the kind of naked fear summoned by original *Hills*' unadorned natural landscape. Likewise, much of the action, which relies on *Survival Run*-like motorbike stunts, feels sanitized, repetitive, and far from scary. Craven's direction, too, lacks the inventive spark that distinguished so much of his work on *Hills* and feels more stylistically akin to his television work from the same period. Many of the suspense scenes lack intensity, and the murder sequences frequently cut away at the moment of impact. Aside from producer Peter Locke, none of Craven's collaborators from the first film encore here, and the film is poorer for it (one especially misses Don Peake's nerve-jangling score). If the filmmakers' intention was to update the franchise for the Michael and Jason era, the result is a half-breed horror weirder than any of Jupiter's inbred children.

While *Hills II* lurks somewhere between the action and horror genres, *The Danger Zone* (1987) firmly emphasizes the former, as a Louisiana-based girl band on their way to a talent competition in Vegas is menaced by a drug-dealing motorcycle gang. After their car breaks down in the middle of the desert, "The Skirts" (no relation to Linnea Quigley's old group) make their way to an isolated ghost town that turns out to be a hideout for biker leader Reaper (Robert Canada) and his scruffy crew of underlings, many of whom go by names like Munch (the towering R.A. Mihailoff, who would go on to play Leatherface in *Texas Chainsaw Massacre III*) and Reptile (Mickey Elders) and whose idea of a good time is setting one of their less loyal members on fire. "What are we gonna do to 'em?" one of the group giggles while sizing up the terrified Valley vixens. Reaper's cocksure answer—"Everything"—actually turns out to be quite an exaggeration, as the girls endure precious little in the way of physical or sexual abuse (the most violent moment in the film has one girl's shirt torn open) before undercover cop Wade (a wooden Jason Williams) comes to their aid, climaxing in an underwhelming shootout which denies the female victims (and the audience) any kind of revenge against their tormentor—but at least The Skirts don't miss the talent show!

Though its "babes versus bikers" premise is ripe with exploitation potential, *The Danger Zone* is decidedly lacking in danger of any kind, as it shies away from the uglier implications of its concept while drowning in a sea of macho posturing, limply choreographed fights, and abrasive pop tunes. Between the six girls and dozen or so bikers, the film is vastly overpopulated with characters, few of which make much of an impression. De facto lead Williams stands out as particularly bad, however, with his detached delivery of lines like "I'm gonna kick the chicken farts out of you" making Chuck Norris look Shakespearean by comparison. The script, which hinges on an utterly absurd method of smuggling drugs over the U.S./Mexico border, is meandering and repetitive, the action scenes are dull and commonplace, and the flat photography fails to capitalize on its desert setting, despite its principal location's obvious western trappings. Lacking the edginess seen in desert terror biker outings like *Werewolves on Wheels* and *Trip with the Teacher*, *Danger Zone* has more in common with the marginally better teens-in-peril flick *Survival Run*. It's a measure of the film's success on video that no fewer than three sequels followed, *Danger Zone II: Reaper's Revenge* (1989), *Danger Zone III: Steel Horse War* (1990), and *Death Riders* (1994).

Unlike *The Danger Zone*, the cheap and cheerful *Blood Frenzy* (1987) at least lives up to its title, kicking off with a gruesome *Halloween*-derived prologue before moving to the present, where Los Angeles psychiatrist Dr. Barbara Shelley (Wendy MacDonald) drives her motley group of six patients—twitchy Nam vet Rick (Tony Montero), frigid Jean (Monica Silveria), nymphomaniac Cassie (Lisa Savage), mean-spirited Ash (Hank Garrett), drunken Crawford (John Clark), and man-hating lesbian Dory (Lisa Loring)—to the desert for a weekend of "confrontational therapy." Arguments between the mean-spirited, high-strung members break out before they've even reached their destination, a rocky, barren stretch of sand near an abandoned silver mine (perhaps the same one the Carters were looking for?). Ash is the first to die when, after a quickie with Cassie, a mystery killer rakes a knife across his throat. The next morning, his body is found, along with the realization that someone has disabled the RV. They're stranded, fifty miles from the nearest town, and the killer could be anywhere, or any of them…

For the most part, *Blood Frenzy*'s plot hues closely to convention, as various characters pair off to look for help and are subsequently butchered by the mystery murderer. Despite director/producer Hal Freeman's long career in pornography (this remains his solo "straight" effort), the film has surprisingly little nudity, with graphic but amateurish gore effects providing much of the production value. Aside from a few cave scenes, Freeman and director of photography Rick Pepin (future co-founder of the infamous PM Entertainment) make only limited use of the desert environment. The film's saving grace is Ted Newsom's screenplay, with its whodunit approach subverting audience expectations for another *Hills*-style cannibal campout. The idea of Dr. Shelley's group of misfits accomplishing anything during a desert sojourn feels more like a jab at new age psychiatry techniques than a serious hook to hang a movie on, but they're still more amusing than most of the bland teens populating the '80s horror landscape, and their over-the-top insults ("So, I'm a dick smoker, huh? That's pretty good coming from a pussy bumper!") often cut deeper than the killer's knife. Of the cast, former "Wednesday Addams" Loring makes the strongest impression as the wild-eyed, venomous Dory, with her extreme hair and makeup and campy meltdowns ("I'm gonna show you what happens to bad girls!").

The appealing VHS artwork for *The Danger Zone* (1987) promises thrills that the movie fails to deliver.

Approached with lowered expectations (and a six pack or two), *Blood Frenzy* is a worthwhile stab at a slasher-themed stranded scenario.

Blood Frenzy would prove to be one of the last desert terror slashers, however, as the late '80s found the genre moving in a more psychological direction. The existential thriller *South of Reno* (1988) is typical of this shift, echoing *Dying Room Only*'s themes of marital discord and *Red Ryder*'s critique of stultifying small-town life while anticipating the neo-noirs which would dominate the genre in the early '90s. We first meet recessive loner Martin Clark (Jeffrey Osterhage) shoveling nails and broken glass onto the highway near his trailer home, hoping to cause a flat which will bring some fleeting social interaction and a welcome break from his daily routine of TV watching (on a set with only one channel). Apart from the random stranded stranger, Martin's only meaningful conversations are with his buddy Hector (Joe Estevez, billed as "Joe Phelan"), who plans to leave for Reno and begs Martin to join him, and his distant, bitter wife Annette (Lisa Blount), who's having an affair with beefcake mechanic Willard (Lewis Van Bergen). Although Martin (along with the rest of the town) is aware of Annette's affair, he avoids confronting her or Willard, preferring to slide slowly into a mind-numbing pattern of television viewing. His longtime dream of leaving his adulterous wife, and the town itself, for Reno is similarly put on hold, replaced with the construction of a secret project deep in the desert.

Unlike many stranded scenarios, which deal with violent clashes between two rival groups or individuals, *South of Reno* adopts a "man against himself" conflict, with Martin, despite his various external troubles, often his own worst enemy. Martin's inability to act on his desires and his own creeping paranoia define the tone and pace of the film, which is built more out of repetition of specific sounds and images (the TV's constant patter, a lonely motel where Annette and Willard have their late-night liaisons) than major plot twists. Certain moments in the script by Mark Rezyka (who also directed) and T.L. Lankford (producer of desert terror film *Scalps*) achieve a fleeting significance—a traveling gun salesman (Bert Remsen) gifts Martin a pistol, Martin arrives at Willard's garage to confront him—only to add up to nothing, with Martin consistently shrinking from making a choice or taking a stand. Even when Martin takes action—as when he finally confronts rival Willard—it feels offhand and casual, and, more importantly, has little to no impact on the rest of the story. The result is a film where the viewer, like its protagonist, feels truly trapped by the surroundings.

Naturally, the deceptively spacious desert setting (which include Roy's Café, familiar from *The Hitcher*, *Kalifornia* and others) is the perfect environment for such a tale of encroaching madness, and Canadian Rezyka accomplishes plenty of strong, evocative images throughout. Particularly impressive is the sequence, about midway through the film, when Martin brings a local woman to see his "personal Reno," a vast network of lights strung across miles of wind turbines. Martin races his truck through the self-made dreamland, laughing wildly as bulbs pop against the windshield, while his terrified companion can only stare in silence. It's a surreal, even transcendent, moment, and as close as Martin ever gets to true happiness (the film repeats the image over the closing credits for added effect). When his passenger doesn't "get it" and wants to leave immediately, one holds their breath for the inevitable explosion of pent-up violence. But like much of *South of Reno*, the scene defies expectations with an abrupt, and depressing, cut to Martin alone at home, once again zombified in front of the flickering TV screen.

Save a mild voyeuristic sequence, *South of Reno* contains very little erotic content;

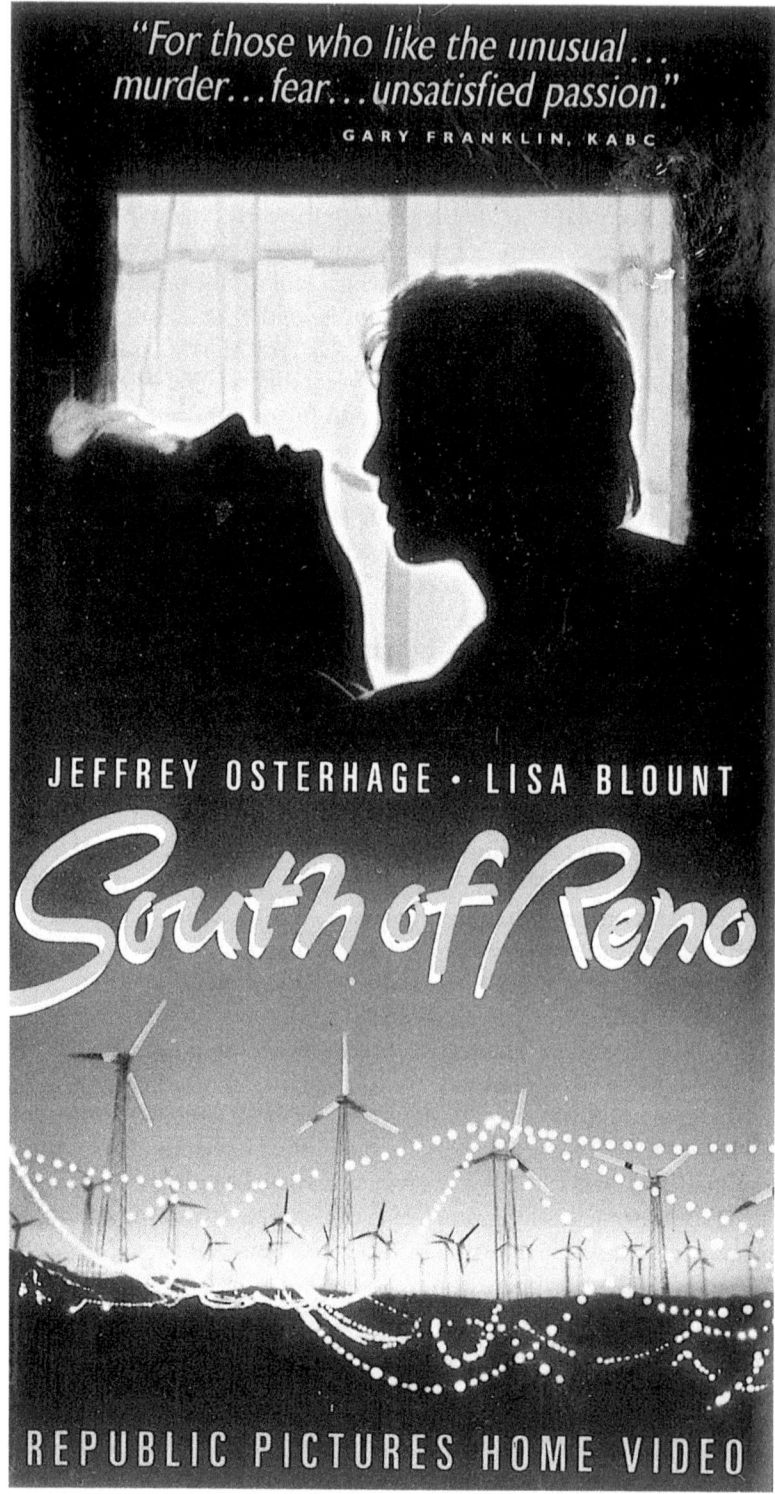

The existential drama *South of Reno* (1988) was marketed as an erotic thriller by distributor Republic Pictures.

the film is more about sexual frustration, as Martin tries (unsuccessfully) to court several local women, all of whom reject him. His only semi-successful romantic encounter occurs in the final act, with an almost improbably sweet Reno-bound blonde who represents the possibility of freedom from his self-created universe. Though attracted to his new lover, Martin is even more excited by the prospect of a TV with multiple channels, so there he stays, clicking the remote as she drives off alone. A final attempt to leave, perhaps spurred on this encounter, finds Martin stuck once again, tire punctured by one of his own nails. Aside from the obvious irony, the scene sums up Martin's character, and predicament, perfectly. The terror lurking *South of Reno* is the not the traditional murderer stalking his victims; rather, it's the internal fear of change that often inhibits the frustrated residents of such out-of-the-way places.

If *South of Reno* plumbs the quiet side of madness, then *White of the Eye* (1988) is a primal scream echoing across the Arizona desert. Atmospheric, disturbing, and weirdly beautiful, the third film by Scottish cult director Donald Cammell (*Performance*) uses a flashback-driven script and striking imagery to explore the duality of a loving husband and father who occasionally commits brutal murder. Familiar desert terror themes of civilization and savagery are introduced over the opening credits, as a hawk's hunt for its prey leads to aerial shots of modern downtown Tucson. Scored to a hypnotic track by Nick Mason (of Pink Floyd) and Rick Fenn, these images lure us into the film's world before it launches into its first violent set piece. Returning to her modernist (and isolated) desert home from a shopping trip, pampered housewife Joyce Patell (Katie Waring) complains on the phone about her "butchered" hairstyle before an unseen killer—urged on

Paul White (David Keith) attempts to explain his murderous tendencies to his wife Joan (Cathy Moriarty) in the superb *White of the Eye* (1988).

by a throbbing electronic beat—chops her to pieces. Aside from a slow-motion shot of the screaming victim's head smashed into glass, the violence here is mostly off-camera, with associative imagery—spilled wine, scattered roses, a fish gulping for air—substituting for onscreen butchery. During a tour of the crime scene, Detective Mendoza (Art Evans) remarks, "I know a goddamn work of art when I see one" as he stares at a bloody set of knives arranged like the four points of a compass.

First introduced singing along while blasting Verdi at top volume as he drives through the desert, ruggedly handsome Paul White (David Keith) has an innate sensitivity to audio dynamics that feeds his thriving stereo design and installation business. Paul's ability (which he describes as "a tuning fork in my sinus cavities") approaches the mystical as he closes his eyes and locates the "four directions" needed for ideal speaker placement. As he and his sexy wife Joan (Cathy Moriarty) make love, Hot Chocolate's "You Sexy Thing" leads us into the first of many subjective, stylized flashbacks. While headed to Hollywood ten years ago, New Yorkers Joan and her then-boyfriend, loudmouth, pistol-toting Mike de Santos (Alan Rosenberg) stop in small-town Globe, Arizona, for car stereo repairs and meet soft-spoken, affable Paul, a part–Indian local who will change all three of their lives forever. Back in the present, Mendoza also takes a liking to Paul, who has become a possible murder suspect after his tires matched the tracks found at Patel's house. Asked if he still hunts, Paul tells the detective, "I quit when I got married."

Long-forgotten memories continue to infiltrate the Whites' present lives as Joan discovers Mike, recently released from prison, now working at an out-of-town garage. "I always loved you, Joanie," Mike tells her as she notices his vehicle's tires are the same as her husband's. "But then he came along and laid his eye on us. The Apaches call it the white of the eye." Joan's own past infidelity to Mike is mirrored in Paul's recent indiscretions with bored, beautiful Anne Mason (Alberta Watson). Ominous flashbacks—of Paul and Joan flirting in his workshop, and Paul and Mike heading into the mountains for a deer hunt—proliferate as Joan finds Paul's van outside Ann's house and angrily slashes the incriminating tires. At the same time, wealthy housewife (and Anne Mason lookalike) Liza Manchester (Mimi Lieber) is murdered by a gloved killer who is "seen" only through extreme close-ups of his twitching eyeballs. In a reversal of Joyce Patel's murder, Lisa's abduction and death occurs entirely on-camera, as a gloved killer holds her underwater while bringing a mirror to her face, *Peeping Tom*–like, so she can watch herself drown.

"I know your act," she screams at Paul during his questioning by police, but, ironically, Paul is guilty of far worse than bedding another woman. Appropriately, it's not Mendoza who discovers the ultimate truth, but Joan. Following a pair of loaded flashbacks—Paul and Joan's sexual union interrupted by a gun-wielding Mike, Mike's horror as Paul arrives carrying a bloody deer—Joan discovers indisputable evidence of her husband's dark deeds. While much of *White of the Eye* breaks from standard thriller convention, the third act really defines the film, as Joan, even when confronted with the awful truth, refuses to surrender her love for Paul. Paul's ravings about being "chosen" inspire not rage or panic in Joan, but an outpouring of sympathy, as she tells him: "I thought I was part of you. But you're all alone." After making love one final time, Joan triggers Paul's anger, leading to one of the film's most "graphic" scenes. Though no blood is shed, Paul's frantic knifing of their bed—which essentially displaces Joan as his victim—is both a symbolic act and the first time we see Paul commit an act of violence. The effect is beyond chilling.

The film's climactic chase veers briefly into conventional thriller territory, as Paul, wearing war paint and wrapped with explosives, hunts Joan within the rusted maze of a copper mine. Mike's sudden appearance, while not entirely believable ("I knew you'd come here ... in the TV in my head"), nevertheless reconstitutes the film's original love triangle, with Joan once again trapped between the loves of two madmen ("Boy, I sure pick 'em," she snorts at one point), along with delivering the final, disturbing payoff to the Mike and Paul's fateful hunting trip. Incredibly, Joan still cares for Paul, even after he has shot at their daughter and tried several times to kill her. Paul, however, is even more dedicated to his own self-destruction, taking his own life (and Mike's) in an explosive ending that, in typical Cammell fashion, glorifies rather than condemns Paul's final act.

The first desert terror film helmed by a European director, *White of the Eye* embraces many of the genre's major themes (civilization versus savagery, a road trip that detours into the unexpected, the maddening effect of rural isolation, fractious husband/wife relations, white/Native American tensions) while introducing new thematic and stylistic elements of its own. Densely plotted, unconventionally directed and rich with visual and auditory information, Cammell's film is impressive, if overwhelming on a first viewing; subsequent revisits allow greater appreciation of the filmmaker's "controlled chaos" approach. Its most obvious attributes are sensual—fluid Steadicam work, specific yet fragmented editing, the use of bleach bypass, a haunting music score—but the film is equally impressive on a plotting and character level. Throughout, the film's style and content work in tandem to create one of the genre's most idiosyncratic, disturbing, and weirdly touching entries.

Most desert terrors favor a stripped-down script that confines most of the action to the present and paints characters with broad strokes, but *White of the Eye* (while taking place over a few days' time) allows past and present equal weight in the narrative as the current investigation of Paul's activities contrasts with his early indications of madness. Interestingly, these 1976 flashbacks (which have the grainier, high-contrast look of an 8mm home movie) are not confined to a single character, but represent the varying perspectives of Paul, Joan, and Mike—though the most significant memories (Paul and Mike's grisly hunting trip, Mike's discovery of Paul and Joan together) always involve Paul. The past events directly affect and mirror the present, as the Paul/Joan/Mike love triangle plays itself out once again, ten years later. Their relationships have changed, but the basic elements—Joan's abiding love for Paul—remain the same. Paul, too, maintains the same ingratiating, good ol' boy demeanor that makes him a hit with both men (Mike, Mendoza) and women (Joan, Anne Mason) in both the past and the present. The common thread that unites the film's temporal halves is the inevitable reveal of Paul's underlying, and largely hidden, madness. In a film riddled with visual and behavioral contrasts, Paul's two faces—loving father/husband and demented killer—are particularly difficult to reconcile.

We rarely see Paul's hidden face—the one that murders random local women under the direction of some sinister, misogynist cosmic force—until his confession to Joan, in which he compares the female sex to a "black hole" that "sucks everything into it" before slashing their bed to shreds. Until then, we only get glimpses of his eyes (a literal evocation of the film's title) during the film's stylized murder sequences, which linger in the mind thanks to Cammell's avant-garde approach, which appropriates both contemporary rock-video techniques (slo-mo, titled angles, fast cutting) and the cold, sexualized tone identified with Italian giallos of the '70s. Joyce Patel's murder betrays an unmistakable

Never released on DVD in the U.S., *White of the Eye* (1988) debuted on Blu-Ray courtesy of Shout Factory in 2016.

Dario Argento influence, while Lisa's morbidly romantic drowning reaches even further back to the Mario Bava's proto-giallo masterpiece *Blood and Black Lace*. Repeated close-ups of twitching eyeballs echo Argento's *Opera* (1987) and Bigas Luna's self-reflexive *Anguish* (1987) along with much of the '80s repertoire of horror maestro Lucio Fulci. Whether intentional homages or not, Cammell gives these sequences a macabre beauty previously unseen in the desert terror genre.

As memorable as its murders are, the film derives its primary impact from Paul and Joan's relationship, which remains shockingly intact through her discovery of his insanity and his attempts on her (and their daughter's) life. Early scenes between them achieve an easy-going, believable warmth missing from most desert terror films, and the flashbacks convincingly depict their initial attraction and sexual connection which fails to be diminished, even after Paul has shown her his murderous dark side. At this point, when most films would throw Joan into "flight or fight" mode, Cammell instead lingers on the couple's final hours together as Joan tries to reconcile the man she loves with the insane murderer while Paul painfully surrenders to the urgings of a diseased mind. Though Paul's later claims ("You and me, we're gonna bore right to the core of this planet!") smack of lunacy, a final exchange with Joan in which they profess their love to each other, after all that had happened, have the undeniable ring of truth. "I was the one!" Paul says triumphantly, rightly referring not only to his "chosen" status, but to his connection to Joan. Mendoza's final, enigmatic comment to Joan—"What's ten years, when you're in love?"—only reinforces the Whites' unique bond.

White of the Eye was not Cammell's first experience with desert filmmaking. Many of its thematic and visual elements can be traced back to Cammell's short *The Argument* (filmed in 1971, but not completed until 1999), a self-reflexive fantasy photographed in Moab, Utah, by *The Sadist*'s director of photography Vilmos Zsigmond (who was, by that point, significantly further along in his career). While adapting the 1984 novel *Mrs. White* (written by Andrew and Laurence Klavan under the pen name Margaret Tracy), one of Cammell's most significant changes was his crucial location shift of the story's action from New England to Arizona. As with its character and plot elements, *Eye* is a detailed exploration of the geography and history of its newly adopted setting, as it contrasts dusty, small-town Globe (where Paul and his family live) with upscale urban Tucson (where his wealthy clients and victims shop). Local sights, such as the victims' modernist desert homes, a vast copper mine, and the surrounding Apache mountains, are well-integrated into the story, as is Paul's Native American heritage. Paul's appropriation of Indian traditions to decorate his crime scenes links well to his bizarre behavior from ten years ago, but one is led to believe his madness extends even further back in time. More important to Cammell is the connection between Paul's mental "tuning fork" and the voice that told him to kill. Inextricably linked, the two voices merge into the film's final, inescapable duality: the impossibility of separating genius from insanity. "I did something with my life. I left my mark," Paul says before igniting the explosives strapped to his chest. With *White of the Eye*, Donald Cammell leaves his own indelible mark on the desert terror genre.

A much younger predator stalks the residents of a trailer park in *Far from Home* (1989), an unusual take on the stranded scenario which focuses its serial-killer tensions through the prism of a teenage girl's sexual awakening. When Los Angeles–bound Charlie Cox (Matt Frewer) and his nubile fourteen-year-old daughter Joleen (Drew Barrymore) run out of gas, they are forced to stay in the tiny desert town of Banco, Nevada (pop. 132), most of whose residents live in the dusty Palomino Trailer Park run by short-tempered Agnes (the always dependable Susan Tyrell). Charlie tries to make the best of the situation, renting a trailer for the night and finishing his overdue magazine article ("this is how real writers live") while waiting for a gas truck to arrive. Joleen is less than enthusiastic about the possibility of spending her fourteenth birthday in the middle of nowhere, surrounded by oddballs and strangers. One of the residents does catch her eye, though: Agnes' wayward teenage son Jimmy (Andras Jones) erotically melts an ice cube along Joleen's arm during their first encounter and later catches her spying on a couple

Andras Jones and a sultry Drew Barrymore star in the underseen erotic thriller *Far from Home* (1989).

making love in one of the trailers. Joleen and Jimmy's sexual spark is interrupted by the nerdy Pinky (Anthony Rapp), another park resident and Jimmy's rival in more ways than one. As the two boys fight over Joleen's affections, a killer starts bumping off residents left and right, causing both Jimmy and Pinky to come under police scrutiny.

Atmospheric, well-paced and populated with kooky characters essayed by an even cultier cast (Richard Masur as burned-out desert rat Duckett, Dick Miller as the sheriff, Jennifer Tilly as a stranded motorist), *Far from Home* solidly balances its thriller plot and murder sequences with Joleen's personal narrative, which is largely defined by her budding sexuality and anchors the film. Her racing emotions are tracked by voice-over journal entries that range from startlingly mature to hopelessly romantic ("I want him to kiss me, but I'm really scared..."). A date with Jimmy starts off sexily before progressing suddenly to a near-rape that is only halted by Pinky's intervention. Joleen's relationship with Pinky, while gentler to start, finds him repulsed by her advances ("Have you ever done it?" she asks as he shrinks away) before revealing his own deep-rooted psychosis. Finally, Joleen chooses neither, with her final voice over, "How can somebody be so right, and still be so wrong?" referring to her father's judgment, but equally applicable to the two boys, each "crazy" in his own way, with whom she has been intertwined.

While balancing Joleen's journey with the madness surrounding her, the screenplay by horror sequel specialist Tommy Lee Wallace (*Halloween III, Vampires: Los Muertos*) paints a convincing portrait of trailer park life, exhibiting a genuine sympathy for even its most monstrous characters. Like *South of Reno*, the opiate effect of television on these forsaken souls is a strong thematic element, whether commenting ironically on Agnes' murder by electrocution or to illustrate Pinky's scrambled, desensitized world view. "I guess living here would drive anyone nuts," Joleen muses at one point and, as with many stranded scenarios, the need for escape, whether physical, sexual, or otherwise, plagues many of the characters. The inhabitants of Banco fall into two categories: those eager to leave and those who have lost their minds after deciding to stay (Pinky is described as having "slipped over the edge" after his mother died). Divorcee Charlie seems almost at peace staying at the Palomino after finding a compatible female friend, and largely ignores Joleen, allowing her to stray even further from his control.

Debuting feature director Meiert Avis, whose resume includes many of U2's best-known videos, brings a strong visual style to the proceedings, with the Palomino, along with other locations, afforded a terrific amount of grungy detail. Memorable set pieces include Charlie's visit to a nuclear dump/trading post deep in the desert and a climactic chase/confrontation at Pinky's television-strewn lair, which takes place during a massive dust storm. All the cast contribute lived-in portrayals, with Tyrell and Masur particularly memorable. But at the end of the day, *Far from Home* rests on Drew Barrymore's teenage shoulders, in the first mature role of her career. In a welcome departure from the typical treatment of women in the desert terror genre, Joleen is neither a helpless victim nor a tough-as-nails heroine, but a real girl who makes mistakes, and struggles to learn from them. Barrymore, who was at the time of production the same age as the character she was portraying, more than brings off the role, and rarely has she been more physically desirable or delivered such a naturalistic performance. She brings a likable, unaffected quality to Joleen that keeps the film centered even when the script wanders into familiar thriller territory. Her performance, along with the film's superior technical and creative aspects, helps make *Far from Home* stand out as one of the best female-driven desert terrors.

The denizens of the Palomino Trailer Park look positively conventional, however, when compared to the dysfunctional family of desert dwellers whose animalistic son answers to the name of *Sonny Boy* (1989). An extended 1970 prologue, set in the small town of Harmony, New Mexico, sets the film's earnestly bizarre tone, as two-bit thief Weasel (Brad Dourif) guns down a husband and wife and steals their convertible. After delivering the vehicle to the isolated desert compound of local crime lord Slue (Paul L. Smith) and his transvestite "wife" Pearl (David Carradine), a hidden surprise is found in the back seat—a baby boy. Slue wants to "feed the kid to the hogs," but Pearl forms an immediate attachment to the infant and threatens to leave if Slue doesn't accept the child as their own. Thus begins the strange saga of "Sonny Boy," whose first memory is of his "father" firing a howitzer at a snooping deputy, exploding the man's body in a shower of blood. As Pearl shields the child, a sensitive voice over explains: "The ground trembles. His hands hold me tight. Warm red liquid covers us both. Now I am his."

A series of increasingly brutal episodes trace the cruel progress of Sonny Boy's development. His sixth birthday is summarized with the following: "Father cut loose my tongue. A present for my birthday. A gift of silence." At age twelve, the mute Sonny Boy is dragged through the dirt by a truck; two years later, the sadistic Slue ties his "son" to a stake and lights a circle of fire around him. Age seventeen—the point at which the story proper begins—finds Sonny Boy (Michael Griffin) living like an animal in an empty grain silo and devouring live chickens like a circus geek. His introduction to the outside world is a late-night visit to the new mayor's residence, where Slue (literally) unleashes the animalistic teen to wreak havoc. After ripping the man to pieces, Sonny Boy looks at his bloodied reflection, disturbed by his actions. "Can this be me? This pitiful thing I see trapped in the mirror?" he wonders before Slue drags him back to his silo prison. Sonny Boy's fractured psyche, caught somewhere between the urge to escape and join humanity and a blind, dog-like devotion to Slue, is felt in his words: "Now I have tasted the blood of a man. I have pleased my father."

Power-hungry Slue continues to use Sonny Boy as a secret weapon against his political enemies, leading others in Harmony to develop their own interests and agendas. Local girl Rose (Alexandra Powers) falls in love with the silent, feral boy, relating his literal imprisonment to her own need for escape, while Slue's devious cohorts Weasel and Charlie P. (Sidney Lassick) "borrow" Sonny Boy without permission for a harebrained scheme to rob and kill a local prospector, which goes badly and attracts the unwanted attention of the local police force. After suffering the infuriated Slue's latest round of abuse, Sonny Boy finally escapes the compound, but his freedom is short lived after a deadly encounter with a biker couple. The sheriff (Steve Carlisle) and sympathetic Doc Bender (Conrad Janis) try to help Sonny Boy, but they can't protect him from an enraged mob that is determined to capture and kill Slue's not-so-secret weapon. In an epic, Peckinpah-esque firefight, Slue and Pearl defend their home and family from hordes of shotgun-wielding locals.

Sonny Boy occupies a unique place in the desert terror pantheon, surpassing simple shock value to tell its disturbing tale of abuse and dehumanization in a surprisingly lyrical, emotionally affecting way. While most desert terrors tend to fall more into the horror/thriller category, *Sonny Boy* boasts a storytelling depth and performance quality that one usually associates with top-shelf dramas. And yet, its down-at-heel atmosphere, extreme characters and over the top scenes of horrific violence make it unapproachable for mainstream audiences. Nearly every scene challenges the viewer, juxtaposing brutality with deadpan humor and following scenes of suffering with sick belly laughs. While initially reeling us in out of a freak show curiosity (David Carradine in drag?), the film holds our attention out of genuine sympathy and care for the main character and his extended family.

Like *The Hills Have Eyes*, *Sonny Boy* is first and foremost a family portrait, and one which clearly favors its colorful weirdos over "normal" citizens. Slue, Pearl, and their associates are the ultimate marginalized outsiders, gathering around the safety of the vast junkyard like pieces of human wreckage. Slue may wield considerable economic and political power, but his eccentric personal tastes doom him to a life on the outskirts of his own community. Pearl, too, is accepted only within the confines of Slue's compound and, unlike the others, never ventures outside the property. Ironically, Pearl is the most normal member of the group, providing genuine love and care for Sonny Boy while the others only exploit and abuse him. Most fascinating of all, of course, is Sonny Boy himself, a tortured soul perennially divided between man and beast. Despite their morally repugnant behavior, Slue and his cohorts somehow remain sympathetic and in many cases, genuinely likable. The community of the ironically-named Harmony, on the other hand, is sketchily developed and represented by individuals who are either ineffectual (the sheriff) or truly monstrous, like lynch mob leader Sandy (Savina Gersak). The few members of the community who oppose the mob are also outsiders in their own ways; Doc Bender is a washed-up alcoholic, and Rose a displaced punkette who, in a sentiment familiar to stranded scenarios, longs to escape to Los Angeles.

First-time director Robert Martin Carroll complements Graeme Whifler's quirky script with a strong visual style, which often expresses much with a few effective images. Early, wordless scenes of Sonny Boy's youth are dramatized with one or two quietly powerful shots, while later sequences, such as his fateful encounter with a biker, or the climactic siege on Slue's compound, are breathtaking in their use of slow motion (several sequences, especially the film's finale, bear a strong western influence). Despite a few narrative lapses, Carroll succeeds in elevating his mute hero's tragic journey to nearly mythic proportions, aided Robert D'Ettore Piazzoli's expansive photography and Carlo Maria Cordio's melancholy score (a *Midnight Cowboy*–like harmonica theme is particularly effective). Carroll's Italian collaborators are the result of producer Ovidio Assonitis, the creative force behind off the wall genre projects such as *Beyond the Door* (1974) *The Visitor* (1979) and desert terror creature feature *Curse II: The Bite*. While there's often a distanced, almost artificial, quality to Italian productions made in the United States (the film was shot on location in Columbus and Deming, New Mexico), that's not the case here; if anything, the more expressive Italian influence may have been exactly what director Carroll needed to achieve such an operatic vision of the American Southwest.

Smith, a physically imposing character actor whose resume includes everything from *Midnight Express* to *Pieces*, leads the impressive cast. Despite doling out much of Sonny Boy's abuse, there's a warmth to his twisted dynamic with Sonny Boy, more akin to a dog and its master than father and son, that's impossibly to deny (their final shot together is one of the film's most touching moments). Carradine's Pearl never lapses into camp or jokiness, and the actor even contributes the film's country-flavored theme song (which is actually quite good). Dourif and Lassick (who together constitute a minor *One Flew Over the Cuckoo's Nest* reunion) are equally effective as the somewhat disloyal members of Slue's gang. And then there's Sonny Boy himself, a no less demanding role that, while largely physical in nature, provides the film's emotional core.

Although the conflict between civilized man and "savages" (and the thin line that separates them) is explored by many desert terror films, few do so with the intensity or directness of *Sonny Boy*, with its main character eternally caught between two worlds. While undeniably the story's one real victim, we fear Sonny Boy as much as we fear for him. His escape from Slue and the compound brings not freedom, only more violence, as the "monsters" of Harmony rise up against him and his family. The compound's destruction signals the end of one life, but not necessarily the beginning of another. Like many great desert terrors, the story closes on an ambiguous note. Saved from both his oppressors and an angry mob of "normal" folks, Sonny Boy finds that, in truth, he belongs to neither group. Like *Hills*' Ruby (who reinvents herself as "Rachel" in its sequel), he has lost his former world, but far from ready to rejoin civilization. Sonny Boy's final voice over, infused with as much loss as hope, sums up his fate: "I have words now. But what good are they? The pain doesn't stop. And I wonder: who am I now?"

Family dynamics also fuel the troubled sequel *Leatherface: The Texas Chainsaw Massacre III* (1990) whose opening crawl informs us that the eponymous masked killer of Tobe Hooper's original classic was never arrested. A quick credits montage finds Leatherface (R.A. Mihailoff) very much alive and still claiming victims since his adoption by a new clan of backwoods cannibals. Bickering California couple Ryan (William Butler) and Michelle's (Kate Hodge) cross-country drive takes a macabre detour while driving through Texas to Florida, as their stop at the ominously-named Last Chance gas station run by gibbering pervert Alfredo (Tom Everett) ends with a hasty retreat down a rural road recommended by helpful cowboy Tex (Viggo Mortensen). Tex's shortcut, however, spells the couple's doom, as they are chased into the night by a monster truck and attacked by the hulking Leatherface before meeting survivalist Benny (Ken Foree). Stranded in the woods, the trio's nightmare odyssey leads to an isolated farmhouse, where more members of Leatherface's crazed "family" (who dub him "Junior"), lie in wait.

Boasting slicker production values than the previous two *Chainsaw* films, *Leatherface* also suffers from an unfocused, overpopulated script by horror novelist/first-time screenwriter David J. Schow that often strains to duplicate scenes and characters from Tobe Hooper's original. The first third of the film, which follows Ryan and Michelle along a convincingly hellish desert landscape, builds tension nicely and benefits from excellent character turns by Everett and Mortensen. Benny's sudden assumption of the lead role sets the film on a shaky new course, as Ryan and Michelle fall into the background. While occasionally managing moments of morbid humor (such as Leatherface's attempted use of a Speak N' Spell), Schow's script fails to explain how "Junior" came to be united with this new clan of killers, along with shying away from any depictions of cannibalism. The final third leans in a more action-oriented direction, as fistfights and explosions play out over a noisy heavy metal soundtrack (including a grating "Leatherface" theme song) before Michelle's final battle with the masked murderer, during which she finally embraces her inner killer. A tacked-on desert denouement finds several previously-deceased characters inexplicably returning for one more round of mayhem.

Too extreme for the casual horror fan yet not rough enough for hardcore gorehounds, *Leatherface* occupies a strange place in the history of the *Chainsaw* franchise. In its Leatherface chapter, Stefan Jaworzyn's excellent *The Texas Chainsaw Massacre Companion* extensively details the creative clashes between then-fledgling studio New Line Cinema (mainly known at the time for the *Elm Street* franchise) and director Jeff Burr (*From a Whisper to a Scream*), who was obliged to make a number of MPAA–mandated cuts made in order to avoid an X rating. Despite all the behind the scenes drama, the film has a surprisingly consistent look and tone, with a strong visual style that benefits immensely from its location shooting. *Leatherface* is the only film in the series to shoot in California; as a result, the film's topography occasionally sports a tangible desert atmosphere. Burr and director of photography James L. Carter (*The Road Killers*) make excellent use of the Valencia locations, with early road and gas station scenes, as well as the otherwise absurd finale, standing in well for Texas. The later woods scenes, however, feel more commonplace and fail to achieve an authentic desert or rural vibe.

Controversial during its original release, *Leatherface* can today be recognized as a valid, if flawed, attempt to blend the scares of Hooper's initial outing and the pitch-black humor of its over-the-top sequel with new characters in a slick new package. If the film occasionally struggles to marry all these divergent interests, for the most part it at least succeeds in providing solid horror entertainment, with Burr directing the various action sequences with a steady hand along with assembling an excellent cast of character actors (particularly Joe Unger, Everett and Foree, the last of whom would team up with Burr again for the *From Dusk Till Dawn*–inspired *Devil's Den*). The only Chainsaw film to qualify as a desert terror movie, *Leatherface* is a textbook example of how studio meddling can affect an indie horror series.

Leatherface was one of the few high-profile horror releases of the early '90s, a quiet period in the genre which saw the familiar (and, by this point, tired) slasher franchises take a hiatus while more interesting efforts (such as *Henry: Portrait of a Serial Killer* or *Hardware*) enjoyed only the briefest of theatrical releases. In the place of the usual genre

R.A Mihailoff as "Junior" in *Leatherface: The Texas Chainsaw Massacre III* (1990), the sole entry of the franchise to have been filmed outside of Texas.

offerings, a spate of neo-noir thrillers—which often bypassed theatres to debut on cable or home video—began to appear, many of them offering more sophisticated, character-driven thrills and chills to terror-starved audiences. Many of these films returned to *The Sadist*'s formula, setting their dark tales of murder and madness in isolated, atmospheric Southwestern settings. John Dahl's debut feature *Kill Me Again* (1989), *Season of Fear* (1989), Dennis Hopper's *Backtrack* (1990), J.S Cardone's *A Climate for Killing* (1991), *Delusion* (1991), *Blue Desert* (1991), *White Sands* (1992), the Drew Barrymore–starring *Gun Crazy* (1992) and Dahl's masterful *Red Rock West* (1993) all flirt with the desert terror genre to various degrees, but their double-crossing plots riddled with hard-luck heroes and femme fatales mostly avoid any truly weird or disturbing content, owing more to polished '40s noirs like *Double Indemnity* or *The Postman Always Rings Twice* than the wilder, more rugged likes of *Detour* or *The Hitch-Hiker*.

The dark psychological thriller *Eye of the Storm* (1991) strays further from the neo-noir trappings of its contemporaries to spin a Gothic narrative of family tragedy, sexual frustration and crippling madness. An ochre-tinted desert prologue sets up the tragic tale as two criminals rob and kill the proprietors of the isolated Easy Rest Inn before trying to shoot the couple's young son Steven. The boy's jump from a second-story window saves his life, but leaves him permanently blind. Ten years later, Steven (Bradley Gregg) lives at the inn with his more responsible older brother Ray (Craig Sheffer), who carries guilt from his absence during their parents' murder. The brothers' private world is interrupted by the sudden, noisy arrival of drunken, loutish Marvin Gladstone (Dennis Hopper) and his tart-tongued spouse Sandra (Lara Flynn Boyle). A competitive vibe immediately sets in between the brothers, both of whom desire Sandra in their own bizarre ways; the grotesquely immature Steven is more obvious, as he snoops through her suitcase and later tries to grope her in the swimming pool. Though rarely sober, the raving, abusive Marvin is acutely aware of the interest in Sandra, leading to a series of tension-filled episodes that ultimately threaten to destroy Ray and Steven's warped bond.

Driven largely by the manipulations and perversions of its unbalanced quartet of fringe dwellers, *Eye of the Storm* is nicely unpredictable for the first hour or so, especially in the scenes between live-wire Hopper (who knows how to deliver a line like, "Home is where you hang yourself.") and ice queen Boyle (who at one point tells her hubby she wants to "spit on his brains"); the pair would be reunited a few years later in the superior desert noir *Red Rock West*. Their dysfunctional dynamic (the two are on their way to renew their vows in Vegas, but fight continuously) lacks motivation, but at least it's not boring; the same can't be said of Ray and Steven's sibling rivalry, which after a time becomes repetitive as Ray slides deeper into psychosis. Though a few scenes (specifically one in which Sandra and Ray kiss in front of Steven, who listens attentively) flirt with the hellish love triangle at the heart of the film, Marvin's abrupt departure pushes the script further into the standard thriller realm, as a visit from the sheriff leads to a storm-swept climax which finds the crazed, knife-wielding Ray reincarnated as an unstoppable, Michael Myers–esque boogeyman. The '80s slasher film is alive and well in the *Eye of the Storm*, but the more disturbing implications of the film's plot are often left twitching by the roadside.

Director/co-writer Yuri Zeltser (whose horror credits include the scripts for *Bad Dreams* and *Mirror, Mirror*) allows his film to float lazily between noir pastiche (Boyle's bleached-blonde look feels less like a character choice and more like a recreation of some long-ago glamour shot) and amped-up slasher antics (most obviously in the *Halloween-*

inspired climax). With Ray and Steven's criminal behavior alluded to early on, the film leans heavily on the considerable talents of its cast and Karl Walter Lindenlaub's photography, which gives the film's motel location an appropriately dusty, wind-blown atmosphere. If all the pieces don't fit together as well as hoped, the film still has enough gonzo moments, most of them provided by the always reliable Hopper and Sheffer (the latter of whom co-starred in desert noir *Blue Desert* the same year, and would go on to contribute an even more uninhibited performance in *The Road Killers*). More unsettled than unsettling, *Storm*'s greatest contribution to the genre may ultimately be its motel set, which was built for the production and remained standing, after which it was subsequently utilized by other desert terrors, such as *The Devil's Rejects* and *No Man's Land: The Rise of Reeker*, over the years.

By the mid-'90s, the neo-noir subgenre was already approaching saturation point, as an increasing number of quirky Southwestern thrillers—*Quick* (1993), J.S Cardone's *Black Day, Blue Night* (1995), *Baja* (1995), *Scorpion Spring* (1996), *Lewis & Clark & George* (1997) and *American Perfekt* (1997)—continued popping up on cable channels and video store shelves. Often featuring the same filmmakers (Cardone, Dahl), actors (Sheffer, Hopper, Michelle Forbes, Robert Forster) and locations, desert neo-noir was verging dangerously close to self-parody by the time two major American filmmakers turned their attention to its stylistic and narrative possibilities. The resulting pair of films, David Lynch's *Lost Highway* (1996) and Oliver Stone's *U-Turn* (1997), both reinvigorated and transformed the previous decade's worth of noir/thriller clichés in their own distinctive ways. Both filmmakers had grappled with desert imagery before—Lynch with his misguided sci-fi epic *Dune* (1984) and Stone with *The Doors* (1990) and *Natural Born Killers*—but neither had embraced the genre's noir history so thoroughly as they did here. On the surface, Lynch's ambiguous, dreamlike exploration of identity and Stone's more playful, blackly comic vision couldn't be more different, but both contain numerous callbacks to desert terror's past inspirations, as well as taking the genre to new levels of darkness and absurdity.

Lost Highway is the less obvious desert terror film of the two, with its frantically undercranked opening credits (set to David Bowie's appropriately ghostly "I'm Deranged") leading not to the desert, but the Hollywood Hills, where beleaguered saxophonist Fred Madison (Bill Pullman) is ominously informed that "Dick Laurent is dead" through his home intercom. Who Dick Laurent is, and why he may (or may not) be dead, is one of the many mysteries that circulate throughout Lynch's film. Fred and his gorgeous wife Renee (Patricia Arquette, sporting a Bettie Page 'do) become the target of a series of anonymously-mailed videotapes, which feature footage filmed inside their house. The pair of detectives sent to investigate cast suspicion on Fred, who "hates" video cameras and prefers to "remember things my own way ... not necessarily the way they happened." Fred's chance encounter at a party with a sinister, pale-faced Mystery Man (Robert Blake, providing a link to the true-crime classic *In Cold Blood*) who defies the rules of time and space leads to a half-remembered night of terror that climaxes with Renee's brutal death.

Found guilty of his wife's murder and sentenced to death row, Fred develops a series of crippling headaches while in solitary confinement. During one particularly powerful episode, Fred has a vision of a cabin in the middle of the desert, burning in reverse until it gradually reassembles itself; the Mystery Man then steps out of the cabin before returning inside. Desert imagery continues as the two-lane highway reappears, dead-ending in front of Pete Dayton (Balthazar Getty) whose appearance signals Fred's transformation—

Alice (Patricia Arquette) and Fred Madison (Bill Pullman) are just two of the troubled souls traveling down David Lynch's *Lost Highway* (1997).

and the beginning of the film's second act. While locked in his cell, "wife-killer" Fred has somehow transformed into Pete, a teenage mechanic with criminal connections. Pete's return to his San Fernando Valley home is cloaked in mystery, as his parents (Gary Busey and Lucy Butler) and girlfriend Sheila (Natasha Gregson Wagner) seem afraid to discuss the details of what happened that night. Gradually, echoes of Pete's former life seep into his everyday routine: Fred's sax solo screams from a radio, crime boss Mr. Eddy (Robert Loggia) is called "Dick Laurent" by detectives, and, most significantly, Eddy's blonde armpiece Alice (Arquette again) seduces Pete, ensnaring him in a convoluted murder/robbery plot that leads the two of them onto the "lost highway" leading, finally, to the desert.

Lost Highway completely embraces the desert for its final—and most disturbing—act. Heightened desert noir imagery (double-crosses, femme fatales, motel rendezvous, bodies left in shallow graves) dominates the narrative as Lynch uses the desert as less a physical destination than a state of mind. When Pete and Alice arrive at the isolated cabin to meet Alice's fence, the result is like intruding on someone else's dream (or nightmare). A slow-motion love scene, lit by the dusty headlights of Pete's car to the soaring strains of This Mortal Coil's "Song of the Siren" acquires a solemn, almost elegiac air, ending with the nude Alice's departure into the cabin (a lovely, surreal image) and Pete's inexplicable transformation back into Fred. After encountering the Mystery Man (who wields an incriminating video camera), Fred escapes to the Lost Highway Hotel, a dreamlike façade where he finds Renee cavorting with Mr. Eddy. Fred drags Eddy to the middle of the desert where, aided by the Mystery Man, he slices the crime boss' throat. Fred returns to Los Angeles only to race back to the desert once again, pursued by a phalanx of police cars as another insane metamorphosis takes place. Whether he is "becoming" Pete again, or something entirely different, remains unknown as the film fades back up on the familiar two-lane highway once again and the credits roll, forming an enclosed loop…

The screenplay for *Lost Highway* (1997) was published in multiple countries, including France.

The first film in Lynch's "Los Angeles Trilogy" which set the filmmaker on a new, more personal journey, *Lost Highway* is also the director's third collaboration with novelist/screenwriter Barry Gifford, whose cult novel *Wild at Heart* had previously been adapted by Lynch into his controversial, Palme d'Or–winning 1990 film. This time around, Gifford worked directly with Lynch on the screenplay, an entirely original concoction bearing the influences of both artists. Lynch had revealed his noir leanings as early as his masterpiece *Blue Velvet* (1986) and continued to develop them throughout *Twin Peaks* (1990–91) and its follow-up feature *Twin Peaks: Fire Walk with Me* (1992). In the introduction to the *Lost Highway* published screenplay, Lynch asserts that his initial description of the film as "twenty-first century noir horror film" is "sort of baloney." It is, in fact, a near-perfect description, as *Lost Highway* displays the filmmaker's most obvious adoption of archetypal noir themes and visuals before surrendering to head-spinning horror. Gifford, who once wrote an entire book about his favorite noirs (titled *The Devil Thumbs a Ride*) and whose *Wild at Heart* also featured a third act rooted in desert depravity, is equally responsible for this new direction. Interestingly, Gifford's presence does not necessarily insure a stronger structural balance to the work anymore than the presence of stars like Pullman or Arquette guarantees a more commercial product; if anything, *Lost Highway* is Lynch's darkest, most nightmarish film since *Eraserhead* (1976) and remains one of his most ambiguous and challenging works.

Lynch's film also functions on an entirely sensual level, with Peter Deming's lush, shadowy photography perfectly merging reality and dreamspace into a continuous whole. Longtime Lynch collaborator Angelo Badalamenti's score is alternately achingly romantic and terrifyingly raw, augmented by soundtrack supervision by Trent Reznor, who performed a similar function on *Natural Born Killers*. While some of Reznor's choice perfectly set the mood (Barry Adamson, Antonio Carlos Jobim), others, like the inclusion of contemporary nu-metal acts Rammstein and Marilyn Manson (the latter of whose members cameo in the snuff film sequence) feel less appropriate and, in a few sequences, badly date the film. The cast of Lynch newcomers (only *Eraserhead*'s Jack Nance is familiar from past films) mostly works, with Pullman finding the perfect shades of paranoia in Fred Madison, Arquette providing plenty of sex appeal in a dual role (this is by far the most brazenly erotic of the filmmaker's works) and Loggia and—especially—Blake registering strongly in competing villain roles.

As a desert terror film, *Lost Highway* is also one of the most deceptively abstract. Despite the title's promise of a desert-bound journey, the first two-thirds of the film delay this trip, instead threading a few selective, borderline subliminal images (the highway at night, the burning cabin) like bread crumbs dropped in Lynch's forest of paranoia. Though infrequent, these "desert moments" signal the film's most significant storyline and tonal shifts; Fred's jailhouse transformation (and subsequent liberation) occurs amidst such imagery, just as Pete's physical return to his alter ego also takes place in the middle of the desert night. Significantly, *Lost Highway*'s final section—which contains many of the plot's revelations—takes place entirely within the desert's dreamlike boundaries. While much of the film remains open to interpretation, Lynch's decision to open and close the film on the "lost highway" of the title (on which the viewer remains as "lost" as Fred Madison) speaks volumes about the desert's meaning in the film's overall design.

Along with its more psychological use of the desert, *Lost Highway* is one of the first desert terror films to openly comment on the desert's proximity to Hollywood in an unusual way. Casual verbal and visual references to Los Angeles abound (Fred and Renee's house is "near the observatory," the Hollywood sign appears in several scenes) and the story takes place in a world of showbiz mansions and parties, yet the film avoids any direct references to the movie business. Instead, it embraces the darkest side of motion pictures, initially embodied by the series of amateurish yet unnerving voyeuristic videos sent to Fred, then progressing to adult movies (Mr. Eddy hands Pete a cassette, asking "You like pornos?"), and finally, to the ultimate taboo of snuff films. Whether this was

Lynch and Gifford's intention or not, the result feels like a mordant commentary on the industry's pandering to public appetites for sex and violence, with both taken to their ugliest, most downmarket extremes. Taking the allusion further, the film's relentless focus on crises of identity (Fred/Pete, Renee/Alice, Eddy/Dick Laurent) can be interpreted as a jibe at the entertainer's chameleonic need to reinvent him or herself, not only for a part, but as a survival tactic in a ruthless business. Lynch would leave the desert behind while continuing to explore these themes in his follow-up films *Mulholland Dr.* (2002) and *Inland Empire* (2008), both of which focus on fractured identities, self-reflexive imagery and looping narratives which directly confront the absurd and tragic world of studio filmmaking.

Just as Lynch strands Fred Madison in a metaphysical netherworld of double crosses and dual identities, *U-Turn* finds its unlucky protagonist mired in an absurdly heightened noir nightmare. Adapted by author John Ridley from his novel *Stray Dogs*, Oliver Stone's big-budget pastiche embraces desert noir themes, archetypes, and imagery as fervently as Lynch's film; the result is the ultimate thinking man's guilty pleasure. Stone employs a top-shelf cast (Sean Penn, Nick Nolte, Billy Bob Thornton) while continuing the experimental photographic and editorial styling of *Natural Born Killers* to breathe life into Ridley's unapologetically amoral and (even more shocking for Stone) apolitical tale of luck-challenged antiheroes, murderous businessmen, triple crossing broads, and the most hellish small town ever committed to celluloid. The film's caustic tone is apparent from the first frames, as Peggy Lee's "It's a Good Day" chirps over a gorgeous aerial view of a Mustang convertible roaring through the desert at sunup. Classic desert iconography (Joshua trees, Indian pictographs) gives way to ill omens—vultures picking over a coyote carcass, a black cat skittering into the car's path—before a blown radiator forces former tennis pro turned gambler Bobby Cooper (Penn), to stop at a crossroads. Bobby's nervous radio twiddling (which, when paired with the amped-up desert imagery, strongly recalls *NBK*'s opening) gives way to the lilting refrains of Ennio Morricone's superb score as California-bound Bobby makes the fateful choice to head toward the ironically-named (though real-life) town of Superior, Arizona.

After depositing his car at a comically filthy junkyard run by literal grease monkey Darrell (Thornton), Bobby walks to Superior (described as "just like a town, only uglier"), which consists of little more than a single mostly deserted, windblown block populated by a smattering of decrepit buildings. An encounter with a blind Native American vet (John Voight) is interrupted by the arrival of the coolly seductive Grace (Jennifer Lopez), who Bobby accompanies back to her lavish, western-themed desert estate. Though Bobby is evasive about answering her questions (he's "from all over," with "unfinished business" in Vegas), a series of quick flashbacks explain his bandaged hand and cash-filled duffle bag. Bobby's attempted seduction of his host is interrupted by her husband Jake (Nolte), a towering bully who assaults Bobby, then offers him a ride back into town. Having immediately pegged Bobby as "a man without scruples," Jake casually asks him to kill Grace. When the disturbed Bobby insists "I'm no murderer," Jake asks, "How do you know if you've never tried?"

From this point on, Bobby's simple stopover grows increasingly absurd, as a chain of fateful occurrences—a botched liquor store robbery, run-ins with the local sheriff (Powers Boothe) and a pair of screwed up teenagers (Claire Danes and Joaquin Phoenix)—leave him nearly broke and stranded. "Is everybody in this town on drugs?" an exasperated Bobby cries out, but local diner patron (Bo Hopkins) offers a more likely

In *U-Turn* (1997), gambler Bobby Cooper (Sean Penn) suffers a breakdown near the desert town of Superior, Arizona.

explanation: "People out here in the desert just go bonkers for some reason." As Bobby's situation worsens, however, the increasingly bizarre situations and aggressive behavior of the locals begin to feel less random and more like interconnected parts of some sinister conspiracy (this is an Oliver Stone movie, after all) to keep him from leaving the town. Equally desperate to escape, Grace convinces Bobby to murder the abusive Jake, after which the pair will (of course) drive to California, leaving both their troubled pasts behind.

Naturally, nothing goes exactly as planned. Jake catches Bobby before he can do the deed, then a tomahawk-wielding Grace finishes the job. Turned on more by Jake's money than sex with her new lover, Grace's loyalties soon become as doubtful as Bobby's. On the way out of town, the pair are stopped by the sheriff, with whom the two-timing Grace has also been carrying on a secret affair (?!). With thousands of stolen dollars (and a few dead bodies) in tow, the increasingly disillusioned Bobby and his "lying, backstabbing psycho bitch" partner make their final stop at the scenic—and deadly—Apache Leap. Bobby's one last bid for freedom lands him right back where he started, only much worse for wear. "You're still lucky," the dying Bobby groans as vultures circle overhead and shadows engulf the canyon. Like *Lost Highway*, the film closes with the same song heard during the opening credits. "It's a Good Day," indeed...

A seriocomic odyssey that flirts with darkness before plunging headfirst into a bloody nightmare, *U-Turn* is the *After Hours* of desert terror movies. The film knowingly

Grace (Jennifer Lopez) strikes one last bargain with Bobby from atop Apache Leap in *U-Turn* (1997).

parades a compendium of clichés from decades of stranded scenarios—the breakdown in a hostile, middle of nowhere town, untrustworthy locals, a sexually manipulative woman who yearns to escape—and reinvigorates them with a potent blend of jet-black humor and mind-bending horror. As artistically groundbreaking as its more "important" companion piece, *Natural Born Killers*, *U-Turn* is the "lighter" and funnier of the two films. Despite the occasional creepy undertone, Bobby's futile quest to escape from Superior is mostly played for sick laughs. Amusing dialogue (Phoenix's character, Toby N. Tucker, is nicknamed "TNT–cause when I go off, somebody gets hurt!") and running gags abound: everyone in town asks about Bobby's hand (and offers the same advice), he can never seem to get a cold drink, and the price of his car repairs skyrockets every time he returns to Darrell's garage.

U-Turn is also the more nihilistic of the two films. *NBK*'s self-consciously corny "happy ending" at least offers some fleeting hope for its pair of misunderstood murderers, but in Superior, "Hope is a four-letter word" (as Grace says), with none for roguish antihero Bobby, nor for anyone else he meets along his cursed path. Ridley's script is far from linear, instead adopting a concentric structure that becomes more and more unnerving as the story continues to turn back on itself, time and again ("One of them days where you feel like you're running in circles ... and you ain't no closer to where you was trying to get than when you started," Darrell muses), like a *Twilight Zone* episode directed by

Sam Peckinpah. The wicked laughter one hears over the closing shot is likely attributed to the "spirits" the film invokes more than once, but it might as well be Stone (who films many key sequences, including the opening and closing shots, from an omniscient viewpoint) and Ridley laughing at the characters, and us.

The third act of the film, after ninety minutes of small-town caricatures and slow-burn tension, echoes *Lost Highway*'s desert-bound final act, as it delivers on some of the darker promises made earlier while embracing the raw terror of the horror film. Stone and Ridley explore the source of Grace's deep-seated madness, which, the film infers, was caused as much by her fucked-up parentage as by the suffocating boredom of small-town life. Jake's death is a gory, drawn-out affair, and the morbidly erotic aftermath perfectly merges sex and death, as Bobby and Grace finally consummate their love beside her ex's butchered corpse ("Let him watch," she sighs). There's no going back after this, and Stone doesn't want to; instead, he ventures even further into the realm of the macabre, in a fight to the finish at Apache Leap that openly mocks the cop-out ending of *Thelma and Louise*. In these final, weirdly tragic scenes, the distanced amusement of Bobby's frustratingly funny adventures in Superior gives way to bloodstained grotesquerie.

A deliberate parody of noir/ thriller/desert horror clichés, *U-Turn*'s only goal is to outdo those films on every level—and it does. The cast lends depth and humor to their knowingly clichéd roles; Penn is the Loser, Nolte the Heavy, Lopez the Femme Fatale, etc. Thornton, Nolte, and Phoenix contribute go-for-broke portrayals, while Lopez has never been so desirable—or delivered a riskier, more nuanced performance. Initially wanting to shoot the film in black and white, Stone and director of photography Robert Richardson ended up mixing various color film stocks to create a distinctive, hyper-real visual style; town exteriors and desert scenes use cheaper reversal film (used primarily for aerial surveillance) to achieve a rougher, more saturated texture, while interiors are muted and silkier. Editing and sound work also adopt many of *NBK*'s formal techniques, amping up every scene to near operatic intensity while on-the-nose rockabilly standards like "Ring of Fire" explode out of nowhere with the force of a mariachi band. Topping it all off is Morricone's lush, playful, Oscar-worthy score, which purposefully recalls not only his iconic Spaghetti western themes of the '60s but also the haunting refrains of his '70s giallo soundtracks.

In the same way *NBK* referenced and updated desert terror's western and true crime origins, *U-Turn* honors the genre's roots while adding a few new wrinkles to the formula: Grace, for example, is the first Native American character to appear (let alone assume a leading role) in a desert noir, and surely the first femme fatale of such descent (interestingly, her closest counterpart in the genre, *Hex*'s "Oriole," was also played by an actress of Latin American ethnicity). The film's only real failing (which is part of the point, really) is a tendency to repeat itself; one gets the suspicion that a few extraneous subplots or characters could probably have been excised with little or no damage to the overall narrative. But as always with Stone, more is more, and *U-Turn* remains one of his most unapologetically entertaining and timeless works. Its middling box office coincided with the relative death of the desert noir movie, along with unfortunately signaling the end of Stone's more brazenly experimental period. The Oscar-winning filmmaker would go on to embrace more prestigious subjects with even bigger budgets, while never achieving the discomfiting power of either of his two desert terror outings.

Unable to top the excesses of *Lost Highway* and *U-Turn*, the desert noir lost steam in the last few years of the '90s, with a handful of latecomers—J.S. Cardone's *Outside*

Ozona (1998), *Clay Pigeons* (1998), *Sand Trap* (1998) and Ray Liotta–starrers *Phoenix* (1998) and *Pilgrim* (2000)—struggling to make an impression before the genre headed south of the border with entries like *Slow Burn* (2000), *Way of the Gun* (2000) and *Desert Saints* (2002). The stranded scenario, however, would continue to occupy a significant role in the desert terror genre in the following years while developing in new and disturbing directions, as new groups of ill-fated travelers found themselves at the mercy of locals while waylaid in "middle of nowhere" towns.

4

Highways to Hell Part I
Death Drivers

"I think everybody got somethin' in their past, some sin, some awful, secret thing. A lot of people walkin' around out there, already dead. Just need to be put out of their misery. That's where I come in. Fate's messenger."—Mickey Knox, *Natural Born Killers*

The desert terror film flourished throughout the '70s, with single-location stranded scenarios like *The Hills Have Eyes* and *When You Comin' Back, Red Ryder?* having a major impact on the genre's development. At the same time, a different, yet equally significant strain of road-based desert terrors began to emerge. Based around the empty highways and lonely back roads of the Southwest, these travel-oriented tales invoked the perils of road trips in the form of murderous motorists (*Natural Born Killers*), homicidal hitchhikers (*The Hitcher*), and inexplicable vehicular violence (*Duel*). Speeding beyond the dusty parameters of the small-town Southwest to encompass miles of murder and mayhem, these faster-paced road thrillers visualize the type of cross-country crime sprees that *The Sadist* (and *The Hitch-Hiker* before it) only hinted at. On these Highways to Hell, evil can just easily be standing by the roadside as behind the wheel, and cars and trucks become the ultimate killing machines. Though sporting a larger scope than *The Sadist*, many elements of these films—a limited cast, isolated locations, life or death stakes—echo its effectively minimalist setup.

The indelible image of the maniacal Tibbs gripping the steering wheel as he doggedly pursues Doris across desert hills hangs heavily over the first group of road-based desert terrors, known as "death driver" films. These movies focus on killers who, like Tibbs, use various gas-powered vehicles to hunt their prey across the desert wastelands of America. The automobile-based predators of *Night Terror*, *Death Valley*, *Victims!* and *Mirage* turn their victims' road trips into desperate races for survival while racking up serious body counts along the way. *The China Lake Murders*, while more restrained in its bloodletting, features perhaps the most disturbing death driver so far: an L.A.–based motorcycle cop whose desert holidays are spent killing off innocent motorists, without an ounce of remorse, pity, or motivation.

The '90s expanded the death driver from an individual menace to pairs or even larger groups of maniacs. Oliver Stone's controversial *Natural Born Killers* updates *The Sadist*'s original "killer couple" Tibbs and Judy with its tale of married serial killers/media darlings Mickey and Mallory Knox, whose multi-state murder spree goes beyond the

Night Terror (1977) is one of many TV movies that are only commercially available on VHS.

type of true-crime carnage that inspired *The Sadist*'s screenplay. Larger, loose-knit "families" of death drivers followed in the Knoxes' wake, such as the psychotic gang of outcasts known as *The Road Killers* and the drug-fueled bikers of *High Desert*, both of whom target civilized families who must inevitably resort to savagery if they are to survive. In the rural paranoia tale *Breakdown*, the white-collar hero must outsmart a community of killer kidnappers, led by a family-man trucker whose appearance is even more outwardly normal than *The China Lake Murders*' badge-wearing menace. Whether traveling on two, four, or eighteen wheels, the death driver remains one of the desert terror's most potent boogeymen.

As with many early desert terrors, the first death driver film was made for television. *Night Terror* (1977) stars Valerie Harper as Carol, a high-strung housewife in the middle of a family move from Arizona to Denver; her husband Walter (Michael Tolan) plans to meet her for a second honeymoon at a Phoenix motel before continuing to their new home together. At the same time, a mute ex-soldier (Richard Romanus, billed simply as "The Killer") drives through the desert with a delivery of semiautomatic rifles in his trunk. Prompted by her husband's delayed arrival and a sick child, Carol decides to make the sixteen-hour drive to Denver on her own. Low on gas and insulted by other motorists ("Lousy women drivers!" snaps one lady after Carol runs a red light) and obnoxious teenage gas station attendants ("Pumps are closed—report us! Big deal!"), Carol's troubles intensify significantly after she witnesses the shooting of a highway patrolman by—who else?—The Killer, whose dog tags suggest (but never explicitly state) his status as a Nam vet.

The remainder of the film plays out as a game of cat and mouse, often unspooling in what feels like real time. Some situations, like Carol's poking around a closed gas station, eventually become tedious, while others, such as a run-in with a drunken businessman on a rainy canyon pass, add a nice touch of irony to the proceedings. The best sequences exhibit an almost Hitchcockian flair, as when Carol accepts a ride from the Killer, who she gradually comes to recognize through a series of telltale clues. With its nighttime setting and suburban female lead, the film almost plays like an inversion of desert terror classic *Duel*; like that film, *Night Terror*'s lower budget works in its favor, with the cost-cutting location shooting and driving sequences adding to the nerve-wracking, middle-of-nowhere ambience. Carol's character is treated with a similar realism, becoming tougher and more resourceful while never transforming into superwoman, though her choice to keep the ordeal to herself, while enduring hubby's condescending remarks ("You're not exactly Gloria Steinem, y'know?") suggests that, even in the late '70s, women's lib still had some ways to go in terms of cultural penetration. Driven (literally and figuratively) by the likable Harper, *Night Terror* is a reasonably effective slice of small-screen desert terror.

City folk continued to be menaced throughout the starkly beautiful landscapes of *Death Valley* (1982), a slasher-styled tale of automotive annihilation, which touts high production values and a solid cast, but is only partially successful at dramatizing the horrors conjured up by its title. Precocious ten-year-old Billy (Peter Billingsley) arrives in Arizona to join his mother, Sally (Catherine Hicks), and her new boyfriend, Mike (Paul Le Mat) for a family trip through Death Valley. As the trio visits old west-themed sights, a sinister-looking black car (bearing the ominous plate HEX-576) appears to follow them. Only Billy notices it, and just when we think we're in for another *Duel* riff, the movie shifts gears, as an attractive young couple parked near an abandoned gold mine

Billy (Peter Billingsley), his mother Sally (Catherine Hicks) and her boyfriend Mike (Paul Le Mat) take a terrifying road trip to *Death Valley* (1982).

is graphically butchered by an unseen maniac. While this double murder is the film's bloodiest, it's far from the last, as the film's death driver continues to claim more victims while pursuing witness Billy from one scenic desert attraction to another.

Juggling family drama with mild suspense and trendy gore, *Death Valley* at times feels just a few stabbings away from a made-for-TV likes of *Night Terror*. But for the most part, the film is a solid ride, thanks to Stephen Burum's excellent location photography, Dana Kaproff's unsettling score and strong performances. Billy is a unique, memorable protagonist (films in this genre rarely include children, let alone make them the lead) who is not only likable, but clearly smarter than any of the adults, including the typically-useless local sheriff (Wilford Brimley). Director Dick Richards stages some nicely tense moments during the family's visit to Frontier Town, a touristy ghost town teeming with cowboys who fire blanks at each other. In one standout scene, the killer (wearing a cowboy costume), stalks Billy through a museum teeming with creepy, tourist trap–like mannequins and artifacts. It's one of many references to the old west throughout the film, from the killer's gold miner past, to the classic westerns Billy (while dressed in full cowboy regalia) watches in his hotel room. Eventually, teary-eyed melodrama wins out over body count, but *Death Valley* still entertains as a western spin on the familiar slasher tale.

The minimalist desert terror offering *Raw Courage* (1984) pits a trio of long-distance runners against a demented cadre of survivalists in the New Mexico desert. Running buddies Pete (Ronny Cox, who also co-scripted and produced), Roger (Canadian horror staple Art Hindle) and Greg (Tim Maier) leave their significant others to take off on a two day, seventy-two mile run across the open desert, with their finish line one of the main attractions at a small-town "Pioneer Day" celebration. Along with the obvious physical challenges of the trek, each man has his own personal issues to overcome: Pete, the oldest and least physically fit, is haunted by childhood bullying, Roger's attractive girlfriend (Lois Chiles) wants to move their relationship to the next level, and twenty-two-year-old Greg's controlling father treats him like a teenager. None of this psychological baggage compares, however, to the sudden appearance of Col. Crouse (M. Emmet Walsh) and his dozen or so "soldiers" who rise out of the sand with machetes and capture the three men, dragging them to their camp as part of a survival exercise. Crouse releases the runners, but a few heated exchanges between Greg and second in command Sonny (William Russ) leads to a later confrontation which ends with Roger (the group's nominal leader) dead, and Pete and Greg forced to fight for their lives against the Crouse's ragtag army of motorcycle-riding death drivers.

Slickly crafted but unafraid to get its hands dirty, *Raw Courage* (originally released theatrically as *Courage*) benefits from the novelty of its concept, which, like the less effective *Survival Run*, pits two groups of desert outsiders against one another. The streamlined narrative is well-handled by first-time director Robert Rosen (a veteran producer of many John Frankenheimer films), who gets excellent performances from his cast (particularly Cox, whose presence can't help but recall his work in the survival-horror classic *Deliverance*) while orchestrating number of muscular action sequences, many of which feature the lead actors performing their own stunts. Shot entirely on location in Las Cruces, New Mexico, the film consistently finds creative ways to utilize its rugged locations, especially in a sand dune skirmish which spells Roger's doom, and a nifty rock-climbing scene which climaxes with Pete's memorable encounter with a rattlesnake. Rosen's use of Steadicam and handheld camerawork often brings the viewer directly in the thick of the action, increasing the tension and excitement of the many chases and fights. While lacking the social critique (or hardcore violence) of other desert terrors, for the most part this is a gripping and supremely entertaining film whose emphasis on action over horror in no way lessens its effectiveness.

The grindhouse golden age that spawned desert terrors like *Barn of the Naked Dead* and *Trip with the Teacher* was pretty much over by the mid–'80s, but apparently nobody told that to the makers of *Victims!* (1985), an unapologetically misogynistic (and technically incompetent) sleazefest that finds a quartet of young women attacked by a pair of killer rapists while on a desert campout. A haphazardly edited opening montage treats us to no fewer than three bloody murders, followed by a robbery/shootout. The death driving duo responsible—who go by the names of Peter and Eric—escape to a rural area where they surprise a pair of lovers, quickly subduing the man and raping his girlfriend. The cumulative effect is of a hastily assembled series of clips tacked on by the filmmakers (or a nervous distributor) to achieve an acceptable running time. The main narrative (and desert-set portion of the film) starts with scantily clad girlfriends Debbie, Jill, Lisa and Janet heading out to the desert for a geology field trip. Their brief stop at a filling station provokes comments from a middle-aged couple ("little hussies ... a good spanking is what they need," the wife snorts while her husband leers), as well as drawing attention from Peter and Eric, who ogle them while waiting to hold up the place.

The rapists don't cross paths with the women until about three-quarters of the way through the film, when they cause a (laughably-executed) rockslide and quickly separate the foursome. From this point on, the film gets progressively uglier; Eric forces Lisa and Debbie to strip and perform sexual acts on each other before raping Debbie, while Peter has his way with Jill. These two goons turn out to be deranged Nam vets (maybe they knew *Night Terror*'s nameless "Killer"?) who met cute over the killing of a "gook" prostitute. Janet, wounded from a falling rock, manages to stab Eric, and Lisa finishes the deed, shoving him off a rock to his death. The girls overpower Peter, lowering a knife between his legs with the immortal line "When it's all over, you'll look just like us!" before the film cuts to an abrupt, unsatisfying epilogue.

Victims' hasty denouement is typical of the film's ultra-conservative tone, which brings up the girls' skimpy wardrobe as suitable grounds for sexual assault again and again. "You like to show it off, teasing. That's all you women do is tease men. And you wonder why you get raped!" says Eric when he first encounters Lisa; he later tells her, "You damn well know you're to blame. You enticed us!" Unfortunately, this point of view seems to be shared by not only everyone else in the film, but the filmmakers as well. Director Jeff Hathcock lingers a little too long on the scenes of degradation, with the rapists' off-camera commands ("Take off the bottom!" "Now do it to her.") blurring the line between character and filmmaker in the most distasteful way imaginable. The women's revenge, on the other hand, is conveyed with fast cuts that barely convey the action. Unsurprisingly, Hathcock does little with his desert setting (the film was shot in Hesperia, California), confining most of the action to the campsite area. Though produced in the mid '80s, the film is rife with the kind of crude filmmaking techniques associated with '60s sexploitation. Shots are over and under-exposed, actors flub lines and look at the camera, dialog is muffled, and the hasty end credits fail to list character names. As indefensible as it is inept, the straight-to-video *Victims!* would be upsetting if it wasn't so dumb.

The latecomer death driver flick *Mirage* (1990) is even more obscure than *Victims!*, as it has yet to be released in the United States, despite popping up on video in Canada and Europe. While it also concerns a desert campout gone bad, the similarities end there, as *Mirage* sports professional production values, an attractive cast, and well-executed gore effects, and makes good use of its desert setting. An ominous black truck circles the area as a group of friends assemble for a get-together in the center of a vast dry lakebed. After nearly half an hour of beer swilling, awful rock tunes and gratuitous boob shots, the partying is interrupted when the truck—whose driver remains unseen—barrels out of the night, destroying one of the group's vehicles and abducting party host Greg (Kenneth Johnson), who is later found buried up to his neck in sand before being dispatched with a grenade. The next day, Mary (Nicole Anton) and Trip (Kevin McParland) also die agonizing deaths, as the black-gloved death driver stalks his prey, materializing out of nowhere at any time.

Finally, only plucky blonde Chris (Jennifer McAllister) is left alive to fend off the maniacal killer (B.G. Steers, billed simply as "Villain"), who taunts his prey with childish remarks ("I always wondered how long you prom queen bitches could last!") as he stalks her around a corpse-littered rock pile. The film's attempts to humanize its formerly faceless killer (at one point invoking *The Sadist* with the line, "I never liked school") fall flat, as his true motivations remain vague. Even harder to swallow is his sudden transformation into an unstoppable, quasi-supernatural boogeyman, as Chris is forced to use a crossbow, shotgun and a knife before the Villain finally expires—or does he? An ambiguous ending suggests, by way of an off-camera voice over and a final shot of the black

Simitar Video's garish artwork for the sleazy desert slasher *Victims!* (1985).

truck rumbling across the desert, that the Villain's death itself may itself have been a mirage.

Along with *Death Valley* and *Blood Frenzy*, *Mirage* illustrates the considerable challenges of making a desert slasher film in a wide-open, sunny environment where, unlike the typical woods or suburban settings, there is literally nowhere for the victims—or the killer—to hide. The film's sole location—a dry lakebed that extends infinitely in every direction—creates a palpable atmosphere of isolation, but the screenplay, which gives the killer a quasi-supernatural ability to appear and disappear whenever convenient to the plot, runs on a kind of nightmare logic which will either be embraced or strongly rejected by most viewers. In some ways, the repetitive monotony of the environment gradually lends the story a profoundly disorienting effect, as the characters seem trapped in a ten-minute loop of murder and madness, where escape is impossible, no matter how far they run or which direction they head. Despite its stubborn adherence to slasher clichés, the misguided *Mirage* is still much more entertaining than its relative obscurity would suggest.

The same year also brought us *The China Lake Murders* (1990), a well-crafted TV movie which introduces a new kind of death driver to the genre. Expanding upon its source material, *Hitcher* director Robert Harmon's 1983 half-hour short film *China Lake*, the film follows Officer Donnelly (Michael Parks), a Los Angeles motorcycle cop who exercises his private demons by taking a yearly vacation to the small desert town of China Lake, where he spends his time abducting (and killing) innocent motorists along an isolated stretch of desert highway. Local sheriff Sam Brody (Tom Skerritt) tries to make sense of the seemingly random killings, first befriending likable loner Donnelly, then gradually coming to suspect his new confidante as mounting evidence points to him as the killer. Director Alan Metzger and screenwriter N.D. Schreiner successfully preserve the rugged beauty and acts of shocking violence that made Harmon's short so memorable, while expanding upon its themes in interesting ways.

The China Lake Murders is one of the first desert terror films to have been based on a short film, which is itself available as one of many extras on the German and British DVD releases of *The Hitcher*. Certain passages from the short remain completely intact in Metzger's feature, such as Donnelly's first murderous act, in which he pulls a woman over for "drunk driving," cuffs her, and roughly tosses her inside the trunk of her car to asphyxiate in the broiling desert heat. A follow-up sequence, also familiar from the short, finds Donnelly at a local diner, fantasizing about roughing up some local construction workers. Shifty, gravel-voiced Parks is perfectly cast, equally capable of turning on the charm or launching into a psychotic rant. A powerful sense of isolation pervades the story, as scenes of Donnelly exercising alone in the desert find an unexpected correlative in Sheriff Brody, a divorced father who has only held the position for a year and lives by himself. When Donnelly is arrested for public intoxication, Brody's first impulse is to arrest him; instead, the two men grow unexpectedly close, with Brody offering his guest trailer and cooking him dinner. While Donnelly is prone to racist or flat out weird remarks ("You can learn a lot about police work from watching pickpockets"), their relationship remains closer than Brody's casual fling with co-worker Cindy (Nancy Everhard).

As bodies keep turning up, Brody finds a connection between the last five years' worth of crimes and Donnelly's "vacations." Despite his suspicions, the sheriff continues to pursue other leads, even bringing Donnelly along on a manhunt for a local "desert

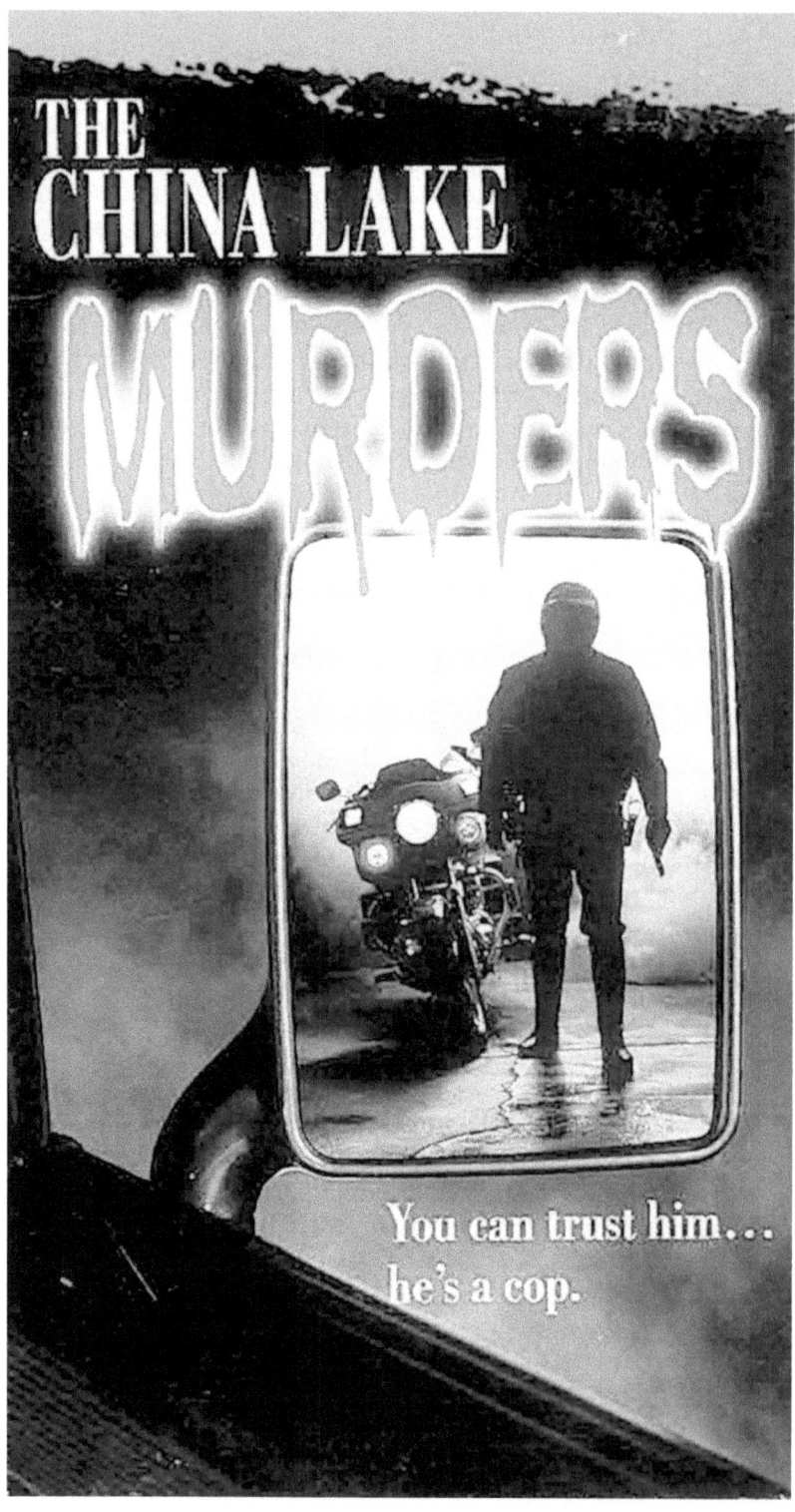

Inspired by Robert Harmon's short film *China Lake* (1983), *The China Lake Murders* (1991) remains one of the best made-for-TV desert terror films of the 90s.

rat" with a criminal past. Brody finally acknowledges the truth, but not soon enough to save his deputy, who is killed by Donnelly after stumbling onto one of his crimes. A standout scene in Brody's backyard finds him confessing his suspicions to his new friend while the two of them shoot at targets. An emergency call interrupts their standoff, and when Brody takes his aggressions out on a white-trash wife beater, it's Donnelly who subdues him, saying, "You lose control, you turn into garbage like that jerk." There's a little of Donnelly in all of us, the film seems to be saying. It's all about being willing to cross that line.

Although Donnelly is provided with flickers of backstory, he remains unknowable, driven by forces that Brody is never quite able to unravel, no matter how close the two men become. "I can do anything I want," Donnelly crows to Brody after escaping from a police lineup, "The system doesn't work anymore." When Brody defends it, Donnelly response—"If it works, then why am I going?"—is hard to argue against. Donnelly lives by his own private code, and like *The Hitcher*'s John Ryder or *White of the Eye*'s Paul White, he exerts similar control over his own death, ordering Sam to shoot him. "You haven't got much choice. Unless you want to let me go." Rendered powerless by Donnelly's own self-destructive impulse, Brody is forced to return to his solitary lifestyle. Bolstered by excellent use of desert locations, the film has a low-key authenticity that gives its twisted plotline the ring of truth; more than any other made-for-TV desert terror film, it feels based on an actual crime case. Despite its short-film origins, *The China Lake Murders* feels fully fleshed out, and yet retains a whiff of mystery that makes it ripe for revisiting.

Throughout the '90s, death driver movies veered away from the previous decade's slasher archetypes and embraced a more action-oriented direction. The low-budget but lively *Driven to Kill* (1991) is one of the first examples of the trend, with its bullet-riddled action and tough-guy clichés offset by a marital-strife drama that hearkens back to desert terrors of previous decades. In the Nevada desert, a group of bikers led by J.B. (Ron Silver lookalike Chip Campbell) rip off a major drug deal, stealing $4 million in cash from the mafia. Back in Los Angeles, alcoholic dentist Harry (Jake Jacobs) is presented with an ultimatum by his unfaithful wife Vivian (Michele McNeil): she'll file for divorce unless he agrees to accompany her on a (sober) road trip to Vegas, the goal of which is to get Harry laid (?!). Harry grudgingly agrees, and the contentious couple are soon taking their hateful act (he won't forgive her for screwing around, she's sick of his drunken behavior) on the road. During an overnight campout, Harry's search for booze leads him to the bikers' van, where he discovers the dirty money. Determined to prove that he has a "sense of adventure," Harry steals the loot and starts driving back to Los Angeles, with both the bikers and mafia soon hot on their trail.

For over an hour, *Driven to Kill* keeps its action on the road in a variety of unexpected ways, with the film's primary focus on its couple's constant bickering. At one point, the pair finds themselves stranded at a roadside café, where Vivian hitchhikes alone back to L.A. while Harry flirts with a lonely female bartender ("You ever seen *The Postman Always Rings Twice*?" she asks coyly). There's an irreverent, almost jocular tone to this section, as Vivian finds herself stuck with a series of offbeat drivers (one of whom is played by producer-director John Gazarian) before returning to save Harry from J.B and his underlings. After a scenic off-road chase through the desert, Harry and Vivian are finally caught and brought to an abandoned mine, where the tone darkens considerably (J.B. is beaten senseless, Vivian gang-raped) before wrapping up in a blood-spattered shootout between

Typically busy artwork for PM Entertainment's release of *Driven to Kill* (1991).

the bikers, mafia goons, and the beaten, bruised, and toughened-up suburbanites, who must unite against their captors to survive.

Though framed by two major action sequences, emasculated Harry and bitchy Vivian provide the film with its plot engine as well as its most amusing exchanges ("You promised not to bring any booze!" "Yeah, well you promised to love and honor."). While not exactly likable, they are far more relatable than J.B. and his cartoonish crew (who utterly fail at being threatening, despite spouting lines like: "We'll bury your bones out here in the desert!") and—even worse—the caricatured mafia "greaseballs." At its best, Harry and Vivian's venomous voyage recalls Georges Simenon's classic 1953 noir novel *Red Lights* (republished in the U.S. as *The Hitch-Hiker* and expertly filmed in 2004 under its original title) while anticipating the funny/bloody cross-country crime antics of Tarantino's script for *True Romance* (1993). The ending, too, if a bit too focused on the peripheral characters, at least forces Harry to consider his ill-fated actions, as well as seeing the couple work together (for once) as they exact some down n' dirty revenge on J.B. and his gang. Though tonally inconsistent and overplotted (the mafia seems almost superfluous after a while), the scrappy *Driven to Kill* is still a more accomplished, and affecting, desert terror movie than its immediate competitors (*Survival Run*, *The Danger Zone*) in the action/terror arena.

A much more convincing gang of death drivers rumbles through the *High Desert* (1993), a nasty little chunk of retro-exploitation which, along with the obscure scarecrow slasher *Dark Harvest*, qualifies as one of the first shot-on-video desert terror films. A shocking opening sequence almost plays like an alternate ending to *Driven to Kill*, as a bickering couple driving along a desert highway is blown to bits by coked-up, gun-wielding biker Frank (Edward Glinski). The action moves to a nearby pool hall, where Frank and his gang scuffle with bartender Pam (Alice Davidson), her boyfriend Dan (Paul Bagley) and bestie Linda (Tyleen Roberts). The enraged bikers tail the trio to their romantic weekend campout at Temple Mountain, leading to an odyssey of rape, murder, and revenge.

High Desert's harsh video look can be off-putting at times, but writer/director/cinematographer Charles T. Lang makes up for it with solid production values, fluid camerawork, and a fast-paced script that packs in plenty of blood and nudity, along with some amusingly over the top dialogue ("I'll blow her brains all over this fuckin' mountain!"), most of it coming from the swaggering, sex and violence-crazed Frank. Glinski's over the top performance is thankfully balanced out by some of the supporting cast, notably Ron Jason as sympathetic biker Joe and Carla Marrero as bisexual, drug-addicted Harley mama Suede, whose attempted seduction of Pam ("I've known a lot of men ... but none of them were any good.") results in some of the film's most heated scenes. The result is not only a fun throwback to '70s desert biker flicks like *Trip with the Teacher* and *Werewolves on Wheels*, but nowadays incurs nostalgia of its own for the analog '90s, when SOV (shot on video) movies earnestly attempted to emulate larger productions, but with significantly lesser means.

Residing at the other end of the budget spectrum, Oliver Stone's *Natural Born Killers* (1994) is not only one of the expensive desert terrors ever made (with a reported budget of $34 million), it is also easily one of the most high-profile, inflammatory and, as is often the case with Stone, politically charged entries in the genre. Here, the Oscar-winning filmmaker utilizes a barrage of multimedia techniques (including multiple film and video formats, found footage, time-lapse photography and even animation), along with an equally schizophrenic soundtrack (which features the most eclectic mix of music in a desert terror film since *Red Ryder*) to visualize this wickedly satirical tale of two psychos in love. While it assimilates elements of the road movie, western, crime and prison genres, *Natural Born Killers* is, more than anything, a romance, albeit one drenched in blood and riddled with bullets.

The film's opening shots revel in desert iconography (rattlesnakes, scorpions, coyotes) before zeroing in on a roadside diner as Leonard Cohen's "Waiting for the Miracle" croaks away on the soundtrack. Inside, flirty Mallory Knox (Juliette Lewis) gyrates to the jukebox while her better half, Mickey Knox

Serial killer superstars Mallory (Juliette Lewis) and Mickey Knox (Woody Harrelson) headline Oliver Stone's blackly comic *Natural Born Killers* (1994).

(Woody Harrelson) munches on a slice of radioactive-green key lime pie. A rowdy cowboy's pass at Mallory initiates a massacre that ends with a single survivor—the one the killers always leave to "tell the tale." Mallory's murderous rage is matched only by her unwavering love for her man, cooing "I love you, Mickey" as the crazed pair dance and kiss tenderly while fireworks explode overhead. A wild opening credits sequence follows the Knoxes through a psychedelic montage of Southwestern imagery (wild horses, the Las Vegas strip) as layers of sound melt together. As the car screeches to a halt in a desert plain, the viewer barely has time to catch their breath.

If *Kalifornia* (released one year prior, and starring Lewis in a similar role) is a cool and calculated death trip through America's collective murderous past, then *Natural Born Killers* is a punk-rock demolition derby smashing through the contemporary cult of celebrity killers, bombarding the viewer with one borderline experimental sequence after another. Mickey and Mallory's initial meeting plays out as an episode of the most disturbing sitcom ever made, "I Love Mallory," which stars Rodney Dangerfield (in an Oscar-worthy supporting turn) as Mallory's grotesque, sexually abusive Dad. It's one of the film's most original and brilliantly realized sequences, down to the tacky décor and insidious laugh track that explodes after every inappropriate one-liner. "Do you believe in fate?" Mickey asks her before being carted off to jail, a stay that is cut short by a fortunately-timed twister that facilitates his escape during a desert work detail. Together, the pair commit their first murder, bludgeoning and drowning Mallory's Dad and burning her mother alive. "I'm a new woman now!" Mallory screams as they ride off to perform a self-conducted wedding ceremony finalized in blood. In truth, Mallory's need for revenge against her father will never truly be quenched, just as Mickey's own childhood demons refuse to disappear.

Like an impatient late-night channel surfer, the narrative reflects the trash-TV aesthetics of *American Maniacs*, a tabloid show hosted by opportunistic reporter Wayne Gale (Robert Downey, Jr., firing on all cylinders) which traces the Knoxes' murderous journey through the Southwest. Deliberately lame re-enactments of murder on "Highway 666" play side by side with idiotically gushing fans who consider the Knoxes "the best thing to happen to mass murder since Manson—but they're way cooler." The lethal lovebirds' motel stay is interrupted by Mickey's insistence on including a sexy hostage in their lovemaking, leading Mallory (in a highly atmospheric sequence) to prowl the empty streets, her sexual fantasies about Mickey merging with sweaty memories of her father. Stopping at an all-night garage, Mallory gets laid by a local mechanic (Balthazar Getty) before blowing his brains out. Seen apart from Mickey for the first time, Mallory comes across as just as deadly—and possibly more uncontrollable—on her own, a trait not lost on Detective Jack Scagnetti (Tom Sizemore), a media whore whose own traumatic past and homicidal acts rival those of his prey.

Mickey and Mallory's reign of terror sputters to an end during a shroom-fueled drive through Monument Valley, which finds the pair stranded in the desert, out of gas and at war with each other. Shot on low-grade Super 8 film and employing skillful use of jump cuts, this sequence achieves the grainy verisimilitude of '70s grindhouse horrors while also boasting the film's rawest emotional payoffs. The Knoxes' encounter with a snake-handling Indian shaman (Russell Means) promises spiritual salvation, as they finally acknowledge their own acts (when Mickey asks Mal if she can "feel the demons here," she replies, "I think we're the demons."). The old man's ritual chanting summons childhood memories of death and abuse, leading Mickey to shoot the Indian in a moment of hallucinatory rage. While trying to escape, the couple is bitten by rattlesnakes; the weakened pair is captured by Scagnetti in a violent, operatic showdown.

After the peripatetic, anything-goes first half of the film, a claustrophobic, dialogue-driven second act finds Mickey and Mallory incarcerated in a maximum-security facility operated by the sadistic Dwight McClusky (Tommy Lee Jones), who plans to have Scagnetti eliminate the celebrity killers ("You'll be bigger than Jack Ruby," McClusky promises). Before their plan can be executed, Gale convinces Mickey to do an exclusive on-camera interview, which will broadcast live after the Super Bowl. As the sexually-obsessed Scagnetti spies on lovelorn Mallory singing "Born Bad" alone in her cell, Mickey sits down with Gale, explaining, "I come from violence. My dad had it. His Dad had it." Like Mallory, Mickey's behavior is the result of childhood trauma: black and white flashbacks show ten-year-old Mickey witnessing his father's shotgun suicide and enduring abuse from his mother.

Between Coca-Cola commercials, Mickey acknowledges his own killer instinct as hereditary, even natural ("Everybody got the demon in them"), saving his strongest attacks for Gale and, by extension, the media. "I used to be you, then I evolved," Mickey says of Gale, who uses the deaths of innocent people to help create celebrity killers, all for the sake of ratings. Before the film can get too heady, a prison riot explodes, distracting McClusky and allowing Mickey to escape. Accompanied by the newly liberated Gale (who quickly locates his "inner Mickey" while continuing to broadcast live), Mickey makes his way through the maelstrom of prisoners, guards, and the media to rescue Mallory from Scagnetti. After a tearful reunion, the pair blast their way out of the prison, with one last pit stop to eliminate their final victim Gale, this time leaving his battered Betacam to "tell the tale" as they live happily ever after.

Armed with a screenplay by Quentin Tarantino (who ultimately requested, and received, a "Story By" credit after his script was substantially reworked by Stone and others) and supported by dependable director of photography Robert Richardson and a gaggle of gonzo performances, provocateur Stone steers the desert terror genre into a new era of self-awareness while simultaneously paying homage to its exploitation-era past. The film's greatest aesthetic and intellectual riches are found in its first half, which is dominated by desert terror content. The opening desert café massacre, Mickey's western-themed escape, the motel room ménage a' murder, the Knoxes' middle-of-nowhere meeting with the shaman … all these and more function as a "Best of Desert Terror" postmodern playlist, reinventing staple scenarios of the genre in one hyper-stylized set piece after another. Venturing light years beyond the experimental photographic and editing techniques Stone first employed on his paranoid epic *JFK* (1991), *NBK* adopts a "zapping" editorial style (foreshadowed in one of the film's first shots, as a waitress turns a dial on an old TV set) to match its outlandish visuals, as Stone switches between reality and fantasy ("I Love Mallory," "American Maniacs," even some of his own work) until we can hardly distinguish one from the other. The result is the first desert terror film to openly acknowledge the genre's bloody cinematic legacy while demonstrating how such once-outré images have, by this point, seeped irrevocably into the mainstream.

The film's most memorable creations, however, are Mickey and Mallory themselves. While clearly descended from a long line of cinematic killer couples going all the way back to *The Sadist*'s original homicidal heartthrobs Charlie Tibbs, Jr., and Judy, they're the ultimate death drivers: sexier, funnier, and more popular (of course!) than any of their forebears. And, unlike *The Hitcher*'s John Ryder or *Kalifornia*'s Early Grayce, they have abusive backstories on which to blame their murderous behavior. Cast successfully against type, Harrelson (whose father was a real-life contract killer still serving time during the film's production) reveals layers of darkness and rage while never losing his inherent easygoing charm; he's especially effective during the extended interview sequence, casually dropping philosophical bon mots ("That's your shadow on the wall") and telling dirty jokes before shotgunning a room full of media twats. The petite, boyish Lewis, who had already cornered the market for unbalanced, sexually fucked-up teens in *Cape Fear* and *Kalifornia*, might seem the more obvious casting choice, but she outdoes Harrelson, delivering a dangerously unpredictable, go-for-broke performance that is alternately feral and coolly seductive.

NBK's gradual elevation of Mickey and Mallory (whose combined pre-incarceration death tally tops out at fifty-two souls) to "hero" status is perhaps its most controversial decision. While the pair were certainly not the cinema's first personable killers (*Silence of the Lambs*' Hannibal Lecter being an obvious recent example), audiences had never been expected to sympathize with, and even root for, multiple murderers in the way Stone's film encourages us to here. The filmmakers stack the deck early on; the Knoxes are "victims" themselves, and most of their murders are discussed rather than shown (the film in general is noisier than it is graphically violent). The only significant on-camera murders are those of Mallory's father and Scagnetti, both of whom are presented as scum, far worse than the Knoxes (even the opening diner massacre is initiated by a lewd cowboy). Wayne Gale is even worse, a self-serving, two-faced ratings whore who, in Stone's view, represents what's *really* wrong with America: the commercialization of mass murder as entertainment. It's a point no one is likely to argue, and an ill-considered move away from a deeper exploration of the Knoxes' pasts.

The film loses its footing a bit in the repetitive final stretch, whose relentless fights and shootouts create an almost numbing effect, and Stone's indictment of the media (which is, after all, nothing without a public to support it) for creating "monsters" like Mickey and Mallory feels over-reaching and half-considered ("Killing you is a statement…. I'm not exactly sure what it's saying," Mickey himself admits before he and Mallory blast Gale to smithereens). Gale may have elevated the Knoxes to household names, but their murders must be considered separately of any media condemnation or glorification. Stone muddles the issue further by dropping in clips from the O.J. Simpson and Menendez Brothers trials, in one of the few sequences that obviously date the film. But for most of its runtime, *NBK* is thrilling even when it stumbles; the few loose ends and half-developed ideas are quickly forgotten amidst Stone's overwhelming visual and aural assault on the senses, which in many ways, has yet to be equaled in the genre.

While divisive upon its release, *Natural Born Killers* has since found many of its techniques (the fragmented cutting, multiple formats to add extra dimensions to a story, use of a music collage rather than a traditional score) borrowed and gradually assimilated into the mainstream; some of its reality-based visuals have birthed entire subgenres. The film's subject matter, however, remains raw and without equal, both inside or outside of the Hollywood system. If anything, the major studios have become less willing to risk substantial budgets on such risky, potentially volatile ventures, and are quick to reshoot and recut films in the event of a perceived backlash. Meanwhile, its cultural criticism has only become more prescient in the years since the film's release. Murderers don't just get interviewed on tabloid programs, they get multi-episode arcs on major cable channels (*The Jinx*, *Making a Murderer*) that are lapped up by critics and audiences alike, while "too much tv" (projected on Mallory's shirt) seems like an understatement in a world whose screen addiction goes far beyond Pink Floyd's proverbial "thirteen channels of shit" to encompass social media and callously violent video games.

Stone has generally enjoyed much of the credit (or the blame) for the film's excesses, but one cannot stress enough the importance of Tarantino's original script, which the frustrated would-be auteur intended to film as a micro-budget indie before finding the funds for his debut *Reservoir Dogs* (1992). *NBK* producer Jane Hamsher's book *Killer Instinct* provides a compulsively readable, first-hand account of the film's tortured journey to the screen, and leaves one wondering what kind of film would have resulted had Stone and company not intervened. Regardless of Tarantino's disowning of the film, the resulting work remains that rare example of studio resources actually amplifying rather than neutering the more politically incorrect aspects of an indie filmmaker's work; beneath Stone's free-associative imagery and sometimes cockeyed political musings beats the heart of an unapologetically violent desert terror film. If Tarantino was dissatisfied with the outcome, his grindhouse aspirations would enjoy more direct expression a year later, when his vampire/crime hybrid *From Dusk Till Dawn* transformed the desert terror landscape yet again, while Stone himself would return to the genre with the pitch black comedy/neo-noir *U-Turn*.

Renamed in hopes of cashing in on *Natural Born Killers*' notoriety and premiering on video on the heels of Stone's masterpiece, *The Road Killers* (1994) is far better than

Jack (Christopher Lambert) tries to rescue his friend from a burning car in *The Road Killers* (1994).

one would expect, boasting excellent production values, one of the best desert terror casts ever, and, most importantly, an unwavering strain of nastiness throughout. The film opens with a bang as two families drive through an isolated stretch of Nevada desert, on their way to San Diego for a group vacation. Easygoing family man Jack (Christopher Lambert), his wife Helen (*Kalifornia*'s Michelle Forbes) and their sixteen going on thirty daughter Ashley (Alexondra Lee) occupy one vehicle; the other is driven by Jack's hothead friend Glen (Christopher McDonald) with his ten- year-old son Richie (Joseph Gordon Levitt, in one of his first films). When Glen stops to cool an overheated engine, Richie wanders into the highway to inspect a "roadflower" (the film's original title) growing improbably in the middle of the blacktop. An El Dorado with four passengers suddenly barrels past, nearly hitting the boy and enraging Glen.

Complications ensue after the families stop at a local diner; after mistakenly wandering into the men's room, rebellious Ashley meets Cliff (Craig Sheffer), a dangerously sexy bad boy who tells her, "If I did what I feel like doin', you'd slap my face and run outta hear screaming." "Been a long time since anyone made me scream," is her inviting reply. She's about to get her wish, as it turns out Cliff isn't just any juvenile delinquent, he's the psychotic death driver of the El Dorado. A subsequent game of chicken on the open road ends badly, with Glen crashing and (literally) burning. Not wanting to be connected to the accident, Cliff has Jack's family, along with Richie, abducted at gunpoint. Cliff's henchman Tom (Josh Brolin) and girlfriend Red (Adrienne Shelley) are sent to shoot and bury Jack, while the others are held captive in the crumbling ruins of a ghost town by Cliff and "artistic savant" Bobby (David Arquette). Conscience-stricken Tom can't go through with it, instead leaving the wounded Jack in the desert. This decision sets a chain

Red (Adrienne Shelley) makes a desperate run for freedom in *The Road Killers* (1994).

of events in motion which spell the gang's undoing, as Jack, the cops, and a mysterious stranger (John Pyper-Ferguson), who may or may not have a connection to Cliff, all converge on the ghost town for a bloody showdown.

Directed by action specialist Deran Sarafian (whose father, Richard Sarafian, directed the 1971 cult car race film *Vanishing Point*), *The Road Killers* has enough car chases, crashes, explosions and shootouts for five death driver movies, but what really keeps its engine humming is its engaging, oddly sympathetic group of outcasts, and the lengths that they will go for kicks, or to avoid going to jail. It recalls the desert terrors of the '60s and '70s, when random acts of violence drove the stories, villains were far more interesting than the heroes, and anyone could die at any moment. Ringleader Cliff, described as a "crazy son of a bitch who killed his mother when he was nine years old," is a force of nature, hurling insults at his gang, lusting after teenage Ashley, shooting cops in cold blood, and hugging it out with Tom before bashing his brains out. He gets all the best lines ("You already killed him once! Why don't you just kill him again?") and exhibits a deadly split personality, switching from touchy-feely to maniacal on a dime.

The other members of the gang are no less interesting and succeed in earning sympathy for their outcast characters: Adrienne Shelly imbues Red with her customary indie quirk, giving her death scene an ironic sense of sadness, Arquette's Bobby is strangely likable, and Brolin is excellent as the morally tortured Tom. "Every family has its problems," Cliff says, and however fractured and fucked up, they are a family, in some ways more so than the "normal" characters. If Cliff ultimately proves to be a self-centered and manipulative sociopath, the film also takes the time to explain how he arrived at that point, making him more than just a stereotypical heavy.

Despite the ongoing conflict between the two families, the tensions worth exploring are between members of Cliff's gang, as they fight to stay together and, perhaps knowing they've crossed a line, stay alive. Once they are out of the picture, we're left with a more conventional, action-packed face-off as Jack dukes it out with Cliff to save Ashley's life. Lambert, never a particularly expressive actor, doesn't quite pull off the transformation that his character is supposed to undergo; he trades his spectacles for a shotgun, but that's about it. He's the one weak link in the chain, but it's not enough to doom the entire film. Slickly produced and handsomely photographed by James Carter (*Leatherface*), *The Road Killers* resonates thanks to its dark subject matter, wild characterizations, and fearless performances.

Boasting an even bigger budget and major movie star, Jonathan Mostow's slick and unnerving *Breakdown* (1997) further emphasizes Hollywood style action and thrills while never forgetting its desert terror roots. Jeff Taylor (Kurt Russell, perfectly cast) and his wife Amy (Kathleen Quinlan) are driving cross country from Massachusetts to start their lives over in California. While passing through an isolated stretch of desert highway, they are cut off by a black pickup. Stopping at a gas station, the pickup appears again, its surly driver Earl (M.C. Gainey) admiring Jeff's shiny new 4×4 before insulting him. When the couple's car breaks down in the middle of nowhere and the truck reappears, conflict seems inevitable. At the last minute, a semi appears, with its driver Red Barr (J.T. Walsh, also excellent) helpfully offering the couple a ride to a nearby diner to call for service. Not wanting to leave the car, Jeff stays behind while Amy accepts Red's assistance. When Jeff finally makes it to the diner, she's not there, and no one has seen her. The local sheriff is (of course) well-meaning but useless. After obtaining some information from local Billy (Jack Noseworthy), Jeff drives to an isolated area, where he is captured by Red and his gang, which includes Billy and Earl. It's all a setup: in exchange for Amy's life, Jeff must give these men an absurdly large amount of money that he doesn't have (in a nice bit of irony, Jeff is no more the "rich asshole" the gang pegs him for than Billy is mentally handicapped, or Red is the devoted family man his wife and son believe him to be).

Just as Red lures Jeff into his trap, writer/director Mostow manipulates the viewer, relying on misdirection and echoes of previous desert terror classics to surprise and confound the viewer. The shadow of legendary genre scribe Richard Matheson hangs heavily over *Breakdown*, with plentiful borrowings from his teleplays for *Duel* and *Dying Room Only*. Amy's unexplained disappearance and Jeff's desperate attempts to deal with the unhelpful line cook and diner customers is drawn from *Dying Room*'s kidnapping setup, while the third act's vehicular mayhem echoes *Duel*'s deadly highway chases. Matheson's theme of urban paranoia, strongly felt in both *Duel* and *Dying Room*, returns here as well, with the usual city/country folk juxtapositions (Jeff and Amy make fun of gas station junk food as "probably gourmet cuisine around here"; a drunk woman barks, "Looks like she got away from you, cowboy" when Jeff inquires about his wife's whereabouts) and plenty of unhelpful cops, eyebrow-raising bankers, and chuckling, squinty-eyed locals who can't be trusted.

The second half of the film focuses more on a series of action set-pieces as domesticated Jeff finally starts to fight the kidnappers on their own terms, including a breathtaking sequence where he climbs to safety from underneath a moving semi. After Jeff finally rescues Amy from Red's farm, Mostow gives us another over-the-top car/truck chase (pointing toward his work on *Terminator 3*) that ends with the two men dangling impossibly off the edge of a bridge. Despite this being a boy's movie through and through,

4. *Highways to Hell Part I* 97

Top: Jeff Taylor (Kurt Russell, left) insists the sheriff (Rex Linn, right) search Red's (J.T. Walsh) truck in the paranoid thriller *Breakdown* (1997). *Bottom:* Amy (Kathleen Quinlan) and Jeff (Kurt Russell) work together to escape Red's farm in *Breakdown* (1997).

Mostow gives Amy the final blow, as she sends the semi crashing down directly on top of her abductor. It's the kind of crowd-pleasing "happy ending" that doesn't happen often in a desert terror movie, but Mostow pulls it off, like most of *Breakdown*, with aplomb, achieving a careful balance between excitement and terror that defines the death driver film.

5

Highways to Hell Part II
Killers on the Road

"He couldn't have walked very far, because I cut off his legs ... and his arms ... and his head. And I'm gonna do the same to you."—John Ryder, *The Hitcher*

In the desert terror genre, the death driver movie is inseparable from its partner in crime, the hitcher-killer film. Even more than death drivers, modern hitcher-killers can trace their roots back to the genre's fact-based noir precursors like *The Devil Thumbs a Ride*, *The Hitch-Hiker* and, of course, *The Sadist*, whose killer couple committed multiple crimes across the Southwest (and eluded capture by police) by hitching rides with unwitting motorists, some of whom ended up dead. Combining the violent exploits of Charlie Tibbs and his predecessors with decades of news reports and urban legends concerning murderous fugitives lurking by rural highways, these hitcher-killers—like *The Hitcher*'s John Ryder—have gone on to become some of the most iconic characters to ever stalk the desert terror landscape.

Hitchhiking horror stories have taken place in all manner of environments, but the most memorable of them occur against Southwestern landscapes. Nowhere is this more apparent than in *The Hitcher*, which derives its disturbing impact as much from its atmospheric desert setting as from its twisted, relentless storyline. Since then, the hitcher-killer film has embraced an astonishingly wide variety of antagonists, ranging from *Prey of the Chameleon*'s personality-swapping temptress to the tortured artist-turned-torturer in *Ultraviolet* to the homoerotic pairing in *Nature of the Beast*. Another significant pair, white-trash Early and Adele on their way to *Kalifornia*, directly recall *The Sadist*'s homicidal lovebirds, with the interplay between them and their "civilized" companions adding layers of psychological and sexual depth to their cross-country journey.

Whereas death driver movies often derive their impact from the physical distance between predator and prey, hitcher-killer movies are more intimate affairs, with a tendency to emphasize the unusual psychic bonds that can quickly form between two strangers. These connections range from the purely sexual (*The Drifter*) to the more complex spiritual "transference" of character traits between charismatic antagonist to their victim(s), leading to disquieting resolutions in *The Hitcher*, *Kalifornia*, and *The Pass*. While their road-movie structures allow for more locations (which tend to favor Route 66 staples like roadside motels, cafes, and gas stations) than other desert terrors, the most telling scenes in these films often occur within the cramped confines of the

The mysterious John Ryder (Rutger Hauer) waits for his next victim in *The Hitcher* (1986).

vehicle itself. In this respect, hitcher-killer films resemble stranded scenarios on wheels, with minimalist plots that revolve around a handful of main players and are built around the antagonist's increasingly shocking actions. Many of these road-dwelling psychos are strangely relatable yet ultimately unknowable, as if having sprung fully formed from the desert environments they haunt. Outwardly normal, initially charming, hitcher-killers wait by the roadside, thumb out, ready to end your life … or change it forever.

"Never pick up a stranger," warns the tag-line for *The Hitcher* (1986), the desert terror genre's first and, in many ways, best hitcher-killer opus. An oppressive atmosphere of fear and isolation is established from the first shots, as a lonely sedan winds through darkened, storm-swept desert landscapes, accompanied only by the foreboding tones of Mark Isham's superb score. Drowsy from a cross-country drive, fresh faced Jim Halsey (C. Thomas Howell) stops to help hitchhiker "John Ryder" (Rutger Hauer) out of the rain. Halsey's hopes of conversation are dashed almost immediately, as Ryder reveals little about himself save his unlikely-sounding name while skillfully avoiding the most basic questions. After producing a switchblade, Ryder admits to murdering the previous driver who gave him a lift, adding that Halsey will be his next victim. "What do you want?" Halsey asks, to which the Hitcher responds, "I want you to stop me" before demanding that his young victim repeat the words "I … want … to … die." (Hauer's low-key delivery makes it less a threat than a suicidal wish). Before he completes the sentence, the terrified Halsey forces Ryder out of the car, speeding away triumphantly. But Ryder is far from finished with the young man, staring down the road in an extreme low angle that, like *The Sadist*'s introductory shot, gives the film's protagonist an otherworldly, almost superhuman, quality.

5. Highways to Hell Part II

The Hitcher returns to menace Halsey in a series of increasingly violent vignettes. A family station wagon reveals Ryder nestled in with the children; Halsey later finds the vehicle pulled to the roadside, the family slain. Halsey stops at a deserted garage to find it empty ... except for Ryder, who silently hands him his car keys before hitching yet another ride in a truck. The next time Ryder appears, he's behind the wheel of the truck, and lays waste to yet another filling station before setting the place on fire. Halsey barely survives, his flaming car screeching away as the station explodes behind him. These sequences, devoid of dialogue and driven by Isham's hypnotic themes, set the surreal, nightmarish tone for the rest of the film, which plays out as a deadly game between Ryder and Halsey across the lonely desert highways of Texas. After being arrested for Ryder's crimes, Halsey finds himself in further trouble when Ryder kills all the cops at the station in a bloody massacre, leaving Halsey as the only survivor—and obviously guilty.

Hiding out at a desert café, Halsey has a brief encounter with his tormentor. "Why are you doing this to me?" Halsey asks once again. This time, Ryder has an answer (sort of), "You're a smart kid. You'll figure it out." But Halsey never really figures it out, and neither does the viewer. As Halsey and Ryder's strange relationship deepens, their encounters become progressively more violent, particularly a standout pursuit sequence during which several patrol cars and a helicopter are destroyed by Ryder, again allowing Halsey to escape, along with sympathetic waitress Nash (Jennifer Jason Leigh). In this sequence, Ryder's sudden appearance and improbable actions (taking down a chopper with a few pistol shots) take him beyond reality, pushing the film's ambience further into that of a waking nightmare. "Why didn't he kill us?" she screams. Halsey's curt answer, sounding more like Ryder than himself, is simply to tell her to keep moving.

Halsey and Nash's platonic relationship is cut abruptly short (the only relationship that really matters in this film is between the two men) when Ryder abducts her and ties her between a truck cab and trailer. In a reversal of their initial encounter, yet still in complete control, the suicidal Ryder hands Halsey a loaded gun and presses the barrel to his forehead, ordering him to pull the trigger. When Halsey declines, knowing that Ryder's death will also insure Nash's demise, the Hitcher calls him a "useless waste" before hitting the gas pedal. With Halsey cleared of wrongdoing and Ryder finally in police custody, the story should reach some kind of resolution—yet the mystery only deepens. The police can find nothing on Ryder: "no prison record, no driver's license, no birth certificate ... we don't even know his name." Only Jim Halsey "knows" The Hitcher, and the separation of the two is only temporary. A final, bloody standoff finds them both back on the road again, with Ryder once more assuming nearly superhuman qualities while Halsey inches closer and closer to becoming that which he formerly most feared.

The Hitcher is not only the best hitcher-killer movie ever made, but remains a strong contender for *the* definitive desert terror movie as well, with its gruesome action unfolding against a beautifully desolate landscape of sand, brush, and deep blue skies. The film has a truly dreamlike, existential quality that is only accentuated by the desolate environment. Inspired by ominous lyrics to The Doors' "Riders on the Storm," the screenplay by debuting writer Eric Red distills years of public fears about psychotic hitchhikers into the character of Ryder, elevates him to mythical dimensions, and turns him loose to wreak bloody, senseless havoc. First-time feature director Robert Harmon, whose acclaimed half-hour short film *China Lake* also featured an enigmatic, well-armed protagonist committing casual acts of violence against a stunning desert backdrop, is a perfect fit for the material. Harmon's confident, muscular direction, however, easily surpasses anything on display

Alone and wanted for murders he didn't commit, Jim Halsey (C. Thomas Howell) contemplates taking his own life in *The Hitcher* (1986).

in the short, as he crafts *The Hitcher* into a frighteningly believable assault on the senses that grips the audience from the first ominous frames and never lets go. Australian director of photography John Seale (*Mad Max: Fury Road*) and editor Frank J. Urioste (*Robocop*) provide excellent support, especially in shaping the film's brutal yet exquisitely controlled action sequences.

The cast are uniformly excellent, disappearing easily into their roles with a much-needed naturalism that balances the script's increasingly outlandish situations. Howell has the most screen time and convincingly depicts Halsey's gradual transformation, while Leigh provides some much-needed "tough love" in a crucial supporting role. At the end of the day, though, *The Hitcher* is Hauer's movie, and he's never been better, oozing a casual, understated menace from his first moments onscreen, yet finding moments of creepy charm and even dark humor in a consistently sadistic, repulsive character. In Hauer's hands, John Ryder remains unknowable, with the film making little attempt to humanize him or explain his origins. Even his name sounds phony, a sick joke he's daring you to laugh at, like "Arnold Friend" in Joyce Carol Oates' excellent short story "Where Are You Going, Where Have You Been?" Like Arnold Friend (remove the R's and what do you have?), John Ryder might be more than just a man, although the film (thankfully) never makes any overt supernatural suggestions.

Ryder's exact intentions toward Halsey remain unclear. There is no explanation for his fixation on this particular young man, and why he lets him live only to torment him time and again. Mild homoerotic overtones persist throughout the film, but the pair's encounters are defined more by Ryder's persistent need for obliteration at Halsey's hands.

In one of the most quietly powerful scenes in *The Hitcher* (1986), John Ryder (Rutger Hauer) and Jim Halsey (C. Thomas Howell) come face to face in a small desert diner.

By the end of the film, Halsey's demeanor has changed; he is colder, more remote, and utterly obsessed with destroying his nemesis. Whether this is the Hitcher's plan all along—to turn a nice American kid who's never even held a gun into a cold-blooded killing machine like himself—is debatable, much like Ryder's intentionally vague background. The film's closing silhouette of Halsey (perhaps a nod to *Duel*, which also ends with an everyman's empty victory) explains nothing. Instead of weakening the film, the mysteries surrounding *The Hitcher* only add to its power to frighten and disturb, thirty years after its release. Although Harmon and Red never worked together again, both men returned to the desert to varied success. Harmon's Van Damme vehicle *Nowhere to Run* (1994) makes effective use of its desert setting, but Red's follow-up vampire road movie *Near Dark*, co-written with director Kathryn Bigelow, is another certified desert terror classic which rivals, and at times surpasses, *The Hitcher*.

The Hitcher was not a major theatrical hit, but it did achieve success on home video and cable, eventually becoming a certified cult film. It was well regarded enough at the time, however, that a few more hitcher-killer films mined the formula, or at least the title, for added visibility. Produced by Roger Corman and written and directed by first-timer Larry Brand, *The Drifter* (1988) at first seems to be a *Hitcher* cash-in, but in fact it has very little in common with Harmon's film, playing more like a noirish take on the same year's hit *Fatal Attraction*. Driving through a small desert town on her way to Los Angeles, feminist fashion designer Julia Robbins (Kim Delaney) passes a "drifter" (Miles O'Keefe) thumbing by the roadside. She encounters him again at a local diner, and again refuses to give him a ride. A flat tire finally forces her to let the hunky, soft-spoken drifter—whose name is Trey—into her life. That night, Julia becomes the aggressor as the two make love in her motel room. While little more than a one-night stand for Julia, for Trey lends their tryst an almost mystical significance. After she drops him off in L.A., he refuses to disappear, stalking and harassing her with phone calls and unexpected appearances at her work and home.

Whereas most desert terrors begin and end on the road, *The Drifter* confines its desert material to the first third; the rest of the film explores the consequences of bringing the desert home with you. Like many of the genre's protagonists, Trey is a stranger not only to Julia's world, but seems to belong to another world entirely (one character sums him up thusly: "He came from nowhere and he's headed for nowhere."). It's never clear what exactly he's doing in Los Angeles (besides shadowing Julia), and as the film's action becomes more concentrated there, his presence diminishes as Julia clashes with her concerned lawyer boyfriend Arthur (Timothy Bottoms), who has hired private investigator Kriger (Al Shannon) to gather information about the mysterious Trey. Kriger's speech to Arthur neatly sums up society's attitude toward such marginalized characters living outside the boundaries of major cities: "He's nobody. He doesn't exist. This country's full of 'em. Drifters. Part of our heritage, you might say. Civilization just doesn't take to everybody." In one of the film's many twists, the obsessive Trey is ultimately the only person Julia can trust, as he saves her from the psychotic Kriger. With its strong female lead, subtle societal commentary and visual attempts to keep the desert alive in the narrative (Julia's apartment is decorated with cattle skulls and cacti, while desert art prints hang in a detective's office), Brand's film allows the hitcher-killer film to drift in new and unexpected directions.

VHS artwork for Larry Brand's modest mystery *The Drifter* (1988).

The gender-blurring road thriller *Prey of the Chameleon* (1992) introduces a female-oriented spin on the standard hitcher-killer premise. Things get off to a bloody start as a sexually active nurse is strangled before her face is smashed through a mirror by an unseen assailant. The reflective imagery serves more than just a casual purpose in the story, as disturbed, mother-murderer Elizabeth Burrows (Daphne Zuniga, in a welcome inversion of her usual "good girl" roles) hitches cross-country from North Carolina to California, leaving a trail of female bodies in her wake. More than just a "garden variety" killer, Burrows' unique method of assuming her most recent victim's appearance and personality keeps her a few steps ahead of small-town Texas deputy Carrie (Alexandra Paul) and Federal Agent Resnick (Don Harvey). Burrows' chance roadside meeting with Carrie's former flame JD (James Wilder) results in an affair that quickly turns deadly, as Burrows uses her new lover's identity to execute gas station holdups, bank robberies, and a series of murders across the Southwest.

Skillfully blending serial killer, road movie, and crime genre tropes, the constantly-changing *Chameleon* is much more interesting than its simple "erotic thriller" assignation would suggest. Burrows' acquisition of her victim's physical traits allows the film a series of arresting images (she is first introduced digging a grave while wearing a nun's habit), but becomes more complex during her burgeoning relationship with JD, which finds her "mousy housewife" turning on the sexy charm before trying on his clothes—and adopting his mannerisms; "You wanna be just like me when you grow up, dontcha?" JD jokes when Elizabeth shows up wearing his jacket (and little else). After seducing her latest conquest, Elizabeth chops her hair short and tapes down her breasts before putting on JD's hat and sunglasses; the inference is that she has somehow absorbed his personality through the sex act. Later, Burrows (now operating as JD) asks a female captive "Don't you like me?" before passionately kissing her. While placed within a thriller context, the androgynous/bisexual overtones of these scenes, and others, go beyond the facile stereotypes of the same year's *Basic Instinct*, flirting with the type of material that would later be addressed in the Oscar-winning *Boys Don't Cry* (1999).

The film is also remarkably femme-centric for a desert terror movie; while JD's fateful pickup of Burrows gets the plot turning, the central conflict remains between Elizabeth and Carrie. Angry with JD for backing out of their engagement (JD expresses small-town anxiety familiar to many desert terror films, explaining, "I saw my future ... never having gone anywhere, done anything."), the tough, even manly Carrie never softens toward him (or to Resnick's advances) but rather focuses her hostility toward her obvious competition, Elizabeth. The muted resolution stops short of suggesting any kind of latent attraction between the two, yet still manages to continue the film's identity-swapping theme, as the two switch outfits before Carrie finally gets the upper hand ("You can force me to dress like this, but it doesn't change who I am—or who you are."). Occasionally falling prey to pedestrian visuals and plotting, *Chameleon* remains fascinating thanks to Zuniga's nuanced portrayal of Burrows and the film's exploration of her fractured sexuality.

Sexual themes also color *Ultraviolet* (1992), Roger Corman's second entry in the desert terror genre. Deep in the rugged, broiling terrain of Death Valley, doctor Kristin (Patricia Healy) and her park ranger boyfriend Sam's (Stephen Meadows) meeting to finalize their divorce is interrupted by the appearance of injured car accident victim Nicholas Walker (Esai Morales). Nick shows his appreciation for their concern by brutally attacking Sam (who is left for dead), abducting Kris, and commandeering her RV for a deadly, extended ride through the area's hellish yet striking landscape. Like *Prey of the*

Chameleon, *Ultraviolet* is more interesting (and kinkier) than its generic B-movie packaging and consignment to VHS limbo would suggest; in fact, it's actually one of the better hitcher-killer movies of the '90s, driven by Mark Griffiths' muscular direction and Gregg Heschong's crisp, naturalistic photography, which captures the profound beauty and isolation of Death Valley from the very first images.

As with many desert terrors, though, the film's success ultimately rests on the performance of its villain, and here Morales delivers in spades with his tortured-artist-turned-torturer, who's just as likely to break into pseudo-mystical rambling ("They say you can't see ultraviolet ... well, I can see it. The desert taught me. Maybe I'll teach you.") as he is to tie Kris to the back of the RV with a rope and drag her along a dirt road. Nick is a literal burnout, creatively "used up" by Los Angeles ("I was dying in L.A. I came to Death Valley, and I died ... and was reborn.") yet driven over the edge by the extreme heat and isolation of the desert ("I am an artist. I deal in truth," he insists as Kris examines sketches and Polaroids of his female victims). The fact that Nick actually has talent, a modicum of wit, and even good taste ("I hate country music," he says before smashing Sam's radio) makes him more sympathetic—and interesting to watch—than your average thrill killer (one is also left wondering if Nick's psychological predicament is screenwriter Gordon Cassidy's response to the maddening frustrations and disappointments of the movie biz).

Kris is similarly strong; while certainly attractive, she is consistently resilient and smart ... and yet Nick is always one step ahead of her. Perpetually one step behind them both is poor Sam, but he's no slouch, either, cauterizing his wounds on a jeep radiator and sucking the venom from a rattlesnake bite. Excepting a brief scene at a country/western bar, *Ultraviolet* is a true three-hander, with Kris, Nick, and Sam the only humans onscreen for much of its eighty-minute running time. In other hands this might have been a liability, but all three performances are consistently strong, and the lack of other characters only accentuates the awe-inspiring desert backdrop of salt flats and rock formations, giving the whole thing a weird existential vibe (Nick more or less states the desert terror mantra when he muses, "There's no one else in this world. There's nothing else. Just you and me, and this place.") Even the sexual scenes bear a disturbing, ugly edge; in one, Nick sucks her bleeding finger ("I can taste you") before forcing himself on her. A later scene finds Nick forcing Kris to have sex with a local for money; before they can undress, Nick stabs the man to death and nearly strangles Kris to death with the victim's belt. Sam and Kris finally join forces against their tormentor in a mineshaft ending that echoes *The Sadist*'s snake-pit finale; the implication, as with many desert terrors, is that the primal experience of survival just might be the ultimate couples counseling.

For years, scrappy, sex and violence-fueled B-movies like *Ultraviolet* were the sole domain of independents like Roger Corman, Charles Band and Ray Dennis Steckler. The early '90s, however, witnessed a hostile takeover of Hollywood by exploitation-loving mavericks who took their inspiration from grindhouse greats like *The Sadist* and *The Hills Have Eyes*. Migrating quickly from arthouse hits like *Reservoir Dogs* and *El Mariachi* (1993) to major studio films like *True Romance*, *Natural Born Killers* and *From Dusk Till Dawn*, filmmakers like Quentin Tarantino and Robert Rodriguez redefined what was acceptable in studio filmmaking—and, in the process, elevated the desert terror genre to new levels of star power and prestige.

Kalifornia (1993) was the first of this new breed, and one of the biggest budget desert terror films produced up to that point. Starring Brad Pitt as white trash serial killer Early

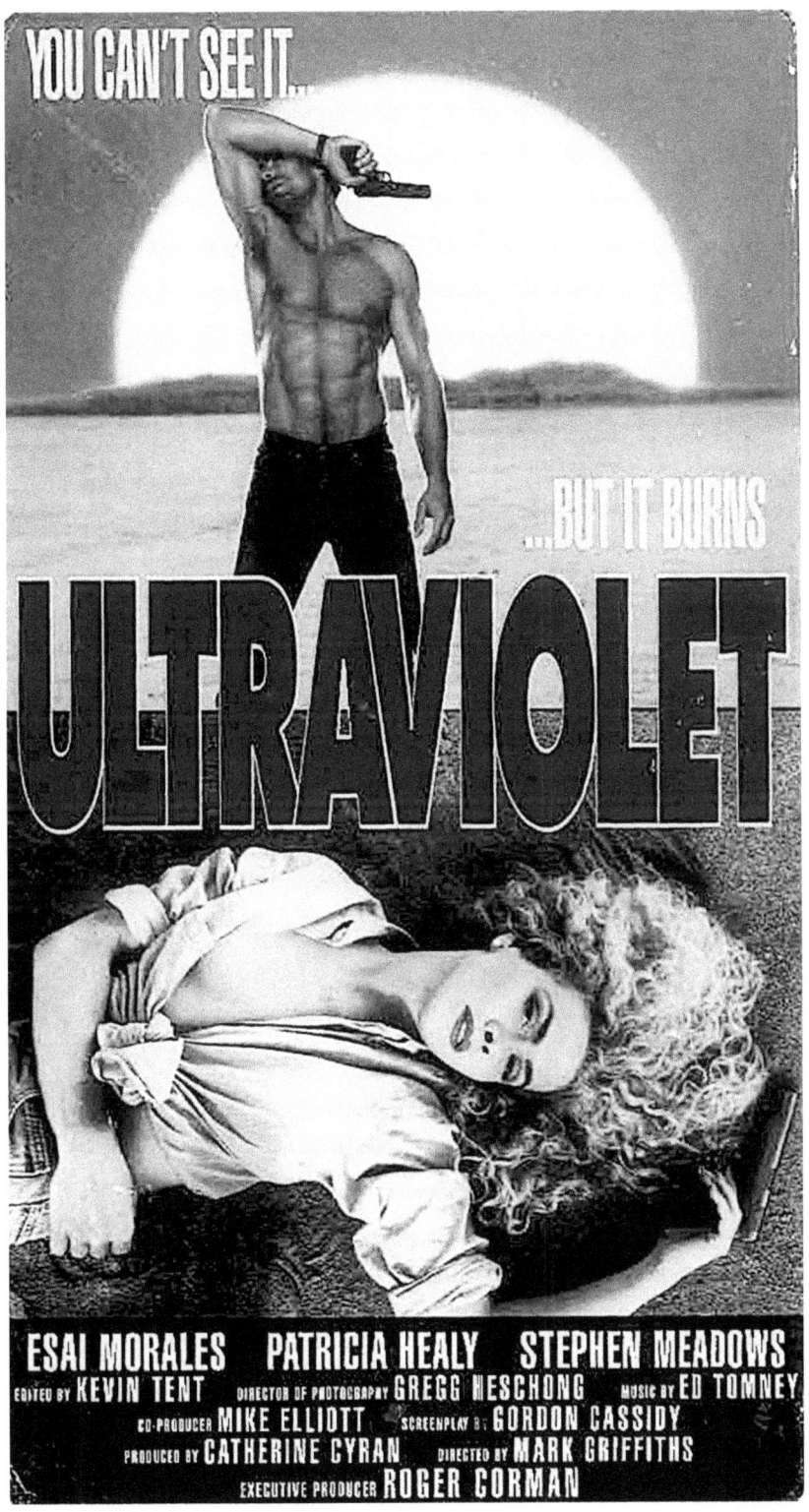

Ultraviolet (1992) was one of the first desert terror films to be released straight to video.

Early Grayce (Brad Pitt) visits his girlfriend Adele (Juliette Lewis) before the two head off to *Kalifornia* (1993).

Grayce and Juliette Lewis as his childlike girlfriend Adele, this road trip through America's murderous past is one of the most well-acted, elegantly shot, and thought-provoking hitcher-killer films of the decade. The twin concepts of Art and Murder intertwine during a darkly stylish opening, as the film intercuts between Early's casual killing of two innocent victims and magazine writer Brian Kessler (David Duchovny) and his chic photographer girlfriend Carrie (Michelle Forbes)'s exploration of a Pittsburgh factory where, years ago, several murders took place. To complete the necessary research for Brian's book about serial killers, the pair elect to drive across the United States, visiting various famous "murder sites" along the way, till they reach California. To ease the financial burden (admittedly a bit hard to swallow given their stylishly furnished, oversized loft apartment), they advertise for another couple to travel along with them and share the expenses.

The only people to answer Brian's ad are Early and Adele, who reside in a ratty trailer park and spend most of their time fighting with the landlord and Early's hook-handed parole officer. These two "primitive but harmless" hicks couldn't be more inappropriate traveling companions for slick urbanites Brian and Carrie, yet before anyone really questions the decision, they're westward bound. "Please don't let them be as boring as Brian's friends," groans Carrie as they drive away. She won't be disappointed. Dynamics between the two couples are established early on, as macho, big-brother type Early challenges intellectual Brian ("How you gonna write a book about somethin' you don't know nothin' about?" he laughs when Brian admits having never killed anyone), while immature Adele forms a quick attachment to "big sister" Carrie. A sexually threatening vibe also develops between Early and Carrie during their first stop, a farm in Tennessee. When Carrie gripes about Early's inappropriate behavior, liberal Brian defends him, saying "he can't help the way he was raised."

The first murder during the road trip occurs at a filling station, where Early pays for gas by stabbing a man to death in the restroom, then stealing his wallet. That night, Bryan gets in touch with his inner redneck as he and Early get in a drunken brawl with some locals at a pool hall. Back at the motel, Adele, who was raped at thirteen, admits to Carrie that she feels "safe" with the abusive Early, who picked her up hitchhiking after getting out of jail. Brian, who now admits being both "frightened and fascinated" by his new friend, continues to dismiss Carrie's concerns. The two men's bond grows stronger the next day, as Early teaches "Bri" how to shoot a gun. At the next murder site, a Texas abattoir, Carrie orders Brian to dump their companions at the next stop, saying "it's him or me," then rushes outside to find Early and Adele having sex in the car. Carrie's voyeuristic side takes over as she snaps photos of the two mid-coitus; Early returns the gesture by staring down Carrie as he fucks Adele.

The desert terror portion of *Kalifornia* kicks in about halfway through the film, as the terrible truth about Early is revealed to the group during a shotgun slaying at a gas station (this same "Roy's Café" location features prominently in *The Hitcher*). Early takes Brian and Carrie hostage, but sticks to their original route, insisting on continuing the murder site tour. During a stop at an abandoned Nevada mine, Early takes Carrie's role, snapping photos on a cheap disposable camera while Brian questions him about the root of his psychopathic behavior. Any possible revelation is cut short by the arrival of two local cops, who Early kills off, *Sadist*-style, before they can help. At an upscale Arizona desert residence, Early passes judgment on Carries sexually explicit art photos ("good thing for you they take all kinds in California") before casually murdering the elderly homeowner. Unable to ignore Early's behavior any longer, Adele prompts a fight with Early, which ends with him scarred and Adele dead. Carrie saves Brian's life by offering herself to Early ("looks like I need me a new woman"), which he is all too happy to accept.

Their road trip dead-ends in *Hills Have Eyes* territory as Early brings Carrie to the Dreamland Nuclear Test Range, an abandoned row of houses adorned with retro furnishings and families of smiling mannequins where he victimizes her in ways we can only imagine. During Brian and Early's final confrontation, the killer uses Brian's own psychoanalytic questions against him ("Do I feel powerful? Do I feel superior?") while nearly thrashing him to death. Together, Brian and Carrie defeat Early, who remains a mystery even after death. "I never knew why Early Grayce became a killer. I don't know why any of them do," Brian's voice over muses as we see him and Carrie at a beach house, having made it to the "Kalifornia" coast after all.

If the plot has a familiar ring, it should; *Kalifornia*'s script, by Tim Metcalfe, is loosely based on the Charles Starkweather murders, the same material that provided the inspiration for *The Sadist*, thirty years earlier (as well as Terrence Malick's excellent *Badlands*, 1977). But whereas *The Sadist* creatively compresses its timeline and focuses almost exclusively on its heavy, *Kalifornia* expands the material with a road-movie structure that explores the psyches of all four main characters, as well as the environments they encounter, as they travel west. Early is, naturally, the most memorable of the group, a good ol' boy gone bad who, with his Confederate flag trucker's cap and utter lack of social "graces," manages to stay just this side of caricature thanks to Pitt's committed performance. Likewise, Lewis takes a character that could have been grating after five minutes and manages to make her, as the only true innocent in the film, an unconventional audience identification figure (Pitt and Lewis, who were a real-life couple at the time of *Kalifornia*'s production, had already essayed another killer couple in the 1990 TV movie *Too Young to Die*). Duchovny makes the weakest impression as Brian, but Forbes more than makes up for it, equal parts strong and sexy as Carrie. The fact that none of these performers was a household name in 1993 only adds to the film's unpredictable nature, as power dynamics shift among the traveling companions throughout the film, with each of them adopting new "roles" as the story progresses. While Early exerts a strong influence on the passive Brian, he does not necessarily want to become him, even if he not-so-secretly covets Brian's woman. Adele, on the other hand, idolizes Carrie, mimicking her hairstyle and harboring a naïve hope that they will all live together once they reach California. Most unexpected, though, is the sexually charged Early/Carrie relationship, which reveals itself early on and finds its logical conclusion in the brutal finale. One can only imagine an alternate version of the film, where Brian fails to come to the rescue, and Carrie and Early duke it out in Dreamland.

As the foursome travel from murder site to another, the specter of death hovers over them like a storm cloud. Early and Adele may be modernized versions of Starkweather and Fugate, but the ghosts of other famous true crime cases haunt the narrative as well: the Tennessee farm recalls the Clutter home from Truman Capote's chilling *In Cold Blood*, a Texas abattoir invokes Ed Gein's human slaughterhouse, and repeated references to hitcher-killers brings to mind multiple murderers from Henry Lee Lucas to Ted Bundy. Even the Dreamland scenes reference death on a mass scale. Like Brian's proposed book, *Kalifornia* probes the serial killer mindset, yet never draws any solid conclusions beyond Brian's admittance that "any one of us is capable of taking a human life"—including Brian himself, as he is forced to do by Early. Early Grayce—like Charlie Tibbs, Papa Jupiter, or John Ryder—is simply born bad, "doing whatever he wanted, whenever he wanted," without motivation, and all the more unknowable—and fearsome—for it.

Contrasting with (and occasionally beautifying) such dark and gruesome subject matter is the slick direction of music video vet (but first time feature director) Dominic Sena, complimented by gorgeous lensing by director of photography Bojan Bazelli (*King of New York*, *Pumpkinhead*), who drenches its scenes of urban decay and desert detritus in bold, painterly colors. Persistent visual motifs—rain, mirrors, cactus—add further thematic richness to an already bracing tale. Critically maligned at its time of release, and subsequently eclipsed by Pitt and Lewis' more successful "serial killer" follow-ups, *Kalifornia* succeeds on many levels and rewards repeat viewings.

Nature of the Beast (1995) also explores the human capacity for evil, pitting two actors who excel at such morally dubious characters—B-movie stalwarts Lance Henriksen and Eric Roberts—against each other in an interesting twist on the hitcher-killer setup. Following the murder of a motorist at a middle-of-nowhere desert motel, the film quickly introduces its dual protagonists: Jack Powell (Henriksen), a straight-laced businessman headed to San Diego by way of Nevada, and Adrian (Roberts), a sleazily charming hitcher with a drug habit and a way of getting under Jack's skin. As in *The Drifter*, Jack doesn't immediately give Adrian a ride, and when they finally meet, Adrian seems to have some extrasensory insight into Jack's (criminal?) past. Roberts' character is a variation on the slimy operator he's been playing so well since *Star 80* (1983), but the real treat is watching Henriksen play the straight man, his rage building as Adrian worms his way into his life. Thanks to constant radio reports, we know that there are manhunts underway in the

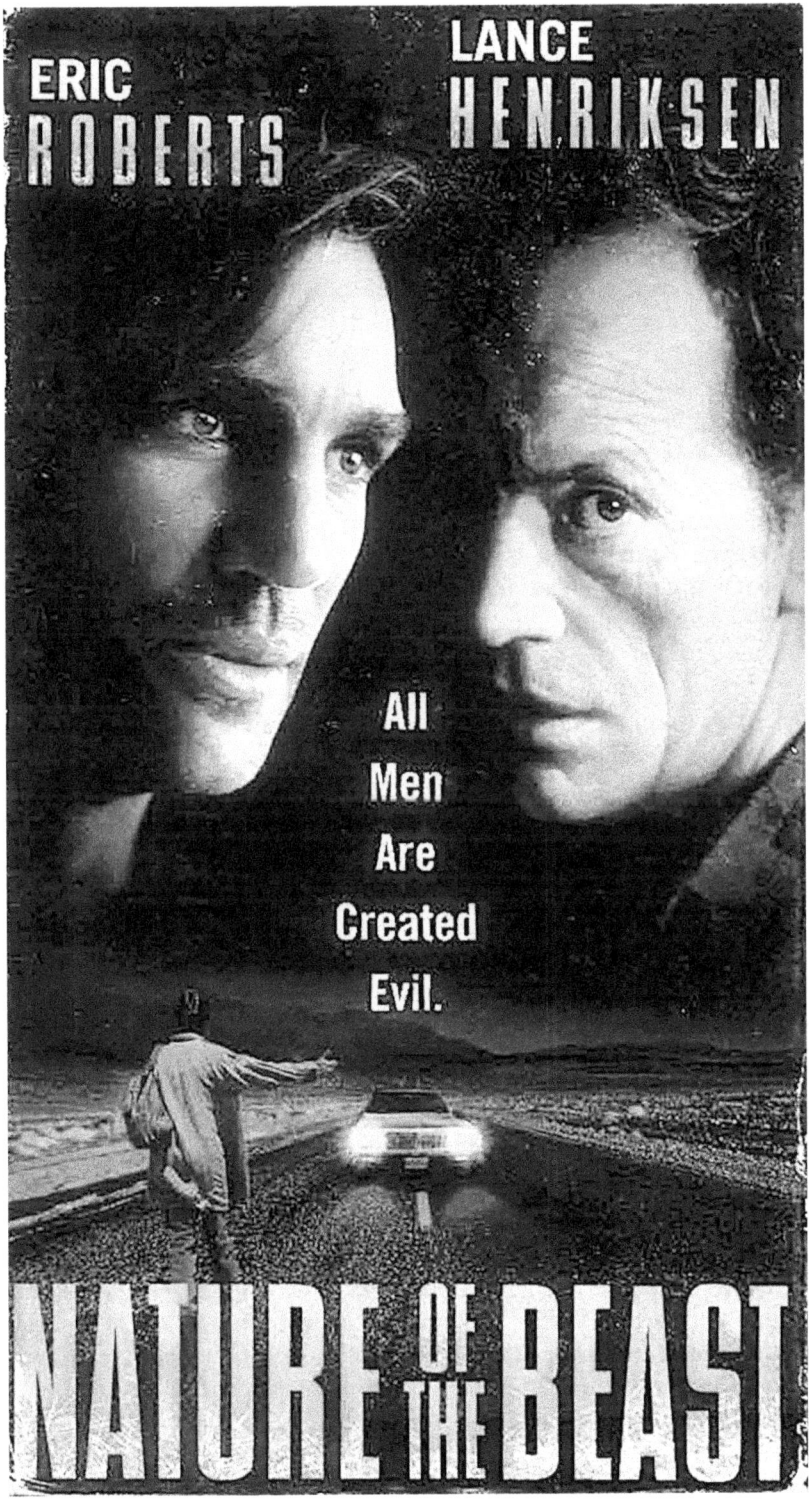

The formidable talents of Eric Roberts (left) and Lance Henriksen (right) drive the two-hander thriller *Nature of the Beast* (1995).

area for two men: a thief who made off with millions from a Vegas casino, and a serial killer dubbed "Hatchet Man" who is hacking his way through the Southwest. Of course, the big question is: which of them is a thief, and which one is a murderer?

More interesting than either question is the strain of barely concealed homoeroticism that pulses throughout the film. Unlike the Ryder/Halsey relationship in *The Hitcher*, it's not exactly arguable; after first meeting in a diner washroom, Adrian asks Jack, "Are you a fag? If it wasn't for homos, none of us fellas would ever get a ride." Later, stuck together in a road trip that becomes progressively more hellish, Adrian delights in Jack's discomfort as he spouts off lines like, "I'll show you mine if you show me yours" and "You know what I am, and I know what you are." Writer/director Victor Salva is canny enough to make these lines work as double entendres, as they further the twisting plot, but the overall effect is to add a consistent sexual frisson to an otherwise conventional thriller. During an overnight pit stop, Adrian elects to party with a pair of swinging hippies. Jack stands outside the hippies' van, fuming, while inside, Adrian indulges in a pot-induced three-way. When Jack starts beating on the van and screaming, it feels less like a man whose conservative values have been offended, and more like the reaction of a jealous (would-be) lover. Adrian returns to find Jack alone in their motel room, saying, "I thought about you. Could you feel it?" The subsequent discovery of the hippies' mutilated bodies only encourages such a reading, with their murder an act of displaced sexual aggression.

Salva uses the hedonistic Adrian to not just challenge Jack's sexuality, but also the hypocrisy of his own judgmental behavior. "Who do you think I am, the Devil?" Adrian says to a sanctimonious Jack, adding, "You've got as much right to moralize as Jack the fucking Ripper." The film's attack on conventional morality feels especially personal considering Salva's own checkered past, which includes serving fifteen months in prison after pleading guilty to sexual misconduct with a minor during production of his first film, *Clownhouse* (1991). This conviction has made Salva a somewhat controversial figure to say the least, especially considering the mainstream success of *Jeepers Creepers* (2001) and its sequels, which reside firmly in the fantasy/horror genre. The lesser-known *Nature of the Beast* trades in a more disturbingly human kind of horror, one that is often best expressed in desert terror films. Even if Salva is more interested in expressive close-ups of his leads than the landscapes they travel through, the stripped-down story benefits from the isolation most closely associated with the desert, as themes of repression and madness bubble to the surface in decrepit roadside attractions, empty motel rooms, and lonely roads. If its final reveal is a bit underwhelming, *Beast* still delivers on its tagline "All men are created evil," emerging as one of the more troubling—and personal—hitcher-killer movies of the '90s.

On the lighter side, the "Chattery Teeth" segment of *Quicksilver Highway* (1997) steers the hitcher-killer tale in a new direction as its traveling companions are joined by a supernatural third party. Written by Stephen King and directed by King specialist Mick Garris (*Desperation*), the half-hour chapter concerns Bill (Raphael Sbarge), a traveling salesman trying to make it home in time for his son's birthday. Complicating matters are a terrible dust storm, and the appearance of a hitchhiker (Silas Weir Mitchell) who Bill first passes on the road, then runs into again at a local grocery store/roadside attraction. Before leaving, Bill notices a pair of toy chattery teeth gathering dust on a shelf, and before you can say Peter Cushing, the kindly old market owner has passed them on to Bill—suspiciously free of charge—as a surprise gift for his son. Bill also offers a ride to the hitchhiker (who answers to the unlikely name of "Bryan Adams"), who promptly pulls a switchblade on his good Samaritan. Unfortunately, "Chattery Teeth" keeps the blood (and scares) to a minimum, even after those damn walking teeth spring viciously to life. While the relentless dust storm is a nice atmospheric touch, and a fair amount of tension is maintained by the two leads, the overall vibe is *Tales from the Crypt*–lite, with its made for TV origins very much in evidence.

Another psychotic thumb-tripper lurks in *The Pass* (1998), a quirkier than usual hitcher-killer film that pays tribute to the desert terror genre's noir roots. Released on video as *Highway Hitcher*, the film opens with middle-aged Charles Duprey (William Forsythe) heading off to Reno on Christmas Eve, hoping to forget about his boring office job and crumbling marriage. Duprey's course is permanently altered once he stops to assist Hunter (James Legros), a bearded slacker stranded by a breakdown in the middle of a mountain pass. Unsurprisingly, Duprey is unable to get rid of his new passenger, who starts out merely annoying ("pokin' the same gal for twelve years?" he laughs at Duprey's marriage) and soon turns downright creepy after casually admitting that he killed a girl. Duprey ditches Hunter at a middle-of-nowhere bus depot, but his vacation trip is again re-routed when a freak rainstorm forces him to spend the night in a fleabag motel in a town called Devil's Gate.

At this point, things get even weirder as Duprey falls for a sexy local tavern owner Zeena (Elizabeth Pena), a heroin addict with a witchy aura about her, burning incense and making proclamations like "stay away from your wife, she's not to be trusted." While at first an unwelcome distraction from the main narrative, the scenes with Zeena, with their downbeat holiday atmosphere and doomed sexuality, serve to form the emotional heart of the film, deepening it in ways that few hitcher-killer efforts attempt (Zeena's is the only death to achieve any real impact). Hunter arrives at the motel, where he spies on Duprey and Zeena's lovemaking before embarking on an all-night murder spree.

If the remainder of the film never quite regains the atmospheric quality of the motel and tavern scenes, the film still has a few tricks up its sleeve, as Duprey finds himself more than capable of dodging Hunter's various attacks. The reveal of Hunter's motivation is a bit hard to swallow, yet ultimately less important than Duprey's own transformation from belittled desk jockey to tough-as-nails survivor, well expressed in his parting speech to Hunter: "It's a funny thing. Yesterday, I was a beaten man, in a slump, going nowhere. Scared of being alone. Scared of the future. But you know what? I'm not scared anymore … and I've got you to thank." It's a journey familiar to many desert terror films, but Voss' film embraces the "transference" between Hunter and Duprey (get it?) by allowing the former victim to literally assume the identity of his tormentor. A parting shot shows Duprey, his former life far behind him, playing blackjack while professing his "killer instinct" to an attractive female companion.

With its philosophical undercurrents (Hunter carries a book titled *Existentialism Made Easy* and Duprey twice asks, "You ever wonder if there's more to life?"), offbeat casting (which includes X guitarist John Doe and Jamie Kennedy), and jazzy musical score, *The Pass* offers yet another idiosyncratic take on the hitcher-killer film. The melancholy Yuletide atmosphere—conveyed both visually and aurally—is unique for the desert terror genre and accentuates the loneliness generated by Denis Maloney's moody desert photography. Writer/director Kurt Voss, whose career has veered between artsy collaborations with indie darling Alison Anders (*Border Radio*, *Things Behind the*

Sun) and low-budget thrillers like the desert noir *Baja*, handles the suspense and action scenes like a pro, but really shines in the film's stranger moments, such as when Duprey discovers a zonked-out Zeena shooting up in the bathroom, or Hunter and Duprey's fiery final confrontation. Like *Nature of the Beast*, it's fun watching both Forsythe and Legros (both underrated actors) playing against type, and Pena provides a welcome, if brief, female presence in the male-dominated tale. *The Pass*' dual emphasis on both character and atmosphere would define desert terror films, both on and off the road, throughout the '90s.

6

Highways to Hell Part III
Murder Machines

"You just never know. You just go along figuring some things don't change ever, like being able to drive on a public highway without somebody trying to murder you. And then one stupid thing happens. Twenty minutes out of your whole life, and all the ropes that kept you hanging in there get cut loose, and it's like you're back there in the jungle again."—David Mann, *Duel*

Just as death driver and hitcher-killer films probe the dark psychology of their automobile-aided antagonists, a third category of films focuses on the awesome destructive abilities of the vehicles themselves. "Murder machine" movies, while making up the smallest portion of road-driven desert terrors, contain some of its most enduring accomplishments. The first (and still best) example of the form, *Duel*, set many of the subgenre's standards: a stripped-down desert setting, minimal cast, clearly delineated "civilization versus savagery" themes, and, most importantly, an immediately iconic vehicular villain. Often imitated but never surpassed, this intense story of man vs. truck would go on to influence subsequent murder machines in *The Car* and a segment of the California-set anthology *Nightmares*, both of whom ascribe more overtly supernatural origins to their four-wheeled fiends.

Later entries introduced new twists to the formula. The celestial supercar piloted by *The Wraith* turns out to be the film's hero, exacting fiery revenge on a group of small-town baddies. The child molester/killer behind the *Wheels of Terror*, however, is one of the genre's most nefarious villains, and, like *Duel*'s unseen trucker, remains strangely unknowable. If these more modern murder machine films prize roaring chases and explosive special effects over disturbing ambiguity, even the least of them benefit from their desert locales, with the empty roads of the rural Southwest proving the ideal environment for these gas-powered predators to stalk their prey. A perfect synthesis of car and driver, the faceless evils behind these movies are both the next evolutionary step forward and the last word in road-based desert terror.

Originally broadcast as an ABC Movie of the Week(end), *Duel* (1971) is based on a short story by acclaimed sci-fi/horror novelist/screenwriter Richard Matheson, (*I Am Legend, Hell House*) which was conceived on the day of Kennedy assassination and saw its first publication in *Playboy* magazine. The rights were quickly snapped up by Universal, who hired Matheson to adapt his twenty-three-page story into a feature screenplay, which would be directed by a then twenty four-year-old Steven Spielberg. Like

Matheson's best work, the resulting film has a deceptively simple storyline: traveling salesman David Mann (Dennis Weaver) is menaced by a tanker truck along a series of increasingly isolated desert highways. At first glance, this synopsis sounds better suited to a half hour TV program (Matheson also contributed to anthology programs like *The Twilight Zone*) than a feature film. But despite its singular protagonist and constricted timeframe, Matheson's screenplay is consistently eventful, surprising, and even provocative. Augmented by Spielberg's controlled direction and Weaver's committed performance, the result is one of the most unrelenting desert terror films ever made.

The film's themes of emasculation emerge as Mann drives out of Los Angeles and into the deserts north of the city; on the radio, a stay-at-home dad admits embarrassment over losing his "head of the household" status. "You're the boss," a gas station attendant quips to Mann, who makes the ill-fated decision to decline a new radiator hose. "Not in my house, I'm not," Mann's responds before calling home, where his wife berates him on the phone for failing to confront an obnoxious party guest at a recent social gathering. Mann is under pressure not only from work (his trip north is to meet with his boss so he won't "lose the account"), but from his wife, and his mother, who is stopping by the house tonight.

These domestic pressures dissipate once a grimy oil tanker truck, adorned with rusted license plates from all over the Southwest, suddenly appears ahead of Mann, blocking his route and belching smoke directly into his path. It's a situation we've all been in, but one which, here, gradually assumes epic proportions. The truck driver remains anonymous, glimpsed only as a hand on the wheel or boots stepping out of the cab. Spielberg deliberately keeps us—or Mann—from seeing the truck driver's face. He is everyman—or perhaps, *more* than a man. Part of *Duel*'s effectiveness comes from its mystery driver's (named simply "Keller" in the short story) unrelenting focus on harassing, and later trying to kill, Mann, giving the film a universally nightmarish quality

Like a bad dream, the truck appears again and again, finally forcing Mann to speed ahead so fast that he loses control and smashes into a fence. Dizzy and sweaty, Mann attracts suspicious looks and derisive laughter as he staggers into a nearby café. It is he, not the unbalanced truck driver, who is the outsider here. After confronting a patron who he assumes is the truck driver (but isn't), Mann is taken for a lunatic and quickly ejected from the café. In his ensuing encounters with the truck, the harried salesman consistently chooses flight over fight. At a faded roadside attraction, Mann's attempt to phone the police is cut short when the truck crashes through the booth, narrowly missing him and smashing open cages full of venomous snakes and tarantulas. The trucker isn't just harassing David Mann, he aims to kill him. Perhaps realizing this, or having exhausted all other options, Mann finally approaches the truck on foot when it blocks him on a mountain road. As he gets closer to the truck's cab, the truck abruptly pulls away, backing down for the first time.

Mann's small victory is short-lived, however, as the truck makes one final effort to destroy its intended victim. In a nerve-shredding final chase, Mann forces his dying car up a treacherous road, screaming, "Come on!" through bloodied teeth as the truck pursues him. Sacrificing his car (and nearly his life), Mann forces the truck off the edge of a mountain, where it tumbles down in a dreamy, achingly beautiful slow-motion shot. Mann jumps up and down, giddy with excitement, as he looks down at the smoking wreck. The driver is gone, either thrown from the wreck, burned up in the blaze, or simply disappeared. A final silhouette of the salesman resting against a burning sunset

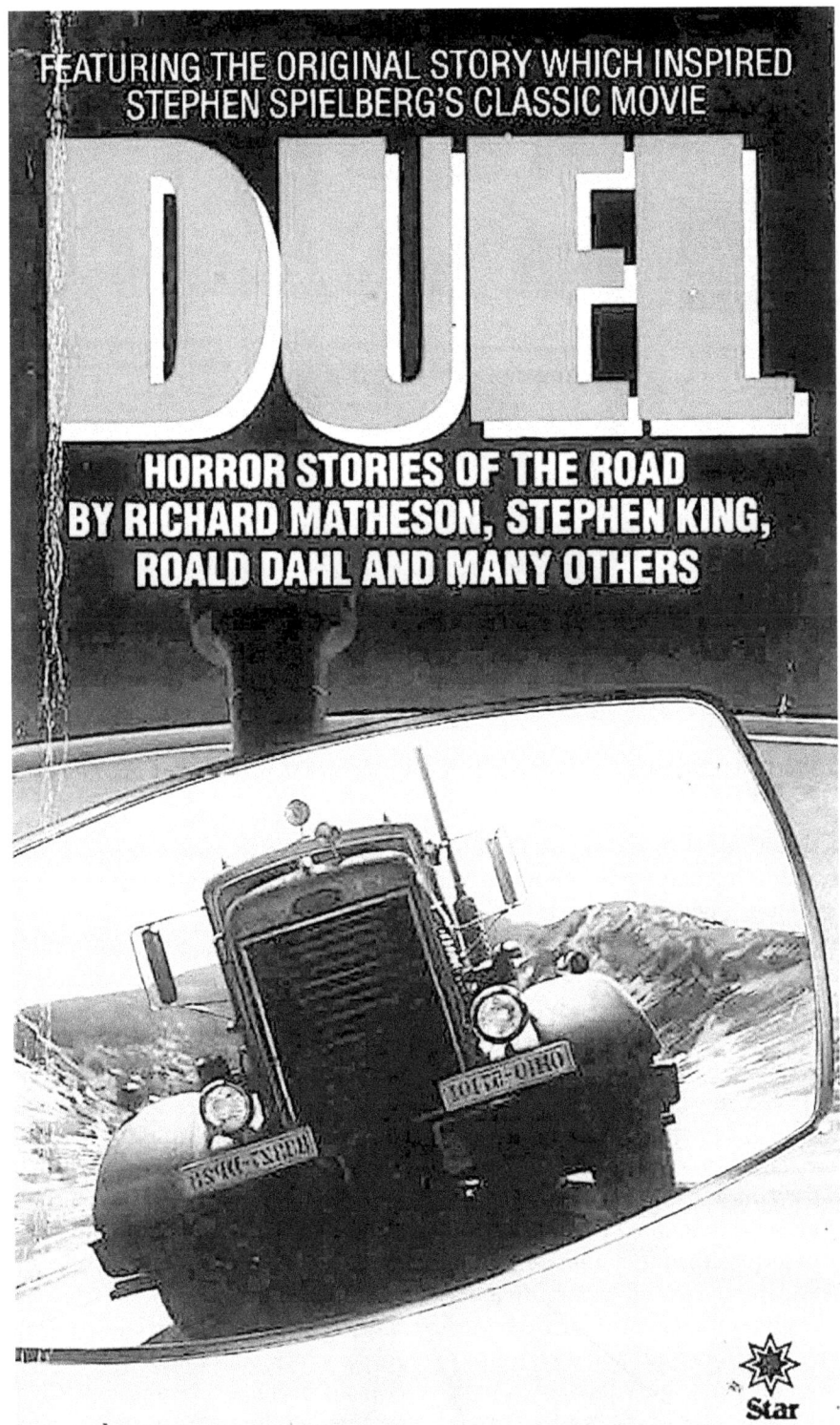

Richard Matheson's short story, which inspired the film *Duel* (1971), was later published in paperback as part of this 1987 collection.

David Mann (Dennis Weaver) tries to outwit a murderous tanker truck in Steven Spielberg's excellent *Duel* (1971).

is less victorious than troubling. David Mann has beaten the truck driver at his own vicious game, but only by descending into the same animalistic mindset. He has regained his masculinity, but at what cost?

In defiance of its small-screen origins, *Duel* is a surprisingly demanding, even exhausting, film. It's hard to imagine a TV movie like this being made today, let alone finding a receptive audience. *Duel*, however, performed so well in its primetime slot that a European theatrical version was commissioned by Universal, with Spielberg allowed to shoot an additional fourteen minutes of material to beef up the running time to a still lean and mean ninety minutes. Predictably, European critics focused more on the underlying social dilemmas presented in the film rather than the straight-up suspense film its director claims to have made (in a 2001 DVD featurette, Spielberg jokingly dubs it his "ghost truck movie"). But to deny *Duel*'s thematic concepts of frustrated masculinity and class warfare is to ignore the explicitly stated content of Matheson's original short story and film script. It is these underlying themes, as much as the desert location and taut action sequences, that allow *Duel* to make such a lasting impact.

The film is visually striking from the first shot to the last, with Spielberg (here helming his first feature film) and director of photography Jack Marta finding endlessly creative ways to film a story that could have been easily become stale and repetitive. The chases are still some of the most intense ever captured on film, due to rejection of both safer studio "process" shooting or traditionally covered, multi-camera stunts. Each time Mann drives off the blacktop, hits a barrier, or is rear-ended by the truck, the viewer feels it acutely. The desert setting receives the same treatment, with real diners and filling stations capturing local flavor. Even lulls in the action are used to emphasize authentic detail: wind whistling through junked cars, tumbleweeds blowing across empty roads, the far-off whinny of a horse. From its first propulsive shots (taken, tellingly, from the point of view of Mann's car, not its driver), *Duel* completely immerses you in its world, with an unforced, almost subliminal, accumulation of detail that adds up to a potent effect.

The film's naturalistic tone is also expressed in Weaver's perfectly calibrated performance, which over the course of the film transforms from snootiness to identifiably flustered to a raving animal. In a role that is surely as physical as it is emotional, Weaver never fails to react believably to the various crashes, scrapes, and fender benders he finds himself in. As a civilized member of the modern world, he's the perfect vehicle (pun intended) to illustrate Matheson's theme of threatened masculinity, which, the film asserts, is retained only by tapping into one's own baser instincts. The filmmakers' decision to render much of Mann's dialogue via interior monologue is a highly effective way of placing us in his increasingly agitated mindset. One significant passage, "overheard" in voice over during the diner sequence (and transposed nearly verbatim from the original short story), sums up the sudden descent into savagery that forms the heart of many a desert terror film: "One stupid thing happens ... and the ropes ... get cut loose ... there you are ... back in the jungle again."

Echoes of *Duel* reverberate through Spielberg's successive films, most obviously in his megahit *Jaws* (1975), while he would revisit the road with *The Sugarland Express* (1974) and the desert in *Close Encounters of the Third Kind*, both of which were photographed by *The Sadist*'s Vilmos Zsigmond. Meanwhile, the murder machine movie was off and running, with more entries to follow, some of them falling into the desert terror genre. Having achieved a surprising amount of critical and commercial success with *Duel*, Universal proceeded to mount a more expensive production, *The Car*, which roared onto movie screens in 1977. Instead of Spielberg and Matheson behind the camera, *The Car* utilizes an original screenplay penned by three different writers, with western journeyman Elliot Silverstein at the helm. While boasting a larger cast and bigger action sequences, the film's sprawling, multi-character plotline only shows how much more effective *Duel* is at creating tension with minimal means.

That's not to say there isn't some fun to be had, as *The Car* opens with a quote from Church of Satan founder Anton LaVey (this was the '70s, after all) while "Dies Irae" booms on the soundtrack. The first time we see the titular automobile is from a distance, its infernal horn blaring as it kicks up dust across a picturesque mesa. Director Silverstein takes a few pages from Spielberg's playbook by only showing us glimpses of his villain—close-ups of wheels, the hood and, most amusingly, its crimson-tinted point of view—as it forces a pair of bicyclists off a bridge to their deaths. The plot stalls as the local police force (which is unusually large for such a small desert community) investigates the cyclists' deaths along with another of the car's victims, a passing hitchhiker. When the sheriff (John Marley) falls victim to the murderous machine, next in command Wade (a passive James Brolin) must take charge and discover the true origins of The Car, which, like *Duel*'s terror-truck, has no visible driver (all windows are tinted a deep black) and seems increasingly otherworldly (if not downright Satanic) as it claims a series of randomly selected victims.

The film has a few highlights amidst the lame subplots about wife-beating locals

The Car (1977) cuts a deadly path through the Utah desert.

and recovering alcoholics. In one, the car attacks a group of schoolchildren and their teachers at a local fairground. All hell breaks loose as cowboys and cops are swept up in a melee of blood and dust, which ends with the kids seeking refuge in a cemetery, which the car refuses to enter. In the middle of an equally demented chase sequence, the car flips itself over, subsequently destroying a pair of oncoming squad cars before somehow righting itself and driving away without a scratch. Skeptical Wade finally starts to accept that they are dealing with more than just a homicidal death driver, as the film invoking both Christian ("It didn't go to the cemetery 'cause the ground was hallowed") and Native American ("Bad things come with the wind") religious motifs in its attempt to literally demonize the evil car. While the film stops short of saying the car is Satan himself, it leaves a distinctly unholy impression when the exploding car produces a set of monstrous facial features through a cloud of smoke and fire. "Whatever he was, he isn't anymore," says an exhausted Brolin. As the end credits roll, we see The Car, improbably shiny and new, rolling through an unnamed metropolis.

For all its supernatural shenanigans, *The Car* is an overly simplistic film, with its four-wheeled fiend killing randomly, then roaring up and zooming away whenever convenient to the plot. Any questions as to why the car has shown up now, in this town, to attack these people, are left unanswered. Suspense or atmosphere are largely abandoned in favor of stunt-based action, which places it more in the '70s trend of car-crash movies like *Smokey and the Bandit* (1977) and *Convoy* (1978) than in the horror genre. Unlike *Duel*'s psychotic trucker, who seems to have a genuine sense of purpose, The Car never displays any motivation beyond running down the next pedestrian. The picture's strongest asset is its stunning Utah location photography by veteran cameraman Gerald Hirschfield, but those wanting more than just dumb fun from their desert terror movies will find *The Car* decidedly lacking.

In the '80s, Universal gave the murder machine concept one more spin with the four-story horror offering *Nightmares* (1983), which stands as the first desert terror anthology. The film's amusing initial segment, "Terror in Topanga" plays like a condensed version of *Night Terror* and stars desert terror vets Cristina Raines (*Hex*) and William Sanderson (*China Lake*) in a tale of hitchhiking horror amidst the dusty canyons of Los Angeles. The film's third chapter, "The Benediction," fully embraces desert atmospherics and introduces a new villainous vehicle to the murder machine pantheon. In it, Lance Henriksen, as Frank McLeod, is a priest whose faith is shaken after the death of a young boy. He leaves his New Mexico parish and, looking to start over, takes to the road. Driving

Pictured left to right, Lauren (Kathleen Lloyd), Lynn Marie (Kim Richards), Margie (Elizabeth Thompson) and Debbie (Kyle Richards) cower in fear after surviving an attack from *The Car* (1977).

along a desert highway, Frank encounters an ominous black truck at a crossroads, which cuts him off before roaring away. The truck appears again, rear-ending him and forcing him off the road. While changing a tire, Frank is nearly killed as the truck rushes past. Frank stops near a field, then watches, stupefied, as the truck literally explodes from underground. The priest finally defeats the malevolent lorry by tossing a canister of holy water at it (?!), after which the vehicle disappears in a flash of light. Faith apparently restored, Frank rejoins his parish…

"The Benediction" builds on *The Car*'s religious themes, with its driverless truck clearly meant to represent some force of evil, perhaps even the Devil himself. Aside from the holy water solution feeling hopelessly old-fashioned and silly, the whole encounter (whether imagined or not) becomes problematic when one considers that the result is to send Frank back to his parishioners—surely not what the Devil would want! Director Joseph Sargent gives the entire segment the sepia-toned look of an old postcard and pours on weird sound effects in some hope of achieving an appropriately nightmarish atmosphere. Henriksen lends much-needed gravitas to the enterprise, with his tortured turn as McLeod one of many fine desert terror performances he would contribute over the decades to follow.

The half-baked spiritual shenanigans of *Nightmares* look positively disturbing, however, next to *The Wraith* (1986), which brings the murder machine movie roaring into the high-octane, effects-and-music driven '80s. A *Close Encounters*–like effects montage of celestial lights flickers over the desert, speeding along a highway, and colliding to form … a sleek silver sports car! A driver, too, appears, dressed in a futuristic-looking spacesuit and helmet, and strikingly backlit as if stepping right out of a Whitesnake video. Which is appropriate, since *The Wraith* is a killer car movie for the MTV generation, down to the great-looking cast of second-gen thespians (Charlie Sheen, Nick Cassavettes, Griffin O'Neal), hot cars and hotter babes (including an early appearance by Sherilyn Fenn), stuff that blows up real good, and a power pop/hair metal soundtrack (including Billy Idol, Robert Palmer and Motley Crue) generously ladled over nearly every scene. Despite its dated excesses, *The Wraith* at least represents one significant change to the formula: this time, the car from another world, along with its alien driver, is seeking retribution.

In a rural Arizona community, brutal gang leader Packard (Cassavettes) and his gang of punks and gearheads spend their time challenging local drivers to high-speed races; the loser forfeits their vehicle, and Packard makes sure he always wins. Packard also operates a chop shop full of stolen vehicles, run by the aptly-named Rughead (Clint Howard). When fresh-faced newcomer Jake Kesey (Sheen) rolls into town on his motorbike, he catches the attention of Carrie (Fenn), Packard's main squeeze, who feels she's met Jake before. Maybe it has something to do with Carrie's former boyfriend Jamie, whose recent murder went unsolved? At the same time, the silver car and its mute, costumed driver (the "Wraith" of the title) keeps appearing, and challenging Packard's punks to a series of deadly races along the winding desert roads, which inevitably end in disaster—for the punks, that is. Sheriff Loomis (Randy Quaid) investigates the increasingly bizarre crimes as Carrie falls in love with Jake, in the process unraveling the truth about his connection to the Wraith and Jamie.

The Wraith has little in common with previous murder machine movies, at times playing more like a souped-up variant on Clint Eastwood's moody revenge–Western *High Plains Drifter* (1973). While lacking that film's eerie desert atmosphere (despite being lensed entirely on location in Tucson, Arizona), *The Wraith* attempts to make up for it with plenty of car crashes and explosions. Unfortunately, the film's automotive chases quickly become repetitive, as they all appear to have been shot on the same stretch of desert highway, and always climax with the same fiery result. A few choice moments of horror-tinged weirdness occasionally liven things up, as when the Wraith pursues Packard into a cemetery (shades of *The Car*), or the spooky reveal that all the Wraith's victims have their eyes missing. Why exactly is never explained, just like the mysterious metal apparatus (assumedly an extension of the Wraith's suit), that disappears from each crash site. Equally odd is the film's merging of '80s film clichés with a '50s aesthetic: the main hangout is a local burger joint staffed by roller-skating waitresses, Packard has a greaser-like look and a switchblade to match, and the drag races homage *Rebel Without a Cause* (1953). The film's real target audience is probably automobile enthusiasts, who will get an undeniable kick out of the various souped-up and customized muscle cars and sports cars—the Wraith's car is itself a sleek Dodge prototype—showcased throughout the film.

Desert terror vets Cristina Raines and William Sanderson team up in the anthology film *Nightmares* (1984).

Slightly edgier, if equally nonsensical, is *Wheels of Terror* (1990), which returns the murder machine to its '70s origins. The unexpectedly harsh opening features the abduction of a stranded little girl who asks "Daddy, are we gonna end up like the Donner Party?" before an evil-looking black sedan roars up out of nowhere, mowing down her father and dragging her inside. Like *Duel*, *Wheels of Terror* (aka *Terror in Copper Valley*) is made for television, though it diverges enough from its obvious model to keep things interesting. When middle-aged single mom Laura (Joanna Cassidy) and her teenage daughter Stephanie (Marcie Leeds) move from Los Angeles to an isolated desert town, they soon learn things are far from quiet. A murderous mystery driver is prowling around, kidnapping and molesting his female teenage victims before dumping their bodies in the nearby woods. As usual, the local officials don't have a clue who the culprit is, or how to stop him. Laura's new job as a school bus driver puts her directly in the middle of the conflict, and once Stephanie is abducted, Laura must face off alone against the mystery maniac.

Wheels' first half differs pleasingly from earlier murder machine outings, with its strong female lead, realistically depicted community and discomfiting notion of an unknown killer abducting, and violating, his underage victims. *Halloween 4* scribe Alan McElroy's script is tight, and director Christopher Cain (*Young Guns*) keeps things visually dynamic, especially in the driving sequences. Familiar city/country tensions between Laura and the sleepy little town pave the way for a truly disturbing reveal of the driver's identity (as with many killer car films, we never see him). Around the halfway point, however, *Wheels* literally switches gears and leaves all previous plot development by the roadside in favor of an extended chase sequence, perhaps the longest ever committed to celluloid. Commandeering a bus full of terrified tykes, Laura pursues the sedan after her daughter is yanked inside. The forty-minute chase takes both vehicles through dusty back roads, construction sites, abandoned factories, and, finally, a copper quarry, where the evil car finally plunges several hundred feet to its doom. As with *Duel*, the sedan's flesh-and-blood driver disappears in an apocalypse of smoke and fire.

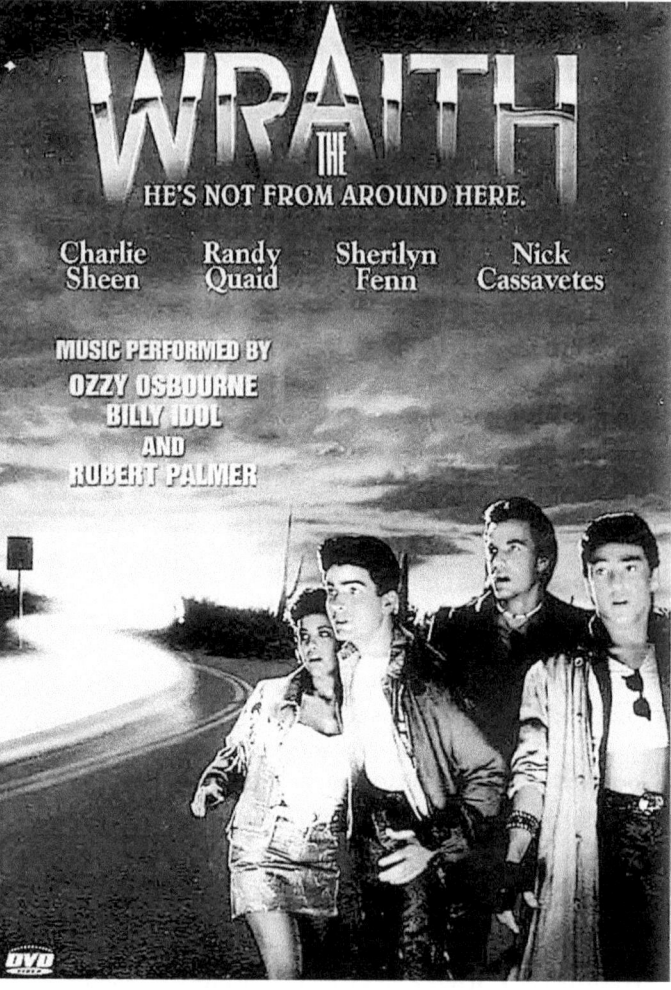

Pictured left to right, Sherilyn Fenn and Charlie Sheen lead Nick Cassavetes and Griffin O'Neal in *The Wraith* (1986).

On some level, it's almost avant-garde the way *Wheels* trades in the previous buildup of story material for automotive action at its most cartoonish. Laura's bus exhibits an unaccountable resilience through a series of crashes, explosions, and walls of flame, and certain moments, such as when the black car goes airborne and smashes headfirst into a motorcycle cop, defy the laws of physics. But the overall effect is numbing and disappointing, as *Wheels*' promising, unsavory first half creates expectations that aren't remotely met by the dragged-out finale. Its closest correlative is probably Quentin Tarantino's overly talky "car slasher" *Death Proof* (2007), which also follows its plot-oriented first half with an absurdly extended car chase. *Wheels* isn't as static (or as pretentious) as Tarantino's picture, but like most of other murder machine films produced in the wake of *Duel*, only serves to demonstrate the difficulties of using a mechanical antagonist to create suspense and terror on the road without lurching into repetition or exaggeration.

7

The Good, the Bad and the Satanic

"I'm gonna tell you a story that'll stick to you like an eyeball on a cactus needle."—Morrison, *Grim Prairie Tales*

If stranded scenarios and road-based desert terrors clearly reference noirs like *The Petrified Forest* and *The Hitch-Hiker*, the western-themed branch of the genre draws its influences less from comic-book style serials of the 1930s and '40s and more from cultural and cinematic trends of the late '60s. Following the lead of popular spaghetti westerns of the 1960s, revisionist westerns like *The Wild Bunch* (1969) and the psychedelic art–Western *El Topo* (1970), the first "weird westerns" to grace the desert terror genre in the '70s emphasize atmospheric location photography, a realistic approach to violence and experimental filmmaking techniques while bearing several distinctive traits of their own. The television movie *Black Noon* is (mostly) set in the post–Civil War past, but most weird westerns reject historical settings, instead transporting western themes and archetypes into the modern age in a variety of creative ways. Perhaps even more importantly, these weird westerns are some of the first American films—in any genre—to feature fully developed Native American characters and story motifs. Though likely influenced by current cultural trends of environmental activism and a return to spirituality, the representation of Indian characters in these films goes far beyond the usual "savage" clichés familiar from decades of Hollywood films, offering characterizations that run the gamut from malevolent ghosts to vengeful "half breed" women to heroic professors.

The initial crop of weird westerns—*Blood Shack*, *Hex*, *Track of the Moon Beast*, *Ghosts That Still Walk*, *Haunted*, and even the big-budget studio literary adaptation *Nightwing*—typify the progressive, experimental '70s. All but one is set in the modern era, and the plots of all six films hinge on Native American characters and entities. Of these, *Haunted* goes the furthest toward deconstructing romantic notions of the cinematic West while addressing the era's troubled history. The '80s continued the contemporary trend with *The Ghost Dance* and *Scalps*, whose supernatural elements often complimented more conventional slasher antics. In the latter half of the decade, progressive-minded films like *Fleshburn* and *The Returning* embraced more complex Native American characters, but even more interesting (and prescient) was a wave of films that—like *Haunted*—allowed the past and present to intermingle. The results, which range from *Natas: The Reflection* to *Ghost Town*, set the stage for the '90s, which saw numerous innovative spins on the "classic" horror western (*Grim Prairie Tales*, *Into the Badlands*, *Silent Tongue*) before returning to the present for the most serious portrait of a Native American character thus far with *The Brave*. Whatever era they inhabit, weird westerns continue to challenge established western conventions while staking out their own unique cinematic territory.

Written, produced, and directed by exploitation auteur Ray Dennis Steckler, the impoverished yet strangely hypnotic *Blood Shack* (1971) is not only the first weird western, it also stands as one of the few desert terrors to boast direct professional links to *The Sadist*. *Sadist* producer, Arch Hall, Sr., worked as (uncredited) producer on Steckler's earlier film *The Thrill Killers*, while *Sadist* director of photography Vilmos Zsigmond shot many of Steckler's earlier films. Neither Hall nor Zsigmond was involved with *Blood Shack*, however, which was filmed in Pahrump, Nevada, on a budget of (according to Steckler) "five hundred dollars tops." The enterprising Steckler assumed most production duties (including photographing and editing the film) under pseudonyms. Despite its minimal production resources and brief running time (under an hour), *Blood Shack* makes a strong impression, thanks primarily to its uniquely decrepit location.

A woman's dreamy voice over warns of a Native American boogeyman named "The Chooper" as a Model T stops at a ranch consisting of little more than a few ramshackle buildings and a rusted water tower. Sassy blonde Connie (Laurel Spring) jumps out, unafraid of "old Indian ghost" stories and determined to spend the night in the shack, against the warnings of caretaker Daniel (Jason Wayne), who tells her "The Chooper will get you!" Connie explores the house, which consists of two small rooms covered with peeling wallpaper and furnished with little more than a few broken chairs and a stained mattress. In an interview on the 2008 Shriek Show DVD, Steckler claims these furnishings were not props, but simply junk left behind by a previous tenant; instead of feeling cheap or lazy, it works, lending a raw sense of believability to an otherwise contrived scenario. Later that night, the girl falls victim to a black-clad, sword-wielding killer, in a claustrophobic, dizzying murder sequence that is punctuated with a high-pitched chirping (chooping?) on the soundtrack. The next morning, Daniel nonchalantly disposes of her body.

Failed actress Carol (Carolyn Brandt, Steckler's wife at the time) arrives after inheriting the ranch from her Uncle Will, a horror movie screenwriter. She learns more about the history of the ranch from Daniel, while local businessman Tim Sanders (Ron Haydock) tries to force her to sell the property to him. More locals are slain by the Chooper (a skinny guy in a black body suit, itself recycled from Steckler's previous children's film *The Lemon Grove Kids Meet the Monsters*) as Carol becomes increasingly suspicious of her surroundings. When the Chooper finally attacks her, Daniel comes to the rescue, in the process revealing the killer's identity as—big shocker—Tim. Carol's curiously blasé voice over has the same sleepy tone as the beginning, lending a time-loop effect to the whole affair: "Tim's dead. Daniel's dead. I don't know what I'm going to do. I think I'll just worry about it tomorrow. If tomorrow ever comes."

Alternately released on video as *The Chooper* and *Curse of the Evil Spirit*, *Blood Shack* is one of the most minimalist desert terror outings of the '70s, its drama stubbornly anchored to the dreary, isolated ranch. Steckler's old-fashioned screenplay plays like a modern retread of early horror westerns like *Haunted Gold*, where schemers dress up as phony "Phantoms" to frighten intruders away from ill-gotten gains. But the script hardly matters, as *Blood Shack*'s pleasures are strictly visual. The film's minuscule budget works in its favor, with an undeniable realism created by the sparse, depopulated collection of structures, which look ready to blow away with the next gust of wind. The grainy, high-contrast film stock (no doubt also chosen for budgetary reasons) accentuates the ranch's rugged beauty and gives the entire film the look of a Polaroid left to bake in the desert sun. Like an Antonioni or Rollin film, the most effective sequences are those where "nothing happens"; establishing shots have a disquieting beauty, and scenes of Brandt wandering aimlessly around the property, or drawn to the house at night, achieve a narcotic pull. By contrast, excepting the reasonably well-edited opening murder, the overtly "horrific" scenes range from unscary to laughable. Filler scenes shot at a local rodeo are even worse, threatening to destroy what little atmosphere the film has achieved. Thankfully, Steckler ends on an ambiguous note, returning the viewer to the same disorienting dreamspace that they found themselves in at the beginning.

Blood Shack's curious combination of realism and fantasy is heightened further by cinéma vérité moments sprinkled throughout the film. The director's daughters Linda and Laura appear in plenty of scenes, and Brandt essentially plays herself. Scenes in the director's cut exhibit an even more personal flavor; in one sequence, Daniel shows Carolyn the room "where your uncle used to write all his horror movies." Its walls are adorned with posters from Steckler's own oeuvre, many of them collaborations with Brandt; "My Uncle Jim wrote some of the best horror movies I ever acted in," she says wistfully. The result is an overwhelming sense of an 8mm home movie which has mutated into a no-budget horror film—or is it the other way around? In this case, one can clearly feel Carol's exodus from Los Angeles mirrored in the Stecklers' move to the Nevada desert, where they decided to make a film literally "by any means necessary." *Blood Shack* demonstrates how independent films made far from the Hollywood factory (as most desert terrors are) can sometimes allow viewers a rare glimpse into the private lives of their creators.

The same year the Chooper haunted grindhouses, the supernatural-themed oater *Black Noon* (1971) premiered on the CBS television network. Like *Duel*, *Dying Room Only* and *Gargoyles*, *Black Noon* was yet another horror-oriented Movie of the Week produced during the '70s. A stark desert opening finds the Rev. John Keyes (Roy Thinnes) and his wife Lorna (Lyn Loring) stranded and near death after their wagon breaks down. They are rescued by kindly Caleb Hobbs (Ray Milland) and his beautiful, mute daughter Deliverance (Yvette Mimeux), who transport them to the small town of San Melas. While Lorna recuperates, Hobbs—who is mayor of the town—informs John of the community's recent "series of misfortunes": the local goldmine is depleted, sadistic gunfighter Moon (Henry Silva) threatens the residents with violence, and the only church has recently burned to the ground. Hobbs asks John to fill in as town minister, leading to a chain of miracles—a crippled boy regains the ability to walk, Deliverance recovers her speech—that coincide with Lorna's worsening physical (and mental) condition. Plagued by cryptic dreams, disturbed by Lorna's hysterical behavior and bewitched by Deliverance, John gradually gives in to Hobbs and accepts a permanent position as the new preacher of San Melas. His first sermon in the newly constructed church may also be his last…

The allegorical tale of a "pure man" caught between two women and corrupted by the dark forces of his own adopted community, *Black Noon* builds a slow-burning atmosphere of paranoia and dread from the first shot of an emotionless Deliverance watching a church burn to the ground. Veteran TV director Bernard Kowalski (whose genre credits extend back to 1959's *Attack of the Giant Leeches*) strikes a successful balance between pacing and mood, sustaining a consistently unsettling tone even when the straightforward script occasionally becomes repetitive and predictable. Although Thinnes and Milland share the most screen time, it's their female co-stars who make the strongest impression. Loring brings a much-needed empathy to a character who could have been merely annoying, and Mimeux personifies the attraction of evil in her mostly-silent role. Deliverance's final words to John, spoken during the church climax, are especially chilling.

Despite its American origins, portions of *Black Noon* bear the look and feel of a contemporary Euro-horror film or spaghetti western. Recurring slow-motion dreams of John running in a misty void from a bleeding doppelganger into the arms of Deliverance play like outtakes from a Leon Klimovsky "sexy vampire" film (one almost expects Paul Naschy to make a guest appearance), while Silva's gleefully evil Moon seems to have rode in on horseback after finishing work on a *Django* sequel. Other sequences, such as Lorna's discovery of a group of children wearing crude animal masks while chanting over a dead owl, have no immediate cinematic precedent and conjure up a genuine sense of fear, as does the disturbing, downbeat ending. Coincidentally or not, both these scenes, along with the basic storyline and many other visual elements of *Black Noon*, strongly prefigure the plot of horror classic *The Wicker Man* (1973), released just a few years later. Though its use of the desert is relegated primarily to opening and closing bookends (the final one set in the modern day), the dusty little town of San Melas has a nicely insular, at times almost unreal, quality shared by many desert terror films. Moody, claustrophobic, and rife with creepy imagery, *Black Noon* is one of the best weird westerns of the decade.

A bewitching beauty also drives the rambling plot of *Hex* (1973), an atmospheric weird western that melds the biker and Native American horror genres within an unusual post–World War I setting. A gang of motorcycle-riding veterans, led by the charming Whizzer (Keith Carradine), arrives in the small town of Bingo, Nebraska, only to be run out by the locals, who banish them to the surrounding plains. There, the bikers stumble onto an isolated farm inhabited solely by sisters Oriole (Cristina Raines, billed here as Tina Herazo) and Acacia (Hilary Thompson), where they plan to hide out before continuing to California. Raised in seclusion by mixed-race parents, Acacia has never heard of airplanes or "picture shows," but Oriole (who goes by the nickname Rio) possesses ancient skills passed on by their father, a Native American who "knew about the seasons … the creatures … and the powers." That night, the attempted rape of Acacia by Giblets (Gary Busey) is thwarted by a fatal owl attack, apparently summoned by Rio, whose dreamy pronouncement "You're going home" foretells the biker's bloody demise.

Despite Giblets' death (and Rio's obvious disapproval of their presence), Whizzer and the others elect to stay with the two "half breed honeys," prompting a series of spooky occurrences while a budding romance develops between sensitive mechanic Golly (Mike Combs) and the virginal Acacia. Whizzer, too, takes a liking to the darkly sensuous Rio, prompting a violent reaction from his girlfriend China (Doria Cook); Rio's response is to cast a spell on her competition. In one of the film's most memorable sequences, the bathing China hallucinates swarms of rats, snakes, and being buried alive. Whizzer falls further under Rio's influence as she continues using various forms of magic (hypnotic suggestion, freak accidents) to dispatch the remaining bikers, while Acacia grows further apart from her increasingly malevolent sister. Whizzer and Golly finally pull up stakes, but Rio, who has by now adopted the persona (and creepy, skull-and-fur costume) of a tribal elder, has other plans…

Residing in a dreamy netherworld between drama and horror, *Hex* (retitled *The Shrieking* and *Charms* for various U.S. home video releases) drifts along on a hazy, unhurried

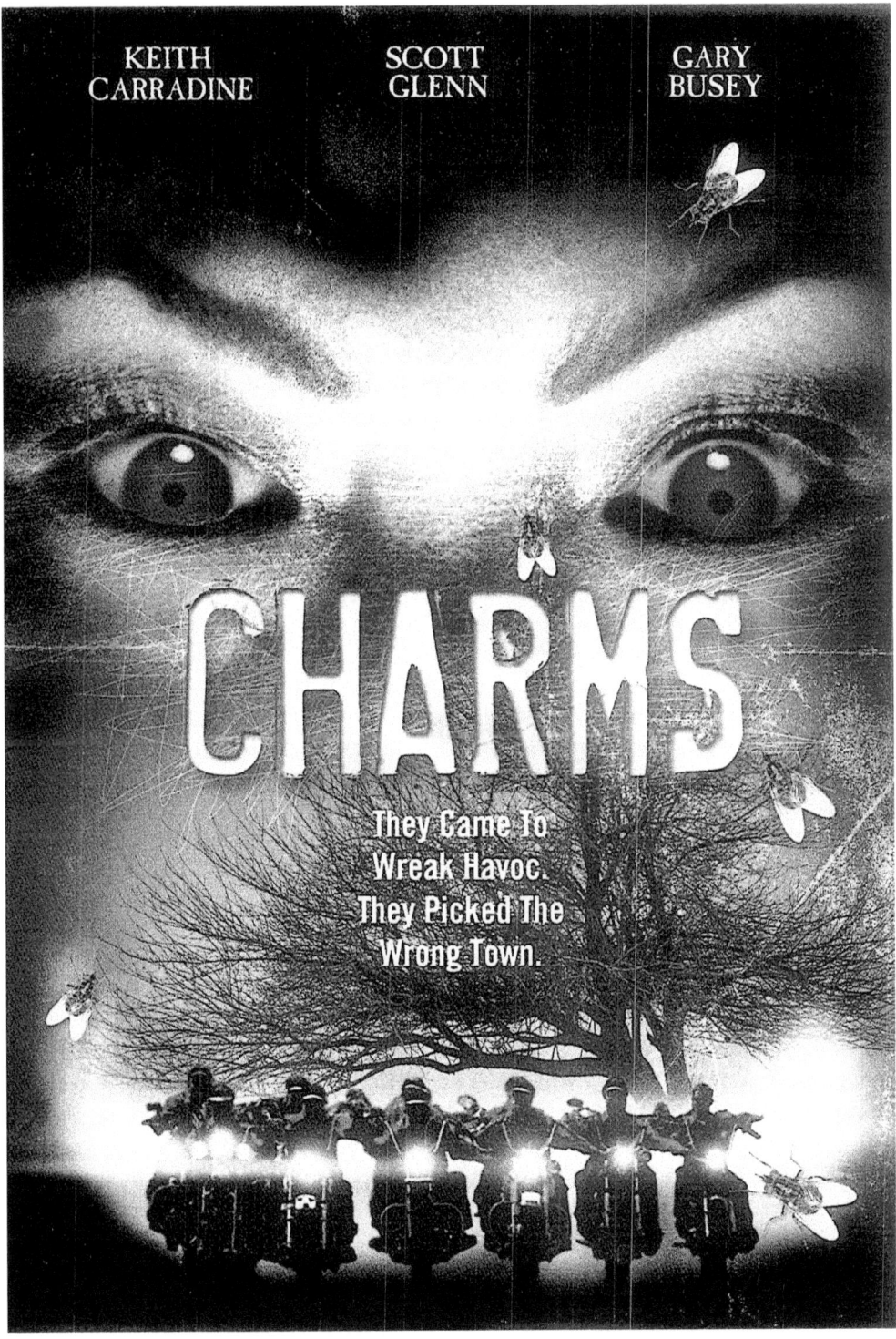

Hex (1973) was retitled *Charms* for its belated DVD release.

ambience that is occasionally interrupted by disturbing death sequences or, more distractingly, slapstick humor. Early scenes in Bingo and the bikers' scuffles with tough-talking Brother Billy (Dan Haggerty) nearly kill the film out of the gate; thankfully, the narrative settles into a more consistently spooky groove once Whizzer and company happen onto the sisters' farm. There, the script, co-written by Vernon Zimmerman (*Fade to Black*), embraces several desert terror themes, as civilization (in the form of Whizzer and his crew) meets savagery (the sisters) with explosive results. Interestingly, the filmmakers invert the usual situation by making the bikers the aggressors, and the locals their victims—for a while, anyway. The film continues to twist our allegiances, however, as Rio begins to kill off the bikers, whether deserving or not.

Alongside this broader conflict, *Hex* contains elements of the stranded scenario, as it examines the stultifying effects of rural isolation, as well as the characters' varied responses to growth and change. Director of photography Charles Rosher contrasts pastoral images of farm life with jumbled, smoky nighttime interiors that practically vibrate with tension. As with many a desert terror film, the arrival of outsiders shatters a carefully composed world, rooted in (and stuck in) the distant past. Acacia's growing need to experience life beyond the boundaries of the farm contrasts sharply with Rio's controlling need to dominate their situation on every level—physical, sexual, and spiritual. The eventual outcome—which rests on the two sisters' inevitable separation more than their tenuous relationships with the bikers—is slightly marred by an uncharacteristically (and frankly unbelievable) happy ending ("Hell of a place, this Nebraska," Whizzer casually quips as he putters away) that threatens to negate much of what has transpired beforehand.

The film's approach to its Native American character and subject matter is surprisingly mature for its time, as the script addresses the inherent biases toward Native Americans and mixed marriages ("They ain't even Americans," one of the bikers scoffs of the sisters). Interestingly, Rio and Acacia, while born of the same parents, have distinctly different looks and personalities: the solemn Rio, with her dark skin, high cheekbones, and handmade jewelry, is clearly her father's daughter in more ways than one, while the virginal, naïve, pale-skinned Acacia (rhymes with Caucasian?) represents the more "acceptable" of the pair (it is, after all, she who is first targeted by the gang). The sisters' haunted history is believably rendered, just as the various totems that decorate the farm possess a genuine authenticity. Even Rio's spells, potentially the most fanciful elements of the film, are downplayed and feel grounded in reality.

Shot on location at the Cheyenne River Sioux Indian Reservation in South Dakota, *Hex* is the first desert terror film to take place (and be filmed) outside of traditional Southwestern environments. Like later weird westerns, it's a reminder of the considerable expanse of the West in the post–Civil War America, and its visual palette of flatlands and wheat fields only adds to its carefully constructed atmosphere. This sense of realism extends to the low-key performances of the entire cast, with Raines (who would later chalk up more horror credits with *The Sentinel* and the desert terror anthology film *Nightmares*) making a particularly memorable impression. With a stronger opening and closing act, *Hex* might have become a cult classic, but it nevertheless impresses through its progressive tone and surfeit of genuinely bizarre imagery.

The New Mexico–set (and filmed) *Track of the Moon Beast* (1976) addresses Native American themes within the parameters of a contemporary (yet traditional) monster movie. Watching a meteor shower with his photojournalist girlfriend Kathy (Donna

Leigh Drake), Paul Carson (Chase Cordell) is struck by a meteor fragment and thereafter begins to suffering from sleeplessness, extreme headaches and—when the moon is full—memory-erasing blackouts. After local people start turning up dead and horribly mutilated, with oversized footprints left behind, the police enlist Paul's friend, Native American anthropology professor John Salinas (Gregorio Sala), to help solve the crimes. Johnny finds uncanny connections between the killings and an old Indian legend about "a big lizard that walked like a man." John's worst fears turn out to be correct, as the meteor fragments imbedded within Paul's skull begin transforming him into a "demon lizard monster" on a nightly basis.

While clearly indebted to *The Wolf Man*, *Moon Beast* follows a somewhat different path, with a fresh blending of science (the meteor shower which instigates the transformation, references to the moon and NASA) and Indian legend (Johnny's "legends about lizards" and their connection to the moon, have a truthful ring to them). Unusual, too, is the film's shift away from ostensible white "hero" Paul (who, for some reason, remains shirtless for much of the film) to focus on Native American Johnny, a character would usually be regulated to a supporting character at best. Instead, he takes on the film's most proactive role, deciphering the meanings behind centuries-old folklore, consulting with local police (who are surprisingly receptive to his far-out ideas), and trying to help Paul come to terms with the terrible symptoms of his supernatural affliction. In fact, it's Johnny (whose tribal name is "Longbow") who devises a novel way to bring down the Moon Beast: an arrowhead made of meteorite.

Conversely, Paul is a distant, barely developed character, and his relationship with the attractive Kathy is similarly dispassionate, with their dynamic more maternal than sexual (she's mostly putting him to bed or making breakfast). Unfortunately, the film often dwells on their "love story" to the detriment of any suspense or scares that might be worked up, with the melodrama intensifying ("Oh, Paul, why couldn't there be time for us?") as he flees the authorities. Aside from questionable dialog ("Maybe there is a dinosaur up in the hills ... now it's on the loose," muses the chief of police), the film is stiffly directed, clumsily edited, and fails to make much use of its desert settings. The primitive special effects, which are mostly limited to the rubbery Moon Beast suit and a few reasonably gory mutilations, occasionally recall the DIY cinema of Don Dohler (one can easily envision a Moon Beast vs. Night Beast monster mash). As ungainly and old-fashioned as its title creature, *Moon Beast* is too entrenched in the past to adequately introduce Native American subject matter into contemporary genre cinema.

The cumbersomely-titled *Ghosts That Still Walk* (1977) eschews *Moon Beast*'s arm-ripping antics for a more cerebral, multilayered account of Native American spiritualism and its effects on white interlopers. The film's fragmented narrative is presented as a series of hypnosis-assisted recollections relating to Mark Douglas (Matt Boston), a teenager who becomes possessed by the spirit of a 500-year-old Indian mummy. After undergoing a series of medical tests intended to diagnose his recent seizures, Mark is sent to medical hypnotist Dr. Sills (Rita Crafts). During the first session with Sills, Mark's elderly, God-fearing grandmother Alice (Ann Nelson) mentions several stressful situations that the family has endured in the past year, including her husband Harold's (Jerry Jensen) heart attack and a nervous breakdown suffered by Mark's mother Ruth (Caroline Howell), who was writing a book about "cliff dweller" Indians at the time. The meeting itself ends on an ominous note when Mark, after hearing whispering voices in his head, smashes his hand through a glass cabinet full of Indian artifacts.

Rather than questioning Mark, Sills puts Alice under hypnosis, leading the prudish old woman to recall a series of strange events that took place during a recent trip to Calico Ghost Town (an attraction in Yermo, California, that dates to 1881, and is still operating today). Alice and Harold's desert vacation is interrupted when some ghostly force takes control of their motorhome, increasing its speed and forcing the vehicle to skid off the road. Later, the couple endures flying "Rocks of Hell" and, again, are nearly killed by their possessed vehicle. The narrative moves in a more eerie—and purposeful—direction as Sills delves into Ruth's journals, which relate the discovery of an "Indian mummy" inside a desert cave, which she subsequently brings home; Ruth's use of the mummy as part of an experiment involving astral projection ultimately results in Mark's current condition. A wheelchair-bound Mark, Alice and Dr. Sills make a pilgrimage to the cave where all the trouble started, hoping to cure the boy and put the Indian spirit to rest, once and for all.

With its shaky structure, salt of the earth cast, and subdued level of terror, *Ghosts That Still Walk* often plays like an educational or industrial film that occasionally strays into supernatural horror. The initial flashbacks involving Alice and Harold (which comprise nearly half the film) are needlessly protracted and contribute little to the narrative—though, to be fair, those flying rocks are cool in a "how'd they do that?" sort of way. Things get weirder and scarier once the film delves into Ruth's "relationship" with the mummy, which takes on an overly intimate, almost sexual charge. Repeated shots of the mummy lying on a slab, heavy breathing on the soundtrack, and Ruth's tender voiceover ("You drew me into the darkness," she coos) combine to create a memorably macabre atmosphere. Later, Mark finds her speaking to it ("You're welcome to live here with me") and runs away, terrified. "It's not what you think," Ruth tells him later, creating more questions than answers (we are told early in the film that Mark was "upset" when his father died six years ago—is this a surrogate?). While far from necrophiliac delirium of Italian horrors like *Lisa and the Devil* or *Macabre*, these scenes are certainly an improvement over the film's first half and only hints at some of interesting directions the story could have gone. Unfortunately, despite a few more effective sequences (Ruth's initial discovery of the mummy in the cave, Mark's out of body possession), *Ghosts* never gets going, with too many static hypnosis scenes and a lack of a central character. Although Mark's plight is technically the focus, all too often the film allies itself with Alice, to the extent that her Christian faith is presented as a viable—and successful—way to defeat a 500-year-old Native American spirit. The result is a film that, while not without interest, is confused—and confusing—on many levels.

Released the same year, *Haunted* (1977) centers its oddball mix of horror and melodrama inside the confines of an atmospheric movie ranch with a cursed history. An 1865 prologue sets up Native American/white tensions that grow to inform the rest of the story, as beautiful "savage" Abanaki (Ann Michele) stands trial for witchcraft and horse stealing. Stripped to the waist, she curses her white accusers—including her lover, cavalry soldier Gordon McCloan (Aldo Ray)—before being banished to the desert to die. In present day Arizona, Hollywood-bound actress Jennifer Baines (Michele again) arrives at the dusty old Apacheland Movie Ranch (a popular movie set once known as "The Western Movie Capital of the World"). Long neglected and in serious disrepair, the set is inhabited by a small, disjointed family of caretakers: crusty old Andrew McCloan (Ray again), his deceased brother Anthony's widow Michelle (Virginia Mayo), and her two young adult sons Patrick (Jim Negele) and Russ (Brad Dearden). Jennifer, whose latest TV project is a "series about reincarnation," moves into the ranch while her car is repaired.

Jennifer soon discovers that Apacheland is built on the same site where, roughly one hundred years before, Abanaki was persecuted. This isn't the only way the ranch is haunted, however, as Andrew not-so-secretly lusts after Michelle (his brother Anthony, who she chose over him, died in a mysterious car crash that left her blind), as well as stalking Jennifer, who he gradually comes to believe is Abanaki reincarnated. Jennifer and Patrick's relationship grows more physical, and he soon makes plans to leave the ranch with his brother. At the same time, Andrew's tortured obsession with the past, and fear of losing his surrogate family, pushes him to commit terrible acts, which eventually lead to his own self-destruction.

Juggling themes of reincarnation, old west/Native American mythology, sexual repression/obsession, and creeping modernization, *Haunted* is an ambitious undertaking which, even more than the self-reflexive *Blood Shack*, qualifies as the desert terror genre's closest equivalent to Dennis Hopper's revisionist quasi–Western *The Last Movie* (1971). Like that film, *Haunted* seldom unites (let alone resolves) all its disparate plot strands, yet remains intriguing throughout thanks to its unpredictable structure, occasionally striking imagery (a pay phone installed in the center of a graveyard, which seems ridiculous at first, gradually acquires a spooky menace), and unusual, atmospheric location. Apacheland, in addition to being a unique location for a horror movie, has a strong influence on many of the characters, in many cases determining their personalities, histories, and futures. Jennifer is mysteriously "brought back" to the ranch by possible reincarnation, Patrick feels suffocated by the weight of its history and wants to escape, while Andrew is desperate to hold onto the past by any means necessary. The ranch's real-life bloody history, which includes Abanaki's punishment by death for crimes she did not commit, comments on the inaccuracy of old west legends as well as the rampant racism of the times.

References to Old Hollywood and the artifice of filmmaking are interwoven throughout the more overtly supernatural content. The neglected ranch speaks for itself, and the characters who mostly closely align themselves with it, Andrew and Michelle, are played by old-time movie stars (Ray and Mayo) familiar from classic westerns from the '40s and '50s. Russell, who is far more attached to the place than his brother Patrick, papers his walls with one-sheets for Universal horrors like *Dracula* and *Frankenstein*. Even many of *Haunted*'s music cues feel borrowed from a '40s melodrama (the entire film has an unusual musical/song fixation, with its strident theme song particularly memorable). It's unclear, though, whether writer-director Michael A. DeGaetano invokes these reminders of the cinematic past for nostalgic effect, or to demonstrate the medium's (and audience) need to move on from such obvious artifice; New Hollywood was in full force at the time of *Haunted*'s production. The film also attains a truly self-reflexive dimension by using the same western town sets for its historical prologue (as "reality") and present-day action. Casting Michelle and Ray in double roles adds to the film's perplexing mix of real and reel life (in an interesting side note, Apacheland survived a few real-life disasters of its own, as the result of fires in 1969 and again in 2004; the remaining buildings live on as part of the nearby Superstition Mountain Museum).

Abanaki's reincarnation through Jennifer, while explicitly stated during the opening card, is vaguely expressed, as Jennifer (who speaks with a British accent for some reason) drives off suddenly at the end, simply telling Patrick: "You'll find someone else." Her purpose seems less to inflict hundred-year-old justice than to simply spur a few events forward. Shots of a topless Abanaki over the end credits do little to explain the situation. Ultimately, it's not the ranch but Andrew who is "haunted," by ghosts of the past and his own diseased obsessions. He alone believes that Abanaki is reborn in Jennifer, his mind warped by years of isolation. Patrick's statement—"You can go buggy out here ... too much aloneness isn't good either"—sums up Andrew's plight while echoing many stranded scenarios. A film that asks more questions than it answers, *Haunted* remains a flawed but significant weird western that points ahead to the more self-reflexive desert terrors of the '80s and '90s.

Indian curses also figure heavily into *Nightwing* (1979), a lavish studio production that addresses current Native American concerns within the context of a "revenge of nature" plotline. Based on a novel by Martin Cruz Smith (*Gorky Park*) and released by Columbia Pictures, Arthur Hiller's film is one of the most well-produced, handsomely photographed desert terrors of the '70s, beginning with a languid opening credits sequence featuring a stunning succession of

Nightwing (1979) was one of several studio SF/fantasy films of the era to receive the short-lived "Fotonovel" treatment.

desert landscapes captured by director of photography Charles Rosher (*Hex*). The film takes its time setting up several characters and storylines revolving around the Maski Indian reservation, including Tribal Deputy Youngman Duran (Nick Mancuso), his privileged white girlfriend Ann (Kathryn Harrold), Duran's modern, greedy rival Walker Chee (Stephen Macht), who plans to sell Maski land to an oil company, and controversial medicine man Abner (George Clutesi), whose mysterious death coincides with the first of several vampire bat attacks on local livestock. "All the Anglo cities ... the time has come for them to die," Abner says cryptically before passing away, suggesting that the bat outbreak—which soon grows to claim human lives—has some spiritual significance.

The conflict between science and the supernatural continues throughout the film, as obsessive bat exterminator Philip Payne (David Warner, who deserves some kind of award for saying lines like "Jesus created the first bat" with a straight face) arrives to track and destroy the vampire bats, which he terms, with Donald Pleasence–like gravitas, "the quintessence of evil." Initially at odds, the more spiritually-attuned Duran and man of science Payne eventually team up to save Anne, who is stranded in the desert after a swarm of bats devour her group of "bible thumper" tourists. Following an even more harrowing encounter with the deadly swarm, Payne, Duran and Ann track the colony of bats to their roosting place, an ancient cave rich with sacred meaning (as well as valuable oil deposits). "There are limits, even to superstition," Payne says as he prepares to exterminate the bats with poison gas, but in the end, Duran's datura-aided mystical visions allow the team to destroy the bloodsucking beasties, along with ending Chee's potential business interests.

Playing more like a social drama with a vampire bat subplot than "*Jaws* with wings," *Nightwing* is often the victim of its own tangled narrative threads and lofty aspirations. In a progressive move, it's the first desert terror film—and one of the first studio films, period—to set its action completely within the Native American community. The script (by Smith and several others) goes beyond the usual clichés associated with Indian-themed horror (rituals, possession) to confront the more serious issues of cultural displacement, economic hardship, and the difficulties of modernization. While this approach grounds the action in a convincing (and previously unseen) milieu, it doesn't excuse the dramatically inert, clearly representational conflicts that populate the story, and eventually drain the film of any energy. Aside from summoning the occasional creepy image (blood oozing from Abner's sheet-covered corpse), Hiller seems uncomfortable with the more overtly horrific material, preferring to focus on the conflict between Duran and Chee (which comes to an unsatisfying end as Chee disappears in the third act) or, even worse, some unnecessary comic relief (Strother Martin, in a pointless, and overacted, role).

The bat attack sequences (there are only two) are reasonably well-orchestrated by FX maestro Carlo Rambaldi (*E.T.*), who uses optics and puppetry to bring the army of bloodsuckers to life. The latter is more effective, especially in close-ups of the little devils sinking their fangs into victims' necks and flapping wildly about in women's hair. The best sequence of the film, which involves the heroes trapped in a metal cage while surrounded by hundreds of hungry bats, is convincingly scary as the creatures gnaw through the electrified mesh. Unfortunately, the canyon climax, which should have generated considerable suspense and excitement, largely ignores the bats to concentrate on a series of hackneyed "Indian" imagery that seems pulled from older, less sophisticated movies. Earnest, well-meaning, but not nearly as scary as one would hope, *Nightwing* is doomed by an unwillingness to embrace the possibilities of its own genre.

Nightwing's late-'70s release (and subsequent failure at the box office) signaled the end of the revenge of nature cycle just as a much more economical type of horror film began to take off. The independently produced, low budget slasher film *Halloween* (1978) was an enormous, unexpected success and forever altered the genre landscape. Its influence can be felt in *The Ghost Dance* (1982), which combines stalk n' slash motifs with mild supernatural content. After Professor Kay Foster (Julie Amato) unearths a mummified body at an archaeological excavation, the grave is ransacked by an unbalanced local Native American man, Aranjo (Henry Bal), who steals a 100-year-old totem from the corpse. After using the totem in a blood ritual, Aranjo is possessed by some unknown force which compels him to slaughter his wife. Tensions develop between Kay and the local tribe, who suspect the dig site is the final resting place of Nahalla, the founder of the "Ghost Dance Cult," an obscure group whose beliefs draw from both Christianity and Native American religions. When her Native American boyfriend, Tom Eagle (Victor Mohica) dismisses Nahalla as a "crazy legend," Kay begins her own investigation. Aranjo begins stalking Kay at home, using his newly-attained supernatural powers against her friends and co-workers. As Kay finally discovers the truth about Nahalla and the reason for Aranjo's fixation on her, it may already be too late.

In many ways, *The Ghost Dance* (its title shortened to simply *Ghost Dance* for U.S. video release) is the first Native American slasher film. It certainly showcases all the familiar genre tropes: plenty of stabbings and impalements (Aranjo's weapon of choice is a large knife), point of view stalking sequences, victims who have sex and die, scares involving the discovery of dead bodies and even a shower scene. Unlike *Friday the 13th* and its imitators, *The Ghost Dance* is fairly restrained in its bloodletting (when you can see it, as many scenes are impenetrably dark) and contains no nudity, leading one to believe that the filmmakers probably intended their film as more of a supernatural thriller. Unfortunately, the film makes even less of an impression in this regard, as Aranjo's powers are severely limited, and film's "mystical" scenes, such as the final showdown between Aranjo and a local mystic Ocacio (Frank Salsedo), are minimal and unimaginative.

The film's most potentially interesting idea involves the past relationship between Nahalla and Melissa Stewart (Amato again), a white woman who "fell under his spell" after he kidnapped her, eventually joining him as the second half of a "murderous team." Like the doomed interracial love affair between Abanaki and McCloan in *Haunted*, *Ghost Dance*'s Nahalla/Stewart pairing informs the present action, as well as influencing it even more directly, as Aranjo is clearly under the control of Nahalla's spirit. Although ripe with potential, any hopes for a supernatural Bonnie and Clyde wreaking bloody havoc in the contemporary West are dashed by the hurried finale, which freeze-frames on a crazed (possessed?) Kay before she can do any damage. With one foot in the slasher stakes and the other in the spirit world, *The Ghost Dance* is a middling hybrid that fails to make a strong impression.

The low-budget supernatural slasher *Scalps* (1983), on the other hand, goes right for the jugular (literally) from its first frames, as a gnarly-looking Indian demon leaps out of the dark to decapitate his victim. The hits keep coming as a lion-man howls at the mountains, and an inebriated prospector stabs himself in the neck after seeing a creepy apparition. And all this in the first five minutes! The story calms down a bit after this initial burst of insanity, as Professor Machen (Kirk Alyn) sends six archaeology students to an excavation site deep in the desert where they hope to unearth some Native American artifacts ("As long as it doesn't include exhuming any dead Indians" gripes one of Machen's colleagues). A stop at a filling station leads to an encounter with older Native American Billy Ironwing (George Randall), who warns them away from their destination, calling it a "bad place ... where many Indians were killed" while random images of gory mayhem flash across the screen. None of Billy's admonitions can hold a candle to the "weird girl" of the group, D.J. (Jo-Ann Robinson), who is against the dig and likes to say things like "the ground is alive with evil" while playing with her prayer sticks.

The first half of *Scalps* is carried primarily by D.J.'s eerie visions and desert atmospherics, all bound together by a surprisingly strong synth score. Things turn nasty relatively quickly, however, after jokester Randy (Richard Hench) stumbles onto an abandoned campfire and, after having a vision of his own, becomes possessed by the spirit of long-dead Indian renegade "Black Claw," who, according to know-it-all Kershaw (Roger Maycock), was known for "black magic and ritualistic murder." Randy claims his victims with old-school Native American weapons like knives, tomahawks, and even arrows in a series of gory murders (including a well-done throat slashing and yes, a scalping) that never become completely predictable thanks to the script's supernatural undercurrent. Randy's physical presence changes, too, becoming progressively more demonic as he is possessed by Black Claw. There's a nice little twist ending, too, which ends the film on an appropriately unsettling note.

An early writing/directing effort by exploitation king Fred Olen Ray (*Hollywood Chainsaw Hookers*), *Scalps* is a scrappy, determined little film that, despite its myriad technical issues, succeeds in entertaining for most of its scant 78-minute running time. With its grainy images, post-synced dialogue, and choppy editing, the film shares the home-movie aesthetic of *Blood Shack* and *Victims!* but, thanks to a more original script, well-chosen locations (the film was shot at California's scenic Vasquez Rocks) and some creative makeup effects, succeeds in overcoming its budgetary limitations. Many scenes are carried by Drew Newman and Eric Rasmussen's throbbing electronic score, especially a chilling drum/chant track that signals Black Claw's arrival. Unlike the bigger-budgeted but more restrained *The Ghost Dance*, *Scalps* successfully balances its spiritual motifs with contemporary slasher elements and delivers on both fronts. Although shot just outside Los Angeles, this is probably the least "Hollywood" film of Ray's entire oeuvre, with a refreshing absence of the B-movie "names" (though Forrest J. Ackerman makes a mercifully brief appearance) or camp sensibility which has defined most of his subsequent output. The end credits instruct us to watch for *Scalps II: The Return of DJ*. I'm still waiting.

It's doubtful anyone, however, is anticipating a follow-up to *The Returning* (1983), a baffling and unnecessarily fragmented story of reincarnation that follows in the familiar footsteps of several previous possession stories. During a family camping trip to an Indian reservation outside Salt Lake City, Utah, John Ophir (Gabriel Walsh) is awakened late at night by strange sounds while, in a nearby canyon, a Medicine Man (Mostea Oshley) intones spells over a pair of glowing red rocks. On a follow-up trip to the site of a famous Indian battle, John's son Jason (Brian Poelman) finds the mysterious rocks and, against the wishes of mom Sybil (Susan Strasberg) brings them home for his collection of totems and dolls. Unable to concentrate on his work at the Bureau of Indian Affairs, John's behavior takes a turn for the worse after Jason is killed in a freak car accident by alcoholic truck driver Al (Victor Arnold). To the dismay of his grieving wife, John begins adopting Jason's behavior and speech patterns, skipping work to hang out at his son's school and demanding to sleep in his artifact-strewn bedroom. In one of the film's most disturbing scenes, John and Sybil's fight about their dead son ("You can't bring him back—no one can!") gives in to a rough lovemaking session in Jason's bed, as the infantilized John paws at her robe.

After John sets his son's bedroom on fire, Sybil is forced to hospitalize her increasingly unstable husband, but refuses to take easy answers ("He's lost his mind," clucks her mother) for his bizarre assumption of their son's personality. At the same time, the tortured Al experiences startling visions of Indian warriors before a gruesome car accident (which, the film suggests, is caused by Sybil's invocation of an Indian spell) lands him in the same hospital as John. Babbling ancient Indian words that he would have no way of knowing, John remains a mystery to the doctors ("there's something locked inside his brain"), but a series of distressing incidents—among them the sudden appearance of the medicine man in her bathroom mirror—send Sybil back to the reservation in a final effort to lift the centuries-old "curse" that has afflicted her husband.

Mostly forgotten since its delayed video release and subsequent VHS retitling as *The Witch Doctor*, *The Returning* is competently produced and acted, but suffers from a deeply confused screenplay and a disjointed editorial style. Chief among its issues is the central question of who (or what) exactly is possessing John; as one of his doctors puts it, "He swings from being a ten-year-old crying for his mother to some strange savage." Unable to fully commit to either option, director Joel Bender further obfuscates the issue by hastily cutting between locations, time frames, and characters in a choppy, almost random way, with abrupt fade outs and awkward transitions that suggest post-production tampering or, more likely, the filmmakers' lack of experience. The film's strongest scenes avoid any overtly supernatural material and deal with the after-effects of Jason's death in a straightforward manner; likewise, its strongest images of horror—such as Sybil's discovery of her son's disinterred corpse lying in her bed—far surpass any of the film's lackluster optical effects.

More interesting than the script's timeworn "past versus present" premise is its marked contrast between the circumstances of the moneyed Ophir family and working-class trucker Al. Though outwardly calm, rifts between brittle housewife Sybil (who suffers through the camping trips and rejects Jason's rock collecting) and distant John are felt from the first moments, with the latter having a much closer bond with his son. Al, on the other hand, seems to have more of a sense of community, as we see in his easy interactions at a local bar and with his sympathetic parents. John and Al are transposed more than once, most memorably in a striking match cut that moves from the uncomfortable lovemaking between Sybil and her deranged husband in their large, nicely furnished home to Al's payment of a hooker (he even comes up a few bucks short). Intentionally or not, these more dramatic scenes are a nice respite from the story's more traditional—and mostly botched—supernatural elements.

Like its characters, *The Returning*'s desert-bound setting of Salt Lake City is poised between present (modern office buildings teeming with whites) and past (represented by the outlying deserts, which seem to be inhabited solely by Native Americans), with city exteriors emphasizing the proximity of the surrounding desert environs to the urban metropolis. While often restricted by the schizoid editing, director of photography Oliver Wood (whose would graduate from low-budget slashers *Don't Go in the House* to blockbuster fare like *The Bourne Identity*) manages to deliver a number of atmospheric desert scenes, especially toward the beginning and end of the film. Harry Manfredini's score, like his music for *The Hills Have Eyes Part II*, leans a little too heavily on *Friday the 13th*–style stingers, but still enlivens many moments and often serves as a much-needed bridge between awkwardly matched scenes or shots. This stitched-together mess of a movie might not be the worst of its reincarnation-themed contemporaries, but it's still one that I doubt many viewers will find themselves returning to very often.

Based on a novel by *Death Wish* author Brian Garfield (titled *Fear in a Handful of Dust*), *Fleshburn* (1984) dispenses with ancient ghosts and curses to offer a more realist, contemporary take on Native American retribution. An opening crawl sets up the basic premise: After leaving several people to die in the desert over a tribal dispute, Native

The *Fleshburn* (1984) VHS sleeve reproduces its memorable theatrical artwork.

American Calvin Duggai was judged insane by a quartet of psychiatrists and committed to a state mental hospital. In the present, we find Duggai (Sonny Landham) making a quick escape from his room, then quickly kidnapping the four shrinks who sent him there. Duggai's plan, we soon find out, is to abandon the group in the middle of the desert and leave them to die, much as he did years before. "I had my Hell. Now, you're gonna have yours," he says cryptically as he drops them from his truck into an arid landscape of rocks and cacti, and drives away into the night.

The quartet of psychiatrists is a motley group, each with his or her personal demons: bickering married couple Shirley (Karen Carlson) and Jay (Robert Chimento), middle-aged homosexual Earl (Macon McCalman), and rugged, manly Sam (Steve Kanaly). Levelheaded survivalist Sam takes charge almost immediately, having the group dig trenches to survive the broiling heat and slice open cactuses for sustenance. Duggai watches the group from afar, performs Native American rituals with animal skins and blood and uses his "witchy" powers to send hawks and snakes after his prey. Earl's worsening leg injury leads an impatient Jay to search for an alternate food source. Finally, Sam takes off to find a road and, after encountering Jay, the two men make a desperate bid to kill their tormentor. Ultimately, the film boils down to Sam versus Duggai, in a contest of strength and smarts (and who looks better without a shirt).

Based on the source material and authentic Tucson, Arizona, location shooting, one would expect *Fleshburn* to be a grueling cinematic experience. Unfortunately, director George Gage mostly pulls his punches throughout, giving the film a watered-down, TV movie sensibility, with very little blood spilled (or flesh burned, for that matter). Despite the film's focus on the harsh realities of survival in such a punishing environment, we never feel the discomfort of Duggai's victims. Duggai is an unconventional antagonist, and Landham (who subsequently moved to the Hollywood big leagues in *48 HRS.* and *Predator* before falling into obscurity) has a commanding physical presence, but his character is underdeveloped, with the film unable to decide whether his "powers" are real or not. Additionally, despite an ideal platform, the film avoids commenting on Native American vs. white relations. Instead, Gage drops in clumsy flashbacks and directs the (few) action scenes in the most pedestrian way, with very little onscreen violence. *Fleshburn* would never have been (nor did it need to be) a high body count picture, but the film consistently misses opportunities to wring suspense or tension from its intriguing premise.

Natas: The Reflection (1986) mixes the western, fantasy, and horror genres in an ambitious, occasionally ridiculous, concoction that feels like three different movies stitched together. Directed by *Fleshburn* stunt coordinator Jack Dunlap, the Tucson-shot film introduces us to Steve Granger (Randy Mulkey), a reporter determined to find out the truth behind the Indian legend of "Natas," an ancient evil supposedly residing in a nearby mountain range. Undeterred even after losing his job at the newspaper, and resistant to the pleas of his girlfriend Terry (Pat Bolt), Steve sets off for the mountains, where he eventually meets Indian mystic Smohalla ("109-year-old Nino Cochise" per his onscreen credit) at a cave entrance. Smohalla gives Steve a canvas map and amulet, warning him to "beware of the serpent" in an echoing voice before disappearing. Encouraged by this encounter, Steve continues through the desert to find a ghost town (Old Tucson Studios, a popular western town set dating back to 1939), populated by pasty-faced ghouls with weird, high-pitched voices who throw him in jail and want to hang him the next day. With the help of a sympathetic female zombie, Steve escapes death and returns to "reality."

Despite its claim of being "Hosted by Elvira," the Mistress of the Dark is notably absent from Avid Home Video's release of *Natas: The Reflection* (1986).

When Steve returns to the ghost town with Terry and news crew members Angie (Kelli Kuhn), Jay (Craig Hensley), and Spec (Fred Perry), the film moves out of the western/fantasy arena and becomes more of a standard body count picture, as the visitors wander around empty buildings, make out and crack lame jokes before they are finished off by the violent undead, who bear little resemblance to the zombies seen earlier. A gooey-faced ghoul (looking like a zombie extra from *Children Shouldn't Play with Dead Things*) shoves a knife through his victim's throat, providing the first real shock of the film. Angie strips off only to be set afire in her sleeping bag, while Jay has the most spectacular demise—graphic decapitation by scythe—while poking around a barn. After once again fleeing the town, Steve and Terry begin the treacherous climb up to Natas' mountaintop lair, where the heroes finally confront the winged demon, who barks out a series of unintelligible threats before being destroyed in a battle of awesomely bad (even for the time) optical effects. A jaw-dropping ending finds Steve musing philosophically, "Who is Natas? Natas was the reflection. Satan spelled backwards."

Despite its schizoid structure, weak acting and muddy day for night photography, *Natas* tries hard to entertain, marching a nonstop parade of mysticism, monsters, ghouls, and gore past the audience. There's a naive earnestness about the film, mirrored by Steve's dogged quest to find the titular demon, that's hard to resist. The breathlessly delivered pulp dialog ("According to legend, he waits there for someone with the faith of a hundred eagles, who can solve the riddle of the Devil's sentry!") and handmade effects lend the film a live-action comic book feel, while the crunchy synth score will no doubt elicit smiles from '80s horror aficionados. The slowest section of the film is ironically its most horrific, as the story slows to a crawl while the news crew waits around to get killed off by random zombies. But even this section has its grisly delights, and the entire project has a hometown haunt sensibility that's often more fun to watch than more "serious" efforts like *Ghosts That Still Walk*. While fans of weird westerns would have to wait a few more years for a more definitive updating of the genre, *Natas* is a shaky step in the right direction.

The "Old Chief Wood'nhead" segment from the omnibus sequel *Creepshow 2* (1987) shares *Natas'* ghoulish comic-book sensibility. Here, a life-size wooden Indian stationed outside a dusty old general store comes to vengeful life after its kindly owners (George Kennedy and Dorothy Lamour) are murdered by a trio of young thugs (led, in a nice reversal of the usual "noble Indian" clichés, by a Native American) intent on high-tailing it to Hollywood with a bundle of stolen cash. In classic EC Comics tradition, Chief Wood'nhead tracks down the killers and exacts bloody justice on them, with the best comeuppance is saved for the group's leader, long-haired Sam (Holt McCallany), who is scalped (off-camera). Though the acting and music in the first half display an almost parodic quality, once the Chief comes to life, this half-hour segment delivers its fair share of thrills and chills.

An underwhelming follow-up to the original *Creepshow* (1982), *Creepshow 2* represents the inaugural forays into desert terror for horror icons Stephen King and George A. Romero (King contributed the stories, which Romero then adapted for the screen). Romero's longtime cinematographer Michael Gornick (who directed all three segments in the film) does a creditable job in his feature debut, with nice use of shadowplay during the murders. Likewise, the *Cisco Kid* reruns playing on all three victims televisions works as not only a callback to western motifs, but acts as an amusing way to connect all three stalking sequences. It might be the least scary of the film's three tales, but "Old Chief

Woodn'head" benefits from its unique monster and points the way toward straightforward, effects-driven efforts to come.

"The Good. The Bad. The Satanic" reads the irresistible tagline for *Ghost Town* (1988), the first (and so far, only) weird western from Charles Band's Empire Pictures, whose previous desert terror entries *Laserblast*, *The Day Time Ended*, and *Parasite* fall into the creature feature category. While thematically different than much of the studio's output at the time, *Ghost Town* retains the signature broad-strokes, comic book approach typical of Empire productions, as it quickly introduces Kate (Catherine Hickland), a spoiled rich girl who has just run out on her wedding day. After her convertible breaks down along a desert highway, she is abducted by a horseman who emerges from a sudden dust storm and drags her away. When local Deputy Langley (Franc Luz) shows up to investigate the young woman's disappearance, he is attacked by a mysterious "man on a black horse," who destroys his Bronco before disappearing into the desert. Langley pursues the rider on foot, eventually ending up in the old west town of Cruz del Diablo, a rotting collection of dust-swept streets and empty buildings. As he meets some of the residents, like the blind Dealer (Bruce Glover) and blacksmith's daughter Etta (Lauren Schaefer), the deputy realizes he is trapped in a time-warped town full of "souls lost between Heaven and Hell" under control of the zombie-like Devlin (Jimmie F. Skaggs), the dark rider who, in a by-now familiar theme, desires Kate as a replacement for his former lover. To rescue Kate, and bring her back to the present, Langley must defeat Devlin and his undead gang of outlaws.

Like many Empire productions, *Ghost Town* relies more on atmosphere and creative special effects rather than character or plot twists to drive the narrative. The story by David Schmoeller (*Tourist Trap*) spins a pleasingly creepy dark fairy tale out of a handful of characters and minimal locations. Luz and Hickland aren't the most engaging pair of actors, but Glover and Skaggs more than make up for it with some solid character work. John Buechler's makeup effects rank among his best and most realistic work of the period, with resurrected corpses erupting from underground, detailed zombie makeups and plenty of graphic flesh wounds and bullet hits. The real star of *Ghost Town*, however, is veteran cinematographer Mac Ahlberg (*Re-Animator*), who gives the film a wonderfully lush, dreamlike look that more than compensates for any script shortcomings (Arizona's Old Tucson Studios, previously seen in *Natas*, is much more effectively used here). Some of the most effective passages of the film occur early on, as Langley first enters the haunted town, passing through dust-blown streets while hanged bodies swing from trees. Another striking (and bloody) sequence, which occurs later in the film, recreates the death of the original sheriff, who Devlin crucifies to a windmill before burying him alive. These sequences, and others, recall Lucio Fulci's gothic horrors of the '80s as well as his brutal, atmospheric westerns like *Massacre Time* (1966).

For all its gruesome set pieces, *Ghost Town* never loses its respect for western conventions, with its colorful townsfolk and several exciting shootouts between Langley and Devlin's gang, culminating with an explosive finale. The film is not only one of the best weird westerns, it also adopts many classic desert terror tropes, with action that begins and ends on the road, and the detailed construction of a self-contained world that is at once both real and unreal. Only the music score—recycled from several other Empire releases—strikes a false note, as it struggles to find a connection with the rich visuals. Minor quibbles aside, *Ghost Town* is a welcome updating of earlier horror westerns like *Curse of the Undead* and easily qualifies as Band's finest desert terror film. The tireless

The stylish and atmospheric *Ghost Town* (1988) is producer Charles Band's finest contribution to the desert terror genre.

producer continued to plumb the western/fantasy genre with *Oblivion* (1994), *Oblivion 2: Backlash* (1996), *Petticoat Planet* (1996), and *Phantom Town* (1997), all of which were filmed in Romania.

Ghost Town, while cosigned mostly to cable and video, nevertheless paved the way for the return of the period piece weird western, as a quartet of past-set spookers appeared over the next few years. The first of these was the macabre anthology *Grim Prairie Tales* (1990), whose action takes place entirely in the late 1800s. Instead of emphasizing special effects, the film focuses more on character and atmosphere, as two travelers—jittery city boy Deeds (Brad Dourif) and rough bounty hunter Morrison (James Earl Jones)—trade progressively scarier campfire stories. Morrison kicks off the evening with the anecdote of an old man (Jim Hare, best known as "Grandpa" from *Silent Night, Deadly Night*) who comes to regret desecrating an Indian graveyard. The bounty hunter continues with a second story (the best in the film) concerning an attractive pregnant girl and the young man who befriends her at his peril. Deeds' attempt to one-up Morrison, a yarn about a Southern family who relocate to the Midwest, but can't escape their racist past, is followed by Morrison's final tale of a fastidious gunfighter (Scott Paulin) who is haunted by the ghost of his most recent victim. The film closes quietly with Deeds and Morrison, having been up all night, parting company in the morning.

Despite Morrison's threats of telling "a story that'll stick to you like an eyeball on a cactus needle," most of his and Deeds' *Tales* are sorely lacking in scares or twists. The "pregnant woman" story is easily the most traditionally horrific, and the gunfighter segment has its creepy moments, but the other two tales, as well as the wraparound, favor drama over horror (the third story plays like a racier-than-usual episode of *Little House on the Prairie*), emphasizing the harsh realities of pioneer life in the post–Civil War Midwest over any overtly horrific content. Cinematographer Janusz Kaminski, who would also shoot the post-nuke creature feature *The Terror Within 2* before photographing major movies for Steven Spielberg and others, handles the daytime material adequately, but many of the night scenes are unfortunately dark and murky (this may be partially due to an inferior transfer, as the film remains stuck in VHS purgatory). The wraparound, usually the weakest part of anthology films, emerges as one of the film's highlights; it's a real treat to watch, or rather listen to, two of cinema's greatest villainous voices (Chucky vs. Darth Vader, if you will) swap macabre tales under the stars; too bad the tales themselves aren't that memorable as the tellers. Apart from its status as the first weird western anthology on record, *Grim Prairie Tales* is a mostly unremarkable effort.

A second weird western portmanteau, *Into the Badlands* (1991), covers similar material much more stylishly and effectively. Comprised of three separate stories linked by the journey of crusty bounty hunter/narrator T.L. Barston (Bruce Dern), *Badlands* defies its TV-movie origins with a haunting, dreamlike structure bolstered by an excellent cast and gritty, authentic production design. The tone is set immediately with strong gothic imagery—dust blows over an abandoned church, an ancient-looking amulet dangles from a rough-hewn wooden cross, a horse-drawn carriage melts into the sinking sun—as Barston's cackling voice over describes the badlands as "stretches of territory that God just plain forgot about … where sensible men never ventured, where dreams and phantoms walked." On the way to claim his latest reward money, the hunter crosses paths with McComas (Dylan McDermott), an outlaw on the run from Sheriff Starett (Andrew Robinson). The ill-fated love affair between McComas and a sharp-tongued prostitute Blossom (Helen Hunt) comprises the first story, based on Heck Allen's short story "The

The made-for-TV Western anthology *Into the Badlands* (1991) sports an excellent cast including Bruce Dern, Helen Hunt, and Mariel Hemingway.

Streets of Laredo." A doom-laden atmosphere, laced with black-clad figures, coffins and desert burials, pervades McComas and Blossom's relationship until the final, haunting image, which sets the stage for more bizarre twists to come.

Barston rejoins the narrative, stopping to dine with settlers Alma (Mariel Hemingway) and her husband John (Steve Tyler) before continuing his quest to find his next target, wanted outlaw Red Roundtree. The second tale, "The Time of the Wolves" by Marcia Muller, begins, as Alma visits her slightly unhinged neighbor Sarah (Lisa Pelikan), whose husband is away for the evening. A violent snowstorm traps the two women together, followed by an invasive pack of wolves, but the real evil plaguing the pair is Sarah's madness, which threatens to infect Alma as well. Trading on psychological rather than supernatural terrors, this middle segment is the film's most effective tale, featuring an oppressively wintry atmosphere, well-balanced drama and suspense, and strong performances from the two leads.

Our narrator takes center stage for the final and most hallucinatory tale, Bryce Walton's "The Last Pelt," as Barston tracks down and kills Roundtree (Michael J. Metzger), then hauls the corpse to the nearly-deserted ghost town of White Rock to collect his bounty. After facing off against a foursome of scruffy locals, Barston barely escapes with his life. Alone with his rotting quarry, Barston's mind unravels as he chats with Red's corpse while circling the moonscape-like craters of the desert. Echoes of trippy '70s outings like *El Topo* and *Bring Me the Head of Alfredo Garcia* (1974) reverberate as Barston falls into a dream from which he will never wake, and is finally buried with his quarry.

In the second segment of *Into the Badlands* (1991), rancher Alma (Mariel Hemingway) meets up with bounty hunter T.L. Barston (Bruce Dern).

A wooden cross marks the grave, on which hangs an amulet, which is quickly pocketed by an unseen rider. The cycle begins again, as the apparently immortal Barston rides off into yet another sunset...

A traveling carnival of free-roving weirdness set (in Barston's words) "between civilization and the ninth circle of Hell," *Into the Badlands* achieves a remarkable narrative fluidity that places it closer to Krzysztof Kieslowski's *Three Colors Trilogy* or *Pulp Fiction* than the jerky, stop-and-start structure of most anthologies. Also unique is a consistent level of watchability amongst the three distinct sections, none of which eclipses the others in terms of atmosphere, pacing or performances. If the film raises more questions than it answers, its lack of closure doesn't detract from its overall effectiveness, and the more surreal elements are well grounded within a thoroughly convincing portrayal of frontier life, with all its regrets, sorrows, and physical hardships. Director Sam Pillsbury (*Zandalee*) does an excellent job unifying the seemingly disparate elements (and genres) with strong support from composer John Debney, whose score contains some truly inspired western/horror themes and melodies.

The slow-burning lycanthropic love story *Mad at the Moon* (1992) transports the werewolf legend to the West, but the results play more melodramatic than monstrous. In the 1892–set tale, Mary Stuart Masterson stars as Jenny Hill, an intelligent young woman in love with rugged, ill-mannered outlaw Miller Brown (Hart Bochner) but forced by her controlling Mother (Fionnula Flanagan) to marry jittery landowner (and Miller's half-brother) James (Stephen Blake). After moving with her new husband to a house in the middle of an isolated stretch of desert, Jenny soon finds that her marital problems have only just begun, as, with every full moon, James transforms into a hairy, howling beast. Jenny's claims of her husband's "moon sickness" result in a dubious arrangement: at the next full moon, Miller will spend the evening with Jenny to protect her from the hideously transformed James.

Moon might be the first "Werewolf Western" in movie history, but it only earns that title by (ahem) a hair, as Argentinean co-writer/director Martin Donovan (best known for penning the effects-driven comedy *Death Becomes Her*) seems more interested in the story's romantic implications rather than its horrific possibilities. The film's lupine elements are only introduced about halfway through, and amount to little more than a few brief scenes of Blake sprouting a few extra hairs and baying at the moon. The sexual repression at the heart of the story (particularly between Jenny and Miller) is left similarly unexplored, with Donovan instead serving up a series of whimsical images—a twilight opera performance, black and white childhood flashbacks, a dreamy cameo by *Prey of the Chameleon*'s Daphne Zuniga—to decorate his overly simplistic adult fairy tale. This chaste and bloodless offering might have worked better as one of *Into the Badlands*' half-hour segments; at feature length, however, the film feels stretched and the end result will likely please neither drama nor horror fans.

The decade's final period weird western, Sam Shepard's *Silent Tongue* (1994), is also one of its most disquieting achievements. Set in 1873 Llano Estacado (a region of the Southwest which encompasses parts of Texas and New Mexico), the picture's melancholy tone haunts from the very first frames, as deranged young widower Talbot Roe (River Phoenix) crouches under a tree strewn with bones and feathers, "guarding" the mummified corpse of his bride Awbonnie (Sheila Tousey), who died during childbirth. Desperate to save his son from complete mental and physical collapse, Talbot's father Prescott (Richard Harris) meets with Awbonnie's father, Dr. Eamon McCree (Alan Bates)

Although relegated to a smaller supporting role, co-star River Phoenix (top), is prominently featured on the artwork for Sam Shepard's troubling western *Silent Tongue* (1994). Richard Harris (middle) and Dermot Mulroney are also pictured.

Writer/director Sam Shepard (top left and bottom) and Dermot Mulroney (top right) on the set of *Silent Tongue* (1994).

to propose a second trade for McCree's other "half-breed" daughter Velada (Jeri Arredondo). When McCree's son Reeves (Dermot Mulroney) rejects the deal, Prescott kidnaps Velada and sets off across the prairie. Over several days and nights, Eamon and Reeves pursue Prescott and Velada while Talbot, tormented by Awbonnie's vengeful spirit, descends deeper into madness.

McCree's pursuit of Prescott gives the film its narrative drive and visual sweep, but the infrequent yet highly charged confrontations between Talbot and Awbonnie provide the film's most powerful moments. Accompanied solely by the sounds of crackling flames and rattling bones, these encounters progress in intensity, from the brutal introduction (after shooting a vulture, Talbot savagely tears the bird's wings off and presses them to his beloved's corpse) to Awbonnie's first appearance as a spirit (her face divided into living and dead flesh by a streak of white paint), building to a hallucinatory exchange in which Talbot's refusal to ritualistically burn his wife's body (and therefore release her spirit) prompts her to demand he take his own life. Echoing the self-destructive wishes of other desert terror protagonists, Awbonnie coldly demands, "Put that gun in your mouth, and set me free." Talbot's response, a last-minute decision to shoot the spirit instead, only results in her disappearance. Awbonnie continues to materialize, however, not only in Talbot's fantasies but elsewhere, as she exacts terrible vengeance on both Prescott and McCree.

Awbonnie's ghost delivers *Silent Tongue*'s most conventionally "scary" moments, but the specter of death permeates every frame. McCree's Medicine Show features a pair of performers who joke about ghosts ("liable to come waftin' around any old time") and play a dirge-like minstrel song titled "The Old Jaw Bone," which uses an actual cattle jaw bone as an instrument. McCree is plagued by nightmares of his own rape of a mute Native American woman ("Silent Tongue," mother to Awbonnie and Velada) in the bone-strewn desert. Prescott traps Velada by playing dead, with coins placed over his eyes. After being abandoned by his son, McCree falls victim to a tribe of "savages" who commit him to an agonizing fate that is eerily reminiscent of his own manufactured "Kickapoo tonic" sales pitch—a speech we later see being delivered, with delicious irony, to a new audience by one of McCree's troupe, now promoted in the Doctor's (permanent) absence. The film's consistent focus on mortality, delivered with a noticeable lack of traditional horror theatrics, makes *Silent Tongue* one of the most subtly frightening weird westerns, with many of its strongest images impossible to forget.

The film takes full advantage of its setting, too, with an impressive accruing of visual detail (particularly in the Medicine Show carnival and its troupe) throughout, as well as a willingness to explore white/Native American relations of the time. In many ways, Shepard's film is the first weird western since *Hex* to feature fully fleshed-out Native American characters, and even more damning of its white (male) characters' attitudes and behavior ("She's an Indian; they were born to suffer," exclaims Eamon). Clearly empathetic toward its Native American (female) protagonists, *Silent Tongue* also adopts *Hex*'s smoky, dreamlike visual texture, which casts a spell over the viewer that becomes more immersive and unshakable as the film progresses. The spiraling story structure is similarly loose, playing more like the existential westerns and moody road movies of Monte Hellman, whose *The Shooting* (1966) and *Two-Lane Blacktop* (1971) also feature rootless characters searching for one another (and yet failing to connect) through a desolate, and increasingly surreal, American landscape.

A noted departure from its more straightforward contemporaries, *Silent Tongue* is a curious creature whose eccentricities will make it irresistible to some viewers while frustrating to others. It's as close to a prestige project as desert terror gets, with Oscar nominees involved on both sides of the camera. Shepard, an old hand at desert tragedy whose credits include screenplays for *Paris, Texas* (1984) and the film adaptation of his play *Fool for Love* (1985) directs his suitably spooky script with a sure hand, working up a convincingly morbid atmosphere throughout. Harris and Bates carry the show, but the lesser-known Tousey and Arredondo (in a less showy role) easily match their co-stars' commitment and intensity. As Talbot, Phoenix plays a supporting role that, while effective, is mostly one-note. His participation lends the film a haunted afterlife of its own, as this was the last commercially released film the gifted young actor completed before his untimely death. The disturbing symmetry between *Silent Tongue* and Phoenix's interrupted follow-up project *Dark Blood*, in which the actor plays another unhinged young widower living in the desert, only adds to the legend surrounding both films.

After a bout of challenging period pieces, Native American horror returned to contemporary tales for the remainder of the '90s. The first of these, the made-for-TV thriller *Seduced by Evil* (1994), revisits the themes of '80s offerings like *The Ghost Dance* and *The Returning*. Based on the novel *Brujo* by Jann Arrington Wolcott, the film stars Suzanne Somers as Arizona-based journalist Leigh Lindsay, who attracts the unwanted attention of mysterious healer Cerio (John Vargas) after she interviews him for a local magazine. Although initially skeptical of "spiritual mumbo jumbo," Leigh soon finds herself besieged by frightening dreams/premonitions, as well as unexpected late-night visitations from the darkly enigmatic Cerio, who is convinced that she is the reincarnation of his seventeenth-century lover ("You are not who you seem to be. Deep inside you, another soul yearns to be set free," he coos in her ear). Against the warnings of her friend, new agey painter Rayna (Julie Carmen), Leigh returns to confront the *brujo*, only to succumb further to his advances. Not content to possess her sexually, Cerio instigates a chain of freak accidents and bizarre deaths that threaten to destroy Leigh and her family.

Occasionally atmospheric and mildly erotic, *Seduced by Evil* is a lightweight effort that never bores but rarely catches fire. Somers is quite good as Leigh, making her a likable, relatable heroine, juggling career and family responsibilities while trying to make sense of her increasingly nightmarish predicament. The initial scenes between her and Cerio are the most intriguing, with Leigh's initial complicity in her seduction suggesting personal issues far deeper than any spell cast by the possessive brujo. These troubling notions are quickly pushed aside, however, as Cerio's pervasive destruction of the family unit drives Leigh to embrace her inner spirit animal and combat him in a shapeshifting finale. Though the film is rife with Native American imagery (wolves and ravens appear throughout), Cerio is described as a "Hispanic boogeyman" with Brazilian origins dating back hundreds of years, lending him a more colorful background than usual for a Southwestern horror tale. Other visual aspects of the film (Rayna's vivid paintings, Cerio's desert dwelling) help *Seduced* rise a few notches above its "woman in peril" plotting, though the end result is worlds away from the serious spookiness of earlier TV films like *Black Noon* or *Into the Badlands*.

The shot-on-video movement took a swipe at the weird western with the ambitious *Ghost Gunfighter* (1995), which fuses slasher, supernatural and time travel motifs in its tale of moviemaking madness. Writer/director/cinematographer Scott Gulbrandsen gets things off to a gory start, as the titular undead outlaw claws his way out of his own desert grave before dispatching a pair of hikers (producer William Burr and David Parker, who also executed the film's makeup effects) before the opening credits have even finished. At a frat-style house party, Pete (Jeff Burr, best known as the director of *Leatherface*) convinces his guitar-strumming pal Shane (co-writer/editor/producer Chuck Williams) to accompany him on a trip to Mexico; along for the ride are their friend Ken (Drew Phillips), his girlfriend Debbie (Kim Day), her friend Marcie (Dena Rae Hayess) plus last minute addition Heather (Stacie Randall). After the group takes an ill-advised shortcut (is there any other kind?), Pete's convertible breaks down deep in the desert, and everyone is forced to hoof it to a nearby ghost town.

The group's overnight stay in the town's sole hotel is punctuated by Heather's prophetic dreams and the murder of the hotel Caretaker (John A. Gammons III) by the "Ghost Gunfighter," who returns to attack Debbie the next day. Forced to stay in the town and searching for weapons, Pete, Shane and Heather stumble onto a dreamlike recreation of a past tragedy: in 1931, during the filming of a western movie, actor Dylan (Tom Wicar) kills his co-star and his cheating girlfriend Jessica (Randall again) during a climactic shootout. Cursed to repeat the macabre scene every day, Dylan stalks the grounds as a putrefying ghoul, chopping up anyone who stumbles onto the town (or the area, it seems). As the gunfighter claims more victims, Heather and Shane, with some help from the spectral Jessica, try and save their own lives and lay the town's tortured souls to rest.

Crammed with enough content for a movie with ten times the budget, *Ghost Gunfighter* stubbornly tries to tackle its confused script with minimal resources. Arizona's Old Tucson Studios once again provides a workable western town, but the cast (excepting Randall, who shines in a triple role) is weak, and many of the stunts and makeup effects come off as awkward and amateurish. Muddy videography, choppy editing (credited to four editors) and poorly mixed sound, which often buries the ridiculous dialogue ("I'm not sticking my neck out for some dead ghost!") under a rock 'n' roll soundtrack, further compromise the film. It still manages to hold one's interest thanks to its "time trap" scenes, which, while reminiscent of *Natas* and *Ghost Town*, tweak the concept further by making its "ghost town" an Old Hollywood film set whose bloody past is directly linked to the motion pictures that were shot there. While far from perfect–Heather's exact connection to actress Jessica is never fully explained, for example—the 1931 scenes have a narrative thrust and visual fluidity that are missing from the rest of the film. An unconscious throwback to similarly uneven, yet entertaining, weird westerns of the past few decades, *Ghost Gunfighter* (which also goes by the titles *High Tomb* and *Last Chance*) wields enough surprises to keep you watching through the rough patches. Like its title character, the film vanished mysteriously following its completion in the mid–'90s, only to resurface over ten years later as part of a bargain DVD set.

Native American–themed desert terror received its most serious treatment to date in *The Brave* (1997), a resolutely contemporary tale which plunges headfirst into a realm of starkly realistic, socially conscious horror. Based on a same-titled 1991 novel by *Fletch* author Gregory McDonald, *The Brave* is best known as the directing debut of cult actor turned unlikely megastar Johnny Depp, who also assumes the lead role of Raphael, a Native American man who, in a desperate bid to provide a better life for his wife and two young children, agrees to participate in a snuff film—as the subject. The queasy, hopeless atmosphere which hangs over the entire narrative starts before we meet any of the characters, as haunting chords play over the desert landscape of Morgantown, a ramshackle community of societal outcasts bordering—and largely built from—a massive trash dump. The wordless first ten minutes of the film follow Raphael as he leaves the trailer home he shares with Rita (Elpidia Carillo) and their children Frankie (Cody Lightning) and Marta (Nicole Mancera) and takes a bus into an unnamed, seemingly deserted city, where he meets the man who will change—and end—his life.

The specific details of Raphael's new job (which he "found out about from some guy at a bar") are kept intentionally vague by both employer and potential employee during a brief interview with the shady Larry (Marshall Bell) inside a generic-looking warehouse. After answering a handful of questions about his past and enduring racial slurs, unemployed "three-time loser" Raphael is brought to an enormous loft on the top floor, which is vacant save for a medieval-looking torture chair. The ghoulish tone continues as a bloated, wheelchair-bound eccentric named McCarthy (Marlon Brando) greets his new hire with the question, "Are you afraid to die?" before casually explaining that "How much you are paid depends on how much you can withstand … how 'brave' you are." McCarthy rhapsodizes about how Raphael's prolonged death will be "a great inspiration for those who are not dying … so that they can see how brave we can be when it's time to go." The repeated use of the word "brave," and its obvious double meaning (in McDonald's novel, *The Brave* is the title McCarthy chooses for the snuff film Raphael will star in), achieves a bitter irony as Raphael agrees to sign over his life for a mere $50,000, a third of which is handed to him in cash on the spot. After a mirthless toast, McCarthy asks Raphael to return in one week.

Over the next seven days, Raphael wrestles with his fateful decision while trying to enjoy the little time he has left with his family. Initially, the sudden influx of money only creates more problems: a skeptical Rita assumes her husband's new job must be another criminal scheme, enforcer Larry makes unexpected, threatening appearances to remind Raphael of his obligations, and brother-in-law Luis (Luis Guzman), a small-time thug who has partnered with Raphael in the past, wants to get in on the suspected score. Additionally, Raphael's own limited lifespan is mirrored in the imminent demise of Morgantown, whose land has been purchased by a salvage company with plans, as one character puts it, to "bulldoze our world away." Confronted with such soul-crushing circumstances, Raphael constructs a miniature carnival (which recalls Martin's "private Reno" in *South of Reno*), complete with rides, a big screen TV, and vending machines—outside their trailer and treats his neighbors to a massive fiesta, complete with fireworks.

Raphael's final twenty-four hours on Earth are marked by a series of physical and spiritual confrontations, beginning with a confession of his fateful decision to Father Stratton (Clarence Williams III), whom he asks for assistance with obtaining the final payment. The priest's harsh response ("You've sold your soul") is more judgmental than helpful. "No, Father. I sold my body like a whore," Raphael counters. "The church forgives whores every day." In a final effort to insure Rita and the children's safety, Raphael tracks down and murders Luis before submitting to a late-night ritualistic cleansing. The following morning poignantly echoes the film's opening, as The Brave kisses his family goodbye before heading off to the city to meet his fate.

Desert terrors are rarely feel-good movies, but *The Brave* is easily one of the genre's most relentlessly grim achievements, with a downward-spiraling storyline and dog-eat-dog worldview that offers little to no salvation for any of its marginalized characters. The script (credited to three writers, among them Depp and his brother D.P Depp), in which desert dweller Raphael travels to the city only to be destroyed by the controlling (white) entities, is a welcome inversion of the usual Native American horror storyline, in which civilized whites journey to the desert and encounter malevolent supernatural forces. The snuff-movie backdrop promises to propel the film into edgy, even graphic, territory, but Depp shies away from explaining, let alone dramatizing, the gory details of Raphael's fate; this is particularly felt during the open, yet hardly unambiguous, ending, which aims for a sickening finality but leaves the viewer feeling curiously empty. Instead, Depp focuses on the dramatic implications of Raphael's decision, as he wrestles with his conscience while attempting to prepare his family for an uncertain future. The result is a film trapped in a no man's land between existential drama and arthouse horror, which

7. The Good, the Bad and the Satanic

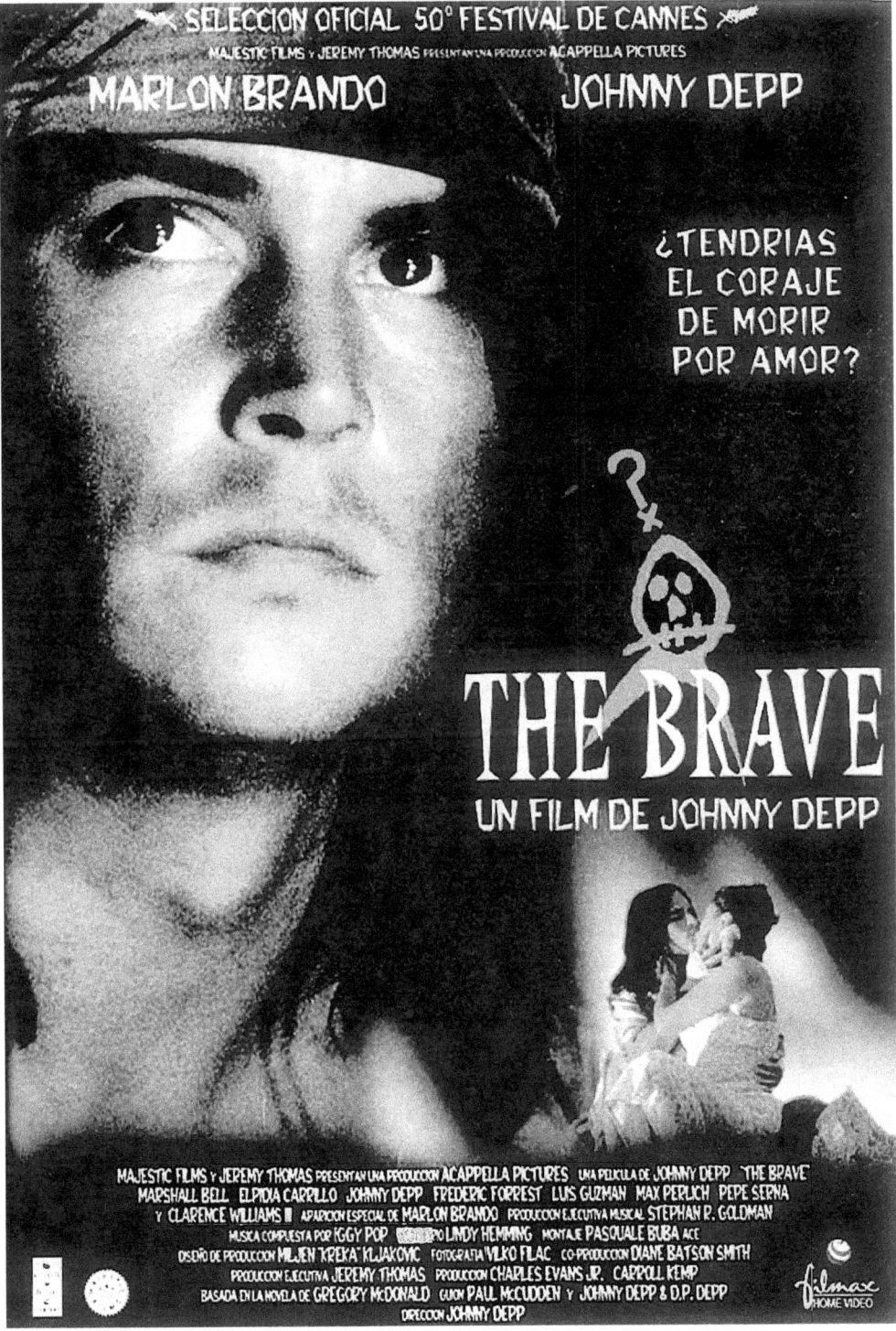

Johnny Depp both stars in and directs *The Brave* (1997), which has yet to be commercially released in the United States.

for most of its running time plays out as the slowest, most agonizingly drawn-out death scene in cinematic history.

To enliven such downbeat subject matter, Depp enlists the talents of several artistic collaborators from past projects, including his *Don Juan DeMarco* co-star Brando along with Serbian director of photography Vilko Filac and production designer Miljen Kreka Kljakovic, along with first-time film composer Iggy Pop, all of whom contributed to *Arizona Dream* (1992), a whimsical desert fantasy in which Depp had previously starred. The resulting fabric of sights and sounds is indeed rich and decidedly European in flavor, especially in the Morgantown scenes, which often unfold in elaborate long takes and possess a vibrant, at times Fellini-esque atmosphere. Outside of the junkyard community (which recalls Luis Albert Urrea's powerful true-life stories of Mexico City's "dump people" as much as the scrap-worlds of *Sonny Boy* or *The Barn of the Naked Dead*), the film grows noticeably colder and less hospitable, particularly in the almost apocalyptic city scenes, where cryptic symbols (primitive graffiti of a skull crowned with a question mark appears more than once, and was later used for the film's one-sheet) scar the walls, the local bar serves a freakish crowd of drunks, and human life is cheap. Pop's versatile score, which alternates gentle, Ry Cooder–like guitar melodies with skin-crawling gypsy gothic, unifies the film's polarized environments while often compensating for the lack of onscreen drama.

Ironically, one of *The Brave*'s weaker elements is Depp's own central performance, which, while probably intended to suggest Raphael's spiritual burden, comes across as overly internalized and lacking energy. Depp injects a few moments of physical humor (his silent film era gags in one sequence recall his physical performance in *Benny and Joon*) and genuine intensity (especially in the third act), but too often allows Raphael to quietly recede into the carefully constructed world of Morgantown and its offbeat residents or, even worse, simply gives us shots of Raphael trudging alone through the desert or staring plaintively into space. Thankfully, the colorful supporting cast makes up for it, with the always-unpredictable Brando (in what amounts to an extended cameo) wavering between menacing and out to lunch while Williams III and Guzman bring some much-needed energy to the proceedings.

Regardless of its triumphs or failings, *The Brave* is unfortunately best known as a "lost" film, as it remains commercially unavailable in the United States nearly twenty years after its disastrous premiere at the 1997 Cannes Film Festival. After receiving several negative reviews, the film (its executive producers include Jeremy Thomas, whose adventurous credits include films for Bertolucci, Roeg, and Cronenberg) failed to secure North American distribution, though it has received theatrical and video releases in countries as varied as France and Brazil. Johnny Depp's presence alone (especially in the post–*Pirates of the Caribbean* climate) should have guaranteed at least a nominal U.S. video release years ago, leading one to suspect there are other factors (such as Depp himself) blocking the release. Understandably shaken by the experience, Depp never directed another film, although visual and thematic elements of *The Brave* and its characters have resurfaced in later Depp projects, from the Gypsy drama *The Man Who Cried* to the big-budget *The Lone Ranger*, in which he plays Native American "Tonto."

The negative energies and unanswered questions swirling around *The Brave* are not solely confined to Depp's film, which was the second attempt at filming McDonald's novel. *Natural Born Killers* producer Don Murphy's meticulously detailed account of the project's first incarnation (which can be read on his official website) begins in 1993, when University of Southern California employee Aziz Ghazal optioned the book and commissioned a screenplay by his associate Paul McCudden (who retains a co-writing credit on the final film). Though McCudden's script caught the eye of major players including Oliver Stone (who was in preproduction on *Natural Born Killers* at the time), the project stalled once Ghazal (whose only previous film credit was producing and co-writing the schlocky 1987 horror film *Zombie High*) insisted on directing the proposed feature. *The Brave*'s dissolution—which unfortunately coincided with Ghazal's recent divorce and firing from USC—led the already unstable would-be filmmaker to murder his estranged wife and teenage daughter before taking his own life. A blood-spattered copy of *The Brave*'s script was allegedly found among his personal items at the crime scene. While Hollywood is haunted by hundreds of tragic stories like Ghazal's, one cannot ignore the eerie parallels with Raphael's own hopelessly self-destructive odyssey.

Owing to its mysterious obscurity and morbid lineage, *The Brave* has, like the snuff films that trigger its plot, attained an almost legendary status among film fans over the years. Due to unreasonably high expectations, the unevenly acted, slow-paced, mostly bloodless film can be a disappointing experience upon first viewing (I personally first saw it on a fuzzy bootleg videotape, with burned-in Portuguese subtitles). Its attributes, however, more than offset its weaknesses, and Depp's film exemplifies just how far the weird western has come in its treatment of Native American characters and subject matter since the '70s, when schlockier, simplistic efforts like *Blood Shack* and *Track of the Moon Beast* were typical of the genre's output. Even the more politically progressive of these films—like *Hex*, or much later, *Silent Tongue*—remain safely ensconced in period trappings. *The Brave*, however, is an unapologetically contemporary effort that jettisons nearly thirty years of clichés in favor of a more realistic, if still bracingly cinematic, vision of the modern West. It remains one of the more significant desert terrors of the '90s, and, sadly, also one of the least seen.

8

Gargoyles and Graboids

"I don't see any eyes. Must be totally subterranean. And those tentacles ... this is probably the biggest zoological discovery of the century."—Rhonda LeBeck, *Tremors*

In *The Sadist*'s penultimate scene, crazed killer Charlie Tibbs falls into a snake pit while chasing sole survivor Doris through the desert. As Tibbs attempts to claw his way out, the riled-up rattlers strike mercilessly again and again, dooming him to the film's most violent death. The inference, of course, is that the seemingly unstoppable Tibbs can only be destroyed by a creature more lethal and cold-blooded than himself. In a bold, naturalistic move forward from '50s B-movies like *Them!* and *Tarantula*, which featured monstrously overgrown ants and spiders, the scene establishes one of the major themes of desert terror "creature features": whatever human evils lurk by the roadside or hide in the hills, the desert's indigenous wildlife often prove to be the most dangerous predator of all.

As with many categories of desert terror, the creature features immediately following *The Sadist* failed to capitalize on its more realistic, contemporary approach. Kid-friendly offerings *Jesse James Meets Frankenstein's Daughter* (1966) and *The Valley of Gwangi* (1969) continued to cling to period settings and Saturday matinee clichés; it was not until the '70s that the more seriously scary creature feature would stalk theatres and TV screens. The first two examples of this new breed, *Werewolves on Wheels* and *Gargoyles*, betrayed a distinctively adult, European influence, as old world evils threatened small desert communities. Later '70s entries like *Phase IV*, *Rattlers* and *Kingdom of the Spiders* were more topical, as armies of ants, snakes and tarantulas overran modern society through ferocious intelligence and sheer strength of numbers. By the late '70s, the revenge of nature cycle was succeeded by a series of milder, sci-fi oriented films that referenced the desert's reputation as a hotbed for extraterrestrial activity, such as *Laserblast*, *The Day Time Ended*, and the Native American–themed *High Desert Kill*.

After the '80s run of low budget, post-apocalyptic monster flicks (*Parasite*, *The Terror Within*), the creature feature returned to its pre–*Sadist* days with the playful, intelligent *Tremors*, which simultaneously referenced sci-fi/horror B-movies of the '50s while skillfully balancing humor, horror and brand-new creatures into a crowd-pleasing whole. While successive creature features returned to using traditional desert critters like snakes and bats to torment small-town residents, many of these films tapped *Tremors*' potent formula of irony and gross-out effects. A select few, like the ambitious *Highway to Hell* and *Phantasm IV: Oblivion*, took a more metaphysical approach, using the desert's inherently dreamlike visuals as a gateway to alternate worlds, with an emphasis on the machinations of all-too human monsters.

The outrageously-titled *Werewolves on Wheels* (1971) may seem an unlikely candidate for the desert terror genre's first official creature feature, but in its own oddball fashion, it's just as representative of the newly emerging genre as the same year's *Blood Shack* and *Duel*. An off-kilter but mostly engaging hybrid of the action and occult genres, the film plays like a typical biker flick of the period for its first third, as the ironically-named "Devil's Advocates" ride their hogs along picturesque desert highways, make out with their old ladies, and brawl with the locals, all to the sound of some surprisingly decent tunes (the main theme is particularly catchy). Card-reading biker Tarot (Gene Shane) spoils the hedonistic fun, telling attractive Helen (Donna Anders/D.J. Anderson, in her last film role), "You'll die in the tower, struck by lightning." Her boyfriend, gang leader Adam (Stephen Oliver) disregards Tarot's dire prediction, laughing, "We all know how we're gonna die, baby. We're gonna crash and burn!"

The film's tone darkens once the Advocates stumble onto a Satanic monastery, where they pass out after gorging on bread and wine offered by a group of monks led by the sinister One (Severn Darden), a wide-eyed servant of Lucifer given to proclamations like, "We must begin in blood, so that we may end in blood." A late-night ritual within the temple begins with One sacrificing a cat while his followers chant and ends with a hypnotized Helen doffing her clothes and performing a snake n' skull shimmy. After busting up the ritual and rescuing Helen, the bikers take off to the desert to "get our heads straight!" The Advocates soon find that no matter how far they ride, they can't escape the monks' curse as each successive night brings bloody death from an unknown, animalistic killer. Tarot's singular awareness of the situation ("someone's controlling the vibes") is, as usual, ridiculed by Adam, who now has a personal reason to deride his friend's claims. As the monstrous truth about Adam and Helen is finally revealed, the quickly diminishing group's "devil trip" comes to a gory end.

The desert terror genre is rife with unique hybrid films, and *Werewolves on Wheels* is one of the more daring, as it takes the strongest elements from biker flicks and post–Manson Satanic Panic creep-outs and gives them an avant-garde spin. Working from a simple but effective script co-authored with David Kaufman, debuting director Michel Levesque concentrates on the visual and atmospheric possibilities of the material, using a variety of striking locations—such as a desolate junkyard and vast sand dunes—that transform the California desert into a psychedelic playground of Burning Man–like bonfires and full moon murders. The monastery scenes are equally hallucinatory, with Helen's trance-dance achieving a macabre eroticism and the mind-bending finale sticking with the viewer long after the credits have rolled. Throughout the film, repeated motifs of flames and flocks of birds intrude on the narrative like ill omens, heightening the tension and invoking the supernatural.

In between these choice moments, the film wanders into overlong biking montages and improvised dialogue, but even these scenes achieve a rough, cinéma vérité quality that helps ground the film's more fantastic elements. Though some will be disappointed by the lack of werewolves (be warned: there are only two in the film, with only one—in the last five minutes—riding a motorcycle), the various lycanthrope attacks are pleasingly savage and bloody. Scarier (and sexier) than expected, *Werewolves on Wheels* is a genre-defying experiment that mostly works, placing it in the select company of other notable California-set desert terrors of the '70s, like *Barn of the Naked Dead* and *The Velvet Vampire* (the latter of which also features actor Gene Shane), in which dark deeds transpire against glaringly sunny environments.

Like *Werewolves on Wheels*, the TV movie *Gargoyles* (1972) also concerns the intrusion of ancient supernatural entities on contemporary American life. Paleontologist/author Dr. Mercer Boley (Cornel Wilde) and his daughter Diana (Jennifer Salt) drive out to the desert to interview Uncle Willie (Woody Chambliss), a crusty old roadside attraction proprietor who claims to own the remains of a previously undiscovered creature. "Them devils used to live up there in the rocks," Willie says as he unveils a winged skeleton with an oversized, horned skull. During Willie's interview, the shed is attacked from above, with monstrous claws ripping through steel as a fire breaks out. Boley and Diana barely escape with their lives, after being attacked by a gargoyle clinging to the roof of their car. Afraid the local Police Chief (William Stevens) won't believe such a wild tale ("Gar-what? You and your old man sniffin' glue?" laughs a skeptical character at one point), Boley lies about the incident, incidentally framing a local group of dirt bikers led by wise-cracking James Reeger (Scott Glenn). Boley's plans to transport the gargoyle skull back to Los Angeles are thwarted by several gargoyle attacks, one of which results in the creatures' winged leader (Bernie Casey, billed simply as "The Gargoyle") spiriting Diana back to his cave fortress, where dozens of newborn monsters are hatching in an egg chamber. The two-man police force, along with Boley and a posse of volunteers, head to the caves to save Diana—and humanity itself—from their ancient enemies.

Though frequently cited as an example of the golden age of '70s TV movies, *Gargoyles* really isn't in the same league as small-screen chillers like *Don't Be Afraid of the Dark* (1973) and desert terror classic *Duel*. The repetitive script is riddled with comic-book dialogue ("It's the end of your age ... and the beginning of mine!"), but the film's biggest letdown is its inadequately designed title creatures, who are (accurately) described as "stuntmen in wetsuits" by director B.W.L. Norton on the Hen's Tooth DVD commentary track. Norton's use of hazy slow-motion during the attack scenes only draws further attention to the cut-rate costuming. One assumes the film's Emmy win for Best Makeup (awarded to Stan Winston and Ellis Burman) was for the masks, which are imaginatively designed but largely inexpressive. The film looks great thanks to its New Mexico location shooting, with the bright, dusty highways of Willie's Desert Museum contrasting nicely with the shadowy caves (shot at Carlsbad Caverns). Salt (best known as Margot Kidder's twin in De Palma's 1972 thriller *Sisters*) has an earthy, girl-next-door sex appeal, with even less money spent on her skimpy wardrobe than the gargoyles' body stockings. Shots of Casey pawing at Salt are the stuff of B-movie fever dreams, and provide the film with its only remotely creepy images. While infinitely preferable to today's CGI–driven Syfy schlock, but for the most part *Gargoyles* fails to transcend its small-screen origins.

Along with the rise of TV terror, the '70s also witnessed a spate of "revenge of nature" films like *Frogs* (1972), *Squirm* (1976) and *The Food of the Gods* (1976), which responded to current ecological and environmental concerns in the same way 1950s creature features like *Them!* and *Tarantula* had commented on atomic-testing fears of the era. While most revenge of nature films were aimed at the drive-in crowd, the killer-ant epic *Phase IV* (1974) elevates the genre to a more sophisticated, at times even transcendental, level. The directing debut of noted film designer Saul Bass, whose achievements include the iconic opening credits sequences of *Psycho* and many other Hitchcock films, *Phase IV* tells its ambitious tale with a relentless, almost obsessive intelligence that mirrors its brilliant but emotionally impaired main characters.

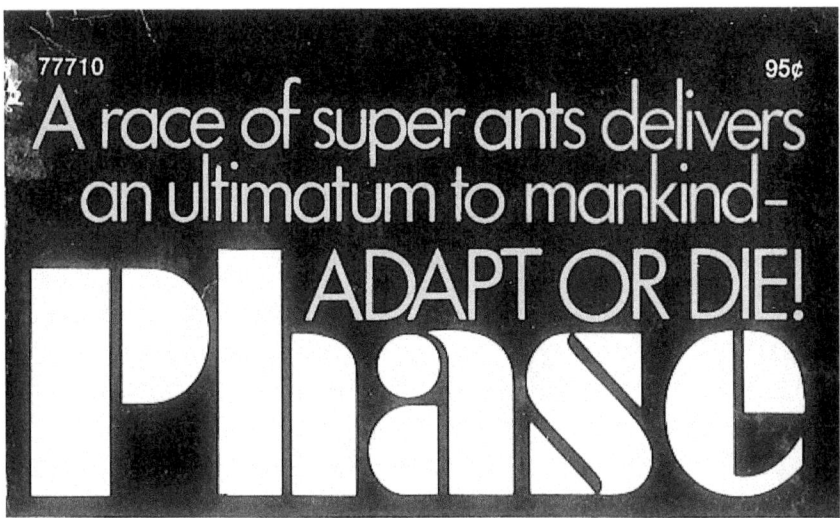
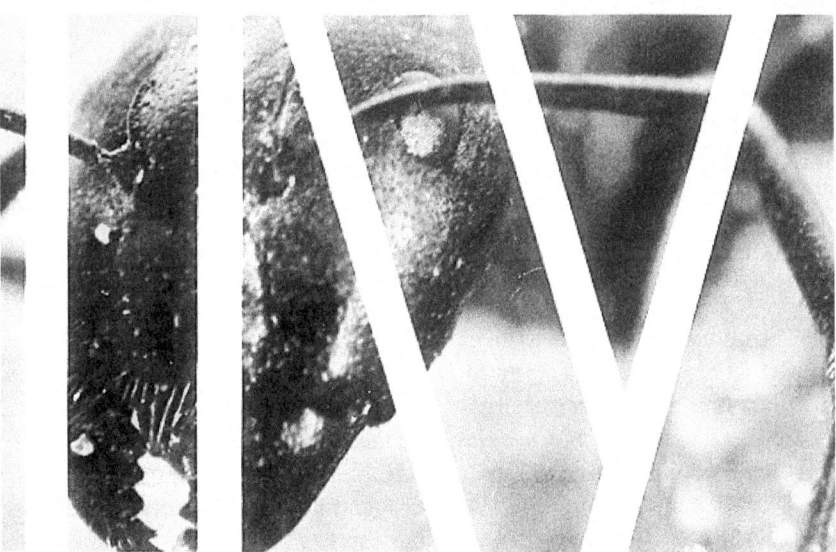

Like many science fiction films of the 1970s, *Phase IV* (1974) was also promoted through a "tie-in" novelization based on the original screenplay.

Dr. Ernest Hubbs (Nigel Davenport, left) and James Lesko (Michael Murphy) combat an army of hyperintelligent ants in the ambitious *Phase IV* (1974).

Bass introduces his intensely visual approach early on as, for nearly ten minutes, we're treated to macro photography of ants racing through underground tunnels and over purple crystals while funereal organs and unsettling voice overs fill the background; it's like watching *The Hellstrom Chronicle* outtakes scored by Tangerine Dream. Humans finally intrude on the narrative as Dr. Ernest Hubbs (Nigel Davenport) and his associate James Lesko (Michael Murphy) arrive at an abandoned community (ironically named Paradise City) in the middle of the Arizona desert to set up an experiment station to document—and control—a recent and unexplained ant infestation in the area. Column-shaped "ant mounds" (recalling the mysterious obelisks of *2001*) tower over the two men, a grim reminder of the advanced intelligence they are up against.

"I did not sign up for a war against a bunch of goddamn ants!" yells a frustrated Lesko, yet that's exactly what happens, beginning with Hubbs' destruction of the mounds. After the ants invade a local farm, Hubbs' poison attack ironically only succeeds in killing off the displaced farmers whose attractive daughter Kendra (the appealing Lynn Frederick) is forced to take refuge in the station. Any chance of a developing romance between Lesko and Kendra is squashed by Hubbs' personal conflict with the increasingly resilient and adaptable ants. After crippling Hubbs with a lethal bite, they sabotage the station's power and sever communications with the outside world. "Now I know how a rat feels in a maze," says Lesko as the insane Hubbs leaves the relative safety of the station for a last-chance mission to destroy the ants' queen, while Kendra slips further under the insect army's control. "Phase IV" has begun.

Using Mayo Simon's cerebral screenplay as a framework, visual stylist Bass concentrates on the formal possibilities of the material, creating a succession of strong, often surreal imagery—corpses doused in bright yellow powder, ants exploding from inside a Dali-esque hand, a resurrected Kendra emerging from under the sand—that, like the film's insect army, gradually eclipses the narrative. Contrasting nicely with the sterile, cramped, confines of the station, the film's desert exterior scenes have a wonderfully alien beauty, especially during the eerie final montage, which, like many of the film's best scenes, is utterly devoid of dialogue. Both hopeful and apocalyptic at once, it's the closest thing the desert terror genre has to *2001*'s star child climax. Sadly, it's only a shadow of its original, much longer incarnation, which was carefully shot and assembled by Bass before being truncated by a nervous Paramount before the film's release (the original ending can be viewed on YouTube). Thankfully, Bass' singular vision is strong enough to survive such studio tampering, and his film remains one of the more challenging, and disquieting, achievements in the desert terror genre.

At the opposite end of the spectrum, the desert eco-horrors *Rattlers* (1976) and *Kingdom of the Spiders* (1977) are less interested in transcendence and more concerned with finding new and creative ways of grossing out their drive-in audiences. The cheaper of the pair, *Rattlers* doesn't waste any time dropping the viewer into a nasty snake pit sequence to rival *The Sadist*'s climax, as, deep in California's Mojave Desert, a pair of unfortunate youngsters fall into a nest of pissed-off rattlesnakes. As more locals are attacked by raging reptiles, the local sheriff (Tony Ballen) calls UCLA herpetologist Dr. Tom Parkinson (Sam Chew) to help explain the sudden outbreak. The sexist, unpleasant Parkinson is paired with an attractive (and outspoken feminist) photographer Ann (Elisabeth Chauvet), described by the sheriff as "better than any male photographer we've used, and prettier, too." The bickering pair eventually trace the snake attacks to an isolated military base, whose experimental nerve gas may have something to do with the rattlers' uncommonly aggressive behavior.

Despite the perfunctory script, wooden acting (particularly Chew, who seems more comfortable handling cobras than his female co-star) and stiff direction, *Rattlers* still manages a few effective, if crudely mounted, horror sequences. In the first, a farm is overrun by an army of the crazed serpents, which kill the livestock and most of the inhabitants before causing a devastating fire; even better is a housewife's bubble bath interrupted by a group of snakes traveling through the pipes and into the tub. The kills (many of which are unfortunately filmed under low light conditions in caves or at night) continue, but for the most part, the story stalls as Tom and Ann circle the desert and spar with the sinister Colonel Stroud (Dan Priest) while eventually falling in love (after finally locating the rattlers' den, the investigative duo make an ill-timed stop in Vegas to "catch a show and grab a steak"). Writer/director John McCauley trades jump scares and ick factor for an atmosphere of spiraling paranoia which, if entirely appropriate for the times, isn't well-developed enough to be truly effective. Likewise, the film's attempt at an action-packed ending feels compromised and anticlimactic, lacking the bite of its earlier snake attack scenes.

Falling in line even closer with the decade's animal-attack pics, *Kingdom of the Spiders* sports a similar storyline to *Rattlers* while borrowing a few elements from recent smash *Jaws*. In the small desert town of Verde Valley, Arizona, cowboy veterinarian Rack Hansen (William Shatner) partners up with attractive city slicker entomologist Diane Ashley (Tiffany Bolling) to solve a recent series of unexplained animal deaths in the

The *Kingdom of the Spiders* (1977) tie-in novel duplicates the film's theatrical one sheet.

community. After finding a massive amount of spider venom in a dead calf's bloodstream, the flirty pair discovers a dirt mound literally crawling with hundreds of tarantulas on a local farm. Diane's theory about the spiders' sudden viciousness ("Excessive use of insecticides like DDT is killing off their food supply!") is ignored by greedy Mayor Connors (Roy Engel), who's more concerned about attracting tourists to an upcoming fair. As the tarantulas upgrade their victims from animals to people and start cocooning the population, the mayor and sheriff finally join forces with Rack and Diane (no John Mellencamp jokes, please) to save Verde Valley from an arachnid takeover.

Kingdom spins its web slowly for the first half of its running time, with an emphasis on small-town melodrama, goofy humor, and a slowly percolating romance between the two leads that, in addition to being sexist in the worst '70s way (Rack hits on "uptight" Diane until she softens to his "women's lib" jokes), ultimately goes nowhere. Journeyman director John "Bud" Cardos shows more confidence orchestrating the film's various spider-attack set pieces, which include a crop duster pilot menaced by a cockpit full of hairy horrors, a single mom stung to death by a bunch of the buggers while her daughter watches, and a full-scale Main Street invasion, with silk-wrapped corpses on every corner. These scenes are well-mounted and give the film a scope far beyond the relatively impoverished *Rattlers*, but the last half hour reverts to a *Night of the Living Dead* type scenario, as Rack, Diane, and a few others find themselves trapped in a arachnid-infested lodge. The downbeat finale, if failing to resolve the situation, at least makes good on the movie's title.

Aside from a nicely photographed opening titles sequence and a few horseback-riding excursions (which suggest an undeveloped western influence), *Kingdom* makes limited use of its desert setting. The stocky Shatner makes an unlikely cowboy, and his stiff performance is about on par with James Brolin's in *The Car* (they could trade places and neither film would be the worse for it). Former Playmate Bolling (whose best film is the sleazy kidnapping drama *The Candy Snatchers*) is easy on the eyes, and does her best with lines like "All species of megalomorphs are cannibalistic!" while (literally) handling her eight-legged co-stars with aplomb. The film gains additional points for its use of real, live spiders throughout the film, granting many scenes (as when a group of them tumble directly onto Shatner's face) a substantial ick factor, although based on the number of scenes of the critters being sprayed with chemicals or crushed under car tires, I'm guessing the ASPCA did not have much of an on-set presence.

That same year's mega-successful release of *Star Wars* (1977) saw science fiction took a turn away from earthbound tales of sinister spiders and anti-social ants and moved to galaxies far, far, away ... as well as budgets that were light years beyond what most exploitation producers could afford. The immediate solution was to bring contemporary sci-fi elements (aliens, space battles) down to earth, as fledgling B-movie producer Charles Band did in his inauspicious desert terror debut *Laserblast* (1978). After a desert-set opening featuring a laser battle between a pair of aliens and a green-skinned humanoid, the film introduces Billy (Kim Milford), a loner who spends most of his time being harassed by just about everyone in his small community, including some local toughs (one of whom is played by Eddie Deezen, who would be a lot more at home in Milford's role), and a pair of stoner cops. Billy gets even, though, with the help of a laser cannon left behind in the wake of the extraterrestrial shootout. Soon, he's rampaging through town, blowing up cars, gas stations, and, in one amusing moment, a billboard for George Lucas' blockbuster. Billy's new toy has adverse side effects, however, as it gradually transforms him into a *Gargoyle*-like creature. With the aliens, girlfriend Kathy (Cheryl "Rainbeaux" Smith, wasted in a generic role) and a man-in-black government agent (Gino Russo) on his trail, Billy's reign of terror is about to come to an explosive end.

Despite its scant 81-minute running time, *Laserblast* feels much longer, with first (and last) time director Michael Rae's lackadaisical pacing and the script's awkward attempts at comedy making the first half of the film a real test of patience. Blond beefcake Milford is miscast as outsider Billy, and his laughable "problems" don't justify his psychotic rampage. Although the alien weapon's takeover of its host suggests some interesting possibilities, the script avoids any of the Jekyll and Hyde type conflicts that might result from such a bodily invasion, preferring to cut away to curiously static, lifeless effects sequences. The desert setting serves mostly as a backdrop, with only the opening battle and cannon discovery sequences capitalizing on any visual opportunities. Future Oscar nominee (and longtime Band associate) David Allen's stop-motion aliens are quaintly amusing, but often seem to have wandered in from an entirely different, and much older, film. Nostalgia, however, isn't what *Laserblast* needs; a stronger script and more energy behind the camera would have helped considerably. Band would recycle the concept over the next few decades, with the family friendly semi-remakes *Deadly Weapon* (1989) and *Alien Arsenal* (1999).

"Yesterday, today and tomorrow are constantly with us … and will be with us for all eternity," a pseudo-scientific voice over rambles at the start of *The Day Time Ended* (1979), sounding more like Criswell than Carl Sagan. Charles Band's sophomore (and sophomoric) creature feature focuses on a nice American family stuck in what one character describes as a "time-space warp." The film opens with *Close Encounters*-like extraterrestrial lights whooshing through the night, passing over an isolated, solar-powered desert home of Grant (Jim Davis). The next day, radio reports mention "trinary supernovas" and various disturbances around the Los Angeles area as Grant and his son Richard (Chris Mitchum) pick up the rest of the clan from the airport: Grant's wife Ana (Dorothy Malone), their younger son Steve (Scott Kolden), Richard's wife Beth (Marcy Lafferty) and their daughter Jenny (Natasha Ryan). Upon arriving at Grant's desert retreat, Jenny discovers a glowing green pyramid near the stables; later that night, Grant and Ana watch, stupefied, as UFOs fly over the house.

This is only the beginning of the family's bizarre twenty-four hour odyssey, as they encounter (literal) little green men, miniature spaceships, and a pair of gigantic wrestling monsters that look like they wandered out of a Ray Harryhausen movie. UFOs fly over Richard's car, causing him to crash. Grant opens the front door to find the front yard transformed into an airplane graveyard. A whirlwind of stars and cosmic lights absorbs Beth and Jenny, later depositing them in the middle of the desert. The upbeat ending finds the family reunited (on horseback!) and apparently transported into the future (or something like that). As the group overlooks a glittering, Emerald City–type landscape, patriarch Grant dispenses a few closing words of wisdom: "Maybe it was meant to be. This is our new way of life."

None of this makes a heck of a lot of sense, but it's rarely boring, with the script, co-written by Band stalwart David Schmoeller (whose story for *Ghost Town* utilizes similar, but much more straightforward, time-travel motifs) throwing one bizarre situation after another at the family, whose reactions range from disgust to fascination. It's almost impressive how much Band and veteran director John "Bud" Cardos (in his second desert terror film after *Kingdom of the Spiders*) manage to pull off with what was surely a limited budget; the picture is literally drowning in visual effects to a near-hallucinatory degree. In this aspect, and many others, it almost plays as a dry run for big budget FX fest *Poltergeist* (1981), which also centers on a family trying to reclaim their young daughter from malevolent forces centered within the home. One thing Spielberg's production lacks is David Allen's stop-motion monsters, which are a definite highlight here and far surpass his work on *Laserblast*. It might not "turn your galaxy upside down" (in the words of one character), but *The Day Time Ended* is still an amusing way to fritter away eighty minutes.

The indefatigable Band struck a third time with *Parasite* (1982), a post-apocalyptic creature feature that is best known today as Demi Moore's film debut, as well as showcasing early effects work by future Oscar winner (and *Gargoyles*' effects whiz) Stan Winston. A confusing dream sequence/flashback introduces Paul Dean (Robert Glaudini), a scientist who, while trying to escape from the sinister Xyrex Corporation, accidentally becomes infected with one of his own experimental parasites. With one creature gestating inside him and another imprisoned in a metal canister, Dean flees Los Angeles for the tiny desert community of Joshua, where he attempts to formulate an antidote with the aid of local farmer Patricia (Moore). Their success is thwarted, however, by local punk gang led by Rickus (Luca Bercovici), a Xyrex rep (James Davidson) who wants their parasite back, not to mention the title creature itself, which manages to escape and cause all kinds of mischief, sucking its hosts dry before slithering on to the next unlucky victim.

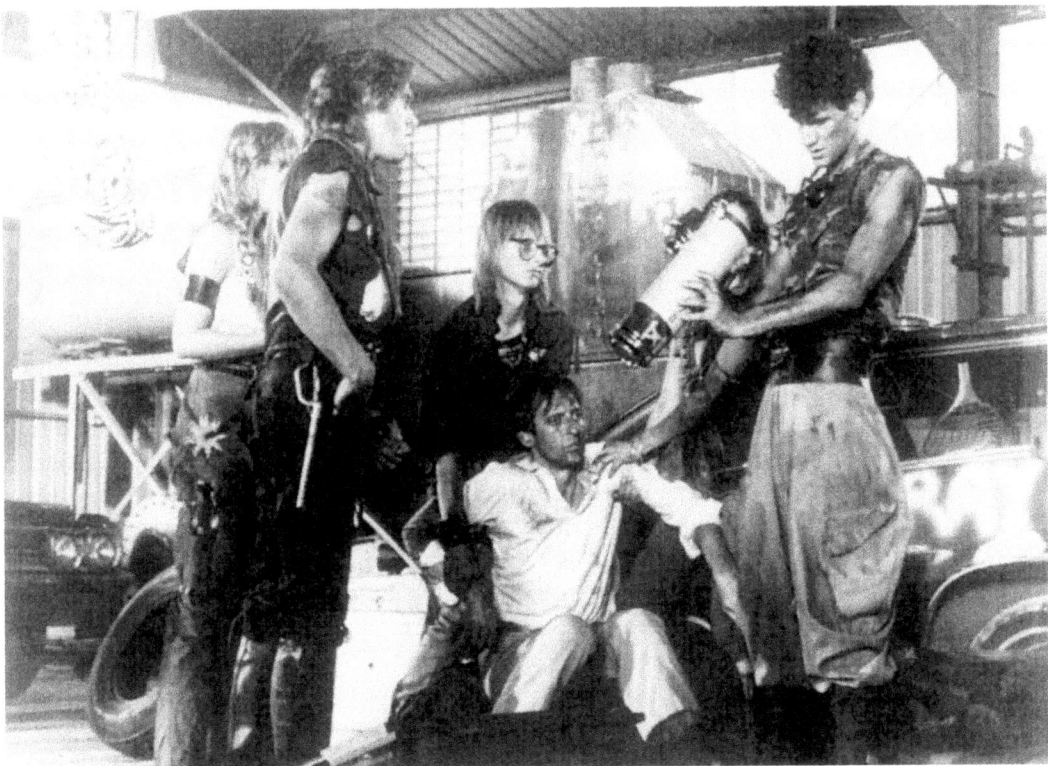

Pictured left to right, desert toughs Dana (Cherie Currie), Ricus (Luca Bercovici), Arn (Freddy Moore) and Zeke (Tom Villard) torment scientist Dr. Paul Dean (Robert Glaudini, center) in the futuristic monster flick *Parasite* (1982).

On *Parasite*, Band not only took the directing reins, but also chose to shoot the film in 3-D, which was at the time enjoying a brief resurgence. The result, however, is far from Jack Arnold's fluid, dynamic work on *It Came from Outer Space*, instead consisting of a series of static, gimmicky shots of people, objects, and—in a few more amusing cases, parasites—being launched directly at the audience. The 3-D gimmick, when coupled with an inexplicable use of slow motion in the film's interminable "action" scenes, results in a plodding, predictable visual style. Not that it matters much, as the script is aimless and uneventful, starting with its bizarre opening and continuing through a pointless sequence in which Dean makes a pit stop at a run-down building where he breaks up a rape, only to be attacked by the topless victim (Cheryl "Rainbeaux" Smith again, providing the requisite nudity)! Pacing/sequencing issues persist during the Joshua material, with many scenes ending with abrupt fade-outs in the middle of the action. Band saves all his money shots for the final reel, as one parasite explodes inside Dean's chest, while the other chews its way through various cast members before being engulfed in flames.

With its *Mad Max*–inspired setting and creature cribbed from *Alien*, *Parasite* is hardly original, but that's not the film's biggest problem; there just isn't enough intelligence, personality, or raw energy on screen to distinguish it from the many other apocalyptic horrors of the time. The desert setting of Joshua, while capably visualized by dependable cinematographer Mac Ahlberg (*Ghost Town*), is used primarily to illustrate the economic hardships of the times (1992!), with its dusty, ramshackle buildings and rocky vistas framing the characters' rugged, survivalist existence. In some ways, the film resembles a western, but this idea is never significantly developed. The cast, too, barely registers, with Moore giving no hint of the future A-lister she'd become, and ex–Runaway Cherie Currie wasted in a throwaway role who plays her biggest scene as a corpse with the parasite sucking on her leg. Band revisited to the desert apocalypse subgenre with the more sci-fi slanted *Shadowzone* and *Crash and Burn* (both 1990), both of which were written by desert thriller specialist J.S. Cardone (*The Forsaken*).

The post-nuke party continued in *The Terror Within* (1989), Roger Corman's contribution to the desert terror creature feature stakes. In the unspecified future, Earth (or America, at least) has become overrun by a biological plague that, along with eliminating most of the population, has turned many of the survivors into genetically-mutated "gargoyles." Deep beneath the Mojave Desert, a small crew of uninfected doctors and scientists remain safe from the prowling monsters, but a dwindling food supply forces them to make occasional trips above ground to scavenge for sustenance. After two team members disappear during one of these missions, alpha male David (Andrew Stevens) and his main squeeze Sue (Starr Andreeff) must venture topside to search for them. Along with the men's mutilated bodies, they discover Karen (Yvonne Saa), a terrified young victim of a gargoyle attack. Soon after being brought into the underground bunker, Karen gives birth to a monstrous critter which kills her before escaping into an air vent. There, like *Tarantula*'s titular beastie, the newborn Gargoyle rapidly grows to adult size and begins slaughtering the crew, one by one.

Although it swaps the interstellar settings of Corman's recent SF/horrors like *Forbidden World* for a more earthbound location, *The Terror Within* does little with its desert setting, with most of the action taking place within the claustrophobic confines of the subterranean lab. The film is heavily indebted to *Alien*, with its gory monster birth sequence, scenes of characters creeping through dimly lit corridors and ventilation shafts, and brief but gruesome monster attacks. More efficiently paced and better made than *Parasite*, it's also more conventionally plotted and largely humorless, enlivened mainly by the "Gargoyle" (which bears no resemblance to the winged demons of the 1972 TV movie), whose lack of facial expression is offset by its propensity to rip its victims to bloody shreds. The film's incessant focus on the Gargoyle's need to mate with human women recalls other '80s Corman efforts like *Humanoids from the Deep* and *Galaxy of Terror*. The scenes encompassing David and Sue's discovery of Karen were shot at California's picturesque Vasquez Rocks, a popular film location featured in numerous sci-fi films and westerns since the early days of cinema and best known to genre fans as the setting of the classic *Star Trek* episode "Arena." Stevens later directed and starred in *The Terror Within II* (1991), an unnecessary sequel that brings back the original film's gargoyles and post-nuke desert setting to little purpose.

The prolific Corman and Band were not the only exploitation producers churning out desert-set creature features during the '80s. Oddball Italian producer/director Ovidio G. Assonitis (*Sonny Boy*) gave the genre one of its first foreign-financed productions with *Curse II: The Bite* (1989), a sequel in name only to the H.P. Lovecraft–inspired *The Curse* (1988). An ill-advised desert shortcut sends California-bound lovers Clark (J. Eddie Peck) and Lisa (Jill Schoelen) onto a stretch of road infested with snakes, which they run over (in one of the film's early gross-out moments) before reaching a garage, where a crusty gas station attendant (Al Fann) calls the area "one big dumping ground for experiments." After stopping at a motel, Clark is bitten in the arm by a snake hiding in the back of the jeep. Traveling salesman Harry Morton (Jamie Farr) offers Clark an anti-venom, but, like other, subsequent attempts to neutralize the poison, Morton's cure isn't strong enough to save Clark as the reptile within takes over.

At first assuming Clark's weird behavior is the result of pent-up jealousy ("I've got plans! I don't need this!"), Lisa gradually realizes that the snakebite is "changing" her boyfriend in more ways than one. Clark's hand soon transforms into—there's no delicate way to put this—a *giant snake head*, complete with rolling eyes, forked tongue, and massive jaws that can crush a victim's throat and chew their face off in seconds. Tracked by his terrified but still devoted girlfriend, Clark and his new appendage go on a rampage through the Southwest, as the snake rips a deputy's still-beating heart out through his throat and lassoes another victim's neck with its tongue. In the truly disgusting finale, Lisa crawls through a mud pit to as her barely human boyfriend vomits oodles of vipers from his mouth before his head splits in half to disgorge his serpentine host. Harry proves an unlikely hero, blasting the damn snake-thing into oblivion as the redneck sheriff (Bo Svenson) pulls Lisa to safety.

Shot in the popular desert terror location of Las Cruces, New Mexico (previously seen in *When You Comin' Back, Red Ryder?* and *Raw Courage*), *Curse II* embraces the landscape more than most creature features, with a peripatetic narrative that occasional swerves into the "death driver" fast lane. The film juggles road movie shenanigans, gooey monster effects (courtesy of the always reliable Screaming Mad George), goofy humor, and earnest relationship drama (one could almost read the film as an examination of how people change in the face of a serious relationship), all of it performed with gusto by a game cast, including Farr, Svenson, and *Sonny Boy* sidekick Sidney Lassick. Schoelen gives the scattershot story a much-needed anchor, contributing a winning combination of girl-next-door sex appeal (the snake POV shot of her stripping in the car is a hoot), pathos, and genuine toughness to her role. If not quite as wonderfully demented as Assonitis' other desert terror entry, *Curse II* remains, like much of its producer's output, a guilty pleasure of the highest order.

The same can't be said, however, of *Chopper Chicks in Zombietown* (1989), a self-consciously quirky horror comedy that, if nothing else, introduces the living dead to the desert terror genre. A female biker gang known as The Cycle Sluts ("Eight broads on the rag," one of them snorts) roars into the tiny desert town of Zariah for some R n' R, most of them getting their jollies with the local guys while former homecoming queen Dedee (Jamie Rose) confronts her loutish ex-husband Donny (Billy Bob Thornton). A few miles outside of town, a busload of blind orphans breaks down near an old mine, which suddenly disgorges a horde of hungry zombies created by the local mortician, Ralph Willum (Don Calfa) and his dwarf sidekick Bob (Ed Gale). With the townsfolk reluctant to attack their deceased relatives, the Cycle Sluts and orphans must join forces to defeat the approaching undead.

The success of Dan O'Bannon's semi-sequel *Return of the Living Dead* (1985) resulted in a plethora of zom-coms throughout the late '80s, many of them bearing a hair metal soundtrack and gross-out makeup effects. *Chopper Chicks* closely follows this model, ladling rock tunes over every other scene and even casting Calfa, who played a mortician in O'Bannon's film, in almost the exact same role! Unlike *Return*, the campier *Chopper Chicks* consistently aims for broad comedy, characterized by over the top dialogue ("I may be a whore but I ain't no heathen!"), and minor-league "splatstick" humor. Despite piling on dozens of characters and events, and introducing its zombies (too) early, the first half of the film is a drag to sit through, with endless scenes of biker girls vamping, Willum and Bob clowning around in the morgue, and—worst of all—the zombie cutaways, which are often accompanied by especially dim-witted comical music.

The pace improves once the bikers take on the living dead, as does the gore quotient; Ed French's dismemberments and decapitations are reasonably well-done, and the script manages a few decent one liners ("Blind, no parents, and now this?" gripes one of the blind kids as their bus is assaulted by zombies). The film makes good use of its distinctive desert locations (an abandoned café, lonely highways, main street), and, in a refreshing change of pace from most creature features, much of the action occurs at night. There's even a bit of social commentary lurking beneath all the silliness, as the outsiders/weirdos (biker girls, blind kids, etc.) initially rejected by the old-fashioned locals (who are, the film suggests, already "zombies" in their own way), ultimately become the saviors of Zariah. None of this is going to make *Chopper Chicks* the ready-made cult item its makers (and distributor Troma, who wisely retitled the film from its original moniker *Chrome Hearts*) clearly hoped it would be, and anyone expecting the cinematic love child of Russ Meyer and George A. Romero will be sorely disappointed.

The made-for-TV movie *High Desert Kill* (1989) takes a more serious approach to its offbeat storyline, which combines creature feature and weird western motifs. In an indeterminately set prologue, a pair of Native American hunters is besieged by an alien presence which forces one of the men to kill his companion. Fast forward to the present and a trio of friends—mild-mannered scientist Jim (Anthony Geary), arrogant Alpha male Brad (Marc Singer) and "new kid" Ray (Micah Grant), the nephew of their recently deceased friend Paul (Vaughn Armstrong)—arrive in the New Mexico desert for their yearly hunting trip. Tensions develop almost immediately between the two vets and Ray, who they view as a lightweight. While hiking to their campsite, the trio comes across older hunter Sam (Chuck Connors) who joins them as they scatter Paul's ashes off a

Formerly known as *Chrome Hearts, Chopper Chicks in Zombietown* (1989) features one of Billy Bob Thornton's earliest film performances.

mountaintop before bedding down for the night. As the men doze, the extraterrestrial sounds and lights return, watching the men through solarized POV shots and reading their thoughts.

Things start to get weird the next day, as Sam's horses run away and a silent stranger who resembles Paul appears, along with a pair of attractive young women campers, Terri (Lori Birdsong) and Kathleen (Deborah Anne Mansy). An orgiastic scene develops that night, as the women throw themselves at the men, who then start fighting over them, crazed with lust (watching bug-eyed Connors and sweaty Singer arm wrestle is itself worth the price of admission). The next morning, a bear hunt turns deadly when three blood-smeared, wild-eyed hunters (Jim, Ray and Sam) attack Brad with their knives, shouting "It's our kill!" when he approaches the animal's bloody corpse. Frightened and confused by their inexplicable, irrational behavior, the group finally decides it's time to cut the trip short, but soon find themselves stranded. A freak dust storm forces them inside the ancient pueblo, where they finally discover the truth behind their extraterrestrial tormentor.

While it takes the characters quite a while to unravel the mystery behind the strange events ("This is like some kind of caveman B-movie," Ray observes, while Jim insists, "This isn't the CIA, or the Russians, or Charlie Manson"), most viewers won't have nearly as much trouble figuring it all out. When the big reveal does come, it's unfortunately in the form of a barely glimpsed, frail-looking insectoid that can barely stand upright, let alone look like it could survive for several hundred years on Earth. The real fun of *High Desert Kill* has nothing to do with cowboys and aliens, but in watching B-movie vets Singer and Connors duke it out in a biggest ham contest. In the end, it's a draw; Connors gets all the choice lines, like "Death rings the dinner bell" and "I'll open you up like a sack of manure," while Singer lets his freak flag fly in the mind-manipulation sequences. The final credit of its director, TV vet Harry Falk, *HDK* benefits from contributions by co-writer Mike Marvin (*The Wraith*) and dependable desert terror composer Dana Kaproff (*Death Valley, The China Lake Murders*) and location shooting at New Mexico's scenic Santa Clara Pueblo. The film trades more on trippy mind games and left-field character moments than special effects, and makes a stronger impression in the process.

High Desert Kill was one of the last desert terror TV movies produced by Universal, whose contributions to the small-screen branch of the genre can be traced all the way back to early masterpieces like *Duel*. The small-town desert setting of the studio's first big-screen desert terror creature feature, *Tremors* (1990), reaches even further back to atomic-age fright flicks like *It Came from Outer Space* and *Tarantula*. *Tremors*' hip, ironic tone, however, is distinctly late-'80s, and its big-name cast and $11 million budget show how far the B-movie had come since the drive-in days. In the tiny desert town of Perfection, Nevada, handymen Earl Bass (Fred Ward) and Valentine McKee (Kevin Bacon), after years of hard, low-paying work, pack up their truck and leave for the "big town" of Bixby. While leaving town, they find several dead bodies along with a strange eel-like creature. Local grocer Chang (Victor Wong) can't wait to make a buck off the "snake monster," and survivalist couple Burt (Michael Gross) and Heather Gummer (Reba McIntire) are ready to set a perimeter in preparation for a possible monster invasion. Earl and Val's attempt to reach help on horseback results in an encounter with a much larger, wormlike beast that attacks from under the sand, swallowing their steeds. While able to successfully kill off their subterranean attacker, Earl and Val soon realize, thanks to plucky

Val McKee (Kevin Bacon, left) and Earl Bass (Fred Ward, right) make a gruesome discovery in *Tremors* (1990).

seismology student Rhonda LeBeck (Finn Carter), that there are three more "graboids" (as one local dubs them) under the sand and headed straight for the town.

A series of well-executed action set pieces follow, as the citizens evade and defend themselves against the slimy subterranean invaders. Highlights include a literal shakedown of Chang's market, as everyone scrambles to the roof after the worm-like beasts burst through the floor, and Burt and Heather's armed response to a monstrous home invasion. Once the townspeople, led by Val and Earl, leave the town on a tractor and become stranded in the desert, the pace slows a bit before wrapping things up in a suitably gooey finale. The graboids' origin is never really explained, with everyone volunteering their own opinion (one character decides they're "mutations caused by radiation," in one of several nods to the past). While the film is a bit too busy and overly noisy at times, the script compensates with a generous dollop of satire (Burt and Heather are the perfect poster children for America's gun fetish, and Chang's "anything for a buck attitude" lampoons capitalism) as well as sporting some truly majestic widescreen vistas courtesy of director of photography Alexander Gruszynski (*The Oasis*) and considerably impressive creature effects by Alec Gillis and Tom Woodruff (who would go on to execute the alien effects on *Alien 3*) and excellent miniature work by *Aliens* vet Robert Skotak.

Tremors strikes a pleasing balance between humor and horror throughout which, while decidedly skewed toward the former, smartly plays its suspense/terror scenes straight; a sequence involving a car sucked underground by the giant worms is extremely well-done, as is the reveal of a victim, his face frozen mid-scream, buried in the sand. Contributing to this are the wry performances by Bacon and, especially, Ward; their early scenes of working together establish a crusty chemistry, which plays far better than the forced Val/Rhonda romance which ends the picture. Sorry, Rhonda, but the only significant relationship in *Tremors* is between Val and Earl, and the film's most important conflict has nothing to do with its wormlike monsters. In this respect, *Tremors* may be the first creature feature to also incorporate elements of another desert terror standby, the

Rhonda LeBeck (Finn Carter) is attacked by a graboid in *Tremors* (1990).

8. Gargoyles and Graboids

stranded scenario. Val and Earl's familiar hesitation between settling for existence in the dull, predictable town of Perfection and moving on to unknown, yet possibly brighter, pastures gives the story an extra shot of realism before the graboids show up to rear their ugly, er tentacles. A sleeper success, *Tremors* would become one of the desert terror genre's biggest hits and spawn an impressive number of sequels and even a cable television series.

Highway to Hell (1991) also successfully combines horror and off-kilter humor to emerge as one of the most bizarre, yet strangely engaging, films ever to enliven the desert terror genre. Its cheeky opening credits sequence, which unfolds against an amusingly hellish postcard, sets the stage for the absurdity to come. On their way to a quickie Vegas wedding, pizza deliveryman Charlie Sykes (Chad Lowe) and his beautiful, virginal fiancée Rachel (Kristy Swanson) take a back road to save time. During a quick gas-up at the Last Chance service station, crusty old owner Sam (Richard Farnsworth) instructs Charlie not to pull over until he's passed two Joshua Trees. Of course, Charlie nods off, after which a police cruiser suddenly pulls him over. But this is no ordinary cop, it's Sgt. Bedlam aka Hellcop (C.J. Graham, "Jason" in *Friday the 13th Part VI*), an unstoppable officer of the damned who abducts Rachel before disappearing into the night. Charlie's only hope is Sam, whose own bride, Clara, suffered the same fate as Rachel fifty years earlier. Armed with a new vehicle, a special shotgun, and a few sage bits of advice ("If you're not back in twenty-four hours, you're stuck there for eternity"), Charlie—and his dog, Ben—sets off to rescue his girl from the underworld.

Hell, it turns out, looks very much like the American Southwest, as the film trades its shadowy desert back roads for blue-skied valleys (the film was shot on location in Page and Phoenix, Arizona). Charlie encounters one bizarre character after another, including a sexy hitchhiker (Lita Ford, the second former Runaway to appear in a desert terror movie), a murderous ice-cream man (Randy Widner), a motorcycle gang led by Royce (Adam Storke), whose main squeeze is Clara (Pamela Gidley), and "Satanic Mechanic" Beezle (Patrick Bergin), and young Adam (Jarrett Lennon), who joins Charlie on his quest to find Rachel. The pit stops are even wilder: at Pluto's Diner, zombified cops munch moldy donuts as the cook (Ben Stiller) fries eggs on the scorching sidewalk; Hoffa's Casino hosts a poker game between Hitler (Gilbert Gottfried) and Attila the Hun (Stiller again). After pursuing Hellcop (and Rachel) from one bizarre outpost to another, Charlie takes a Styx-like ferry to Hell City, where the Devil himself—who bears a distinct similarity to Beezle—tempts Rachel with promises of a better life. While Charlie manages to liberate his true love from Satan's clutches, further challenges await him and Rachel as they struggle to return to Earth.

A stylish and smart creature feature that also fully embraces the episodic, road-oriented dynamics of the hitcher-killer and death driver movie, *Highway to Hell* is one of the few desert terrors to fully embrace the fantastic. Its ambitious central concept, which could have lapsed into silliness or pretentiousness, is brought to life with a loose and breezy style by Dutch director Ate De Jong (who also helmed the cult comedy *Drop Dead Fred*), working from a highly intelligent and creative script by Brian Helgeland (*Nightmare on Elm Street 4: The Dream Master*, *L.A. Confidential*). While its basic plot amounts to little more than an extended chase with a few outlandish (and, at times, far-fetched) twists, the "devil" is in the details, as the filmmakers sprinkle textual humor, visual puns, and auditory jokes in nearly every shot, from Hellcop's "hand cuffs" made of living human hands to the Good Intentions Paving Company, a road crew of Warhol lookalikes who grind up sinners' bodies for gravel.

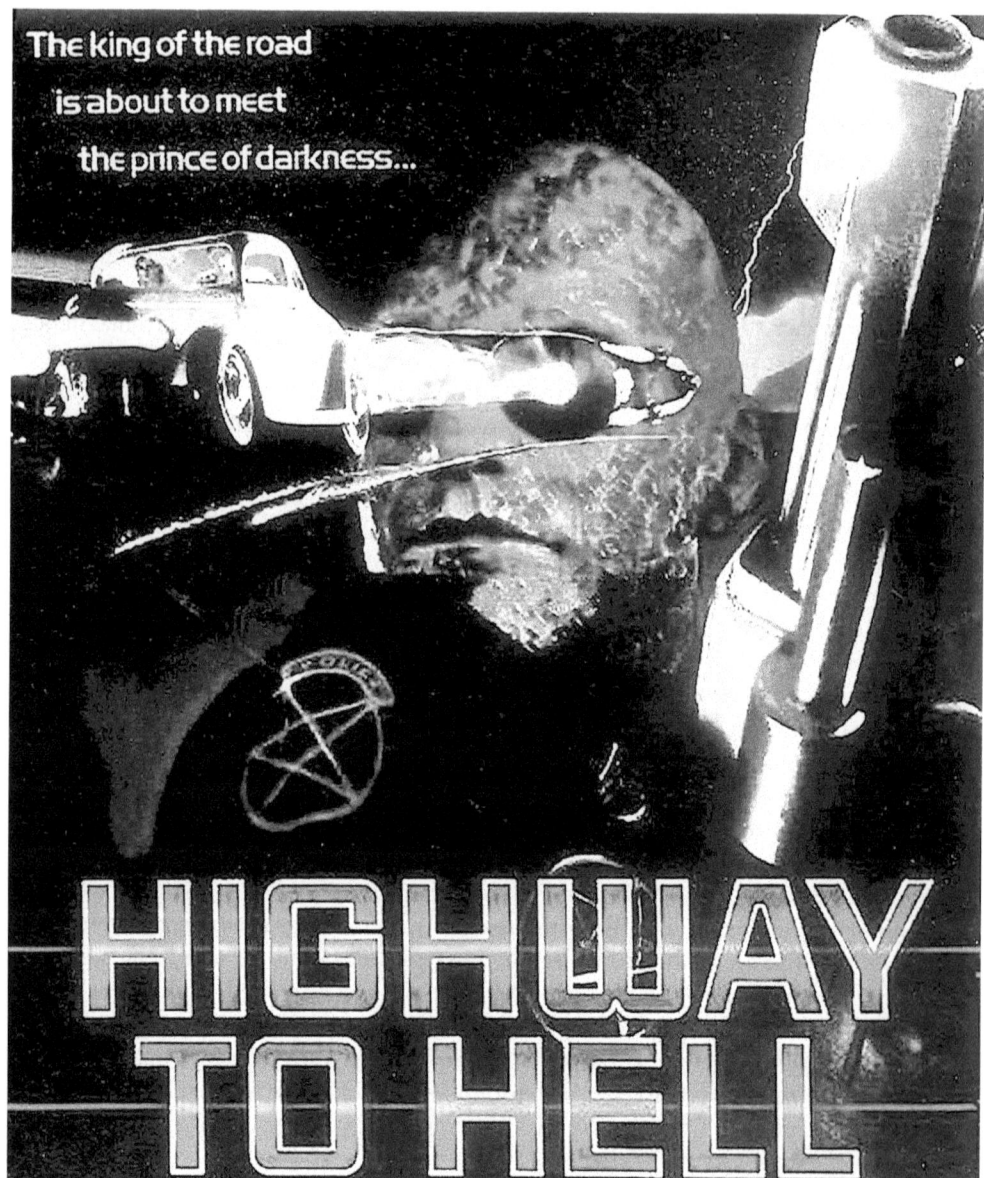

Hellcop (C.J. Graham) is just one of many bizarre characters populating the *Highway to Hell* (1991).

For all its cleverness, there's an equally impressive sense of tension maintained throughout the story; we never stop caring about Charlie and Rachel, no matter how absurd their predicaments become. While the horror elements in horror/comedies often end up feeling neutered, De Jong never downplays the film's racier or more violent aspects (such as a sexy female demon that tries to seduce Charlie) and brings a real intensity (and surprising emotional investment) to the various fights and car chases. In many ways, *Highway to Hell* plays as an R-rated live action comic book in the style of adult-oriented magazines like *Heavy Metal*, with one highly original (and surprisingly graphic) image after another thrown at the viewer. *Hellraiser* cinematographer Robin Vidgeon takes full advantage of the impressive locations and surreal visuals, giving the film an epic feel on what was surely a less-than-epic budget. His clean, colorful photographic style is especially effective at depicting and delineating the film's two distinct (but visually similar) desert worlds, whether in the blue-hued nighttime scenes back on Earth or the sun-scorched deserts of Hell.

Chad Lowe isn't the most charismatic lead (which is kind of the point, in a way), but the supporting cast—Bergin in particular—makes up for it, with plenty of familiar faces popping up throughout. Graham deserves special mention for his performance as Hellcop, as he brings a terrific physicality and real sense of menace to his character without uttering a single word. His various clashes with Charlie give their struggle a real sense of danger, and his exit is one of the film's more memorable moments. Despite its 1991 release date, *Highway to Hell* has a decidedly '80s aesthetic, placing it in the company of fellow culty genre-blenders *Radioactive Dreams* and *Cherry 2000*. The film's ninety-odd minutes breeze by faster than Hellcop's supercharged cruiser, and it's perfect for repeat viewings, as there's such an abundance of visual and auditory detail filling every frame that one watch isn't nearly enough. Who knew going to Hell could be so much fun?

Highway to Hell ultimately ended up in distribution limbo for several years before finally struggling onto video shelves, where it joined a growing number of smaller independent productions made directly for the video market. The supernatural slasher *Dark Harvest* (1992) is an early example of this new wave of DIY filmmaking, and stands as the very first "shot on video" Desert Terror film. An obligatory pre-title sequence manages to pack in splashes of nudity and gore while introducing one of its unlikely monsters—an undead, pitchfork-wielding scarecrow rampaging through the desert. The film then wastes no time introducing its main victims, er, characters, a group of three men and six women headed for a doomed horseback riding excursion. Led by one of the most inept guides in movie history and characterized primarily by their relationship status (one couple is married; another engaged), these nine strangers prove easy prey as night falls.

The first two acts of *Dark Harvest* pile on the desert terror clichés—dire warnings, a breakdown off the main road, ill-advised separation from the group—before unleashing a series of skirmishes between the survivors and the scarecrows, who often materialize in the strangest places (one ghoul appears to be trying to piloting a helicopter!). Ugly encounters with psychotic locals and bizarre dream sequences keep things lively too, along with a smattering of awkward sex scenes and (largely bloodless) murders. Unfortunately, writer/director/producer James I. Nicholson rarely takes advantage of the various desert settings to imbue his film with a sense of style or atmosphere, and the scattershot script never offers any real explanation for its bag-headed boogeymen (are they zombies, possessed scarecrows, or what?), offering only some mumbo-jumbo about a "cursed Indian tribe" before ending on a highly cryptic note. Like many early shot-on-video features, *Dark Harvest*'s ambition exceeds its resources, yet it still roughly paves the way for microbudget desert terrors to come.

Although *The Hills Have Eyes* generated the desert terror genre's first sequel, the *Tremors* films have proven to be its most enduring (and prolific) franchise. The first of several straight-to-video sequels, *Tremors II: Aftershocks* (1996) manages to rope together a few of the cast and filmmakers from the first installment. After a new group of graboids surface in Mexico, famous "monster hunter" Earl (Fred Ward, reprising his character from the first film) and his ambitious new partner Grady (Chris Gartin) are hired to hunt down and destroy the giant worms, who are being studied by attractive geologist Kate (Helen Shaver). Using old-school techniques borrowed from the first film, Earl and Grady blow up several of the creatures before calling in paramilitary nut Burt (Michael Gross, also encoring) for additional firepower. Plenty of goo is spilled as Earl and Kate fall for each other while trying to evade, then destroy, a new breed of bipedal, hermaphroditic "Shriekers."

Despite its location change and reduced budget, *Tremors II* will probably please fans of the original, thanks to a lively script by original *Tremors* scribes Brent Maddock and S.S. Wilson, the latter of whom assumes the directorial reins this time around. While a tad overlong, the pace improves once the new creatures appear, with lots of fun FX work from Alec Gillis and Tom Woodruff. Once again, the filmmakers poke fun at American militarism, addressing the global political shift since *Tremors*' 1990 release (Burt blames his romantic woes on "the collapse of the Soviet Union") It's also more self-aware than your average sequel, satirizing Hollywood merchandising (Earl is bitter about his lack of residuals on a Tremors arcade game, while Grady dreams of opening a theme park called Monster World) and even film franchises, as Grady tells a beaten-down Earl "maybe this is your second chance." The Mexican setting is felt more musically than visually, with only a few Latino characters in tiny supporting roles, and the generic green hills of Valencia, California, are no match for the classic, western-style look of the original's desert landscapes. Though lacking the scope (and most of the cast) of the original, *Tremors II* still serves as a better than average continuation of the first film's eccentric blend of creatures n' comedy.

Another straight to video sequel, *Phantasm IV: Oblivion* (1996) continues the adventures of unlikely heroes Mike (A. Michael Baldwin) and ice cream vendor-turned-monster slayer Reggie (Reggie Bannister) against the otherworldly Tall Man (Angus Scrimm) against—for the first time—a stark desert backdrop. After a barrage of flashbacks culled from the previous three films in the franchise, *Oblivion* cuts back and forth between the separate road journeys of Mike and Reg, who were separated at the end of *Phantasm III: Lord of the Dead* (1994). During a pilgrimage to Death Valley, tortured Mike undergoes a series of spiritual visitations and hones his own supernatural powers before traveling back to the 1860s to discover the origins of his nemesis. Wise-cracking Reg's path is defined more by sardonic humor and explosive action, as he battles a female hitcher (Heidi Marnhout) with a ghoulish secret and a "Demon Trooper" (Bob Ivy) whose appearance recall's *Highway to Hell*'s iconic Hellcop. In the time and space-hopping third act, Reg and Mike join forces in Death Valley in attempt to destroy the seemingly unstoppable Tall Man once and for all.

One of the horror genre's quirkiest franchises, the *Phantasm* films are characterized by dreamlike, effects-driven storylines that are as imaginative as they are nonsensical. Working with a noticeably lower budget this time around, writer-director Don Coscarelli trots out the series' trademark iconography (flying silver spheres, killer dwarves, tuning forks that send characters into other dimensions) and established characters while delivering a jumbled plotline that will test even the staunchest "phan" of the series. The most distinctive aspect of the film, aside from its desert locations, is its notably somber, elegiac tone. Since the original *Phantasm* (1979), the series has traded in morbid, funereal imagery, but *Oblivion* is positively drenched in melancholy, with a large portion of Mike's

Straight to video sequel *Tremors 2: Aftershocks* (1996) finds Grady (Michael Gartin, left) fighting graboids alongside Earl Bass (Fred Ward, middle) and Burt Gummer (Michael Gross).

desert sojourn spent conversing with the ghost of his older brother Jody (Bill Thornbury), writing out a will, and attempting to take his own life. In this aspect, the well-shot desert locations (shot in Lone Pine, California) contribute to the hallucinatory atmosphere of Mike's spiritual quest, and provide a welcome change from the anonymous small-town locales of previous entries.

As the first (and so far, only) example of an established franchise dipping into the desert terror playground, *Phantasm IV* works more as an interesting side trip than a satisfying conclusion to the series (a fifth entry, 2016's *Phantasm V: Ravager*, serves as a final installment). Like *Lost Highway*, *Oblivion* presents the desert more as a state of mind than an actual place, with much of the conflict (especially Mike's psychic duel with the Tall Man) attaining an unexpectedly existential vibe that pushes the film out of the generic horror arena and toward a *Zabriskie Point* (1970)–like head trip. Coscarelli takes further advantage of the setting to indulge in occasional western and noir imagery (a hanging tree in the middle of a desert plain, the abandoned motel where Reg and Jennifer stay the night) which openly reference desert terror's roots. That said, the film still suffers from many of the same issues that plague earlier entries: flat performances, wobbly scripting, and a boy's club dynamic that prizes muscle cars, customized weaponry, and male bonding over any serious treatment of its (few) female characters. After nearly twenty years of terrifying his heroes with all manner of monstrosities, Coscarelli himself still seems most afraid of the opposite sex.

The '90s climaxed with a high-pitched screech as, twenty years after the earnest but plodding (and commercially disappointing) *Nightwing*, Columbia Pictures gave bloodsucking beasties another shot at the big screen in the unimaginatively titled *Bats* (1999). Dispensing with the stultifying drama and Native American politics of Arthur Hiller's earlier effort (and in a nod to the contemporary slasher revival), *Bats* sends a swarm of the critters after a teenage couple before the opening credits have rolled. The pace rarely lets up over the next hour and a half, as attractive "bat-ologist" Dr. Sheila Casper (Dina Meyer, who gets to say things like, "The Chinese consider bats good luck.") and her wisecracking African American assistant Jimmy (Leon), and local Sheriff Kinsey (Lou Diamond Philips) try to contain a recent lethal bat outbreak in Gallup, Texas. After tracing the source of the rabies-like virus to a pair of infected Indonesian bats bred by sinister— and possibly insane—Dr. McCabe (Bob Gunton), the team sets about trying to save the citizens of the town and locate the bats' roost before further contamination occurs.

Light on plot but foaming at the mouth with frenzied, over the top action, *Bats* plays like an over caffeinated update of '50s B-flicks, or even 70s drive-in fodder like *Rattlers*. The script by debuting feature writer John Logan, who would go on to write the 1997 Best Picture winner *Gladiator*, is for the most part played remarkably straight, not that the cast has much time to breathe (let alone wink) amidst a constant barrage of "battacks" both big (a winged invasion of Kinsey's high school headquarters) and bigger (a *Kingdom of the Spiders*–style main street massacre). Many of the film's main story elements—from the white female scientist/Native American sheriff pair to the duo's final invasion of the roost—shrewdly mimic the humorless *Nightwing*, but *Bats*' relentless pacing and concentration on special effects easily identify it as a definite product of the adrenaline-rush, Tarantino/Rodriguez–inflected '90s.

In an effort to outdo Logan's action-intensive script (or to capitalize on his big break) Corman vet Louis Morneau directs with exhaustive fervor, piling on swooping bat POVs, shaky hand-held camerawork and rapid-fire editing that often obscures rather

8. Gargoyles and Graboids   181

than highlights KNB EFX's fun prosthetic bat effects. Combined with effective CGI for the swarming scenes, the film's most horrific scenes (which push the PG-13 rating to its limit) mostly take flight despite Morneau's unnecessary technical meddling. Much of the film is set at night, which helps considerably in bringing the bat attacks to life, but tends to obscure the various desert locations, which include rocky hills and caves outside of town. In many ways, it's hard to complain about *Bats*; it delivers exactly what it promises (and then some) and never bores. Morneau's film also inadvertently set the template for the following decade's rash of mid-budgeted, straight-to-video creature features, many of which would premiere on Syfy and prize computer generated effects, dumbed-down plots and familiar faces over narrative complexity or any attempt at genuine atmosphere or terror. Though a few of these films adopt desert settings, the majority—like the Afghanistan-set, Bulgaria-filmed sequel *Bats: Human Harvest* (2007)—take place against considerably more generic, less photogenic, and increasingly budget conscious environments.

9

Desert After Dark

"My father kept a secret once. He had been bitten by a vampire. He kept it a secret from me and my mother. By the fifth day, he was turning. That night, he attacked my mother. And then he came after me. I killed my own father, Padre. I got no trouble killing you."—Jack Crow, *Vampires*

An interesting offshoot of the desert-set creature feature, yet worthy of special consideration, is the desert vampire film. At first glance, there's nothing more visually incongruous than a vampire—a ghoul who can be destroyed by sunlight—living amidst the sweltering, sun-drenched environment of the desert, where shade is the rarest of commodities. However, the inherently animalistic vampire is more at home in the desert than one might think. Aside from their mythic associations with bats and wolves (both of which are indigenous to the Southwest and hunt at night), vampires are by nature nomadic beings, constantly on the move or in hiding, a quality that closely allies them with the protagonists of hitcher-killer and death driver films. On a more intellectual level, vampires traditionally bear conflicting desires about their own condition; like the characters who inhabit small-town stranded scenarios, they are the ultimate societal outsiders. A small but substantial selection of desert vampire films, which includes the first desert terror films directed by female and Latino filmmakers, demonstrate these themes in a variety of ways.

The first desert vampire films focused heavily on sexuality, a subject familiar to the desert terror genre yet rarely explored with such sensual appeal. Like *Werewolves on Wheels* and *Gargoyles*, *The Velvet Vampire* combines traditional Old World monsters with updated American settings and social attitudes. The following decade's *Near Dark*, a masterpiece of the genre which pairs sex appeal with explosive violence, largely writes its own rules while incorporating influences from the road movie and western genres. The western influence is even more clearly felt in *Sundown*, the first horror western in thirty years; desert vampire films of the '90s would further emphasize action and humor over atmosphere and sexuality. The decade closed with a pair of heavyweights—*From Dusk Till Dawn* and *Vampires*—both of which revert to more traditional vampire and religious elements. Existing apart from the standard vampire horror and often encompassing aspects of other genres (true crime, road, western), the desert vampire film continually finds new and creative techniques to bring these children of the night out of the darkness and into our cinematic nightmares.

The initial desert vampire film, *The Velvet Vampire* (1971), also bears the distinction of the first desert terror movie to be directed by a woman; in this case, Corman affiliate

Stephanie Rothman (*Terminal Island*). A wordless opening follows the statuesque Diane LeFanu (Celeste Yarnall) who, during an attempted mugging, stabs her assailant to death. After nonchalantly washing her victim's blood from her hands, Diane arrives at The Stoker Gallery, where she cozies up to attractive young couple Susan and Lee Ritter (Sherry Miles and Michael Blodgett). Clearly attracted to Lee, Diane invites the pair to her desert place for the weekend. Lee can't wait to go, but Susan is considerably less enthusiastic. On the way to their host's residence, the couple's car breaks down in the middle of a desert landscape of cactus and Joshua trees. They are rescued by Diane, who appears out of nowhere in a dune buggy and sweeps them away to her estate, where she lives alone with her manservant, Native American Juan (Jerry Daniels). That night, after a dinner filled with sexual innuendo, Diane views Susan and Lee's troubled lovemaking through a two-way mirror. In the first of several connected dream sequences, which are attributed to both Susan and Lee, the couple lay in bed, now in the middle of Sahara-like dunes, while a red-robed Diane attempts a slow-motion seduction.

The next day, Diane takes the pair on a tour of the area, stopping by an abandoned mine (where Susan is frightened by bats and Diane unearths a "bloodstone"), and a ghost town. While Diane attempts to seduce Lee inside an abandoned saloon, the sunbathing Susan is bitten by a snake. Diane sucks the venom out, getting a taste of Susan's blood in the process. An even more macabre scene follows, as Lee accompanies Diane to a desert cemetery (one of the film's most atmospheric locations), where she places flowers in her husband's still-open grave. Susan/Lee's recurring dreams intensify, gradually becoming indistinguishable from the reality. The film's theme of voyeurism continues as Susan watches Lee caress Diane's pale, naked body, not looking away even when Diane meets her gaze. As Susan's feelings about Diane shift from revulsion to sexual curiosity, Lee pressures his wife to leave. When he accuses her of wanting Diane, his wife replies, "Maybe I do. How does it feel?" Eventually, Lee literally falls victim to their host's hedonistic charms, his ecstasy becoming a death scream as she bites his neck. Susan flees back to Los Angeles, where a final, unexpected encounter seals the fate of both women…

A modern reworking of J. Sheridan Le Fanu's 1872 novella *Carmilla* against a Southwestern backdrop, *The Velvet Vampire* is a highly effective slice of California gothic, with a languorous, dreamlike tone, minimalistic aesthetic and an array of startling images. Unlike many erotic horror films, the various couplings drive the narrative, as the plot's romantic triangle shifts from Lee/Diane to Diane/Susan. The film questions the sexism inherent in the sexual revolution of the time, as Lee makes no secret of his affair with Diane, but balks once Susan shows interest in their bisexual host. While Susan's sexual confusion is not fully explored (the film slyly dodges the issue, as Susan finds Lee's body just as she is about to succumb to Diane's seduction), its importance to the plot gives the film a notable transgressive edge. Also noteworthy is the film's ambiguity regarding Diane's "vampire" status. Despite her proclivity for blood-drinking, love of raw meat and intimations of being hundreds of years old, she shows none of the usual supernatural symptoms: she casts a reflection, walks around comfortably in sunlight, and never bares any fangs. The epilogue suggests that Diane may have merely been a disturbed woman who was acting out a personal fantasy, but ultimately the issue is left tantalizingly open for interpretation.

In these and many other aspects, *The Velvet Vampire* serves as an American counterpart to Euro-horror classics like *Daughters of Darkness* (1971) and *The Blood-Spattered Bride* (1972), the latter of which also references Le Fanu with its lesbian vampire named

Mircala. Additionally, Velvet's morbid eroticism—Diane sucking blood from Susan's breast, a nude Diane splayed atop her husband's coffin—recalls the works of French erotic horror auteur Jean Rollin. Its desert setting, however, is completely unique, and adds a further layer of otherworldliness to Lee and Susan's nightmarish journey; Diane's isolated mansion and the neighboring old west environs, while far from menacing, are completely alien to the pair of Angelenos. The film is not perfect; several scenes suffer from minimal coverage and awkward transitions, and the final scenes in Los Angeles feel rushed and threaten to break the spell woven by the previous seventy minutes. Barring its lackluster ending, Rothman's best film remains one of the few films to successfully explore the erotic possibilities of the desert terror genre.

Writer/director Michael Cartel's one-of-a-kind oddity *Runaway Nightmare* (1982) also mixes desert settings, erotic energy and creatures of the night to lesser effect. The opening sequence, in which bored Death Valley worm farmers Ralph (Cartel) and Jason (Al Valetta) discovering an unconscious, naked woman (Sijtske Vandenberg) buried alive in a box, strikes an appropriately surreal, macabre tone. Soon afterward, a group of shotgun-toting sisters arrive to reclaim their lost member and forcibly transport the hapless guys (who don't put up much of a fight) to a large house deep in the desert. There, a female cult of brainwashed hippies with Manson-esque names like Sadie and Leslie force Ralph and Jason to undergo a week of initiation rites (most of which involve sexual slavery) before enlisting their services in a loopy plan to steal a suitcase full of platinum from the mafia.

In a film that encompasses a head-spinning variety of genres and tones, one character in particular sticks in the memory: Vampiria (Alexis Alexander), a bewitching babe clad in a black-and-red cape and ghoulish makeup. Given only one cryptic line ("Every man I've touched has died a violent death.") and appearing sporadically throughout the film, her presence not only carries a genuine air of mystery (is she real or not?), but helps provide some much-needed Gothic atmosphere to balance out the more banal sequences. Unlike the restless *Velvet Vampire*, Vampiria never venture outside the walls of the house into the surrounding desert heat. In many scenes, she barely occupies the same space as the other women, instead floating in infinite blackness or smirking knowingly from inside a picture frame. She also serves as an unusual "love interest" for Ralph; while ladies' man Jason shacks up with every available girl in the house, Vampiria and Ralph execute a dreamlike *pas de deux* which finally pays off in the film's final horrific moments.

Unfortunately, Vampiria's campy charms are not enough to rescue *Runaway Nightmare* from its awkward plotting and stilted direction, as the final half hour replaces witchy ambience for limply executed (and Vampiria-free) shootouts and chases. Even more annoying is the film's relentlessly sexist point of view, which extends from the characterizations (all the women are feminazis or double-crossing bitches) to the dialogue ("Maybe they've just been away from men too long") to the jaw-dropping ending. Although the overall vibe is more Playboy Mansion than Spahn Ranch, Cartel shows a noticeable lack of confidence in his handling of the many sexual scenes, which display a prudish self-censorship uncommon in exploitation films of the time (production began in 1978, but the film was not released until 1982). The schizophrenic result, which plays like a PG-rated clash between Jack Hill and Jean Rollin, is strangely conservative for a desert vampire movie.

It took more than another five years for another desert vampire film to sink its fangs into screens, but the result was well worth the wait. Directed (and co-written) by Kathryn

9. Desert After Dark

Bigelow (*The Hurt Locker*) and co-written and co-produced by *Hitcher* scribe Eric Red, the western-styled vampire road movie *Near Dark* (1987) takes the desert vampire film down new and dangerous paths. First introduced swatting a mosquito, bored small-town Texas cowboy Caleb (Adrian Pasdar) finds his life forever changed after a chance romantic encounter with the strangely seductive Mae (Jenny Wright). "You haven't met any girls like me," she purrs coyly, and Caleb finds out just how different after an all-night date ends with a bite on the neck. On the way home, the weakening Caleb is abducted by a Winnebago piloted by Mae's misfit "family" of vampires: leader Jesse (Lance Henriksen), his main squeeze Diamondback (Jenette Goldstein), wild card Severen (Bill Paxton), and "big man in a little man's body," teenager Homer (Joshua Miller). Having already "turned," Caleb is given a week to make his first kill—or else perish forever.

As Caleb's father, veterinarian Loy (Tim Thomerson) searches the state for his son, Mae educates her new lover about their new, after-hours lifestyle, explaining that "the night has its price" as each member of the group claims a victim. After botching an initial attempt to draw blood, Caleb is given "one more night" to prove himself as the group sets upon an isolated bar. "What do you people want?" the bartender asks, after

Pictured left to right, Jesse (Lance Henriksen), Homer (Joshua Miller), Diamondback (Jenette Goldstein) and Severen (Bill Paxton) are bloodsuckers stalking the southwest in *Near Dark* (1987).

Diamondback slits a waitress' throat (and lets the blood drain into an empty glass). "Just a couple minutes of your time, about the same duration as the rest of your life," Jesse responds laconically, and the drawn-out massacre that follows skillfully alternates shocking gore with the blackest humor imaginable ("I hate 'em when they ain't been shaved," Severen gripes before biting into his scruffy victim), all perfectly scored to The Cramps' "Fever." Caleb once again fails to draw blood, but redeems himself the following day, as he rescues the group during an explosive shootout with the local police.

"You're one of us now," Mae assures Caleb after the narrow escape, but his acceptance is short-lived as the two families unexpectedly cross paths at a roadside motel. The jealous Homer's attempt to turn Caleb's little sister Sarah (Marcie Leeds) as payback for Mae's induction of Caleb leads to conflict between the two groups, ending with Caleb's escape and return home. A blood transfusion restores Caleb's humanity, but Caleb is forced to confront Jesse and the others one final time after they abduct Sarah. A series of western-themed showdowns finds Caleb outmatched by Jesse, who proclaims it "too late" for Caleb to return to the group—or be spared. Torn between her love for Caleb and her allegiance to Jesse and the others, Mae's choice spells the end of her blood-drinking brethren—and gives her a second chance at humanity.

Homer (Joshua Miller) is incinerated by sunlight during the stunning climax of *Near Dark* (1987).

Powered by a terrific ensemble cast, whip-smart dialogue, Adam Greenberg's gorgeous photography, and a moody, throbbing synthesizer score by the always-reliable Tangerine Dream, *Near Dark* remains one of the desert terror genre's most enduring—and wickedly entertaining—accomplishments. Though surely worthy of discussion based on its own merits, the film must be recognized first and foremost as a companion piece to desert terror classic *The Hitcher*, with which it shares executive producers Edward Feldman and Charles Meeker along with, courtesy of Red, numerous script similarities. Beginning with Caleb's random yet life-altering meeting with Mae (which, like *The Hitcher*'s Halsey/Ryder relationship, begins with giving a stranger a ride) and continuing through its increasingly bloody and explosive action sequences (the motel shootout and Caleb's battle with Severen on the truck could easily double as deleted scenes from Robert Harmon's thriller), Red and Bigelow's screenplay repeatedly invokes the spirit of John Ryder, down to the purposely enigmatic nature of its antagonists (the word "vampire" is never uttered and fangs are never seen).

At the same time, *Near Dark* differs in several significant ways from its more streamlined, male-oriented counterpart. It's easily the warmer and more humanistic film of the two, with Caleb and Mae's tortured love story complicated by the clash between Caleb's old and new families who, despite their merciless and predatory behavior, emerge as oddly likable, driven by the need for companionship as much as their thirst for blood. Unlike *The Hitcher*, whose sole female character contributes little to the Ryder/Halsey conflict, *Near Dark* boasts a triumvirate of strong female characters—Mae, Diamondback, and Sarah—whose actions propel the story's development. It's also a funnier film, with plenty of gallows humor provided by its ghoulish gang; when asked his age, Jesse chuckles, "I fought for the South. We lost." While it's convenient to attribute the film's more sensitive tone to female co-writer Bigelow, then one must equally acknowledge her influence on the level of violence, which is often nastier, gorier, and more intimately felt than *The Hitcher*'s bigger-scale but more detached scenes of vehicular carnage.

Visually, Bigelow's film differs significantly from its cinematic cousin, favoring the same fire-and-ice palette Greenberg employed on *The Terminator* (1984). Like that film, most of *Near Dark*'s scenes transpire at night, in strong contrast to *The Hitcher*'s more naturalistically photographed daytime settings. *Near Dark*'s locations (the film takes place across several states, but was chiefly shot in Arizona), while appropriately isolated and dusty, also tend to reflect a more rural, low-key ambience than *The Hitcher*'s more vivid Southwestern landscapes. If its plains and prairies are bit of a departure from the usual desert terror environments, the film's western callbacks (Caleb literally rides a horse into town to confront Jesse's gang) and winding road-travel narrative more than compensate for it, conveying strong feelings of loneliness, transition, and societal displacement that easily place the film as much within the hitcher-killer or death driver category as its more obvious desert vampire designation.

While undoubtedly improved by her script contributions, *Near Dark* benefits most from Bigelow's assured direction, which skillfully unifies dark romanticism with hard-edged violence. In only her second feature after co-directing the rockabilly road movie *The Loveless* (1983), Bigelow gets great, lived-in performances out of her cast and serves up one arresting image after another while never losing track of the winding storyline. Co-leads Pasdar and, especially, the androgynous, otherworldly Wright perfectly exemplify Bigelow's delicate tonal balance between earthiness and fantasy, while the suspenseful, often brutal, action sequences speak for themselves; *Near Dark* is the first of many films (including the Red-scripted *Blue Steel*) that would cement Bigelow's status as the leading female director of traditionally male-directed action movies. The influence of James Cameron (with whom Bigelow was romantically involved at the time) is indisputable, from the casting (Henriksen, Goldstein, and Paxton all appeared in *Aliens*, which can be spotted on a theatre marquee in one scene) to the choice of cinematographer (Greenberg later photographed Cameron's *Terminator 2*) but, ultimately, Bigelow's artistic vision for the film is really all her own.

Many vampire films over the years have pontificated on the implications of eternal life, but few as effectively as *Near Dark*. Always on the move and lacking a true home, Jesse seems almost relieved when Caleb's arrival throws their endless predatory cycle into chaos, finally forcing the displaced, world-weary bunch to make choices that will, ultimately, result in their destruction. Severen burns in a joyful act of self-annihilation, while Jesse and Diamondback attain a bittersweet release in their final moments together. In these moments, the film mirrors *The Hitcher*'s self-destructive themes, but with an added crucial emotional pull. Mae's initial speech to Caleb, in which she insists, "The night will blind you," sums up her own divided feelings about immortality and its accompanying pressures. Visually sumptuous, thematically ambitious, and possessing a character and emotional depth absent from its more cerebral predecessor, *Near Dark*, like its cast of weirdly sexy vampires, both enchants and repels in equal measure.

Lance Henriksen as Jesse in *Near Dark* (1987), just one of the actor's many fine desert terror performances over the years.

Thirty years after Universal's *Curse of the Undead*, Anthony Hickox's *Sundown: The Vampire in Retreat* (1989) moves away from *Near Dark*'s progressive new western styling and returns the desert vampire film to its traditional roots while adding more than a dollop of humor to the mix. A thundering, *Red River*–type theme plays as an opening crawl explains how, many years ago, Count Mardulak led the remaining vampires out West to the former copper mining town of Purgatory, where they began creating and consuming synthetic blood. In the present day, unsuspecting scientist David Harrison (Jim Metzler), along with his stunning wife Sarah (Morgan Brittany) and two daughters, arrives in the vampires-only community to help repair their "blood plant." David immediately locks horns with plant supervisor Shane (Maxwell Caulfield), a former classmate (now a vampire) who carries a torch for former girlfriend Sarah. David and Shane's rivalry over Sarah plays out against a larger conflict between master vampire Mardulak (David Carradine)—who advocates for peaceful co-existence with humans—and rival Jefferson (John Ireland), who wants the vamps to return to their old, savage, blood-drinking ways. As Jefferson's army of cave-dwelling nightwalkers prepare for bloody battle against Mardulak's adherents, David and his family become caught in the middle. And did I mention Van Helsing's bumbling great-grandson Robert (Bruce Campbell) arrives in town to destroy Mardulak before falling for sexy vampire Sandy (Deborah Foreman)?

Overstuffed with more intrigue, affairs, illegitimate children, and revenge plots than an entire season of *Dark Shadows*, *Sundown* is all talk for over an hour, as subplots and supporting characters pile up one on top of another until there is barely room for the characters—or the viewer—to breathe. It's almost as if co-writers Hickox and John Burgess didn't trust their basic setup—which is highly original and rife with possibilities—to engage the audience, and so resorted to adding new characters and situations every five minutes. Thankfully, the excellent cast of character actors keep things lively (save Carradine, who seems bored most of the time) until the vampire revolution begins, at which point the film delivers plenty of western-style shootouts that feel dull, repetitive and strangely anemic for a vampire movie. Rather than emphasizing horror or western motifs, the film falls back on broad comedy, with every kill (including the first decapitation) a chance for a wink and a nod. There are no real scares to be found in *Sundown*, but plenty of time spent on kiddie hijinks, Campbell's trademark slap-shtick, and the antics of bumpkin bloodsuckers The Bisby Brothers, the funniest of which is played by M. Emmet Wash ("Didn't get these in 7-11," he snaps at a terrified female victim while baring his fangs). Unfortunately, most of these gags fall flat, and the mix of R-rated violence and goofy jokes gives the film a schizophrenic feel, as if unsure what audience it's intended for.

The film's visual style is similarly uneven, cutting from stunning vistas (the picture was shot in picturesque Moab, Utah) to astonishingly flimsy-looking interior sets. Special effects are also a mixed bag, with decent vampire makeups and burning meltdowns rubbing elbows with some crudely animated stop-motion vampire bats. Clearly intended as a cheeky postmodern updating of the cinematic legacy of Universal and Hammer, with a dash of John Ford thrown in for western flavor, the film is directed with enthusiasm by Hickox, son of director Douglas Hickox, whose *Theater of Blood* cameos via a poster on a bedroom wall. His excitement, and the novelty of the concept, carries the film for a while, but by the end, the whole endeavor simply collapses under its own weight. *Sundown* might be worth a watch for fans of its cultish cast, but its primary significance remains its unique status as the first desert terror movie to fuse the western and vampire genres together in a contemporary setting.

Near Dark at least enjoyed a nominal theatrical release before distributor DEG went bankrupt, but *Sundown* fared even worse; after languishing in legal limbo for a few years, the film was unceremoniously dumped to video along with most of struggling studio Vestron Pictures' slate. Vampires stayed out of the West for a while afterward, finding more gainful employment in big-budget, literary-based period pieces like *Interview with the Vampire* (1992) and Francis Ford Coppola's cheesily enjoyable *Bram Stoker's Dracula* (1992), both of which were major successes, paving the way for an endless flood of subpar erotic horror tales which were short on scares and big on skin.

During this dire period, then-aspiring screenwriter Quentin Tarantino penned a different kind of vampire movie, one which combined *Sadist*-type hostage drama, *Hitcher*/*Near Dark*–like road games and monster-movie gore, all bound together with fusillades of rapid-fire, pop culture-infused dialogue. Based on a story by KNB EFX's Robert Kurtzman, Tarantino's script for *From Dusk Till Dawn* (1996) wouldn't go before cameras until 1995, by which time its writer was an Oscar-winning filmmaker, as well as the literal poster child for the new American indie cinema. With *Dusk*, DIY auteur Robert Rodriguez, who Tarantino met while both had films in competition at the 1992

Sundance Film festival, stepped behind the camera for his third theatrical feature, while Tarantino himself assumed a hefty co-starring role aside George Clooney (at the time best known for popular television show *ER*). The resulting film, produced and released by Miramax genre division Dimension Films, is an entertaining, if bumpy ride, as two distinctive authorial voices attempt to merge their considerable talents into a cohesive whole.

In many ways, *Dusk* plays like a pair of hour-long movies that have been roughly stitched together by some crazed cinematic surgery. The first half of the film clearly bears Tarantino's stamp, as a long-winded, verbose opening sequence at a middle-of-nowhere Texas liquor store introduces the bank-robbing Gecko Brothers, level-headed Seth (Clooney) and hair-trigger psycho Richard (Tarantino) as they kill the sheriff (Michael Parks, from *The China Lake Murders*) and set the clerk (John Hawkes) on fire before high-tailing it to a desert motel. The brothers' ticket to Mexico, where they plan to meet up with the mysterious "Carlos," arrives conveniently in the form of former preacher Jacob Fuller (Harvey Keitel) and his teenage kids Scott (Ernest Liu) and Kate (Juliette Lewis, in her third desert terror film in as many years), who are traveling in a motorhome. After taking the family hostage, Seth and Richie commandeer their vehicle through a tense border checkpoint, after which they finally arrive at their destination: an all-night bar called the Titty Twister.

At this point, Dusk assumes the look and style of a typical Rodriguez picture, with an emphasis on visual gags, outlandish production design (the bar looks like a leftover set from a *Mad Max* movie), and over the top weaponry and violence. After a few altercations with the doorman (Cheech Marin, in one of three roles), and bartender (Danny Trejo), the Geckos and their hostages settle in to enjoy an outrageously sexy dance routine of the even more absurdly named Satanico Pandemonium (Salma Hayek), who shows an unhealthy interest in Richie's bleeding hand wound. Suddenly, everything literally goes to Hell as the club doors are bolted shut and the strippers transform into ravenous vampires. The vamps massacre most of the club's customers (including Richie, who Seth is forced to stake through the heart), leaving only a few survivors, among them Seth, Jacob and his family.

From then on, long bouts of yakking ("Has anybody here read a real book about vampires, or are we just remembering what some movie said?" Jacob asks in one of many referential moments) alternate with chaotically staged and edited action scenes, which become progressively more outrageous. Genre icons Tom Savini and Fred Williamson (as exaggerated versions of themselves) join in the fun before becoming vampire food. While much of the violence is played for sick laughs, a few surprising moments toward the end (Jacob's transformation into a vampire, Scott's death) achieve some emotional weight. Carlos (Marin again) finally arrives, inadvertently saving the day by blasting open the doors (a light-reflecting disco ball comes in extremely handy in one of the film's most inspired moments) and causing the vampires to explode in an orgy of blood and guts. A final stinger reveals the ruins of an ancient Mayan temple beneath the ruins of the Titty Twister, suggesting an evil that is thousands of years old.

A slap in the face to the last few years of tasteful vampire costume dramas, *From Dusk Till Dawn* is unapologetically lewd, rude and crude, with Tarantino's blisteringly profane dialogue competing with KNB's graphic special effects. On a deeper level, though, the film is surprisingly conservative, as it hints at, yet carefully avoids, any truly transgressive situations. Nominal anti-hero Seth is more bark than bite (we hear about, but

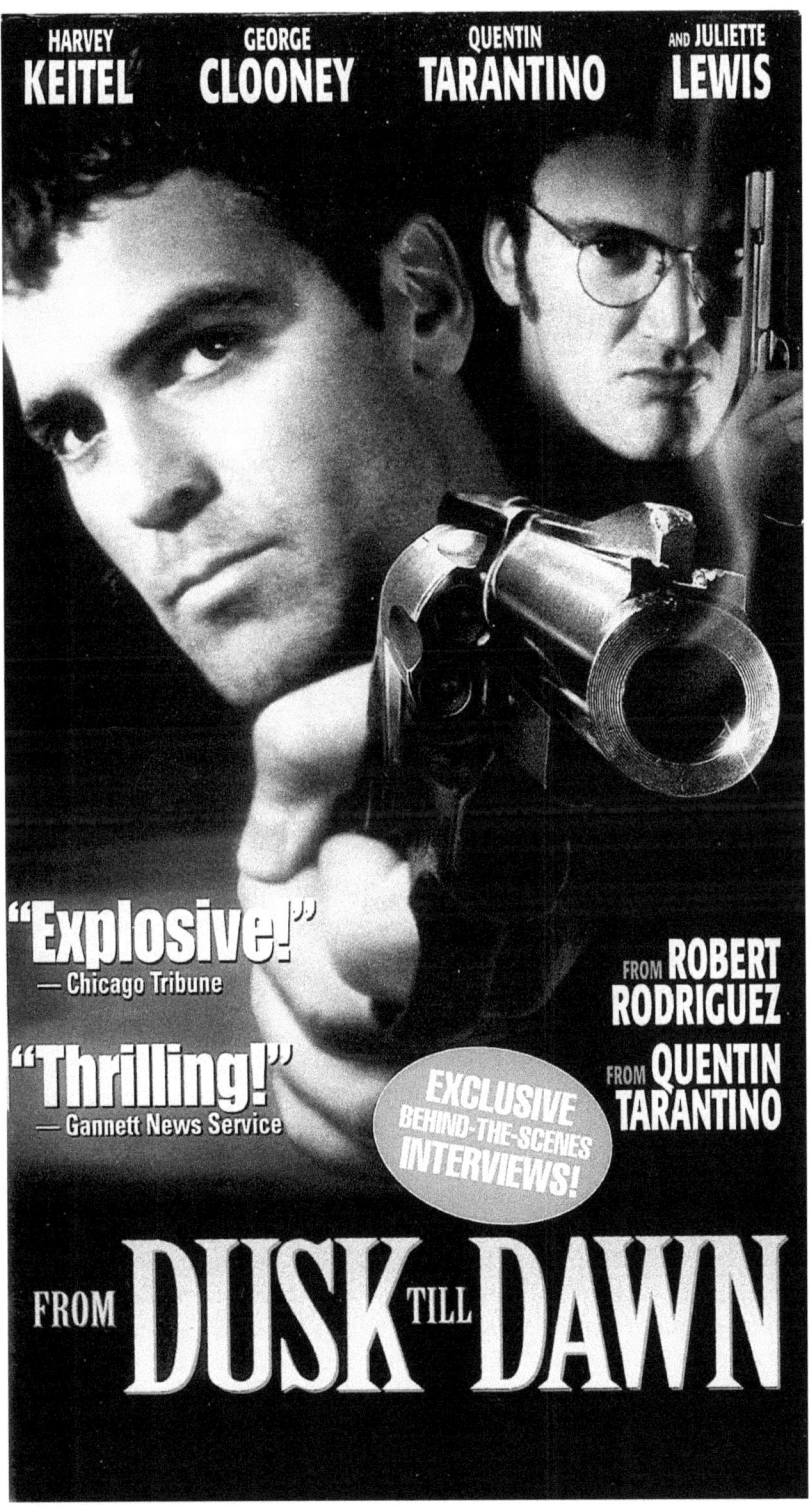

George Clooney (left) and Quentin Tarantino play the bank-robbing Gecko brothers in *From Dusk Till Dawn* (1995).

never see, the bank robbery bloodbath he perpetrated), leaving Richie to execute the film's more violent acts. At the same time, Richie's lusting after Kate—which provides some of the film's most uncomfortable, *Sadist*-like moments—goes nowhere. The Titty Twister also emerges as more of a tease, with only fleeting glimpses of nudity provided by the dancers and a decidedly PG-13–rated routine from "main attraction" Hayek. Here, Rodriguez replaces the heated sexuality intrinsic to the vampire film (and its strip club setting) with an overload of splattery special effects, which range from excellent full-body vampire suits to surprisingly poor CGI. While some of these gags (such as a giant vampire rat) exhibit an almost manic creativity, Jacob and Seth's vampire-slaying methods (crosses, stakes to the heart) feel not just old-fashioned but at odds with the film's overall cliché-busting intentions.

As a desert terror film, *Dusk* lacks a proper sense of scope, with its location-hopping first act taking place mostly within confined spaces of the liquor store, motel or Jacob's motorhome. There's little sense of its Texas locations, and the claustrophobic feel only intensifies once the characters reach their final destination. The casting, too, suffers from a schizophrenic nature; Keitel, Lewis and (to a lesser degree) Tarantino himself are borrowed from QT's previous endeavors, while Rodriguez ports over Marin, Trejo, and Hayek from his previous film *Desperado*. Savini, Williamson and Parks, on the other hand, typify the fanboy casting that Rob Zombie would take even further in his own desert terror epic *The Devil's Rejects*. Unfortunately, most of the principals are miscast; Tarantino and Clooney just aren't believable as brothers, and Keitel continuously slips in and out of his Texas accent. Lewis performs adequately, but Kate ranks as the weakest role in her Trilogy of (desert) terror.

Dusk remains, like *Duel*, *The Hills Have Eyes*, and *The Hitcher*, a game-changing desert terror film that, along with *Natural Born Killers* (not coincidentally, also based on an early Tarantino script), gave the genre a definitive commercial boost in the '90s. The first Latino filmmaker to helm a desert terror film, director Robert Rodriguez steers the genre into exciting new cultural territory while taking on the most creative responsibilities, including camera operation and editing, since Ray Dennis Steckler on *Blood Shack*. Almost in defiance of its studio origins, Rodriguez' highly personalized, DIY filmmaking approach gives his film a lively, anarchic quality that successfully invokes into its '60s and '70s exploitation roots. For the next ten years, *Dusk* would be the new model for vampire films, many of which emphasized contemporary narratives, experimental cross-breeding with other genres, and rip-roaring gore.

Interestingly, the genre-blending *Dusk* proved inspirational to the studios and independents alike, as its success eventually led to both a big-budget grindhouse revival (resulting mostly in a parade of sequels and remakes) and a renegade wave of micro-budget desert terrors, which, while varying in quality and budget, would help keep the genre alive and edgy through the next decade. *Dusk* was a big enough hit to inspire the direct-to-video sequel *From Dusk Till Dawn 2: Texas Blood Money* and prequel *From Dusk Till Dawn 3: The Hangman's Daughter*; a theatrical documentary about its production, *Full Tilt Boogie* (1998); and, fifteen years later, an eponymous TV series.

One of the first, and most significant, post–*Dusk* desert vampire films to appear was *Vampires* (1998), which shares with Rodriguez's film a contemporary western setting, anti-hero leads, snappy dialogue, and a messier, more animalistic approach to vampirism. Based on John Steakley's 1990 novel *Vampire$*, the film represents director John Carpenter's first foray into desert terror, a surprising fact considering his noted affection for the western genre, to which his only contributions thus far had been the screenplays for TV movies *El Diablo* (1990) and *Blood River* (1991). With *Vampires*, Carpenter takes full advantage of the film's Southwestern setting and larger-than-life storyline and characters to forge his own unique, ironic, and action-heavy take on the desert vampire film.

The film begins promisingly, as a team of working-class vampire hunters led by foul-mouthed, hot-headed Jack Crow (a terrific James Woods) invade a New Mexico nest full of undead "goons," spearing their targets before Crow's right-hand man Anthony Montoya (Daniel Baldwin) uses a wench to drag the vampires into the sunlight, where they promptly explode into multicolored flames. The gory follow-up sequence is equally memorable, as the hard-partying hunters are slaughtered at a nearby motel by 600-year-old master vampire Jan Valek (Thomas Ian Griffith), who leaves only Crow, Montoya and vampire-bitten prostitute Katrina (Sheryl Lee) alive. After sending Montoya away with Katrina, Crow stakes and beheads his fallen team members, then sets the motel ablaze before reporting to his employer, Cardinal Alba (Maximillian Schell). Crow is assigned Father Adam Guiteau (Tim Guinee), an inexperienced young priest with questionable allegiances.

The ill-matched Jack and Father Adam reconnect with Katrina and Montoya, who, after being bitten by his charge, has also started to turn. Using Katrina's telepathic link with her master, the three hunters track Valek as he slaughters priests and monks across the state in his quest for the Berziers Cross, a fabled relic that supposedly wields the power to allow vampires to walk in the daylight and essentially renders them invincible. Jack uncovers unparalleled levels of corruption within the church as the master's bloody trail ends in the ghost town of Santiago, where Valek and other master vampires plan to use the Cross in a restaging of Valek's original "reverse exorcism." With Montoya weakened, Father Adam becomes part of the team, and, as Katrina loses the last traces of her humanity, the slayers are pitted against a literal army of bloodsuckers.

In many ways, *Vampires* is a welcome return to the stripped-down style of Carpenter's '70s and '80s classics, sporting an uncluttered yet expansive narrative which offers plenty of opportunities for action and suspense set pieces. Visually, the film is probably the best-looking collaboration between Carpenter and his longtime cinematographer Gary Kibbe (*In the Mouth of Madness*), as they take full advantage of the gorgeous New Mexico landscape, using sweeping mesas and rocky plains as inspired backdrops for vampire/slayer showdowns. Aside from handling the film's action with customary finesse (the opening nest invasion is framed and edited for maximum impact, compared to the helter-skelter jumble of *Dusk*'s vampire attacks), Carpenter manages to serve up an occasional truly nightmarish image, as when Valek and several other master vampires erupt dramatically from their resting places like undead extras from Lucio Fulci's *Zombie* (1979).

While playing to the director's strengths, the script by genre vet Don Jakoby (*Lifeforce*, *Invaders from Mars*)—which distills and improves upon its literary source material—is surprisingly multilayered and character-driven, as it plumbs the tortured pasts of adversaries Jack and Valek—both of whom are, in their own way, molded by the forces of organized religion. Rebellious contrarian Jack, who was raised by the church to be a master slayer after his parents were killed by vampires, lives for vengeance but bristles against his employers (and pretty much everyone else, too); Valek, on the other hand, is described as "the first vampire created by the Catholic church," an accusation that defines the clergy—and not Valek—as the film's true monsters. This notion, more than Jack's rewritten rules on vampire slaying (apparently, only sunlight and stakes do the trick), is

Jack Crow (James Woods, center) leads (from left to right) Mark Boone, Jr., David Rowen, Thomas Rosales, Jr., and Cary-Hiroyuki Tagawa, a team of church-financed vampire slayers in John Carpenter's entertaining *Vampires* (1998).

Vampires' most revolutionary idea (as well as echoing Carpenter's *Prince of Darkness*, which also revolves around the church's concealment of an ancient evil) and gives the film an edge over other vampire films based on more conventional "good versus evil" conflicts.

The film also boasts one of Carpenter's best acting ensembles since the late-'80s, with Woods contributing a live-wire, sometimes unscripted lead performance that feels refreshingly alive, Lee channeling her *Twin Peaks* character Laura Palmer in a series of "vampossession" freak-outs, and action star Griffith (best known for action programmers like *Excessive Force*) surprisingly effective as Valek. Baldwin and Guinee provide strong support, holding their own against Woods, whose rapid-fire, profanity-laced outbursts can be more painful than a stake through the heart. KNB EFX's makeup effects are just as unabashedly gory as their work on *Dusk*, but less cartoonish and emphasize practical effects over CGI. While not as sexy as those in *Dusk*, Carpenter's vampires are wonderfully feral creations, with the dirty, dusty look of deranged Burning Man refugees. The film also benefits from Carpenter's last great score, a pleasing mixture of crunchy guitars and whispering synths that marries traditional horror ambience with a honky-tonk western twang.

The film is not, however, without its missteps. Dissolve-heavy editing (whose visual gaps suggest a lack of footage in some cases) detracts from some sequences, particularly

Katrina (Sheryl Lee) is about to become the latest victim of Valek (Thomas Ian Griffith) in *Vampires* (1998).

the motel massacre and Jack and Valek's final battle. After a ballsy opening and entertaining middle (the scenes with Katrina and Montoya being highlights), the last act drags a bit, with Jack and Father Adam's convoluted vampire hunt followed by an old-fashioned climax that, like *Dusk*'s, is an odd fit with the film's modernized take on vampire lore. For all its fresh ideas, the script runs dry toward the end, lapsing into juvenile, homophobic, dialogue as Jack calls his nemesis a "pole smoking fashion victim" and asks, "After six hundred years, how's that dick working?" His exchanges with Father Adam go even further in this direction, often ending with the question, "Did it give you wood?" Whether intended to compete with *Dusk*'s explosively profane dialogue or an inescapable by-product of Woods' on-set improvisation, these comments quickly become tiresome, as do repeated scenes of Katrina (the film's sole female character) being cold-cocked, shoved to the ground, or similarly abused. While not quite misogynistic, much of *Vampires* radiates a macho swagger that often suggests suppressed homoeroticism.

Despite these issues, *Vampires* remains the most entertaining of Carpenter's '90s outings, with the director appearing to be having fun behind the camera for the first time since his underrated *They Live* (1987). The script's road-movie structure keeps the narrative twisting and turning in unexpected directions while never losing sight of its central conflict. For the first time since his classic collaborations with Kurt Russell, Carpenter has a hero that perfectly echoes his anti-establishment sensibilities, and Woods imbues Jack Crow with an extra level of manic energy. Aside from the film's obvious jabs at the church, there's a familiar ring to Jack's clashes with his superiors; one could easily read Cardinal Alba's threat to have Jack's "funding withdrawn" if he does not take on Father Adam as Carpenter's jibe at the studios' creative interference in his work over the years. While assimilating images and themes from Carpenter's best works, as well as other desert terror films both past and present, *Vampires* stakes out its own flawed yet fiercely individualistic place in the desert vampire genre.

"What the hell are vampires doing robbing a bank?" asks Sheriff Otis Lawson (Bo Hopkins) in *From Dusk Till Dawn 2: Texas Blood Money* (1999), an anarchic blending of the heist and horror genres that bears little connection to the Rodriguez/Tarantino original. After a frenzied bat attack opener (featuring Bruce Campbell in his second desert vampire appearance) that is completely unrelated to the main storyline, the film focuses on escaped bank robber Luther Hegg (Duane Whitaker), who enlists his former partner Buck (Robert Patrick) to assemble a Texas-based crew for a Mexican bank job. While Buck compiles a not-so-elite team of grizzled safecracker CW (Muse Watson), hot-tempered getaway driver Jesus (Raymond Cruz) and dim-witted Ray Bob (Brett Harrelson), Luther is attacked by a pair of vampires (one of whom is played by Danny Trejo, reprising his "Razor Charlie" bartender character from *Dusk*) after stopping at the Titty Twister. Now a vampire himself, Luther continues with his plan, executing the break-in and theft while turning his accomplices into bloodsuckers, one at a time. This clearly isn't going to be your average heist...

Like its predecessor, *Texas Blood Money* follows a talky first half with a second act full of nonstop action and gore as "goddamn fearless vampire killers" Otis and Buck join forces against Luther's fanged foursome. In one amusing scene, a vampire is defeated by the Red Cross logo; in another, vampire Jesus is impaled on the cattle horns mounted on the front of his Lincoln. While these gags exhibit a certain amount of creativity, they fail to compensate for a scattershot script (co-written by Whitaker and Scott Spiegel, who also directed) that lacks a defined hero or even a villain with a sense of purpose. Aside from lacking the wicked humor or occasional pathos of Tarantino's script, it's also plainly sexist; while *Dusk*'s resourceful Kate emerged as one of the few survivors, *TBM* offers only its few females only unnamed supporting roles as girlfriends or prostitutes. Spiegel (best known for co-writing the 1987 cult classic sequel *Evil Dead 2*) seems more interested in bizarre camera placement than character development, as we're treated to POVs of electric fans, telephone cords, and even a pair of fangs as they chomp into a victim's neck!

On the positive side, this sequel is at least a less claustrophobic undertaking than its parent, with a large part of its action (particularly the drawn-out climax) taking place outside at night. Many of the best scenes–Luther's late night, middle of nowhere encounter with the undead—surface early in the film and summon up a genuinely nightmarish, unpredictable atmosphere. Luther's subsequent attack (as a bat!) on a showering prostitute (Playmate Maria Checa, providing some much-needed eye candy)—and her rebirth as a hungry vampire who attacks the team—is also good tasteless fun and represents a more outrageous side to the film that is gradually eclipsed by a focus on cartoonish shootouts and explosions. In this respect, Spiegel's film appropriates the manic, noisy, yet neutered style of Rodriguez' picture a little too well, as any sense of real danger is buried in an avalanche of pyrotechnics and meltdowns.

Creatively speaking, *From Dusk Till Dawn 2* adds little to the desert vampire genre, but its status as the first U.S.–financed desert terror film to be shot outside the United

States lends it an ominous significance. While runaway production (to Canada mostly) had been an issue since the '90s, it had not yet affected the desert terror films, whose scripts were often dictated by (or often written around) locations found only within the Southwestern United States. In a cost-saving decision which would be repeated in the coming decades of desert terror films, U.S.–based production company Dimension Films chose to shoot both *TBM* and its successor, *From Dusk Till Dawn 3: The Hangman's Daughter*, in South Africa, which featured the necessary desert environments as well as cheaper, professional, English-speaking crews. In *TBM*'s case, the change in scenery is not especially noticeable (the film's expressly desert content is limited to a few establishing shots), but consistent studio outsourcing of desert terror to other continents both near (Canada) and far (South Africa, Morocco) would have a profound effect on the genre's creative and visual development in the twenty-first century.

10

Franchising Fear

"We're lost in the middle of nowhere! We've been attacked by a fucking psycho. I watch you commit murder and help you bury a body in the first day of our fucking marriage. This is not how it's supposed to be."—Gina, *Dark Country*

By the beginning of the twenty-first century, desert terror had been a mainstay of the American cinematic landscape for nearly forty years. The genre had survived three full decades since *The Sadist*'s release, with each period yielding many distinctive films. The desert terrors of the '70s (*Werewolves on Wheels*, *Hex*, *The Velvet Vampire*) emphasized counterculture themes with a tendency toward artistic and technical experimentation and a questioning attitude toward the establishment, whether represented by the family unit (*The Hills Have Eyes*, *Duel*) or big government and corporations (*Kingdom of the Spiders*, *Nightwing*). The more conservative cultural and political views of the '80s, along with a valuing of style over substance, resulted in slicker and more violent offerings like *Death Valley*, *The Hitcher* and *Near Dark* before closing with the inoffensive crowd-pleaser *Tremors*, which would give the genre its first franchise. The '90s indie invasion of Hollywood gave birth to some of the highest profile—and most controversial—desert terrors yet, with groundbreaking postmodern films like *Natural Born Killers*, *Lost Highway* and *U-Turn* sporting A-list casts, acclaimed auteurs and studio-level budgets and releases. The box office success of these films inspired not only further sequels, but a mini-boom of straight-to-video desert terror thrillers.

The popularity—and increased visibility, thanks to major studio releases like *From Dusk Till Dawn* and *Breakdown*—of desert terror in the '90s would have serious repercussions in the following decade, as the studios seriously embraced the genre for the first time. While every decade since the '70s featured a handful of studio offerings, there were more studio-financed desert terrors produced between 2000 and 2010 than any other period in the genre's history. The initial run of studio-backed desert terror films was comprised primarily of straight-to-video sequels (*From Dusk Till Dawn 3*, *Tremors 3*, *Vampires: Los Muertos*), which were often produced outside of the United States, with the deserts of Mexico, Canada, and South Africa substituting for domestic locations. Alongside these films, the studios released the occasional big-budget theatrical outing (*The Forsaken*, *Eight Legged Freaks*), which were driven by name talent on both sides of the camera and received some of the widest releases ever accorded a desert terror film. Aside from *Joy Ride* (which ended up birthing its own franchise), few were major hits.

Poised squarely in the middle of the decade, Rob Zombie's stand-alone sequel *The

Devil's Rejects revived studio interest in the type of grindhouse goodies that the desert terror genre was founded upon. Much as the first half of the decade was littered with cost-conscious sequels, the remaining five years were defined by a series of big-budget retro remakes of desert terror classics like *The Hills Have Eyes* (which was once again sequelized to ill effect) and *The Hitcher*. The results were a mixed bag of major hits and disappointments, and the remake trend continued to flourish outside of the desert terror genre. Later, a handful of mid-budget original productions (*Dark Country*, *The Burrowers*) began to appear, pointing the way toward the next decade's quirkier, individualistic slate of desert terrors.

The first of many studio-funded desert terror sequels, *From Dusk Till Dawn 3: The Hangman's Daughter* (2000) was shot back to back in South Africa with previous chapter *From Dusk Till Dawn 2: Texas Blood Money* and released straight to video less than a year after its predecessor. Intended as a prequel of sorts to the original *Dusk*, *Hangman's* story is based around the real-life legend of short story writer and journalist Ambrose Bierce (*An Occurrence at Owl Creek Bridge*), who, after traveling to Mexico in 1913 to join Pancho Villa's revolutionary forces, was never heard from again. Lifting its title (and part of its story concept) from Bierce's 1892 novel *The Monk and the Hangman's Daughter*, Alvaro Rodriguez's ambitious script (based on a story co-authored with Robert Rodriguez) uses the mysterious circumstances of the author's disappearance to spin an enormously entertaining tale that encompasses drunken writers, outlaw lovers, sadistic executioners and, of course, plenty of vampires.

In the dusty Mexican town of Purgatorio, Ambrose Bierce (desert terror regular Michael Parks) boards a stagecoach bound for Tierra Negra, where he hopes to meet up with General Villa. At the same time, The Hangman (Temuera Morrison) drags condemned outlaw Johnny Madrid (Marco Leonardi) to the main square for a public execution. At the last second, Johnny's life is spared when killer-on-the-lam Reece (Jordana Spiro) fires into the crowd, leading to a chaotic shootout/stampede that ends with Johnny escaping with the hangman's beautiful daughter Esmerelda (Ara Celi). On the way to Tierra Negra, caustic atheist Bierce spars with recently married missionary couple John and Mary Newlie (Lennie Loftin and Rebecca Gayheart), before their coach is overtaken by Johnny's band of outlaws, which now includes Reece. After finding only the pages of Bierce's most recent story, the gang leaves the Americans stranded in the desert. Angered by her false claims, Johnny abandons Reece, where she is later saved by the hangman and his posse, hot on Johnny's trail.

The myriad plot threads coalesce as the various parties converge on an isolated, ancient-looking inn known as "La Tetilla de Diablo." Early arrivals Bierce and the Newlies meet bartender Razor Charlie (Danny Trejo, the only performer to act in all three films), whose appearance gives a not-so-subtle hint as to the demonic origin of the inn's seductive dancing girls. An orgiastic vibe takes over as vampire madam Quixtla (an apparently ageless Sonia Braga) seduces both the straight-laced John and—after licking blood from the girl's fresh wounds—Esmerelda, while Johnny's gang has their way with the inn's dark beauties. After fresh blood is spilled during a bar fight, the whores reveal their vampiric nature and attack the clientele in a frenzy of erotically-charged mayhem. A motley group of survivors—along them Johnny, the Hangman and Bierce—escape and try not to kill each other while searching for Esmerelda, who is re-christened "Satanico Pandemonium" (the character played by Salma Hayek in the original *Dusk*) in the ritualistic finale. Although the ending is less spectacular than one would hope for, it retains a nice sense of melancholy as Johnny joins Bierce on his Quixote-like adventure.

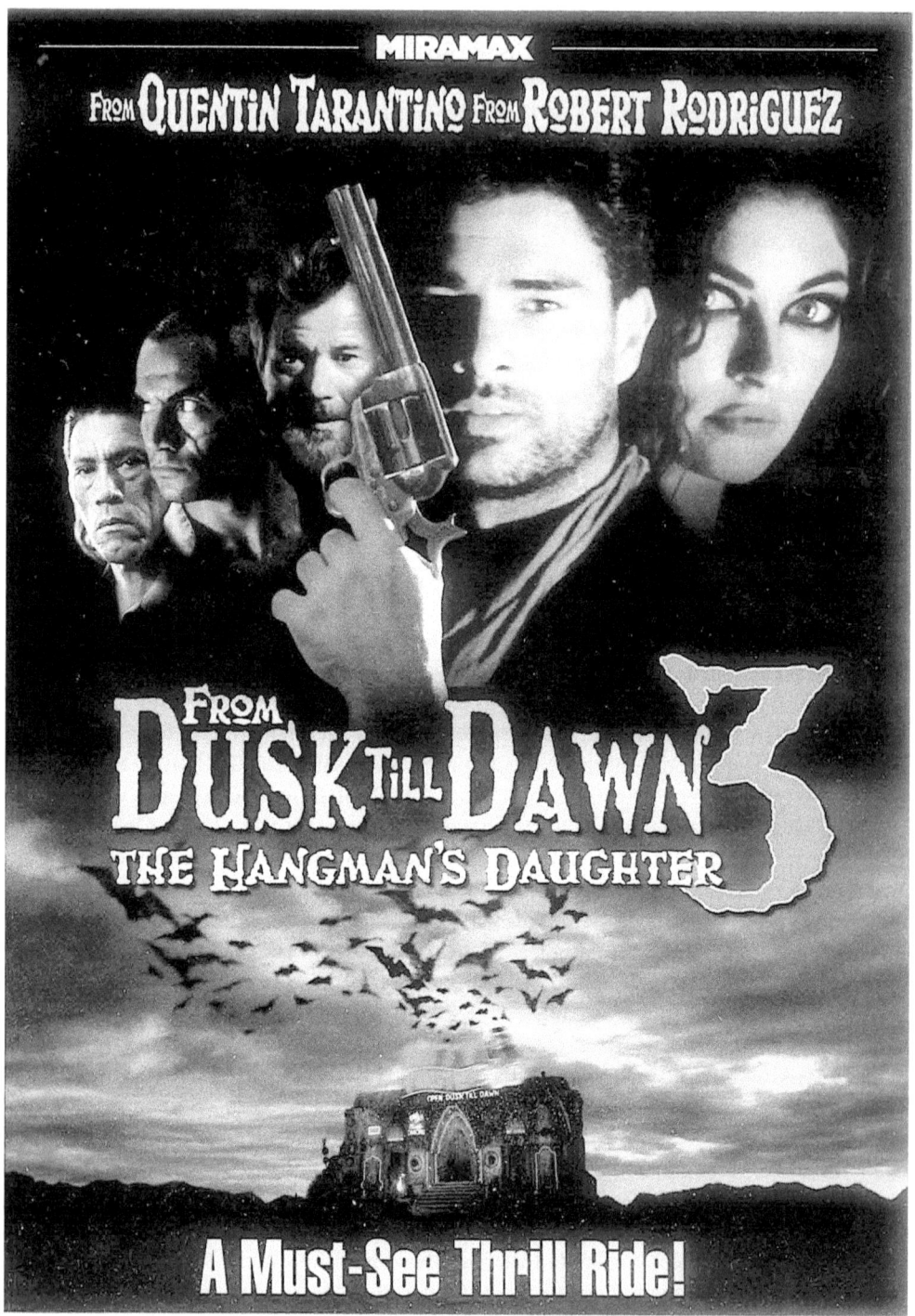

Pictured left to right, Danny Trejo, Temuera Morrison, Michael Parks, Marco Leonardi and Rebecca Gayheart star in *From Dusk Till Dawn 3: The Hangman's Daughter* (2000), one of the first U.S.–financed desert terror films to be filmed outside North America.

By their third chapters, most horror franchises either try and reinvent the wheel (*Halloween III: Season of the Witch*) or resort to desperate gimmickry (*Friday the 13th Part III, Jaws 3D*), but *Hangman* defies conventional wisdom, emerging as the clear frontrunner of the trilogy by honoring and expanding the world originally created by Tarantino and Rodriguez. Its multilayered, period-piece script, which combines historical figures with fictional creations to tell the origin story of a minor character from the first *Dusk*, sounds unwieldy and overstuffed, but under P.J. Pesce's confident, stylish direction, the various narrative threads congeal smoothly while still retaining the ability to shock and surprise. The action scenes have a scope beyond anything in either of the previous *Dusk* films, but more importantly, the two trademark aspects of vampirism—sex and death—are treated with an adult tone previously unseen in the franchise. This is easily the sexiest of all three films, with copious amounts of skin on display and a pleasingly hedonistic atmosphere that grows more depraved as the film continues. The film's acts of violence, beginning with the Hangman's brutal whipping of both Johnny and his own daughter, and climaxing with Esmerelda's evisceration of her own ancestor, also feel more personalized than the cartoonish carnage of the previous two installments.

Interestingly, the most flagrantly sexual film in the trilogy also boasts the strongest female characters, with the titular daughter not the sole woman of interest. A variety of interesting and powerful femmes—hyper-sexual, manipulative Quixtla, prudish Mary (who has a show-stopping vampire tango), the androgynous, slippery Reece—all have memorable moments throughout the film, often leaving a more lasting impression than their male counterparts. While Morrison and Loftin make strong impressions, and Parks brings his usual laconic wit to Bierce, the film remains dominated by the fairer sex, with Esmerelda's physical and spiritual journey from humanity to vampirism gaining an unexpected poignancy which, once again, represents a high mark for the series. Beautifully shot and skillfully edited, the film occasionally goes astray in certain CG-heavy moments, but these flaws are easily ignored when one considers the overall achievement. Few franchises count their third entry as their best, but, with a little help from Ambrose Bierce, Razor Charlie, and some of the sexiest vampires you'll ever find south of the border, *The Hangman's Daughter* manages to pull off such a feat.

The more family-friendly *Tremors* franchise also chalked up a third installment with the video debut of *Tremors 3: Back to Perfection* (2001). After the previous sequel's Mexican sojourn, this chapter wisely brings the action back to its original Southwestern setting, with supporting character Burt Gummer (Michael Gross, in his third *Tremors* outing) assuming the lead role. Returning home to the tiny desert town of Perfection, Nevada (Pop. 5) after an overseas worm-exterminating gig, Burt finds the community overridden with competing entrepreneurs, including general store owner Jodi Chang (Susan Chuang), tour guide Jack (Shawn Christian) and budding real estate mogul Melvin (*Tremors*' Robert Jayne), who plans to build ranchettes in the valley. Most of these newcomers have never even seen a graboid, but that all changes when one of the creatures erupts from the ground to gobble down Jack's assistant in the middle of a tour. The armed-and-ready Burt quickly enlists a few locals to hunt down and kill the giant worms and their hideous offspring before they reproduce and become unstoppable.

After setting up some new characters and bringing back a few from the first *Tremors*, like Miguel (Tony Genaro) and Nancy (Charlotte Stewart), the film gets down to business as Burt and his ragtag team set off after the creatures. In one amusing sequence, Burt is ingested by a graboid and radios Jack from inside the belly of the beast, instructing him on how to kill it. The funniest, and most suspenseful, scenes, though, come courtesy of the amusingly-named "ass blasters," a new, deadly breed of winged wonders that can blast off like a rocket. "It's always something new with these things," Burt sighs wearily as he, along with Jodi and Jack (who start off business rivals and—big surprise!—fall in love by the end), takes on a horde of flying foes. If the first half of the film (which, like the previous chapter, is a tad overlong) is overrun with go-nowhere subplots and characters (including *Leatherface*'s Tom Everett, in an uncredited role), the final third, which encompasses Burt's junkyard standoff against the ass-blasters and an albino graboid known as El Blanco, provides some genuinely spectacular, and creative, action scenes.

A welcome return to the desert settings of the first film, *Tremors 3* is a noticeable improvement over the previous entry, with appealing characters, a nicely irreverent tone, and plenty of old fashioned guts and goo. Original *Tremors* co-scripters S.S. Wilson and Brent Maddock return as executive producers and contribute an original story, with Maddock also taking the directing reins this time around. The script by newcomer John Whelpley honors and expands the established *Tremors* universe, name-checking characters from the first movie (Chang sells books by Rhonda LeBeck), getting in the usual digs at Burt's anti-authoritarianism along with satirizing big government (graboids are considered an endangered species) and capitalism (there's a special fate in store for real estate developer Melvin). At the same time, the film never takes itself too seriously and has more fun with its monsters than any of the previous installments. More than ten years after the original film, *Tremors 3* may not achieve perfection, but it's surprisingly adept at finding new ways to mix humor and (mild) horror in a desert setting.

In a refreshing break from the last few years of sequels, Fox released the first original studio-produced desert terror film of the new century: *Joy Ride* (2001), a slick road thriller that shifts gears between college comedy and torture-porn horror. Co-written and produced by J.J. Abrams (known primarily at the time for creating cult TV hits like *Alias*) and directed by neo-noir specialist John Dahl (whose *Red Rock West* remains one of the all-time best desert noirs), the *Duel*-influenced tale finds college student Lewis (Paul Walker) driving from Berkeley to Denver to pick up childhood friend-turned-hottie Venna (Leelee Sobieski). Lewis' plans are slightly derided after making a detour to bail out his older brother, perennial loser Fuller (Steve Zahn), who purchases a CB radio to avoid speed traps. Lewis and Fuller soon find another use for the device, as they create a fictional female trucker named "Candy Cane" as a come-on to potential listeners. Gravel-voiced trucker "Rusty Nail" (voiced by an uncredited Ted Levine) takes the bait, and the resulting prank—though innocent enough—ends badly, with an unwitting victim horribly maimed, and Fuller and Lewis pursued by the psychotic, retribution-seeking Rusty Nail across one state after another.

The first act of *Joy Ride*, while convoluted in its plotting, yields its greatest pleasures. Walker and Zahn (the latter of which easily steals the movie) have a natural rapport, particularly in the CB scenes, which achieve genuine laughs and tension. The conversations with Rusty Nail, and the later motel room sequence, feature some of the best use of sound in any desert terror movie, with an impressive amount of suspense and terror created by what is heard rather than seen. Later scenes go for more visual thrills, as the brothers are pursued by Rusty's big rig. Like the anonymous driver in Spielberg's *Duel* (which, thirty years after its release, is still scarier than anything in this slicker offering), Rusty is barely glimpsed; he exists primarily as a disembodied radio voice. Once Venna joins

The slickly entertaining and financially successful *Joy Ride* (2001) birthed one of the first desert terror franchises of the new millennium.

the pair, the film wanders briefly into love triangle territory before Rusty returns, using Venna's kidnapped roommate to force the trio into one ridiculous situation after another (including forcing the brothers to walk fully naked into a coffee shop), culminating in a cornfield truck chase that ends with Venna's capture by the vengeance-bent trucker. Lewis and Fuller are forced to endure a deadly replay of their own initial motel prank, with Venna's life—and possibly theirs—hanging in the balance.

Though it flirts with the death driver and murder machine genres, *Joy Ride* mostly pulls its punches, with the noncommittal script by Abrams and Clay Tarver maintaining a distanced, ironic tone throughout (sample lines include "this is the part where you kiss the girl" and "this is like an old-fashioned western. I want you out of Wyoming before the sun goes down."). Lewis and Fuller are well-written and performed, but Venna is a cipher whose presence both confuses and dilutes the entire narrative. Dahl directs with his customary technical finesse, but unfortunately, the film lacks the distinctive desert atmosphere of his earlier neo-noirs. Although the protagonists travel through several Southwestern states, the exteriors are limited to establishing shots; the bulk of the film takes place inside cars and motel rooms, the latter of which director of photography Jeff Jur glazes in bright hues of green and red to create some visual interest. An unappealing array of generic rock and pop songs are poured over many scenes, further disrupting any possible middle-of-nowhere ambience. One-third of a great movie followed by two-thirds of an average one, *Joy Ride* makes one too many wrong turns, losing the audience along the way.

In *The Forsaken* (2001), desert thriller specialist J.S. Cardone (*Black Day, Blue Night*) puts bloodsuckers behind the wheel for a Southwestern vampire odyssey. The film looks like a clear descendent of *From Dusk Till Dawn* and *Vampires*, but its true inspirations date back to the '80s. *Hitcher* overtones permeate the opening scenes, as cash-strapped trailer editor Sean (Kerr Smith) agrees to drive a car from Los Angeles to Miami so he can attend his sister's wedding. After a flat tire strands him in small-town Arizona, smart-ass slacker Nick (Brendan Fehr) ingratiates himself into riding along. Along the way, a group of strangely attractive young men and women, led by the predatory Kit (Johnathon Schaech) appear and disappear randomly. Sean and Nick's journey takes a nightmarish turn after they meet vagabond vampire Megan (Izabella Miko), who carries a psychic link to her "master," Kit. When Kit's gang (which, in a nice twist, is composed of humans and vampires) slaughter a group of dune-buggy driving locals, Megan reacts wildly, biting Sean as he tries to subdue her. "You've been bitten by a vampire," Nick casually informs him.

After administering a homemade antidote to Sean and Megan, Nick explains that he's been hunting Kit for almost a year after being bitten himself. In a nod to Vampires, Nick uses Megan as a homing device to find Kit, one of an elite group of original vampires known as "The Forsaken" whose destruction will free Nick—along with Sean and Megan—from the curse of vampirism. The two groups engage in a series of increasingly violent chases and shootouts during which both humans and vampires alike meet gory endings; vampiress Teddy (Alexis Thorpe) bursts into flames after being tossed into direct sunlight, a highway patrolman is shotgunned and burned alive, and, in one particular bloody sequence, some good ol' boys are messily devoured by sexy African American vampire Cym (Phina Oruche), a "full blown feeder" described by Nick as "The Penthouse Pet from Hell." After Kit tracks his prey to an isolated farmhouse built on an old Spanish graveyard, the stage is set for a hellish collision course which few will survive.

Johnathon Schaech (top left), Phina Oruche (top right), Kerr Smith (bottom left), Izabelle Miko (bottom middle) and Brendan Fehr star in *The Forsaken* (2001), one of many desert thrillers written and directed by J.S. Cardone.

Although certain aspects of *The Forsaken*—the noisy, pop-laden soundtrack, some peripatetic editing—grate, it has aged surprisingly well in the fifteen years since its initial release. Writer/director Cardone is no stranger to desert-set filmmaking, with over twenty years of credits in both the thriller (*Outside Ozona*) and post-apocalyptic (*Shadowzone*) realms, but *The Forsaken* stands apart from the rest of his filmography as his first (very) red-blooded desert terror film. Cardone's screenplay successfully merges the death driver, hitcher-killer and desert vampire genres into a pleasingly ragged, unpredictable framework, but the film's real pleasures are sensual, with the sexiest cast of vampires since *Near Dark* and a keen eye for detail throughout, as every coyote howl and moonlit canyon contributes to its potent, hell-bent atmosphere. Photographed at a variety of picturesque locations in Yuma, Arizona, the film really comes alive in its third act, which appropriately takes place entirely at night.

Like *The Hitcher* or *Near Dark*, *The Forsaken* is as much an action movie as a horror film, with Kit more likely to use a shotgun to kill his prey than fangs (which we never see). The second half of the film works as an extended chase, with dialogue kept to a minimum while the audience is slammed with a barrage of car crashes and gunfights. Despite its concentration on action, the film doesn't shy away from the erotic aspects of vampirism, with several moments—such as a bloody, sweaty scene between Kit and Cym—merging sex and death in a way that rivals the adult-oriented *From Dusk Till Dawn 3*. Along with providing the requisite thrills and chills, Cardone drops in pointed commentary about the movie biz, addressing everything from the importance of "connections" and the industry's snobbery toward B-movies (Troma posters line the walls of Sean's workplace) to film people's lack of real-life experience (when Nick asks how much he knows about vampires, Sean replies that he "saw Coppola's *Dracula*"). Such asides occasionally place *The Forsaken* in the company of other self-reflexive desert terrors (*Blood Shack*, *Haunted*) but never distract from its unapologetically violent, "less talk, more rock" style.

Cardone's film may not have been the franchise-spawning hit that Sony hoped for, but that didn't stop them from double-dipping into the plasma pool once again with *Vampires: Los Muertos* (2002). A straight-to-video sequel to John Carpenter's *Vampires*, *Los Muertos* retains its predecessor's horror western vibe while introducing an entirely new set of characters and moving its action to Mexico. After minor-league slayer Derek Bliss (Jon Bon Jovi) is hired by an anonymous client to put together a new team of hunters, his first stop is a monastery supposedly inhabited by *Vampires*' well-known hunter, Father Adam Guiteau. With Guiteau long since passed away and all other prospective candidates recently turning up dead, Bliss is forced to assemble a ragtag team consisting of enthusiastic but untrained teenager Sancho (Diego Luna), half-vamp Zoey (Natasha Wagner), who pops pills to combat the virus, secretive Padre Rodrigo (Christian de la Fuente) and hired gun Ray Collins (Darius McCrary). Together, the unlikely group of hunters must face off against female master vampire Una (Arly Jover), who, like the first film's Valek, aims to perform a reverse exorcism that will allow her to walk in the daylight.

While utilizing the same basic plot structure as *Vampires* (including Derek's use of Zoey as a telepathic link to track Una), *Los Muertos* differs from its parent in several narrative and visual aspects, many of which are informed by its culturally unique and richly atmospheric Mexican locations. Writer/director Tommy Lee Wallace, a longtime Carpenter associate whose resume includes co-scripting the desert terror film *Far from Home*, has made a career out of crafting worthy sequels that distinguish themselves from their

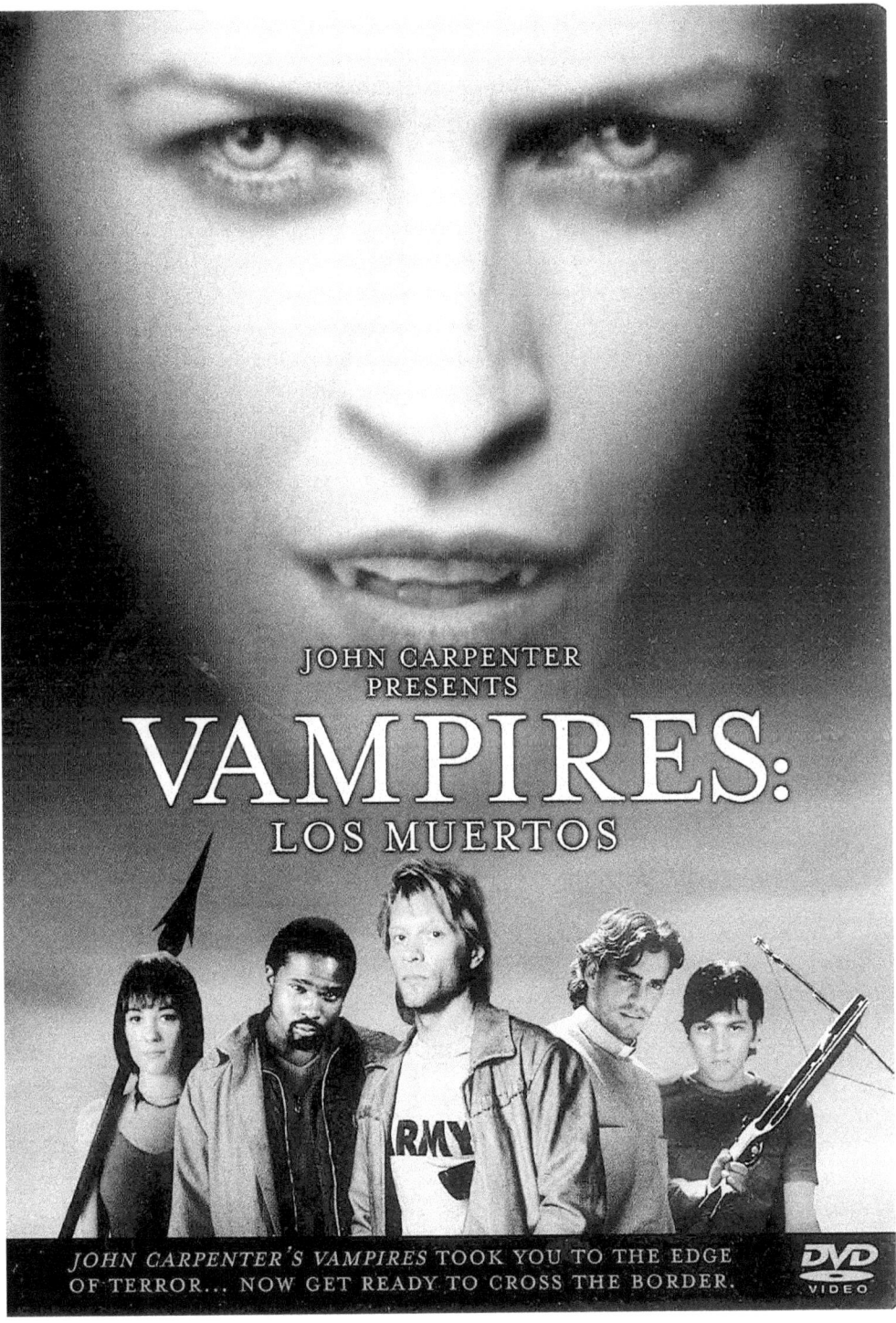

Vampires: Los Muertos (2002), starring Arly Jover (top) and, left to right, Natasha Gregson Wagner, Darius McCrary, Jon Bon Jovi, Cristian de la Fuente and Diego Luna, moves its vampire-hunting action south of the border.

predecessors, and *Los Muertos* is no exception, beginning with its novel approach to its slayers. While his profession may be the same as Jack Crow and his team, Derek Bliss lacks their calling; he's a loner with no Church affiliations who "just wants to surf." His eventual team, too, is far from the from the grizzled pros of Carpenter's film, but rather desperate people enlisted into the profession through financial necessity (Derek, Pancho, Ray), medical need (Zoey) or a personal thirst for vengeance (Rodrigo). In Pancho and Zoey's cases, the characters' situations are directly tied in with the film's Mexican setting; Pancho initially joins the team to combat his family's poverty, while, in a smart commentary on FDA regulations, Zoey has come to Mexico City to buy drugs that stave off her sickness of vampirism. While Una's quest is overly familiar, her borderline androgynous nature opens several new and interesting possibilities, only some of which the film explores. Unlike the well-defined slayers, the primarily silent (she has only two lines of dialogue in the entire film) Una ultimately remains too much of a mystery, without even the faintest hint of a backstory.

Visually, *Los Muertos* at least equals its precursor, with Henner Hoffman's stunning location lensing giving the film a much bigger look than its budget likely allowed. The last half of the film, a cat and mouse game between Derek's team and Una amid the crumbling temples and underground catacombs of ancient Toltec ruins, summons up the kind of eerily gothic atmosphere more common to European horror films of the '60s and '70s. While none of the film's action scenes can match *Vampires*' opening nest invasion, there's still plenty of slayer/vampire combat and plenty of KNB–created stakings and immolations on display. Ironically, one of the few areas in which *Los Muertos* too slavishly copies the original is in its drawn-out, unnecessarily convoluted third act, which inverts *Vampires*' nest hunt/ritual structure to little effect. Making up for it, though, is one of the film's most innovative ideas, as Derek undergoes a *Near Dark*–like reverse transfusion, becoming half-vampire to destroy Una. It's an intriguing concept, and one that echoes the first film's Montoya/Katrina pairing as Derek and Zoey drive off together into the sunset. Unfortunately, Sony chose not to continue their adventures, instead moving the franchise to Thailand with a new set of characters for the disappointing *Vampires: The Turning* (2005), the third (and likely final) chapter in the series.

For their first desert terror offering since *Natural Born Killers*, Warner Brothers released the big-budget giant spider flick *Eight Legged Freaks* in the summer of 2002. *Freaks* co-writer/director Ellory Elkayem had already proven himself adept at the creature feature with his charming short film "Larger Than Life" and the TV movie *They Nest*, but the real guiding influences behind the film are mega-producers Roland Emmerich and Dean Devlin (*Independence Day*), who turn what could have been a clever, small-scale homage to atomic-era SF flicks into a bombastic, overbearing CGI showcase. The film's first few scenes set up the silliness to come, as a truck passing through Prosperity, Arizona (an economically disadvantaged town described by one local as "stuck in the 1950s") accidentally dumps a barrel of toxic waste in a local pond. After a spider farmer (Tom Noonan) feeds crickets from the pond to his arachnids, it causes them to grow to enormous size, eventually breaking free of their cages before disappearing into a local mine, where, in a clear homage to films like *Them!* (seen playing on TV at one point), they get bigger and bigger...

After a ten-year absence, Chris McCormack (David Arquette) returns home just in time to combat the oversized arachnids, with more than a little help from "the sexiest sheriff in the county" Sam Parker (Kari Wuhrer), her rebellious teenage daughter Ashley

(Scarlett Johannson), and a paranoid radio DJ Harlan (Doug E. Doug). While the cast does a more than serviceable job, the film's title (changed from the original "Arach Attack" after the events of 9–11) tells you who the real stars are: the spiders. And there are plenty of them, the most memorable being the jumping spiders who leap several feet in the air to pounce on their prey, and Consuela, a massive female "orb weaver" which presents the greatest challenge to our heroes (Chris' method of combating the beast is, if nothing else, original). Some of the film's early sequences are genuinely amusing; one such is a *Hills Part II*–style dirt bike chase (one of the few scenes to take advantage of the film's Arizona location shooting), in which a group of teenage racers are pursued by a horde of plus-size jumpers. Another borderline kinky scene finds Ashley menaced in her bedroom by a giant arachnid that crawls through the window, pins her against the wall and sprays her with goopy webbing (better not to read too much into it).

Unfortunately, later scenes depicting the "giant spider invasion" (to borrow the title of Bill Rebane's cheaper but much more fun 1974 movie) have a distinctly Emmerich/Devlin sensibility, favoring widespread chaos and rampant overuse of CGI over isolated attacks, as armies of computerized arachnids skitter over cars, buildings, and people. In a mad race to top itself every five minutes with ever-more-preposterous set pieces, logic or intelligence fall by the wayside, as the locals retreat into a mining tunnel which conveniently connects directly to a shopping mall. Although the filmmakers strive for a *Tremors* vibe, *Freaks* lacks that film's careful tonal balance, one of a kind graboids and easy, naturalistic rapport between its leads, instead feeling like the less campy cousin of Warner's recent SF/comedy *Mars Attacks!* (1996). Though far from unwatchable, *Freaks* misses the creeping terror—and more purposeful use of desert locations—found in those early big-bug movies that it so desperately wants to emulate.

While most installments of the various budding desert terror franchises managed to reach shelves within a few years of their previous entries, *The Hitcher II: I've Been Waiting* (2003) is a much more belated affair, arriving (in what must be some kind of record for time passing between installments) a staggering *seventeen* years after the first film's release. Whether mainstream audiences were "waiting" for it or not, this straight to video sequel to one of the all-time desert terror classics easily qualifies as a must-rent, if only to see how a new team of filmmakers (only lead C. Thomas Howell and producer Charles Meeker encore) would extend a story which ended on such an uncomfortably ambiguous note. Much like the ill-fated *Hills Part II* (which at least saw Wes Craven return as writer/director), *Hitcher II* is not a complete disaster, but a mostly competent effort that inevitably suffers from comparisons to its far superior parent.

A storm-swept opening finds Jim Halsey (Howell), now a cop, rescuing a small boy from a kidnapper. After Jim is fired for using excessive force, his pilot girlfriend Maggie (a likable Kari Wuhrer, in her second desert terror movie in as many years) convinces him to take a therapeutic road trip to Texas to visit his old friend Captain Esteridge (Stephen Hair), who intervened on his behalf in the first film. Plagued by traumatic flashbacks to his encounter with the Hitcher, Jim resists picking up a stranded motorcyclist during a blinding dust storm. Maggie, who doesn't know Jim's troubled past, allows "Jack" (Jake Busey) into their car, and before you can say John Ryder, their evasive new passenger pulls a gun. While they're able to force him out, Jack quickly commandeers a passing big rig, posing as a trucker (wearing a wig and cowboy hat, in the first of many disguises) while killing a cop (an uncredited Steve Railsback) and wounding Jim in a bloody shootout. After escaping, Jim finally confesses his dark past to Maggie, groaning, "it's starting again."

It seems The Hitcher is back for a second round of mayhem, as Jack channels the sadistic spirit of the original film's relentless psychopath. Although Jim insists "He doesn't look the same, but it's him. I know it's him," Jack *does* bear a more than passing resemblance to Rutger Hauer's Ryder—at first, anyway, sporting a dark trench coat and blonde hair. And yet Busey's over the top performance (which recalls his father's shameless mugging) couldn't be more different than Hauer's cold, enigmatic portrayal, which suggested infinite evil beneath a stoic surface. Instead, Jack is given to Freddy Krueger–style wisecracks (when asked "Why are you doing this?" his jaw-dropping response is "Sometimes you just get tired of watching television.") and adopting one increasingly ridiculous look after another, the most laughable being a line cook's apron and hat, as he severs his own finger and chucks it in the deep fryer as a half-hearted "homage" to the original film's french fry scene. In many ways, the film's schizophrenic treatment of its title character is typical of the storyline, which jumps from one character or plotline to another, failing to truly involve the audience as the first film did.

Along with retooling its main villain's persona into that of a merry prankster, the script (which remains the sole writing credit of all three screenwriters, one of whom is producer Meeker) makes a drastic decision to kill off Jim more than midway through, effectively severing its only connection to the original outing and leaving the film to rest on the shoulders of Wuhrer. The remainder of *Hitcher II* mimics the first film, as Jack frames Maggie for a series of violent crimes; unlike the original's surreal creepiness, there's a tiresome repetition to these frantically edited, overly noisy sequences, finally leading to a combustible finale which tries to outdo Harmon's film, as Maggie, piloting a plane, faces off against Jack, behind the wheel of a big rig. While surely more outrageous than anything in the first film, it's also highly unbelievable, and lacks the emotional pull necessary to sweep us up in the action. "Who the hell are you?" Maggie screams as, in another homage to the original, she ties the Hitcher between the cab and trailer of his truck. "What? And spoil all the fun?" is his smartass response. As before, the Hitcher remains unknowable—only this time, we don't care.

Although *The Hitcher II* disappoints on several levels, the dogged professionalism of the filmmakers and cast keeps it from becoming a complete embarrassment. Howell does the most with his truncated part, while Wuhrer turns in one of her most memorable performances with a physically and emotionally demanding role. *Bats* helmer Louis Morneau directs in a frenzied, eager-to-please visual style, with frequent use of Steadicam, jumpy editing, and colored filters, which make the negative looks like it went through a dust storm. While lacking in atmosphere, at least the film's not boring, with its many well-executed action sequences retaining a more expensive (and explosive) look than one usually expects of straight-to-video sequels. In yet another example of runaway production, *The Hitcher II* was shot entirely on location in Alberta, Canada, yet most of its desert locations display an authentically rugged, occasionally majestic, Southwestern feel. Unfortunately, the film's technical prowess is in service of a mediocre screenplay which, by diluting its villain and killing off its only link to the past, fatally ignores what made the first film great.

The same year *The Hitcher II* debuted on video, Universal brought its favorite creature feature franchise to the Syfy cable channel with *Tremors* TV series (2003). Canceled after one season (four episodes of which were directed by *From Dusk Till Dawn 3*'s

P.J. Pesce), the show picks up where the third film left off, bringing back series hero Burt Gummer (Michael Gross) and his personal "white whale," the albino worm El Blanco. The series' untimely demise, however, did not stop the studio from green-lighting *Tremors 4: The Legend Begins* (2004), which, as the title implies, serves as both an origin story of both the town of Perfection and the franchise's most enduring monsters. Following in the footsteps of *The Hangman's Daughter*, *The Legend Begins* is a period piece set around the turn of the century (1889, to be exact, which places it roughly one hundred years before *Tremors*' release date), when the West was still wild and no one had yet seen (or even heard of), a graboid.

After a mine outside the town of *Rejection*, Nevada ("Maybe we need a different name," remarks one character early in the film) is invaded by giant worms (dubbed "dust dragons" by the locals), most of the surviving townspeople flee, leaving only a small collection of hardy souls behind, including Chinese shopkeeper Pyong Chang (Ming Lo), Mexican miner Juan (Brent Roam), hotel proprietor Christine Lorde (Sara Botsford) and Native American Tecopa (August Schellenberg). The motley group is soon joined by wealthy, and unworldly, mine owner/Burt's ancestor Hiram Gummer (Gross), who, eager to reopen the mine, attempts a search and destroy mission with Juan and a few remaining miners. After the creatures feed on everyone but Gummer and Juan, a more radical solution arrives in the person of experienced, and slightly sinister, gunfighter Black Hand Kelly (Billy Drago). Kelly is no match for the monsters, either, leading Gummer and the desperate locals to take up arms against the underground invaders in a series of showdowns above, and beneath, the streets of Rejection.

Although conceptually promising, this western-inflected chapter in the *Tremors* saga comes as somewhat of a letdown after the irreverently entertaining *Tremors 3*. Scott Buck's script takes far too long setting up the situation and characters, with an overreliance on corny platitudes ("being full-growed don't make you a man") and silly sight gags. *Tremors II* director S.S. Wilson (who once again shares story and exec producing credit) applies a stately visual style that accentuates the film's pacing issues while also drawing unwanted attention to some of the less-than-impressive production values. Most of the monster action (handled by the ubiquitous KNB EFX this time around, whose new contributions include a baby graboid) is heard rather than seen, with the first on-camera attack not occurring until halfway through the film, and those that follow feeling overly familiar. Despite its western theme, the film's scope is sadly limited, with its desert material mainly confined to horseback-riding montages or a few nighttime scenes.

Over four films and fourteen years, Gross' "Burt Gummer" has become increasingly significant in the *Tremors* franchise, growing from an oddball supporting character to an unlikely leading man. He's fun in this, too, as an opportunistic, selfish man who undergoes a metamorphosis of his own, gradually coming to care for the inhabitants of Rejection while simultaneously discovering a passion for firearms. The lampooning of America's gun fetishism, which traces its roots back to the old west, has been a series trademark, but here, the irony of previous chapters is discarded in favor of a more straightforward, and softer, approach. Similarly, the film's attempts to address the realities of immigrant life through a mixed bag of ethnicities come off as unrealistic (there are no real racial tensions within the group) and reductive. While the townspeople's final stand is intended to invoke fond memories of Ron Underwood's original, it feels forced and indicative of a franchise which, after years of re-inventing itself with different writers, cast members and locations, has finally run out of ideas. Perhaps sensing this, Universal allowed the series to lie dormant for ten years before putting anther sequel into production.

Although mid–'90s hits like *Natural Born Killers* and *From Dusk Till Dawn* had bolstered mainstream interest in the desert terror, by the mid–2000s the studios had largely consigned the genre to lower budget, straight to video productions. While some of these films diverted from formula, none of them reached as wide an audience, or were nearly as impactful, as their forebears. At the same time, a second wave of grindhouse-inspired filmmakers, like Eli Roth, Alexandre Aja, and James Wan, continued the trend begun by pioneers Tarantino and Rodriguez a decade earlier, creating a series of gory horror hits like *Cabin Fever* (2003) and *Saw* (2003). One of the best-known and most controversial members of this new breed was Rob Zombie, the former White Zombie frontman-turned-filmmaker, whose long-delayed debut *House of 1,000 Corpses* (2003) was an obvious love letter to drive-in and exploitation greats of the '60s and '70s. While the dark and claustrophobic *House* mimicked the rural horror vibe of films like *The Texas Chainsaw Massacre* and *Tourist Trap*, its road-movie sequel *The Devil's Rejects* (2005) clearly looks to the desert terror genre for inspiration, with visual and thematic references to *The Sadist*, *The Hills Have Eyes*, *Blood Shack* and many more.

Appropriately set in 1978, the story opens with self-proclaimed "devil slayer" Sheriff Wydell's (William Forsythe) raid against a literal Barn of the Naked Dead occupied by the murderous Firefly family, along with dozens of their victims' bodies. During the ensuing shootout, Otis (Bill Moseley) and Baby (Sheri Moon Zombie) escape while Mother Firefly (Leslie Easterbrook, replacing *House*'s Karen Black) is captured. Firefly patriarch, the clown-faced Captain Spaulding (Sid Haig), gets a call from Baby, asking him to meet her and Otis at an out of the way desert motel, the Kahiki Palms. There, Baby and Otis make captives of touring country act "Banjo and Sullivan" (Lew Temple and Geoffrey Lewis) and their wives, on whom the pair of deviants inflict a series of increasingly brutal acts. Otis forces Roy's wife Gloria (Priscilla Barnes) to strip, then violates her while the gleefully unhinged Baby forces Adam's young spouse Wendy (Kate Norby) to strike Gloria repeatedly. Otis takes Roy and Adam to an isolated stretch of desert, where he murders them both. Baby eventually slays Gloria but the worst is saved for Wendy, who is forced to wear a mask made from her husband's facial skin before being turned loose outside, where she's swiftly splattered by a passing big rig.

After this section, which plays like a hyper-sexualized (and more graphically violent) version of *The Sadist*'s by-now iconic hostage scenario, Zombie moves the reunited Firefly family back on the road for an extended visit with Spaulding's pal Charlie (Ken Foree), who runs a backwoods whorehouse. After Wydell and his bounty hunters crash the party, the sheriff transports the Fireflys back to the farmhouse where it all began, torturing them by staple-gunning photos of their victims to Baby's chest and driving nails through Otis' hands. A last-minute appearance by deformed giant Tiny (Matthew McGrory) saves the freakish family from the psychotic lawman, but they still can't escape their fate, as a police barricade blocks their escape route. As Lynyrd Skynyrd's "Free Bird" fills the soundtrack, Spaulding, Otis and Baby trade bullets with the law in one final, gleefully self-annihilating *Bonnie and Clyde*-style bloodbath.

The first significant studio-financed desert terror film of the 2000s, *The Devil's Rejects* is a true road trip to Hell, in every way bigger, brighter, and bolder than its predecessor's oppressive yet repetitious carnival of carnage. Louder, more sadistic, and even more proudly derivative than the groundbreaking *From Dusk Till Dawn*, Zombie's sophomore effort is also more expansive, yet suffers from scattershot scripting and a forced, exaggerated stylistic approach. Despite the title, the film's only narrative thrust is provided by Wydell, whose obsessive quest to avenge his lawman brother's murder compels him to track the Fireflys from one location to another. Despite clearly being in love with his own creations, Zombie restricts his focus to the superficial, with no interest in seriously exploring the individual family members' pasts, or even establishing strong, distinctive personalities for them (as one finds in, for example, the families of *Chainsaw* or *Hills*). While its visuals and locations are authentically grungy, the film remains psychologically vacuous, lacking the occasional attempts at insight found in *Natural Born Killers* or *Kalifornia*.

Zombie's unadulterated love for the '70s golden era of exploitation is much in evidence, as he ladles on gratuitous nudity and gore from the very first shots and frequently indulges in flashy mannerisms (freeze frames, slow motion) associated with the period. The casting, too, tries hard to revive the spirit of classic cult films, with even the smallest roles played by genre icons (Michael Berryman, Steve Railsback, PJ Soles). While it's fun to see so many familiar faces together in one project, the overall effect is weirdly distancing and, like many of the director's creative choices, feels overly self-conscious. Of the principal cast, only Forsythe's Wydell registers as a three-dimensional character, convincingly batshit whether giving a speech about "the cleansing of the wicked" before raiding the farmhouse or repeating "Lord, I am your arm of justice" while staring down his reflection. In a film in which everything is hyperreal, Forsythe keeps pace with the insanity around him while never straying into campiness.

The Devil's Rejects is the logical extension of the blood n' guts B-movie revival begun by *From Dusk Till Dawn* ten years earlier, with its emphasis on gross-out gore, fanboy casting, and frenzied storytelling that dispenses with character depth, logic, and any truly transgressive content. More than Rodriguez' film, *Rejects* is truly a movie about movies, and therefore never reaches the depraved heights of its more inspired and unselfconscious inspirations. Far from a serious updating/rethinking of the genre, the result comes dangerously close to the most expensive, well-made fan film ever produced. Its flaws, however, are almost as fascinating as its attributes, and it remains worthy of examination, with many desert terror classics name-checked throughout its two-hour running time. While failing to add anything truly new to the desert terror pantheon, *Rejects* was nevertheless essential for its growth, as its successful release, along with the well-received remakes of *The Texas Chainsaw Massacre* (2003) and *Dawn of the Dead* (2004), would lead to a period of renewed studio interest in the genre over the coming years.

Ten years after the mediocre *Quicksilver Highway*, Mick Garris and Stephen King reteamed to create a much more complex, and satisfying, slice of desert terror with a large-scale adaptation of King's novel *Desperation* (2006). An original, atmospheric, and at times genuinely chilling work, the made-for-TV film spins a richly layered (but rarely confusing) tale out of a handful of characters, a middle-of-nowhere desert town, and an ancient, immortal evil. Despite its small screen origins, the King/Garris collaboration boasts the cast and production values of a theatrical film, as well as a level of intensity and violence that goes far beyond network allowances (while originally broadcast in a softer version on ABC, Lionsgate's subsequent DVD release reinstates some R-rated language and gore). At 131 minutes, *Desperation* is not only one of the lengthiest desert terror films ever made, it just might qualify as the genre's first epic.

The story unfolds at an unhurried pace, as the amusingly-named Peter Jackson

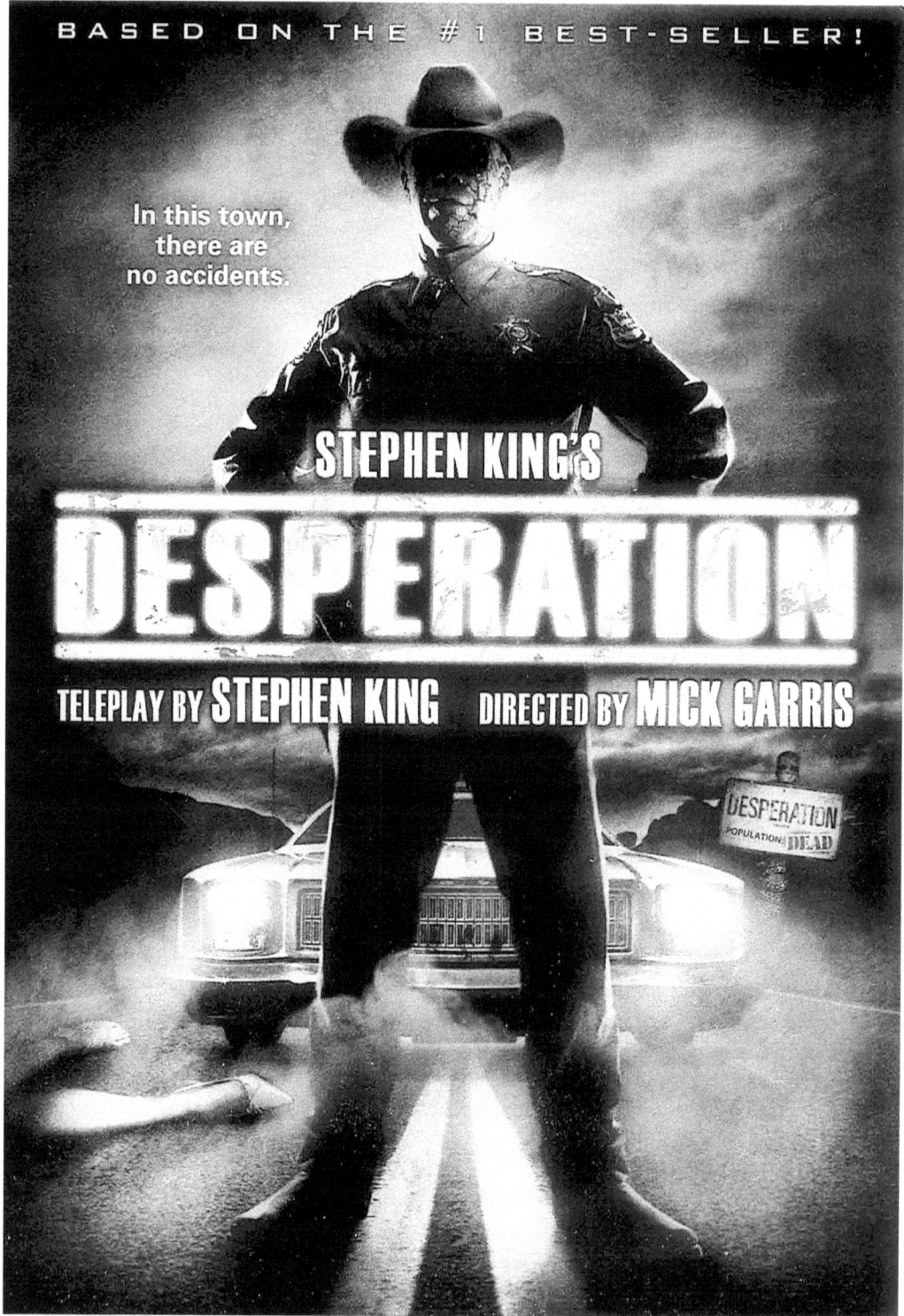

Originally broadcast on ABC, *Desperation* (2006) was later released in a longer, R-rated version on DVD.

(Henry Thomas) and his wife Mary (Annabeth Gish) are pulled over and arrested by physically threatening and psychologically unbalanced local cop Collie Entragian (Ron Perlman) while driving along a barren desert highway. After transporting them to a literal ghost town whose main street is strewn with corpses and vultures, Collie kills Peter and locks Mary up with fellow prisoners Ralph Carver (Matt Frewer), his wife Ellie (Sylvia Kelegian), their son David (Shane Haboucha), and the town's only surviving resident, historian Tom Billingsley (Charles Durning). Soon to join them is famous novelist and reformed alcoholic John Marinville (Tom Skerritt), whose book tour is interrupted by the increasingly monstrous Collie. While searching for his boss, Marinville's roadie Steve (Steven Weber), along with quick-witted hitchhiker Cynthia (Kelly Overton) eventually arrives in the cursed town of Desperation, Nevada, which feels like the more macabre sister city of *U-Turn*'s comically hellish Superior, Arizona.

After Collie takes Ellie to the local mine, David (who has extrasensory abilities and speaks in religious platitudes) finally escapes the jail and—after a hellish tour of the town—sets the others free. After meeting up with Steve and Cynthia, who have also uncovered plenty of horrors in Desperation, the group takes shelter in a long-shuttered movie palace. While discussing their nightmarish situation, Tom mentions the "China Pit," a mineshaft full of Chinese laborers that collapsed 150 years ago, burying everyone alive. The town's cursed history is cleverly presented as a silent film, as miners accidentally release the ancient, malevolent spirit "Tak," which quickly possesses the workers and causes them to turn on each other. Though sealed up during a company-sanctioned cave-in, a recent reopening of the shaft has released Tak once again, leading to a revolt of the local wildlife and the decimation of the residents. "Something came out of that mine that never died, and never will," Tom says before his own life is cut short by one of the demon's four-legged followers.

There are plenty more twists (and scares) to come, as well as further character development (especially concerning King doppelganger Marinville, who emerges as an unlikely hero) along the way, and much of the enjoyment of Garris' large-scale stranded scenario is in following its twisted trail of supernaturally gifted kids, possessed lawmen and slithering desert denizens all the way till the hellish, Lovecraftian ending. While a few subplots stray a bit too far from the main narrative and David's Biblespeak feels a bit cloying at times, overall this is a compulsively watchable, original, and immersive desert terror film packed full of creepy imagery, quotable dialogue and memorable characterizations. Perlman's Collie, in particular, is one of the nastiest, most unpredictable desert terror heavies of the new century, chanting lines like (in a possible nod to *NBK*'s Mallory Knox?) "Eany, meany, miney, moe. Catch a tourist by the toe. Don't you scream, don't you shout. The time has come to take you out" with gleeful menace that approaches, but never completely verges into, parody. In fact, Collie's presence is so strong that once he disappears from the narrative, a void is left that Tak, for all his armies of carnivorous critters and zombified slaves, is never able to fill.

Shot on location in Bisbee, Arizona, *Desperation* makes great use of the town's visual qualities and its troubled mining history is cleverly fictionalized in Tak's unusual backstory, which illuminates aspects of western history rarely seen in the genre. Striving for more than just simple frights, the film also functions as a thoughtful (if not always successful) consideration of the true power of one's faith in times of crisis; as Marinville remarks to David in one scene: "You want to know how cruel God is? Sometimes he lets us live." King also drops in several personal (and often self-deprecating) moments, such as Steve's comment that "I pretty much stick with Dean Koontz" or, on a more serious note, confronting Marinville's hard-drinking past or his literary demons (when Tak calls Marinville "a joke," the author dryly responds "I hate critics" before blowing the place up). Though not the first King work to reflect on the writer's life (*Misery* and *The Dark Half* are just two novels that come to mind), it is one of the few desert terror films to explore the subject with such thoroughness and lack of pretense. Garris applies just the right balance to King's sprawling vision, knowing exactly when to let the narrative breathe, and when to go for the jugular. In some ways resembling a scaled-down version of King's masterpiece *The Stand* (adapted by Garris into an eight-hour TV miniseries in 1994), *Desperation* is an effective miniature apocalypse and one of the better studio-produced desert terrors of the new millennium.

Only a year after Rob Zombie killed off his colorful family of killers at the end of *The Devil's Rejects*, the grindhouse remake trend was in full swing, with every studio searching for the titles to acquire and "reimagine." One of the first, and most commercially successful of these was *The Hills Have Eyes* (2006), a big-budget remake of Wes Craven's 1977 desert terror classic. Arriving almost thirty years after its predecessor, the new *Hills* (backed by 20th Century–Fox) saw original filmmakers Craven and Peter Locke returning as executive producers, with the creative reins handed to Frenchman Alexandre Aja, a relatively new talent whose previous feature, *High Tension* (2004), had opened to mixed reviews and dismal box office a few years earlier. Aja's *Hills* is a bigger, slicker, bloodier ride that benefits from its experienced cast (among them desert terror vets Ted Levine and Kathleen Quinlan), KNB's disturbingly realistic makeup effects, and a script that, most of the time, wisely honors its source material while attempting to creatively expand Craven's universe.

A gory prologue sets the stage for the carnage to come, as a group of scientists checking radiation levels in the New Mexico desert are massacred by a monstrous, pickaxe-wielding killer. An opening credits montage littered with mushroom clouds and hideous deformities gives way to the main narrative, as the all-American Carter family familiar from the original film—Big Bob Carter (Levine), his wife Ethel (Quinlan), and their children Brenda (Emile de Ravin), Bobby (Dan Byrd) and Lynn (Vinessa Shaw), along with her husband Doug (Aaron Stanford), their infant daughter Katy and the family German shepherds Beauty and Beast—arrives at an isolated gas station on their way to San Diego. Craven's character dynamics remain intact, with an extra edge given to the dialogue between macho Bob and cell-phone salesman Doug (described by Bob as "a Democrat … he doesn't believe in guns.") Rather than insisting the family stay on the main road as in the first film, the station's shifty attendant (Tom Bower) advises Bob to take a time-saving shortcut, essentially guiding the Carters straight into the hands of the freakish family living in the desert's mines and hills.

The film continues mimicking the original film's scenario as a hidden spike strip causes Bob to crash his truck, stranding the family deep in the desert where the surrounding hills prevent cell or radio service. Bob and Doug take off to look for help, while Bobby finds Beauty's mangled corpse far away in the hills. Doug's discovery of a crater full of junked cars and abandoned possessions is mirrored by Bob's return to the gas station, where he finds news clippings ("Military razes mining town") and photos of children with birth defects. The late-night invasion of the Carters' camp by mutants Pluto (Michael Bailey Smith) and Lizard (Robert Joy), which ends with Bob and Lynn dead, Ethel dying, and Katy abducted, provides Aja with a chance to fashion his own take on one of its predecessor's most grueling sequences. Though some aspects (such as Bob's fiery death) feel overdone, others, such as Brenda's rape and Lynn's humiliation and subsequent murder, improve effectively on the source material. We also get our first real look at the film's villains, who up till now have only appeared fleetingly. In a clear departure from the original film's inbred, animalistic yet recognizably human family, these hills are home to a group of raging, freakish, barely coherent monsters. While it's debatable which film's antagonists are scarier, any attempt to create a comparison between the two families, or show how one must mimic the other to survive, is replaced by a more simplistic "humans versus monsters" viewpoint.

The next few sequences delve further into the mutants' world as Brenda and Bobby stay behind while Doug and Beast leave to find Katy. After traveling through a mine tunnel, Doug finds a haunting, abandoned nuclear test village where the mutants have been surviving for years. There, he encounters a few new members of the family, including the grotesque Big Brain (Desmond Askew), a wheelchair-bound freak with a massively oversized and misshapen cranium who rasps, "Your people asked us to leave ... destroyed our homes. You made us what we've become." While this lends the mutants an interesting (and unique) backstory and gives the film an unexpected political dimension, it's largely lost in the subsequent barrage of gore and body parts, as Doug is pursued through a claustrophobic, *Chainsaw*-like house of horrors before finally killing Pluto. The film reverts to the original's structure for its final act, as Brenda and Bobby kill Papa Jupiter (a barely glimpsed Billy Drago) as Doug takes on Lizard, with the assistance of helpful mutant Ruby (Laura Ortiz), to save Katy. Doug's final reunion with Bobby and Brenda looks to be short-lived, as a pair of eyes (whose?) watches them from afar.

One of the better-received remakes of the period, *The Hills Have Eyes* preserves the original's potent atmosphere of danger and desolation while continuing its theme of normal folks pushed to animalistic extremes. Standing apart from other contemporary remakes (*The Fog, When a Stranger Calls*), Aja's hyper-violent, gore-drenched update not only embraces the savagery that defined Craven's film, but pushes it even further. Even more importantly, the film avoids mocking its inspiration, with its departures from the original narrative executed in roughly the same spirit of the first *Hills*. Aja is crueler to his characters than the more sensitive Craven, but it's nice to see the Carter clan return wholly intact, even if de Ravin's transition from spoiled but likable teenager to hardened (but still shaken) survivor is more believable than Doug's shift from helpless nerd to Doug the Monster Slayer. The film's new family of mutants, however, makes less of an impression than the twisted brood in Craven's original. Despite their extreme (and unique) physical features, Big Brain and company lack both the individual personalities and social structure (patriarch Jupiter, so commanding in the first film, is curiously relegated to the sidelines here) that allowed Craven to easily draw provocative comparisons between the two groups.

If Aja and co-writer Gregory Levasseur fail to create a recognizable family unit for their freaks, they make up for it with their politically charged backstory. Craven's script only hinted at the atomic-age origins of the cannibal clan's desert home, the new *Hills* uses it as a chance to create an entirely new race whose physical deformities and animalistic urges are, the story implies, less caused by inbreeding than by the radioactive effects of postwar nuclear testing in the area. It's an interesting, if shakily developed, idea, as only Ruby (whose role here, like Jupiter's, is diminished) is remotely sympathetic, while her brethren are portrayed less as suffering victims of nuclear fallout than psychotic, drooling monsters that derive sadistic pleasure from raping and pillaging. In the end, the script abandons any attempt to humanize its mutants, in the process drawing an uncomfortable line between early images of babies with birth defects and bloodthirsty adult "monsters."

Alongside its conspiracy theory subtext, *Hills* 2006 also attempts a muddled critique of American conservatism. Trigger-happy Bob mutters "praise God and pass the ammunition" as he whips out a pair of pistols, while Ethel's family prayer gathering feels hopelessly old-fashioned. The stars and stripes appear repeatedly (Ethel has a flag on her sweater, Doug uses a decorative flag from the family truck to kill Pluto) and Big Brain is first introduced singing the national anthem. Aja's "ironic" appropriation of such patriotic imagery comes off as immature and undercooked, with any progressive politics abandoned as pacifist Doug goes Rambo and exacts bloody revenge on the mutants, one after another. Far from the tortured soul of Craven's original (who only committed one murder, with Ruby's assistance), Aja's battle-scarred Doug is framed as a western-style hero, complete with low angle framing and triumphant theme music. More interested in delivering bigger and better shocks than developing its own personality, the remake remains more of a technical achievement than a successful advancement of the themes and situations set forth by Craven's film.

If granted a larger budget and wider release than any of the decade's previous desert terrors, Aja's *Hills* subscribes to the contemporary studio trend of shooting in desert environments outside the United States. In this case (and a first for the desert terror genre), the film was shot entirely on location in Morocco, whose serviceable yet slightly alien desert environments differ considerably from their more familiar Southwestern counterparts. The topography's flattened-out, featureless appearance lacks the distinctive homegrown details one associates with the original *Hills* (gone is the first film's iconic rock pile, and the only time we see a Joshua tree—which appears frankly phony—is during Bob's fiery death), or other stranded scenarios taking place in similar settings. To distract from the bland backdrops, Aja sends his camera swooping through a series of intricate, overly stylized sets (gas station, crater, the nuclear test village), most of which fail to duplicate the lived-in realism or cramped intimacy of the original film's environments.

After *Hills'* over-the-top take on desert terror resulted in box office success ($41 million gross on a budget of $15 million), a theatrical sequel was immediately put into production, shooting once again in Morocco and with Wes Craven assuming a more active creative role. Scripted by Craven and his son Jonathan Craven, *The Hills Have Eyes II* (2007) continues the casually violent, dehumanizing tone established by Aja's remake, introducing an even more monstrous (and sadistic) gang of mutants along with more obvious political content in a storyline that occasionally recalls Craven's own much-derided 1984 sequel. Set two years after the events of the previous film, the sequel's grim tone is established as a bloodied, naked young woman chained in a darkened cell gives painful birth before being bludgeoned by an unseen figure. In the New Mexico desert, a group of military technicians are attacked by cannibals while installing surveillance equipment. A group of national guard trainees are next to arrive in the infamous hills, where a routine equipment delivery turns into a struggle for survival as the would-be soldiers come under attack from a hideous clan of cave dwellers far worse than anything they might encounter in Afghanistan.

The first half of *Hills II* plays like a slasher-style body count picture, as a rescue expedition leads to a series of bloody encounters with a new, more vicious tribe of savages led by the brutish Papa Hades (Michael Bailey Smith, Pluto in the *Hills* remake), whose interest is primarily in abducting the female members of team for "breeding." After picking off most of the trainees (by high falls, dismemberment, and—most creatively—literally drowning in feces), the mutants capture female member Missy (Danielle Alonso) and hide her deep within a network of mines, where she is raped by the drooling Hades. Trapped on the hilltop with no other way down, survivors Amber (Jessica Stroup), Napoleon (Michael McMilian), Delmar (Lee Thompson Young) and hot-headed Crank (Jacob Vargas) journey into the mines with hopes of escaping to the bottom, and saving Missy along the way.

Like recent follow-ups to *From Dusk Till Dawn* and *Vampires*, *Hills II* functions as more or less a stand-alone sequel, featuring an entirely new group of characters (humans and cannibals) doing battle in the previously established desert/mine setting. This is not necessarily a bad thing, as such attempts to integrate previous characters with a new narrative can often feel forced and awkward (see Craven's *Hills Part II*), and using a group of untested trainees as protagonists has all kinds of possibilities. Although the opening test exercise (in which dusty sets double for Kandahar) prepares us for further political commentary to come, the closest the film comes to exploring such ideas is throwaway lines like: "It's not the fucks in caves halfway around the world that keep me up at night. They're right here in the middle of our own goddamn base." The trainees are mostly interchangeable until whittled down to the final four survivors (Stroup stands out here, while McMilian, as Napoleon, inherits the "Doug" role), as are the cannibals, who are barely visible most of the time, and possess even less personality (or humanity) than the previous film's clan.

The film's biggest misstep, however, is its decision to set over half of the action within the mines, leading to a series of claustrophobic, shadowy standoffs that start to feel numbingly similar after a while. Director of photography Sam McCurdy (who shot the superior cave-horror movie *The Descent*) does a fine job with the limited space, but the shift to interiors ultimately makes *Hills II* feel like just another "kids in a house" horror flick, and less of an exercise in desert terror (The Cravens are clearly enamored of this type of scenario, as the original *Hills Part II* and 1995's sort-of Hills sequel *Mind Ripper* both use mines or underground bunkers in their storylines). Though lacking in character or atmosphere, *Hills II* does stand out as the most unconscionably cruel and ugly film in the series. Starting with its exploitative "mutants need women" premise, the film is relentlessly mean-spirited, with its scenes of rape and physical abuse passing from excessively brutal into the realm of misogyny. Hades' death, on the other hand, is almost comically drawn out, with Missy, Amber, and Napoleon using sledgehammers and bayonets to finally destroy the drooling monster. Aside from providing a not-so-spectacular ending to the franchise (for now, anyway), the film also initiated a spate of Middle-East themed "war horror" films including *The Objective* (2008), and *Red Sands* (2008), both of which were filmed in Morocco.

Hot on the heels of the *Hills* remake and its unnecessary sequel, another desert terror classic was re-imagined courtesy of Michael Bay's Platinum Dunes, the production outfit behind *The Amityville Horror* (2005) and *The Texas Chainsaw Massacre: The Beginning* (2006). Repeating the formula which Bay and company used on their previous films (hot young TV-friendly cast, novice screenwriter, experienced commercial/music video director), Dave Meyers' remake of *The Hitcher* (2007) differs less from its source than previous remakes, with a screenplay that apes the twenty-year-old original nearly beat for beat—to the extent that original screenwriter Eric Red was granted a co-writing credit on the film. Despite its slavish appropriation of familiar situations and dialogue, the updated *Hitcher* bears little resemblance to its predecessor, with its atmospheric visuals and twisted character dynamics transposed by a slicker, more "commercial" sensibility.

Like Louis Morneau's so-so sequel *The Hitcher II* (which had hit video stores just a few years earlier, and bears no connection to this film), the new *Hitcher* adds a third, female character to the story who eventually supplants the male lead to become the film's heroine. Driving late at night through the desert, plucky college student Grace (Sophia Bush) and her boyfriend Jim Halsey (Zack Knighton) have their Spring Break road trip interrupted by the arrival of psychotic vagabond John Ryder (Sean Bean). After making a few inappropriate comments about Grace ("How long you been fucking her?"), Ryder pulls a switchblade on Jim in a repeat of the first film's famous "I want to die" scene. While Grace and Jim kick the maniac out, he's not nearly done with them, as the film replays the original's most memorable sequences (the Hitcher riding with a family, the police station massacre) and dialogue ("Why are you doing this?" "You're a smart kid. You'll figure it out.") as Ryder perversely frames the duo for his own sadistic crimes.

The remake continues to crib as Grace and Jim seek refuge at a motel/truck stop, where the Hitcher attacks Grace (exclaiming "I'm horny, too!" as he leaps out at her) before capturing Jim and tying him between the cab and trailer of a big rig. In a predictable gender reversal of the original sequence, Grace must reckon with her tormentor while he threatens to release the brake. While her exchange with Ryder duplicates the Howell/Hauer original, the scene lacks the sickening horror of its inspiration; it is, however, more explicit, as this time, we *see* Jim getting ripped in half. Presumably hardened by the experience, Grace faces off against her nemesis after he escapes from police custody and kills every cop in sight, leaving only the two of them standing. "Feels good, doesn't it?" Ryder croaks after she shoots him in the back. "I don't feel a thing," she mutters before blowing his brains out.

I didn't feel anything, either, and that's the problem with this *Hitcher*; even more than the *Hills* reboot, the 2007 film merely ports over and amps up key horror/suspense scenes from the original while jettisoning the accompanying character or story content. While Grace's graduation from screamer to ass-kicking heroine is typical of the period (a standard begun in Bay's *Chainsaw* redux), it's not an unwelcome change, and even has the potential to steer the Hitcher/Halsey relationship from the first film in new and interesting directions. Instead of capitalizing on the opportunity, the script simply repeats key situations with the Hitcher's focus split between two protagonists rather than one. While this approach might still have worked if Grace and Jim were more engaging characters, they're sketchily developed and spend much of their time either reacting to the Hitcher's attacks or arguing over whose fault it was to pick him up in the first place. Her boyfriend's death allows Grace to assume the "Jim Halsey" role C. Thomas Howell portrayed in the original film, but by this time, it's too late; the film has already lost its chance to create the crucial interpersonal dynamic between Grace and the Hitcher, robbing their final confrontation of any power it might otherwise have had.

Music video vet Meyers directs with a penchant for pop song montages, saturated colors and frantic editing that attempt to distract the script's deficiencies, but most of the time only makes them more apparent. A faintly sexual vibe between Grace and Ryder never amounts to anything, nor does the director's random use of religious imagery throughout, culminating in a car/helicopter chase improbably scored to Nine Inch Nails' "Closer." This sequence perfectly illustrates what's wrong with this remake; while Robert Harmon turned each car chase into a carefully orchestrated ballet of destruction, Meyers simply dumps the footage into an editorial blender and cranks the volume to eleven. Despite a fair amount of New Mexico location shooting, the desert environments are even weaker than those in the Canada-shot *Hitcher II* and are often obscured by the film's gloomy photography. On a more positive note, Bean stands out as a major improvement over *Hitcher II*'s manic Jake Busey, and his attempts to channel Rutger Hauer's otherworldly persona are occasionally effective. But like the rest of the cast, Bean is limited to the slavish conventions of a script that, while plagiarizing the 1986 film's text, utterly fails to capture (or continue) its spirit. Until some enterprising producer decides to update *Werewolves on Wheels* or *Blood Shack*, the 2007 *Hitcher* stands as the last of the desert terror remakes.

Exhibiting more originality than the *Hills* or *Hitcher* retreads, if still disappointing, is the Syfy channel movie *Sands of Oblivion* (2007). One of the few desert terrors to be based on historical facts (which have, over time, mutated into Hollywood legend), *Sands* opens with not one but *three* separate prologues. The first, set in ancient Egypt, introduces the film's monster, an Anubis-like "god of chaos" known as Im-La-Ra. The film then segues to 1923, where filmmaker Cecil B. DeMille (Dan Castellaneta) is shooting his epic *The Ten Commandments* in the Sahara-like landscape of Guadalupe Dunes, California. Im-La-Ra's spirit, imprisoned in Egyptian artifacts imported to the set as props, escapes and causes several unexplained deaths. Hoping to contain the danger, DeMille has the massive sets buried under the sand before departing. Lastly, the action moves eighty years forward to find Dr. Alice Carter (Morena Baccarin) and a team of students excavating DeMille's Lost City Site in a preservation effort before the entire area falls victim to coastal erosion. Unsurprisingly, Im-La-Ra is unearthed once more, to wreak further havoc in the present.

Aside from the dreadful Egyptian sequence, which leans heavily on a lethal combination of virtual sets and shoddy visual effects, the first half of *Sands* is mostly captivating. The '20s section successfully mixes fact (DeMille did shoot *The Ten Commandments* on location in Guadalupe Dunes and destroyed the sets afterward, to prevent their use in other filmmakers' productions) with obvious fiction, and the early present day scenes aren't bad either, as a variety of appealing characters are introduced. One of them, the elderly John Tevis (George Kennedy), we first meet as a boy on the silent film set (Tevis, too, is loosely based on various locals who frequented DeMille's set as children and returned to collect various artifacts from the Lost City over the years). Tevis' grandson, Iraq vet Mark (Victor Webster), lends a refreshingly realist point of view to the proceedings, as well as competing with Alice's estranged husband, archaeologist Jesse Carter (Adam Baldwin), for her attention.

The unearthing of the Lost City and Im-La-Ra's gradual escape from his tomb set the stage for a low-budget desert variant on slow-burn supernatural thrillers like *The Keep* (1982) and *Prince of Darkness* (1987). Unfortunately, the filmmakers are more comfortable with the usual monster-in-a-suit mayhem and even worse, more half-baked CGI manifestations (a giant snake made of sand is particularly cringeworthy) that conform to the usual (low) standards of Syfy-channel silliness. The second half of *Sands*, which unwisely leaves the desert behind for some dune buggy chases and even more visual effects, often feels like a different film entirely and effectively destroys whatever fragile atmosphere had been created by earlier excavation sequences. A missed opportunity in many ways, *Sands* is still worth watching for its unique historical angle and splendid location work; though not actually shot at Guadalupe Dunes, the vistas of California's Dumont Dunes provide a wonderfully scenic backdrop to the bloodletting.

The underperforming *Hills II* made Fox loathe to green light a third film in the franchise, but the studio wasn't above sequelizing one of its other recent desert terror hits. The direct to video *Joy Ride 2: Dead Ahead* (2008) is, like *Tremors II*, a bit late to the table, with seven years having passed since the modestly successful original. While lacking its predecessor's marquee names or major writing/directorial talent, it's in many ways more of a proper desert terror film than its slicker, more restrained predecessor. In his third desert terror credit, director Louis Morneau announces his more exploitative intentions during the pre-credits opener, as series boogeyman Rusty Nail finds a cruelly creative way to decapitate a topless prostitute. After incurring a breakdown on their way to Vegas, fiancées Bobby (Nick Zano) and Melissa (Nicki Aycox), her troublemaker sister Kayla (Laura Jordan) and Kayla's date Nik (Kyle Schmid) "borrow" a car from an isolated farmhouse. Responsible Mel mistakenly leaves her phone number at the house, which, of course, belongs to Rusty Nail. Rusty's abduction of Bobby from a diner restroom triggers a series of demands—communicated primarily through a CB radio—that force Mel (who Rusty gives the handle "Goldilocks") and her friends into increasingly dangerous situations.

"Heck of a joyride, isn't it?" chuckles the demented Rusty (this time, not voiced by the distinctive Ted Levine) as he plays one devilish prank after another on the terrified trio. Beginning with Rusty's request for Kayla's middle finger ("She gave me the finger. Now, I want it.") and progressing to a sleazy sequence in which shapely Mel is forced to strip to her undies in front of her tormentor's big rig, things get seriously warped after self-described "third wave emo punk" Nik is forced to infiltrate a trucker hangout in a quest for meth while dressed as a transvestite. Easily the film's most obnoxious character (and instigator of the car theft that sets off Rusty's revenge), Nik gains unexpected audience sympathy as he is made to endure a Russian roulette–style torture game as brutal and grisly as anything seen in the *Saw* or *Hostel* films. Kayla's fate, too, will shock for anyone expecting more of the jocular, bloodless thrills seen in the original *Joy Ride*. Several other gory incidents, many of them punctuated with black-humored punch lines ("Did you see the way that guy's jaw dropped?" Rusty laughs after bisecting a victim's skull), transport the unrated *Joy Ride 2* out of the thriller category and firmly into the rougher realm of hardcore horror.

In his second Canadian-shot desert terror sequel, Morneau again creates a serviceable desert atmosphere out of British Columbia's rocky landscapes, empty back roads, and out of the way motels and diners. In the process, the film achieves a more convincing desert atmosphere than John Dahl's original, even if the photography is occasionally marred by focus and exposure issues. The script, while lacking the novelty of the first film's CB concept, is well-paced and engaging, especially once Bobby is abducted. Aycox contributes a committed lead performance, and the entire enterprise has an endearingly scrappy, run-and-gun quality often missing from studio-produced desert terrors, especially sequels. The climactic confrontation between Mel and Rusty, which ends with the trucker's flaming vehicle taking a slow-motion tumble off a ravine, is more satisfying than *Joy Ride*'s tiresome multiple endings—and the closest approximation of *Duel*'s parting shot attained by any film since *Breakdown*. An unnecessary (and non-desert) coda sets up a third chapter, which arrived in the form of *Joy Ride 3: Road Kill* (2014). Declan O'Brien's Canadian-shot threequel dispenses with the desert locales of the series' prior entries while upping the sleaze and gore content in a manner more reminiscent of his contributions to Fox's other straight-to-video horror franchise, the *Wrong Turn* series.

After the expensive yet empty-headed violence of the last few years of sequels and remakes, a pair of more interesting studio offerings returned to the desert terror precursor genres of western and noir. The first of these was Lionsgate's *The Burrowers* (2008), which marries the creature feature and weird western genres. The film's understated tone, pastoral imagery (courtesy of *Devil's Rejects* director of photography Phil Parmet) and reserved approach to special effects represent a marked change from the rock n' roll excesses of the Rodriguez/Tarantino era. Set in the Dakota Territories in 1879, the story begins with the brutal murder of one family and the disappearance of the other. Assumed to be the work of the local Sioux Indian tribe, a search party led by local rancher Will Parcher (William Mapother) heads out to find the missing women, one of whom is engaged to be married to Irishman Coffey (Karl Geary). Accompanied by a military escort led by the sadistic Victor (Doug Hutchison), Parcher's group—which includes Coffey, teenage Dobie (Galen Hutchison), and old hand John Clay (Clancy Brown) soon spar with Victor over treatment of a Sioux captive. The Indian's mention of "burrowers" is largely ignored, even after several of Victor's men disappear unexpectedly during the night.

After separating from their escort, Parcher's men find further evidence of burrowers—strange holes in the ground, a woman buried alive—before the hideous quadrupeds themselves attack Parcher. "They were here before white people ... before humans," explains Faith (Alexandra Edmo), an Indian woman whose family was massacred by the monsters, who have turned to a new food supply following rampant slaughter of the buffalo. The burrowers' technique is akin to a spider, injecting their victims with a paralyzing poison and burying them underground before returning to feed on the host's organs and fluids. Coffey's determination to find his fiancée clashes with the ailing Parcher's plans, leading to a creepy confrontation with a horde of burrowers deep in the woods. While Coffey manages to destroy some of the creatures, an ironic, downbeat ending suggests that his efforts have mostly been in vain.

Written and directed by JT Petty (*Mimic 3*), *The Burrowers* joins *Hex, Into the Badlands* and *Mad at the Moon* as one of the handful of plains-set weird westerns. Unfortunately, the New Mexico locations lacks the dusty, rugged ambience or extreme topography typical of the genre, with its visual palette further muted by the filmmakers' choice to drain the images of color (much of the film appears almost black and white). Though intelligently written (Petty's script does a better job than say, *Tremors 4*, acknowledging the various ethnic groups who settled the West) and capably directed, for the most part this is still a cheerless, dour excursion that rests more on the tensions between the men than it does with their encounters with the title creatures. Seen only in darkness, the burrowers themselves are finally revealed more than halfway through the film, and truth be told, they're not that memorable, with a blobby, vaguely humanoid appearance and CGI-augmented movements that lack distinction. Coffey's climactic face-off against the creatures, while conceptually ambitious, is murkily photographed and suffers from the same lack of energy that hampers much of the film. Perhaps intended as a "thinking man's *Tremors*" and undoubtedly well-intentioned, *The Burrowers* resuscitates the weird western only to bury it under layers of pretension and dullness.

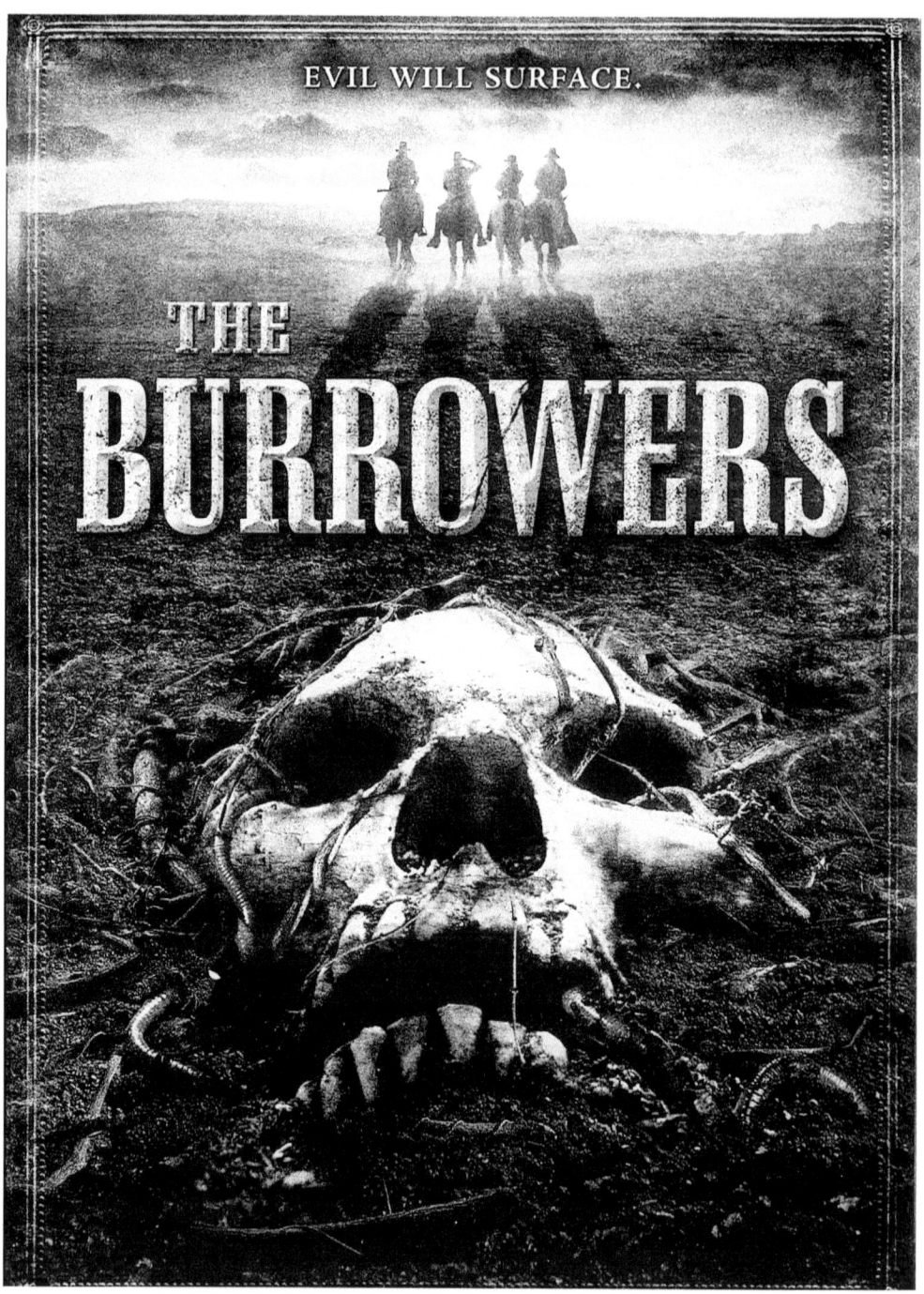

The Burrowers (2008) is a welcome if uneven return to traditional horror/western hybrids of the past.

Just as *The Burrowers* mines the genre's horror western past, the psychological thriller *Dark Country* (2009) celebrates nasty '40s and '50s noirs like *Detour* and *The Hitch-Hiker* as it follows a trio of shifty protagonists travel through an increasingly nightmarish desert landscape. The opening shots at a desert motel are bathed in seedy imagery, as Dick (Thomas Jane, who also directed) and his young wife Gina (Lauren German) start their new life together after a quickie Vegas wedding. Tough guy voice-overs and stylized lighting create a heightened, almost campy atmosphere, which becomes even more aggressive once the newlyweds hit the road. Driving through the night on their way to Sedona, Dick and Gina flirt (via a laughably unsexy sequence involving Beethoven's Ninth symphony and an ice cube) before almost hitting a horribly disfigured accident victim. Their attempts to help the aptly-named "Bloodyface" (also played by Jane)—who seems to know dark secrets about both of them—causes their honeymoon to go quickly to Hell amid a flurry of mistrust, recriminations, and violence.

Like the fractious relationship at its core, *Dark Country* is an ambitious yet flawed marriage of style and content. The film's merging of noir elements (femme fatales, double crossings) with gothic horror (the grotesque Bloodyface, bodies buried beneath the sand) is conceptually promising, but the schizophrenic visual approach and nonsensical screenplay work against its own modest goals. In a misguided attempt to mimic the comic book look of *Sin City* (2005), Jane douses his naturalistically lit New Mexico locations with gratuitous amounts of green screen, high-contrast color correction, and unnecessary visual effects. If this wasn't enough, the film was shot in 3-D (a decision ultimately made pointless by financier Sony's refusal to release it theatrically), which only registers in its most gimmicky moments. The result appears more like a post-production salvage job than the stylized homage that was probably intended.

The film's uneven visual approach doesn't completely spoil the film, but Tab Murphy's script frequently fails to provide the necessary twists and turns that would elevate the project beyond its obvious inspirations. While the "Vegas wedding" setup smartly illustrates its theme of hidden secrets and former lives, Dick and Gina remain ciphers from start to finish, with only a few amusing exchanges and dramatic meltdowns throughout their journey. Bloodyface's arrival threatens to push the film into more macabre territory ("Have you ever been murdered before?" he asks Dick cryptically) before eventually being discarded in favor of a third act which introduces new characters (including *Desperation*'s Ron Perlman as a highway patrolman) before spinning into a head-scratching, pseudo–Lynchian finale. The overall impression is of a promising yet overstretched concept that might have played better as one of the segments of a road-tripping anthology like *Nightmares* or *Creepshow 2*.

While intended as theatrical releases, both *The Burrowers* and *Dark Country* ultimately made their debuts on home video. The fate of these two flawed but interesting films amply demonstrates the prevalent studio attitude toward the desert terror genre at the end of the decade. Having retired (or relocated) all their desert-oriented franchises (*From Dusk Till Dawn*, *Vampires*, *The Hills Have Eyes*, *Joy Ride*) and uninterested in launching new ones, corporations like Sony and Fox simply moved on to less demanding locations and more generic subject matter. The studios' abandonment of big-budget desert terror, however, was far from fatal for the genre, as a new breed of independent filmmakers—working on budgets ranging from micro to millions—would once again return the form to its edgier roots while expanding it in many new and exciting directions.

11

Indie Invasion

"There is no place like the desert. It'll let you live off it for a while, and then one day, it just severs the friendship and swallows you up whole."—Jackie, *The Mummy an' the Armadillo*

The rise of the studio-financed desert terror film throughout the aughts coincided with an even more intensive spike in production on the independent side; for example, ten indie offerings were released between 2008 and 2009. Many of the new breed of desert terrors, however, were produced on budgets significantly lower than those in the past. While the consistently independent genre had traditionally been defined by films with smaller budgets and new talent, each successive decade witnessed desert terror moving further from its scrappy grindhouse and TV movie beginnings to a more comfortable "middle ground" budgetary area characterized by recognizable actors, solid production values and limited theatrical (or at least major home video) releases. This middle ground, however, began to erode throughout the 2000s, as the film industry endured a series of technological and infrastructure shake-ups that found the studios producing fewer, more expensive movies each year while independents scrambled to find financing and (even harder) return a profit. This dire state of affairs affected all movie genres, but was especially hard on the desert terror staples of mid-range, quirky horror films and thrillers.

Thankfully, the decreased budgets of the period did little to stop enterprising filmmakers from achieving an astonishingly diverse array of desert terror visions. Encouraged by the conspicuous successes of fans-turned-filmmakers like Tarantino, Rodriguez, and Rob Zombie as well as significant advances in digital cameras and editing software, numerous impassioned first-timers explored the genre from a variety of angles, often wearing many hats and supported with little more than a tiny cast and crew and some stunning desert locations. The most memorable of these works, like *Hell's Highway* or *Whispers from a Shallow Grave*, transcend their limitations, while others succumb to their lack of funds or (even worse) lazy storytelling. At the same time, the rise in popularity of film festivals allowed many independently-produced desert terrors to reach worldwide audiences and generate positive buzz and, in some cases, limited theatrical play in advance of their video debuts. There, these films joined a multitude of direct-to-video genre efforts (such as *Evil Sister II* and *666: The Demon Child*) financed and distributed by a new breed of scrappy upstarts like Brain Damage Films and The Asylum.

As a likely result of financial restraints, desert terror filmmakers working on all budget levels began to adopt a "New Minimalism" style, which pared their plots, casts, and locations down to the barest essentials. Initiated by controversial art-house dramas *Gerry* and *Twentynine Palms*, the loose movement soon grew to include genre-oriented likes of *Bone Dry, Dreamland, Blood River* and *The Canyon*. These minimalist desert terrors recalled the genre's humble beginnings, using as few as two or three actors, unpredictable plotting, and—most importantly—atmospheric desert locales to engage their audiences. In most of these films, stunning natural landscapes like Death Valley, the Mojave Desert and the Grand Canyon are explored with a heretofore unseen level of detail, resulting in some of the most impressive visual achievements in the genre since the more experimental '70s.

The increased focus on U.S.-based location shooting was a necessary antidote to the studios' outsourcing of their desert terror to overseas countries as distant as South Africa and Morocco, whose cost-saving yet generic backdrops failed to compete with their American counterparts. At the same time, a noticeable globalization slowly crept into domestically produced desert terrors on both sides of the camera. Directors from the UK, France and the Netherlands contributed to the genre, while casts also took on a truly international flavor, with Australian, British and Russian actors sharing screen time with American talent. These foreigners were not always cast as Americans, either; the more commercial *Reeker* films, for example, showcase main characters of South African and British descent. An unusually turbulent yet fruitful period, the years between 2000 and 2010 contain some of desert terror's bravest artistic accomplishments, with even the least of these films keeping the genre not only alive but vital as it marched into the next decade.

Twenty-first century desert terror began with a bumpy ride down *Carnage Road* (2000), a shot-on-video desert slasher that recalls the bare-bones filmmaking style of *Blood Shack*. Like that cash-strapped effort, Massimiliano Cerchi's film combines a Nevada desert location, some local talent, and the occasional spurt of blood to create horror on a pocket-change budget. After a photographer and his half-naked model are slaughtered by a maniac in a flight suit and a bizarre-looking mask, we meet four students on their way to *another* desert photo shoot; their white-trash driver (Mack Hail, director of indie horror movie *Mr. Ice Cream Man*) mentions a local legend called "Quiltface," who wears a mask made of human skin. When one of the group chuckles, "Sounds so cliché," the viewer can only nod in agreement. The remainder of this stranded scenario skews more *Friday the 13th* than *The Hills Have Eyes*, as the ill-matched group wanders around and bickers before Quiltface arrives to butcher them, one by one, with his trusty machete. The ending detours into *Texas Chainsaw* territory, as sole survivor Robert (Dean Paul) stumbles onto the junkyard dwelling of a Nam veteran (Mike Paulie) who reveals the maniac's true origin. Despite a "gotcha" ending that leaves the door wide open for *Carnage Road II*, a sequel has yet to materialize.

Triple-threat writer/director/producer Cerchi deserves credit for realizing his project with such obviously meager funds, but *Carnage Road*'s failings have nothing to do with budget. Aside from its bleak, rugged desert setting, the movie simply has nothing new to offer, serving up the same old tired characters and situations we've seen before in decades of third-rate slashers. Technically speaking, it's a disaster: scenes are filmed in jerky, excruciatingly long takes, with apparently improvised dialog (the cast get the giggles more than once), the victims all die in the exact same way, and sound effects and music are limited to a few basic effects/cues repeated ad nauseum. Far from earlier shot-on-video yet professionally-mounted productions like *High Desert* and *Ghost Gunfighter*, the micro-budget *Carnage Road* (released on video as *Carnage: The Legend of Quiltface*) lacks the necessary ambition or imagination to transcend its DIY roots.

Miles ahead of *Carnage Road*, *Route 666* (2001) is a slicker, more action-driven stranded scenario with a supernatural twist. Despite playing a significant role in defining westward expansion and tourism (and generating many of the accompanying fears of cross country travel), America's venerable "Mother Road" had never been portrayed in a horror film before. *Route 666* references established ideas of the nation's first superhighway, with its now-forgotten pit stops and roadside attractions, while creating its own original mythology along the way. Somewhere in Arizona, an intense gunfight takes place between a team of U.S. Marshals, led by Jack La Rocca (Lou Diamond Philips) and his colleague Stephanie (Lori Petty) and the Russian mob over federal witness Rabbit (Steven Williams). Barely escaping with Rabbit (and their lives), the agents have a limited amount of time to deliver their charge back to Los Angeles in time for a trial. Pressed for time, Jack chooses to venture onto an officially condemned road deep in the desert. Closed since 1969, "Route 666" is haunted by a quartet of vengeful ghosts who can appear and disappear at will and make bloody messes of their victims. Traveling along this cursed road leads to death and destruction for most of the agents, but allows Jack, who has a personal connection to one of the ghosts, a chance to make peace with his past.

Co-written and directed by William Wesley, whose *Scarecrows* remains a minor masterpiece of late–'80s indie horror, *Route 666* trades that film's slower pace and atmospheric chills for a testosterone-driven thrill ride peppered with high tempered shouting matches and bullet-riddled shootouts. Clearly indebted to recent action/horror/road hybrids like *From Dusk Till Dawn* and *Vampires*, the script is a nonstop gabfest peppered with scatological humor and pop culture chatter (the worst offender is Rabbit, who becomes tiresome very quickly but unfortunately makes it till the end). Thankfully, the film slows down enough now and then—usually via Jack's sudden flashbacks—to develop the four ghosts, a group of prisoners whose chain gang uprising was punished with violent death and burial beneath the road. While devoid of dialogue and not defined much beyond their weapons of choice (the end credits list three of them as "Pickaxe," "Sledgehammer" and "Jackhammer"), the convicts are at least original and make a strong visual impression, with grey skin the same color as their uniforms and hollowed-out eyes.

Wesley's decision to shoot most of the attack scenes with a constant shaky-cam effect may have been *au courant* at the time, but does nothing to increase the scare factor and quickly becomes confusing and annoying. Apart from this creative misstep, director of photography Philip Lee (*From Dusk Till Dawn 2*) gives the picture a bright, clean look, making the most of the stunning Joshua Tree State Park locations and the various outdoor sets (a desert cemetery, roadside attractions). The genre-friendly cast (which includes *Far from Home*'s Dick Miller in a small role) is mostly game, with Philips finding a nice balance between sincerity and humor, and western fixture L.Q. Jones bringing a nice sense of menace to his Sheriff Conaway. It's eerily appropriate that the final showdown with the undead takes place at an abandoned drive-in theatre, as by the time of this film's release, even medium-budgeted desert terrors (like this one) were bypassing theatres altogether and released straight to video. While it's never really disturbing, there are far worse places you could get your kicks than *Route 666*.

Two of my own directorial contributions to the desert terror genre, *Evil Sister II: Bound by Blood* (2001) and *Mad Jack* (2001) were also released around this time. A sequel in name only, the Euro-horror influenced *Evil Sister II* follows a handful of oddball char-

U.S. Marshal Jack LaRocca (Lou Diamond Philips) must combat the undead along *Route 666* (2001).

acters traversing the Mojave Desert whose paths occasionally cross, often with catastrophic results. Tam (Heather Branch) and her father (Joe Haggerty) search the roads for Tam's mute twin sister Lorna (also Branch), who inexplicably ran away from home and now occupies a trailer on the border of a dusty junkyard. The psychologically imbalanced Lorna occasionally draws men into her abode where she seduces and graphically murders them in an orgy of bloodshed before conducting even weirder private rituals in the middle of the desert. A pair of small-time thieves, Widow (Jarrod Robbins) and Jake (Jeff Loughridge), are drawn into the ever-tightening web of madness after Jake becomes Lorna's latest victim. Widow's chance encounter with Tam and her father leads to a series of revelations and conflicts, which ultimately result in the two sisters' tragic, bloody reunion.

LEO Films' artwork for *Evil Sister II* (2001) features a cover model who does not appear in the movie.

Although produced with more resources than *Evil Sister II*, *Mad Jack* is a smaller-scale affair, with a three-hander hitcher-killer plot modeled on European thrillers like *Knife in the Water* and *Hitch-Hike* (1977). Transposing the Polanski film's setting from open waters to the desert environs of the Southwest, *Mad Jack*'s story follows just-married couple Peter (Christopher Rydman) and Angel (Angela Ford)'s chance encounter with psychotic drifter Jack (Jack Wareing, who also executive produced), who is first introduced dispatching a terrified prostitute (Sarah Greenberg). Following a freak driving accident, Jack proceeds to manipulate the couple's trip, stranding them at a middle-of-nowhere desert motel where he carefully draws out their past transgressions, eventually driving the couple apart—and Angel into his arms. Angel's morning-after realization of her mistake leads to her discovery of the truth about Jack's murderous ways. A final, bloody desert showdown between Peter, Angel and their relentless, cold-blooded adversary finds the fractured husband and wife descending to new levels of savagery.

I'll leave it for others to discuss the comparative merits or flaws of these two films, both of which are low-budget attempts to marry Euro-horror narratives and visuals with the unmistakably American ambience conjured by the Mojave Desert locations (both

11. Indie Invasion

Widow (Jarrod Robbins) discovers the bodies of Tam (Heather Branch, left) and her father Frank (Joe Haggerty) in the gory climax of *Evil Sister II* (2001).

films were shot in and around Rosamond, California). In this respect, *Evil Sister II* is the more obvious of the two, with the mostly-silent Lorna/junkyard scenes clearly inspired by the works of Jess Franco and Jean Rollin; Oscar-winning film editor Bob Murawski once compared *Evil Sister II* to Franco's *Female Vampire* and *Blood Shack*, the latter of which I had not seen at the time. *Mad Jack*, on the other hand, is more indebted to American thrillers like *The Hitcher* and *The Drifter*, while twisting their plots in a more psychosexual direction. Both movies benefit from David Smith's photography, and they share some of the same locations (including the Bel Air Motel, which also features prominently in the first act of *From Dusk Till Dawn*). If nothing else, together they represent two of the first micro/low budget desert terrors to be shot in California, which would eventually become the new epicenter of the genre.

The debut in-house production of Arizona-based indie horror label Brain Damage Films (who released *Carnage Road* on video), *Hell's Highway* (2002) begins as a female variant on *The Hitcher* and gradually heads off on its own strange, individualistic path. Multihyphenate filmmaker Jeff Leroy (who wrote, directed, photographed, edited and contributed to the special effects) opens his idiosyncratic tale with a gruesome pair of killings, as a psychotic preacher (*Evil Sister II*'s Joe Haggerty) viciously stabs hitchhiker Lucinda (Phoebe Dollar) to death, then is murdered himself when Lucinda (now wearing red makeup) returns from the grave to split his head open with a shovel. Along the same desert road (nicknamed "The Devil's Highway" after a Donner Party–type legend), a pair of couples on a cross-country road trip notice Lucinda thumbing by the roadside. "This is how a lot of horror movies start," says blonde Monique (Beverly Lynne). "It's also how a lot of porno movies start," laughs her boyfriend Chris (Jon Prutow). They quickly come to regret picking up Lucinda, as she spins creepy stories, confesses to the

Top: Writer-director Brad Sykes and actress Angela Ford during a break in the filming of *Mad Jack* (2001). *Bottom:* Angel (Angela Ford) and Peter (Christopher Rydman) survive their savage encounter with *Mad Jack* (2001).

murders of Chris' brother and friends, and—after producing a pistol—violates Sarah (Brittany James) while forcing her boyfriend Eric (Mark Overholt) to videotape it. "My name's not Lucinda—but it's close enough," she giggles before the group finally forces her out of the car. As with the Robert Harmon classic it emulates (for a time, anyway), the seemingly immortal Lucinda continues plaguing the group in a series of nightmarish confrontations, as her *Vampires*-like psychic "link" with Sarah forces them all on a truly hellish journey from which few will return.

Shot on video on a tiny budget, *Hell's Highway* packs an absurd amount of entertainment value into its lean and mean seventy-minute running time. In many ways, it's an exploitation fan's dream, serving up wildly over the top gore, stylishly handled nudity, off-the-wall humor, and some surprisingly effective acting (along with Dollar's crazed performance, the four leads have decent chemistry, with Overholt and James particularly good in their roles). The real fun of the film, though—and what sets it apart from its contemporaries—is found in its repeated divergences from the expected hitcher-killer clichés. An adult anime-inspired nightmare finds Sarah menaced by a horned, tentacle devil-beast. Chris' wait for a phone call turns into a Sergio Leone homage, with pagers in place of six-shooters. Best of all, Lucinda hitches a ride with guest star Ron Jeremy (making good on that porn quote), playing a low-budget movie producer on his way to Arizona to sue the company who ripped him off. Leroy's skewering of the treacherous indie film business is dead-on and Jeremy is shockingly good in his brief role, but the funniest part is the punch line, as Lucinda dispatches her victim in a very uncomfortable (for male viewers) way. The use of old-fashioned miniatures to depict a subsequent car crash pushes the whole sequence even further into the realm of the bizarre.

For anyone expecting a straightforward *Hitcher* knockoff, *Hell's Highway*'s kitchen-sink approach can become dizzying, but for those who appreciate such irreverence, the film is a treasure chest of weirdness. Leroy plucks out a series of environmental details to create a hallucinatory Mobius strip of a desert terror film, where all roads inevitably lead to Lucinda—and death. Eric's video camera point of view adds an extra dimension of visual interest to several scenes—notably Lucinda's first meeting with the group and a revealing flashback witnessed through a flip-screen. While the storyline weathers most of its narrative digressions surprisingly well, the film goes slightly off the rails toward the end, as the formerly supernatural atmosphere is replaced with a head-scratching explanation out of a '70s sci-fi flick. Even this last twist, however, is somehow in character with the film's relentlessly bonkers, go-for-broke atmosphere, which conjures up a true grindhouse vibe better than the better-known (and far bigger budgeted) *Devil's Rejects*.

The following year's *Detour* (2003) was also filmed under the title *Hell's Highway* (and retained it for some overseas releases), but has very little in common with Jeff Leroy's far more original effort, and even less connection to Edgar G. Ulmer's classic noir. Produced by The Asylum, Steve Taylor's excursion into desert terror aims to imitate *The Hills Have Eyes* (certain story elements strangely predate the big-budget remake), but, in the end, falls far short of its modest goals. A by-now *de rigeur* pre-credits sequence features scream queen Tiffany Shepis (the only familiar cast member) and Renee Madison Cole as a pair of lesbians on their way to a desert rave whose plans are cut short by a hulking madman (Curtis Davidson, billed as "King Freak" in the credits) wielding a pair of meathooks. Post-rave, a group of seven ill-matched "friends" riding back to Los Angeles in an RV make a detour to check out a supposed peyote stash that they plan to steal and sell (such a nice group of kids). Following the warnings of a gas station attendant

The Asylum production *Detour* (2003) borrows its title and little else from the classic 1945 noir.

(Anthony Connell), the group finds themselves stranded, to use one character's eloquent expression, "a million miles from dick." It's only a matter of time before King Freak shows up to party, this time bringing along a posse of murderous maniacs.

Technically spotty and abysmally acted, *Detour* is an obnoxious little programmer that practically thumbs its nose at the audience with a smarmy, "we're so much smarter than this" attitude. The filmmakers tick off a grocery list of genre clichés (pre-credits kill; unlikable group of kids; creepy gas station guy) without adding a single new wrinkle to the formula. Among the most mean-spirited and superficially hip bunch of victims ever seen in a desert terror movie, the worst offender is wannabe rapper Loopz (Aaron Buer), whose look can best be described as "early–'90s Corey Haim" and whose rhyming act grows old after the first few minutes. Unfortunately, Loopz lives till the end of the film, by which time we've seen (get out your checklist): one pair of boobs, a few primitively-executed impalements and some of the lamest, most nondescript villains ever seen in the genre. The film does little with its generic north of L.A. desert locations and rarely attempts any kind of atmosphere, let alone set up a single convincing scare. Despite a prominently featured sign reading "Trespassers will be eaten," no actual cannibalism occurs in the film's excruciatingly inane ninety minutes. The Asylum would go on to produce and release an even less-inspired (but equally cynical) series of "mockbusters" timed to hit video stores at the same time as their better-known counterparts opened in theatres, including desert terror rip-offs like *Hillside Cannibals* (2006) and *The Hitchhiker* (2007).

Alongside the slashing antics of Quiltface, Lucinda, and company, the weird western enjoyed a mini-revival in the 2000s, with contemporary-set pictures including *Miner's Massacre* (2002), *Death Valley: The Legend of Bloody Bill* (2004), *After Sundown* and *The Quick and the Undead* (both 2006), and the Tim Thomeron–starring *Live Evil* (2009) introducing vampires, zombies and undead killers to classical ghost town and abandoned mine environments. The conceptually ambitious *Legend of the Phantom Rider* (2003) stands apart from its contemporaries in several ways, most noticeably in the filmmakers' choice to set their supernatural tale entirely in the past. The film's opening reaches even further back in time (to AD 1165), where a pair of Indian warriors fights to the death in the middle of a barren desert. This ancient battle for supremacy between good and evil replays itself, seven hundred years later, in the frontier town of Saugus, where murderous outlaw Blade (Robert McRyan, who also wrote the screenplay) and his gang of outlaws have taken control. Only strong-willed survivor Sarah Jenkins (Denise Crosby)—who is determined to exact vengeance after losing her family to Blade's attacks—dares challenge them, eventually invoking the assistance of the unfortunately-named Pelgidium (also played by McRyan), a silent, otherworldly gunfighter who might be the townspeople's only hope.

Bearing a title which smacks of '30s serials (smartly changed from the tongue-twisting *Trigon: The Legend of Pelgidium*) and marked by a straightforward photographic style, measured pace, and distinct lack of visual pyrotechnics, *Phantom Rider* is determinedly old-fashioned in its approach to the genre. The film's biggest issues rest with its enigmatic title character, who is initially set up as the good to counter Blade's evil, but gradually takes on a more muddled role in the proceedings. Conjured by a Native American medicine man, appearing only to scare off or kill Blade's men, and never interacting with other characters, Pelgidium remains frustratingly ill-defined, as if his sinister presence alone (in some scenes, the long-haired, black-clad figure looks like an Ozzfest refugee) is enough to keep audiences riveted to their seats as the film reaches its predictable conclusion. Blade is similarly undeveloped, with McRay's over the top performance failing to make up for a lack of backstory. The beleaguered Sarah is easily the film's most relatable character, but even she is saddled with spiritual baggage, as Blade allows her to live ("You are the one," he repeatedly tells her) only as some kind of conduit to his supernatural opponent.

Alex Erkiletian's stately direction, which favors wider compositions and longer takes, lends a nice sense of scope to the Arizona desert locations and allows the more dramatic scenes to breathe, but fails to conjure the necessary excitement during the more action-oriented scenes. Though teeming with shootouts, rapes, hangings and other gory acts of mischief, most of the film's violence is curiously muted. Thankfully, the filmmakers resist the impulse to indulge in trite visual effects during the film's supernatural passages, relying more on sound work and impressionistic lighting to convey the appropriately spooky atmosphere. Saddled with a script that demonstrates more imagination than consistency yet occasionally elevated by several memorable performances (Crosby and *Phantasm IV*'s Angus Scrimm as the town preacher are standouts), *Phantom Rider* emerges as a respectable stab at the weird western.

After several years dominated by lower-budget, "nu-grindhouse" films like *Carnage Road* and *Detour* (which predated the studios' own bloated efforts to capture the drive-in spirit), a pair of auteurist works steered the desert terror genre in a more dramatic, experimental direction while redefining its traditionally minimalist aesthetic. At first glance, Gus Van Sant's *Gerry* (2003) and Bruno Dumont's *Twentynine Palms* (2003) share more similarities than differences, as both films eschew traditional notions of both plot and character, instead tracking the meandering actions (or, in some cases, inaction) and non-sequitur dialogue of a pair of largely unknowable protagonists through a hostile desert environment. If less provocative than *enfant terrible* Dumont's sex-and-violence soaked treatise on the American (or is it European?) nightmare, the softer, quieter *Gerry* is perhaps the more surprising of the two films. Here, Van Sant reteams with his *Good Will Hunting* (1997) co-star/co-writer, Matt Damon, for a self-consciously artsy detour from the big-budget studio projects (remakes of *Psycho* and *Ocean's Eleven*) which had, for the past few years, defined both men's careers.

Gerry opens with one of many extended, fixed position shots, as Damon and Casey Affleck (both of whom, absurdly, play characters named Gerry) drive silently along a winding desert road, finally coming to a stop at a nondescript turnoff labeled "Wilderness Trail." For what seems like miles, the two men trudge through the desert, uttering only the occasional oblique comment ("We're halfway to the thing") to break the monotony. As the sky darkens, so does the mood; the self-assured Damon's decision to retrace their steps only gets the two men further lost amidst the nondescript terrain. The two friends (neither of whom carries gear or supplies of any kind) spend the night huddled around a makeshift campfire, muttering improvised dialogue (when Damon says, "I hate you," Affleck asks, "Not really, right?").

The following days, which increasingly bleed together to erode conventional notions of space and time, find the two Gerrys navigating a variety of threatening environments, from rocky peaks to breathtaking dunes to windswept mountain passes. Never particularly gregarious to begin with, the pair grows further apart both figuratively and literally, with the occasional disagreement (they never really agree on anything) replaced by oppressive silence. As they travel in circles, Van Sant's camera pulls further and further back to emphasize the two men's insignificance against a vast—and indifferent—landscape. Damon continues to assert control of the situation while Affleck crumbles under the strain, hallucinating before finally collapsing in the middle of an infinite salt flat. Soon, the film itself devolves into a series of sequences which approach the truly nightmarish, climaxing with an act of violence that feels both inexplicable yet weirdly natural.

As if testing Jean-Luc Godard's famous remark that all he needed to make a movie was "a girl and a gun," Van Sant employs only two actors, a desert setting, and a single understated murder to bring desert terror to extreme new levels of minimalism. Like so many other desert terror movies, *Gerry* is loosely based on a true crime case; here, the 1999 murder of hiker David Coughlin by his companion Raffi Kodikian after the two became lost in New Mexico's Rattlesnake Canyon. The resulting film, however, is less interested in recreating the circumstances of Coughlin's death than radically deconstructing the genre on both a narrative and visual level. There is no plot and the (few lines of) dialogue is mostly improvised; Damon and Affleck's monosyllabic exchanges do little to illuminate their characters beyond a thinly established strong/weak dynamic. The filmmaking is even more austere, with the two men's fateful journey presented in a series of excessively long, unedited tracking shots, many of which will test viewer patience. Though usually employed to convey a heightened realism or build suspense, Van Sant's extended takes serve only to exaggerate the stifling monotony of his characters' absurd predicament.

Just as *Natural Born Killers* and *From Dusk Till Dawn* rejuvenated desert terror by embracing its pulpy roots, *Gerry* heads the complete opposite direction, focusing on the dull realism of getting lost in the desert. Gone are the usual colorful roadside settings, over the top locals and bizarre atmosphere of most desert terror films. Missing, too, is any kind of John Ryder or Papa Jupiter–type boogeyman to get the story cranking. Instead, the empty protagonists are their own worst enemies: directionless, inexpressive, and almost comically unequipped for even a minor outdoor hike. Similarly, the desert itself barely registers as a specific entity; when the film cuts between material shot in Death Valley and Argentina's Salt flats, the purpose isn't to denote a visual progression so much as confuse the audience's perceptions, placing them in the same headspace as the increasingly aimless characters. The only way to relieve such maddening repetition, it seems, is death. Damon's attack on the weakened Affleck occurs without warning, yet is presented so casually that it feels less shocking than inevitable. There is no buildup nor release, and the stoic Damon remains, like the audience, unaffected by the tragic outcome.

Gerry earns, if nothing else, the designation as the first mumblecore desert terror film, as it arrived at the dawn of the notoriously low-key, largely plotless indie movement. Though strewn with a few stray kernels of malcontent and arresting imagery, the film never quite transcends its experimental status. Failing to fully engage the audience on an emotional, intellectual or even aesthetic level, *Gerry* failed to make much of a splash even on the arthouse circuit despite its A-list director, stars, and distributor (Miramax). While Damon returned to the safer waters of studio fare, Van Sant has stubbornly revisited *Gerry*'s morbid existential themes over a series of low budget, minimalist efforts—*Elephant* (2003), *Last Days* (2005), and most recently, *The Sea of Trees* (2015), which share its environmental exploration and re-imagining of real-life tragedies. If not completely successful in its reinvention of desert terror, *Gerry* nevertheless spearheaded the New Minimalism trend, which would influence many films in the genre throughout the decade and beyond.

While *Gerry* is an extreme departure from its makers' usual output, the artsy shocker *Twentynine Palms* is a typical Dumont film, characterized by an unconventional narrative and frank approach to sex and violence. Originally conceived while the director was scouting locations for a larger-scale production, the virtually plotless *Palms* represents Dumont's American debut and shares several commonalities with Van Sant's effort, among them a two-hander cast, largely improvised dialogue, lack of discernible plot, and a disturbing finale. Its opening shots directly recall the Damon/Affleck outing, as dysfunctional duo David (David Wissak) and his Russian girlfriend Katia (Yekaterina Golubeva) drive out of Los Angeles toward the titular desert city. Like the two travelers in *Gerry*, the exact nature of David and Katia's relationship is as unclear as their purpose, which is ostensibly some kind of location scout. Conversation, when it occurs, is pointlessly banal; Dumont is more interested in contrasting his crudely contemporary characters with the desert's threatening beauty, as when Katia leaves David's obnoxious red Hummer to blithely urinate in front of the enormous, vaguely menacing wind turbines that tower over the landscape.

The next few days are marked by the ill-matched couple's repeating patterns of rough, animalistic sex and petty bickering that explodes into drawn-out fights, occasionally interrupted by brief moments of calm. David forces himself on Katia in the motel pool before crying out (as if in horror) as he climaxes. Later, during dinner, the unstable Katia behaves hysterically after David glances at another woman. The following day's off-road excursion at first seems like a welcome escape into nature, but soon devolves into impromptu screwing amongst the boulders, followed by David's near-drowning of Katia after he tries to force her to pleasure him underwater, and (literally) climaxing with a borderline pornographic motel room coupling that ends with yet another bizarre response from David. Sex temporarily resolves some of David and Katia's largely unexpressed issues, but fails to exorcize their personal demons.

The confrontations worsen the following day, as a series of mounting tensions ends with David tossing Katia out of their motel room. The two scream at each other in the streets until David finally pins Katia to the ground and slaps her while screaming "I hate you!" again and again. The violence of that night seeps into the following day as, while exploring an isolated stretch of desert, David and Katia are suddenly forced off the dirt road by a nondescript white truck. In a shocking sequence that comes literally out of nowhere, a trio of locals leaps from the truck and strip Katia naked while David is beaten with a baseball bat, then brutally sodomized. After finishing (in a way uncomfortably close to David's own sexual responses), the skinhead-type rapist and his friends drive off just as abruptly as they arrived. Katia reassumes her regular routines but David, physically and emotionally shattered by the experience, gives in to his worst impulses in a shattering final scene.

Utilizing only two characters (who bear the same names as the actors), a handful of locations, and the slimmest trace of a story, *Twentynine Palms* shares *Gerry*'s minimalist aesthetic while transporting the desert terror film to new levels of vulgarity and misanthropy. While utilizing tropes often found in stranded scenarios and death driver movies (civilized city folk meet desert savages; a road trip gone bad; violence that explodes in the middle of nowhere), the film does so in a completely unconventional way that is equally fascinating and frustrating. Beginning with its pair of psychologically fragile, utterly unlikable characters (especially David) that we will never know or understand, Dumont consistently departs from expectations. Scenes play out in agonizingly extended takes that sometimes play like raw footage but are nonetheless stunning to behold (particularly the desert scenes), the frequent sex acts are graphic but decidedly unerotic, and the third-act detour into graphic violence feels forced, yet retains an undeniably disturbing aftertaste in its wake.

For hardened desert terror fans, though, there's something refreshing about Dumont's rejection, and reinvention, of familiar motifs, and his film, for all its faults, refuses to be easily dismissed. The potentially off-putting mixture of improvisational dialogue (much of it communicated between an American and a Russian in broken French) and anything-goes, often public sex scenes creates a truly unbalanced ambience, subconsciously preparing the audience for further transgressions to come. The pleasingly naturalistic photography (which often seems to be working off available light) encompasses not only some of the most starkly beautiful desert imagery of the decade, but gives the run-down desert community of Twentynine Palms a strong visual and aural presence, with specific sights and sounds (whooshing turbines, receding train horns, and the constant rumble of traffic) complementing the action in a raw, subtly discomfiting, way.

The film's most radical departure from previous desert terrors, however, is felt in its approach to David's violation and his delayed, yet equally violent, response. Aside from defying the usual clichés (most films would have made Katia the victim), the film denies the audience the usual "revenge" response commonly associated with the genre, in films as diverse as *The Hills Have Eyes* and *Victims!* Instead, it focuses further inward, provoking David to fully embrace his barely latent aggressions, which emerge continuously throughout the film and grow more intense and physical with each passing day. Viewed this way, David's penultimate act is less another chance to shock the audience, but an inevitable outcome of the character's personal predisposition to violence, which is exacerbated by (but, significantly, not solely caused by) the evils lurking in the desert. Once again, *Twentynine Palms* breaks from the usual stereotypes by making outwardly "normal" but clearly deranged David the film's real villain, not the barely glimpsed locals, who are far more forgettable than the rural grotesques who bring *Easy Rider*'s traveling duo to a similarly shocking end.

Even as Dumont deconstructs a uniquely American genre, his film (the first desert terror movie to extensively feature foreign language dialogue) can't escape its own European cinematic lineage. Its themes of alienation (from the environment and from others), intentional lack of dialogue and character development, and emphasis on breathtaking yet menacing landscapes recall the work of Michelangelo Antonioni, specifically his desert-based (and English language) masterworks *Zabriskie Point* and *The Passenger* (1976). The film's graphic sex and violence, however, are more typical of contemporary French art-shockers *Baise Moi* (2000), *Fat Girl* (2001) and *Irreversible* (2002), all of which ground their excesses in a more dramatic, non-genre context. *Twentynine Palms*, however, is the only entry in the cycle to be set (and filmed) in the United States, an important distinction that not only places it apart from its brethren but also allows it an additional layer of cultural commentary. The director takes the expected shots at American excess (David fixates on waxing his oversized Hummer, *Jerry Springer* on TV) but is not above self-critique, as the bored pair watches a laughably pretentious German art film on television.

Arguably the most "European" film in the desert terror canon, *Twentynine Palms* (not to be confused with the 2002 desert-heist flick *29 Palms*) is ironically closer in spirit to earlier desert terror classics like *The Sadist* or *The Hitcher* than many post–Tarantino entries, which prize rapid-fire dialogue and explosive special effects over character, atmosphere, or genuinely transgressive content. In its own inimitable manner, Dumont's difficult work explores the dark heart of desert terror while pissing all over every rule along the way. The result is one of the most challenging, boring, offensive, irritating, and disturbing desert terror movies of the new millennium. Like *Gerry*, the more effective *Twentynine Palms* went unnoticed by most audiences, yet maintains a lasting influence on the desert terror genre, as many future entries adopted its New Minimalism trappings to varying degrees of success.

"There's two types of people who travel the desert: those on the run, and those up to no good," states one of the members of the deranged family who run an isolated café/roadside attraction in *The Mummy an' the Armadillo* (2005), and both types figure largely in this single-location, dialogue-driven slice of Southwestern Gothic. Written and directed by J.S. Cardone, *Mummy* trades the striking locations and explosive action of the filmmaker's previous desert vampire flick *The Forsaken* for a claustrophobic tale driven by biting exchanges and perverse behavior, as long-kept secrets are revealed over one long, dark, and—yes—stormy, night. Conservative preacher's wife Sarah (Clare Kramer) arrives out of the rain to find herself the sole customer at the Armadillo Café (named after its mascot, one of many stuffed critters who share space with a "mummy") run by sharp-tongued bartender Billie (Lori Heuring), who is having an affair with Deputy Temple (Wade Williams) and yearns to leave the family business behind. "There's nothing special about the desert," Billie snaps after Sarah waxes romantically about the "shapes and colors" of the area.

After Billie's sudden departure, Sarah's snooping is interrupted by the arrival of drunken, gun-wielding family matriarch Let (Betty Buckley) and her retarded relation Wyatte (Brad Renfro), who tie the intruder to a chair. Sarah's physical and emotional torment has only begun, however, as Let's sexually confused, abusive son Jesse (Johnathon Schaech, *The Forsaken*) arrives, saying "I can do anything I want in my house," before banishing his little brother to an underground "Scare Hole" (an alternate, earlier title for the film) before plying Sarah with personal questions while applying lipstick and eyeliner taken from her purse. Jesse's attempted rape of Sarah is thwarted by Billie's timely return, leading to a series of disturbing—if predictable—revelations about the family's—and Sarah's—tragic past, both of which are intertwined with that of the mysterious mummy.

The genre's first stage adaptation in the twenty-five years since *When You Comin' Back, Red Ryder?*, *Mummy* resurrects that film's rundown diner setting and hothouse dramatics, but lacks its virtuoso lead performance and broader visual and sociological scope. With literally no exterior scenes to work with, Cardone (adapting his own play) uses stylized visuals and dramatic lighting and sound effects to successfully conjure a stylized, immersive inner world out of the cluttered details of the café while managing to probe the hearts and minds of the people who populate such inhospitable and largely forgotten places. Billie, with her dreams of selling the café and escaping to California, is the classic stranded scenario hopeful who itches to leave the desert (i.e., the past) behind, while Let, who has already warped the minds of Wyatte and Jesse, represents the madness generated by rejecting the outer world. Sarah, on the other hand, is the outsider who, in this case, does not merely stumble into the family's demented world but does so intentionally, with her own need for personal closure. In yet another interesting departure from genre norms, *Mummy*'s strongest characters—Billie, Let, and Sarah—are all women.

Aside from *Red Ryder*, echoes of other desert terror films permeate the film as well: introductory scenes with Sarah and Billie bear a strong similarity to *Dying Room Only*; *Mummy*'s freakish family recalls everything from *The Hills Have Eyes* to *Sonny Boy*; and the café itself typifies the kind of stultifying, self-created nightmare worlds found in *Barn of the Naked Dead* and *Haunted*. The overheated dialogue, which plays like some unholy marriage of Tracy Letts and S.F. Brownrigg, occasionally strays into camp ("Curses, like chickens, come home to roost."), but most of the cast—especially Heuring, Schaech, and, in a brief but effective supporting role, Jodi Lyn O' Keefe—keep it grounded with credible, realistic performances. A worthy (and underseen) companion piece to *The Forsaken* and an extension of the filmmaker's previous desert noirs, *Mummy* represents the more personal side of Cardone's continued exploration of the genre.

Nearly twenty years after penning one of the first desert terror slashers, *Blood Frenzy* writer Ted Newsom returned to the genre with the even darker true-crime thriller *Whispers from a Shallow Grave* (2006). Based on Raiderette/Playboy model Linda Sobek's 1995 murder by photographer Charles Rathbun, *Whispers* tells its sordid tale with a dizzying mix of real news footage and dramatic recreations of the events leading up to, and following, Sobek's death. A grim disclaimer of authenticity plays over shots of an anonymous vehicle driving through a dry lakebed before the unseen driver disposes of his female victim's body and belongings in the Angeles National Forest (ironically described on signage as "Land of Many Uses"). Rather than laying out the events chronologically, writer/director/producer Newsom structures the film as an extended flashback, allowing Sobek (star/producer/editor Trudi Keck) to appear in court as a witness to her own death. Her sobering testimony gradually expands to include not only her own tortured past, but the checkered background of Rathbun (Gerald Brodin), as well.

Adopting a fragmented, documentary-style approach, *Whispers* plumbs the depths of entertainment biz desperation and depravity like a microbudget version of the downbeat biopics of Bob Fosse *(Lenny, Star 80)*. Though hardly as well-known as Dorothy Stratten (whose infamy was insured by not one but two motion pictures as well as plentiful media coverage), Sobek emerges as even more relatable, with modest cheerleading and modeling gigs rubbing shoulders with failed past relationships, suicide attempts, and therapy sessions. Alternately damning (an off-camera lawyer describes Sobek's physical appearance as "a lie") and shamelessly titillating, the film turns even nastier in its second half, which concentrates on Rathbun's own catalog of cruelty. Including dramatizations of rape (one of which stars B-movie queen Michelle Bauer as Rathbun's unfortunate roommate) and other physical and mental abuse, Rathbun's past is examined in uncomfortable detail, with the film's harsh video look, for once, serving to enhance the raw immediacy of these moments.

As evidence mounts against Rathbun, the film returns repeatedly to the pivotal day of Sobek's murder, which takes place almost entirely in the desert. Encompassing the uncomfortable drive north (which finds Rathbun flirtatious, then openly hostile), the ill-fated photo shoot, and its horrifying aftermath, the desert material occupies just a small percentage of the entire film, and yet also contains its most powerful imagery and most uninflected performances (especially from Keck). Perhaps realizing its unique visual appeal and obvious story significance, Newsom makes the most of his dry lake bed location by presenting two different versions of the day's events (later becoming three or four as Rathbun changes his story), using color and black and white to differentiate the accused's fantasy/lies from reality. These *Rashomon*–like sequences, many of which unfold

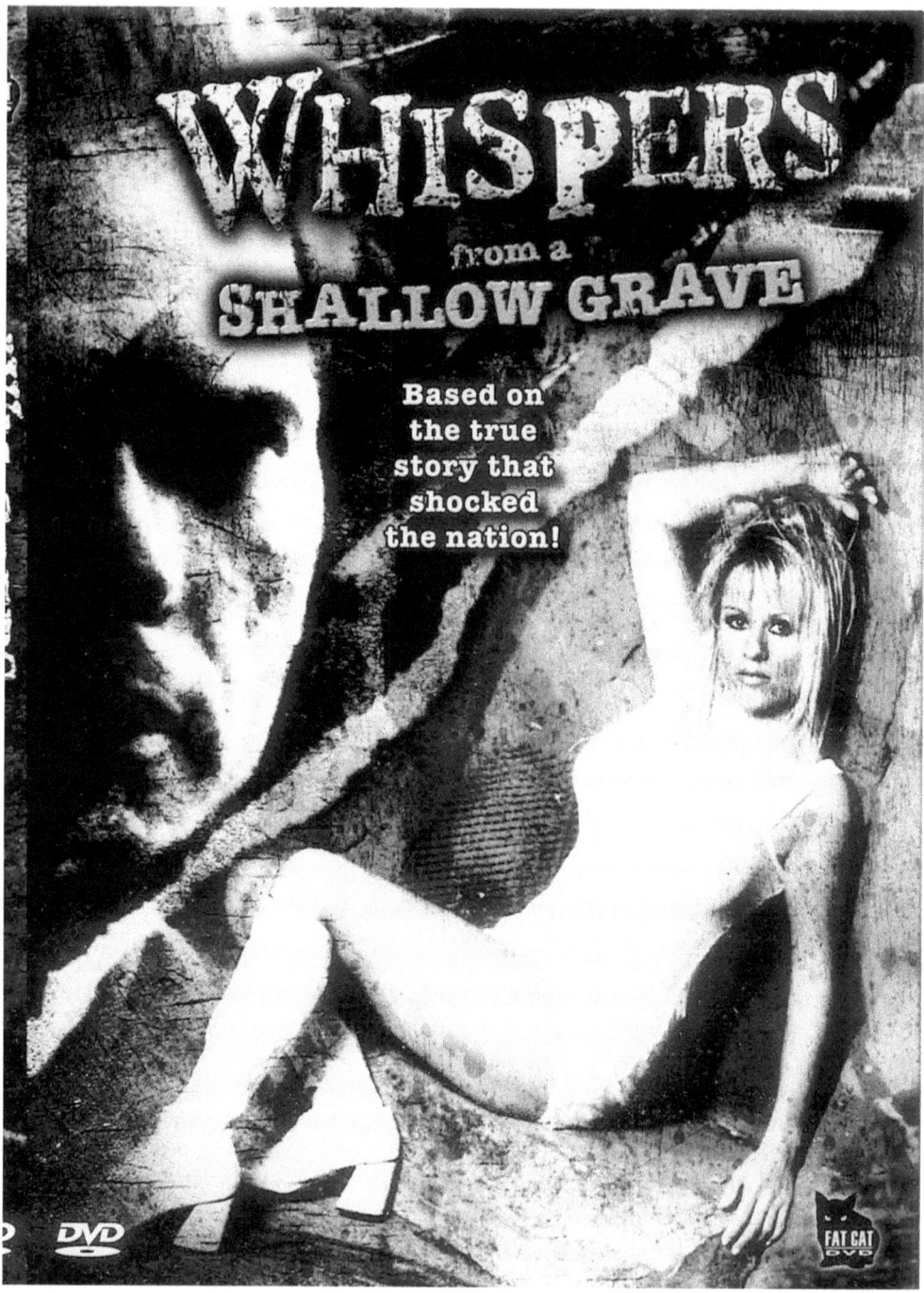

The video artwork for *Whispers from a Shallow Grave* (2006) stresses the titillating aspects of its true crime subject matter.

in real time, allow the somewhat schizophrenically edited film to slow down a bit and breathe. The film's last scenes, which dramatize the awful circumstances of Sobek's last hours on earth, are as unforgettably ugly as anything in the desert terror genre.

Going beyond the genre's true crime progenitors like *The Hitch-Hiker* and *The Sadist*, *Whispers* uses real names, places, and events (and sometimes, even authentic news footage) throughout its fictional narrative. By acknowledging her flaws as much as her own naïve ambition, Newsom effectively uses Linda Sobek as a stand-in for every wannabe starlet who ever dreamed of fame and fortune, with Rathbun the classic predatory creep. Equal parts cautionary tale and expose, Whispers references and criticizes the entertainment industry more directly than self-reflexive works like *Blood Shack* and *Haunted*. The film isn't without its flaws, not the least of which is Keck's flat lead performance (in an eerie parallel with the subject matter, she never acted again after this film) and the extensive use of post-dubbed dialogue, which gives many exchanges between characters a hollow, distanced quality. Treading (and occasionally crossing) the fine line between exploitation commentary and genuine exploitation, Newsom's ambitious effort illustrates the real-life horrors at the heart of many a fictional desert terror film.

Whispers' hard-edged, analog look betrays its '90s origins; though completed in 1999, it was not released on DVD until seven years later. By then, digital cameras and editing software had progressed significantly, allowing even the clumsiest DIY filmmaker to make a marginally slicker-looking (if not necessarily more watchable) product. One of the first examples of this second micro-budget wave was *666: The Demon Child* (2006), a lo-fi creature feature which takes the supernatural scares of Native American–themed monster flicks like *Track of the Moon Beast* and *Natas* on a road trip to Hell. On their way to an excavation in the Arizona desert, a group of archaeology students encounter a Native American man (Grady Hill) carrying a pair of oversized "eggs" that look more like spray-painted volleyballs. Before leaving, sticky-fingered Daryl (David Carchidi) stows an egg on board their RV, figuring, "What was he gonna do with it, make a giant omelet?" when the others question his decision. Unsurprisingly, the egg soon breaks open to hatch a screeching, horned "demon child" with a serious appetite that chews Darren up and drags his body into the dark. From then on, it's a game of survival as the students are picked off, one by one (including a tastelessly fun, *Psycho*-inspired shower murder) by the hungry humanoid. "Pretty smart little tyke," notes final girl Karen (Jennifer L. Jackson) before finally using an ancient sword against the infernal infant.

Armed with little more than a mini–DV camera, a handful of actors, and a rubbery puppet, Arizona-based producer/writer/director Cary Howe (whose past credits include work as a sculptor on the desert vampire movie *Sundown*) works hard to provide an hour and a half of entertainment with only an hour's worth of story material. The filmmakers' decision to have much of the action take place at night lends *Demon Child* a spooky, middle-of-nowhere ambience (and helps hide the special effects fakery), but having a few more lights on hand would have helped tremendously, as many of the students' skirmishes with the fast-moving fiend are terribly difficult to make out. The practical effects aren't bad (when you can see them), particularly a skeletal beast that's never really explained but way creepier than the title creature, whose effectiveness is diminished by a droning loop of whiny sound effects, which quickly grow annoying. Howe's script is mostly formulaic, but the opening and closing bookends (which explain the demon child's origin—sort of) lend the story a nicely ominous atmosphere. A lightweight little creature feature with an apocalyptic chaser, *Demon Child* makes the most of its limited resources.

If *Demon Child* occasionally stumbles in its effort to entertain, the watered-down desert slasher *Delirium* (2007) barely even tries. Its *Kalifornia*-inspired setup finds a motley group of college students sharing the expense of a Spring Break road trip, which rapidly disintegrates once the argumentative group takes the ill-advised "Route 69" (ha, ha) through the open desert. A subsequent breakdown creates even more conflict amongst the travelers (who have all the bile of *Blood Frenzy*'s therapy group but none of that film's acidic wit), who trade insults (and, in a few cases, blows) during the twelve-mile walk to the nearest town. Along the way, a black-clad killer (who bears a curious resemblance to the phantoms of early horror western serials) appears like a mirage to randomly dole out death in a series of occasionally gory, but lifelessly directed, murders.

Delirium's deceptively smoother visual presentation might be easier on the eyes than the washed-out videography of past analog desert terrors, but it does nothing to improve the by-the-numbers plot, unpleasant characters (accurately self-described as "six assholes stranded in the desert") and juvenile dialog, which is rife with slurs ("flaming faggot," "carpet munching lesbo"), smartass self-referencing (as in *Carnage Road*, a character mentions "cheesy straight to DVD horror flicks") and pseudo-philosophical musings ("In the end, it's all about respect—and love."). Even at less than eighty minutes, the movie feels padded, with a series of lazy montages substituting for genuine suspense or plot development. The desert setting is little more than a backdrop, with flatly photographed daytime exteriors leading to a series of muddy night scenes which are even more luminance-challenged than *Demon Child*. Bereft of original ideas and indifferently directed, *Delirium* adds nothing new to the desert slasher canon.

The proliferation of independent films of all genres throughout the '90s and aughts coincided with the rise of film festivals, many of which catered to horror and Fantasy films. One of the first desert terror films to benefit from the increased exposure of festival play (at the 2005 South by Southwest and Tribeca film festivals, among others) was the slickly made *Reeker* (2007), written and directed by Corman alumnus Dave Payne. The film juggles several elements—a supernatural boogeyman whose can be smelled before he's seen, *Twilight Zone* ambience, and a M. Night Shyamalan–esque twist ending—in a semi-successful attempt to "class up" the desert slasher subgenre. A bizarre pre-credits sequence establishes the film's "WTF?" tone early on, as an unseen force attacks a family driving through the desert. Like 2003's *Detour* in reverse, the main story concerns a grab bag of victims (er, characters) heading from Los Angeles to a desert rave, among them Gretchen (South African actress Tina Illman) and blind, wisecracking Jack (Devon Gummersall). After discovering that one of their fellow passengers, slacker Trip (Scott Whyte), is carrying stolen ecstasy pills, Gretchen dumps him at the eerily-named Halfway Travel Oasis. Her choice to stop there proves ill-fated, however, as subsequent engine trouble, and the unexplained loss of all communication (cell phones, landlines, radios) strands the group there for one very long night.

The events that follow will either be intriguing or annoying, depending on your tolerance for unexplained phenomena and a mysterious killer who can appear and disappear at will. Garbled voices erupt from phones and TV sets. Cryptic inscriptions appear in blood on the walls. A legless man inexplicably tumbles out of a dumpster and scurries away. Character actor Michael Ironside arrives in an RV, raising the spirits of viewers acquainted with his excellent past work, then dies off without impacting the plot in any significant way. Despite its efforts to build a foreboding atmosphere, *Reeker* follows the same '80s slasher template as earlier desert terrors like *Blood Frenzy* and *Mirage*, with characters pairing off to have sex or wandering in the dark when they'd be much better off staying with the group. Progressing from a CGI mist to a gas-masked freak with a whirling blade apparatus, the "Reeker" is not in the film enough to make a real impact, and is never really explained. Outside of an improbable outhouse murder (seriously, the motel room didn't have a bathroom?), the kills are mostly unremarkable, relying more on the twist ending (the motel's name is a clue) for their impact.

Sporting a bigger budget than many of its desert terror contemporaries, *Reeker* aims for a more intellectual approach to horror but for most of the time, fails to engage the audience. Payne's script is well-paced, and the characters—notably Gretchen ("I'm from Johannesburg—it takes a lot to scare me.") and Jack, whose affliction gives him an advantage over the Reeker—are not your stereotypical horror heroes. Unfortunately, the film never really works up a head of steam, either, especially in the crucial third act as the Reeker starts claiming victims and real panic sets in. The "smell" concept, while novel, doesn't really translate cinematically, ultimately leaving the Reeker just another slasher wielding an edged weapon. Also disappointing is the film's visual style, which applies a high-contrast, colorless look to its early desert exteriors, and becomes even more pronounced during the nocturnal scenes, which are often murky and underlit. Although entirely set (and shot) in the deserts north of Los Angeles, desert atmosphere often takes a backseat to the film's random, freakish images of horror which, much like the Reeker himself, achieve momentary impact but fade from the film (and the mind) just as quickly.

Reeker's frustrating "head-fake" storytelling approach encores on a smaller level in the sci-fi/horror tale *Dreamland* (2007), which mines the desert's notorious history of UFO sightings and government cover-ups for chills. Driving through rural Nevada late at night, high-strung Megan (Jackie Kreisler) and her slacker boyfriend Dylan (Shane Elliott) stop at a roadside diner (whose sign reads "Welcome UFOs and Crews") for a bite. Over burgers and Groom Lake shakes, owner Blake (Jonathan Breck) tells the pair wild tales of flying saucers and government spooks while, in the parking lot, a surly local is vaporized by a mysterious white light. Back on the road, the increasingly contentious couple (he's unemployed, she's off her meds) is interrupted by strange radio broadcasts from the past before their car breaks down in the middle of nowhere. Dylan collapses unexpectedly, leaving Megan to

The supernatural slasher *Reeker* (2008) is one of many late–2000s desert terrors to attempt a *Sixth Sense*–like ending.

wander the desert while being assaulted by visions of creepy kids and wounded soldiers. After being reunited with Dylan and resuming their trip, the unhinged Megan notices a series of troubling changes in her boyfriend's looks and behavior. Is there truth behind the rumors of alien entities haunting Dreamland, or is Megan simply losing her mind?

The answer, it turns out, is both much more, and much less, as *Dreamland*'s jumbled narrative unspools through a series of bizarre, if mostly repetitive, incidents before arriving at a corny conclusion. Although it employs two of the genre's most underused angles—alien visitation and time travel—debuting writer-director James P. Lay fails to create either a sense of extraterrestrial wonder or even pull off a simple scare. Lead actress Kreisler tries hard in an occasionally unlikable role, but is forced to spend much of her time waking from nightmares (three in the first ten minutes!), shrieking at her loser boyfriend, and stumbling from one absurd encounter to another before her fate is revealed. The poorly lit desert locations are drab and generic and much of the dialogue overreaching ("There's nothing out there for you ... except a dream you can't wake up from."). Riddled with images that verge from the subpar (a ghost girl feels like the ultimate modern horror cliché) to the ridiculous (Adolf Hitler?), *Dreamland* saves its biggest misstep, however, for the head-scratching finale, which strives for emotional weight but ultimately fails to approach even *Reeker*'s cold cleverness.

When a movie opens with quotes from both Shakespeare's *Richard III* and Roman philosopher Lucretius (whose name is misspelled), you know you're in the hands of a filmmaker with an overly high-minded approach to their material—and that's *before* the end credits announce *Bone Dry* (2008) as a "Brett A. Hart Vision." In achieving his vision, co-writer/director/editor Hart (who, in a desert terror first, financed his film mostly through crowd funding) strips the genre down to its core elements, with just two principal performers and some breathtaking scenery carrying its noir-influenced storyline. At a roadside diner, Eddie (British actor Luke Goss) flirts with waitress JoAnne (Dee Wallace Stone, in her first desert terror film since *The Hills Have Eyes*) before heading back onto the road. After being captured by the mysterious Jimmy (desert terror vet Lance Henriksen), Eddie wakes up in the middle of Death Valley with little more than a compass, a walkie, and orders to march dead north—or face certain death from the mysterious Jimmy, who constantly watches, and tracks, him from a distance.

As a sunburned Eddie treks further into the desert, Jimmy puts him through one grueling ordeal after another. One morning, Eddie wakes up buried to his neck in the sand (a la *Mirage*) and left to perish. Later, he's chained to the hood of Jimmy's vehicle as it crashes through a brush-strewn landscape. Most memorable (and painful) of all, Eddie finds himself stripped naked and handcuffed to a cactus, which he must saw through to attain freedom. In between these punishing trials, Jimmy makes small talk on the walkie, posing questions both philosophical ("You think God gives a shit what we're doing out here?") and banal ("What's the worst job you ever had?"). Eddie, however, has only one question for his torturer—"What do you want?"—for which he receives no answer. Instead, the film explores the two men's growing interpersonal dynamic, which is mostly created via their radio chats, as Jimmy confesses his past and Eddie slowly loses his grip on reality. A drug-dealer subplot temporarily breaks the film's spell before the adversaries face off in yet another big reveal that aspires to operatic levels of tragedy, but feels overwrought and, frankly, predictable.

Bone Dry's survive-or-die premise and two-hander cast reference several past significant desert terrors including *Duel*, *The Hitcher*, and *The Oasis*, and while not in the

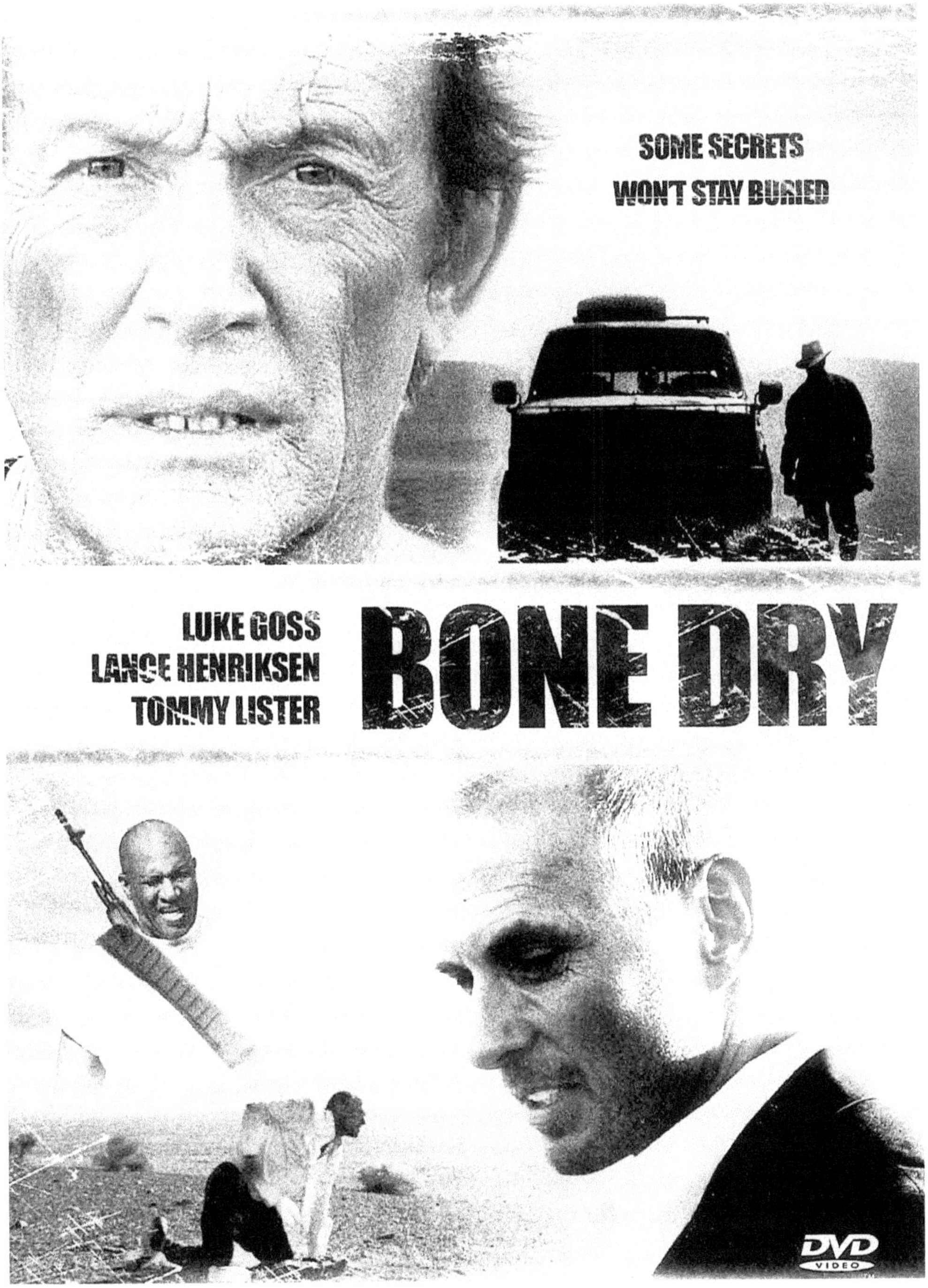

The survival thriller *Bone Dry* (2008) was one of the first desert terror films to utilize crowd funding.

same league as those classics, the film still manages to carve out a unique place for itself in the genre. After a spate of horror-skewed entries, it's nice to see a return to the genre's noir roots, even if some of its torturous set pieces (particularly that cactus scene) smack of the more recent *Saw* franchise. The minimalist script leans heavily on the talents of Henriksen and Goss (who share little screen time), both of whom rise to the challenge.

Visually, the film is stunning throughout, with some of the best use of desert locations (including Death Valley, California, and Yuma, Arizona) seen in years. Told in a series of atmospheric, often wordless, passages, Eddie's journey perfectly captures the harsh beauty—as well as the overpowering isolation—of the environment. At the same time, Hart's repetitious, self-indulgent landscapes occasionally cause the sparse storyline to meander, waiting until the final five minutes (in a trend affecting several post–*Reeker* desert terrors) to explain the loopy plot. *Bone Dry* remains worth seeing for its committed lead performances and gorgeous location work.

Meanwhile, the micro-budget wave continued with *The Craving* (2008), a modest creature feature that follows a generic quintet of hard-drinking, horny kids headed to Burning Man (now *there's* a novel setting for a desert terror film). The story diverges from the expected slasher/*Hills Have Eyes* template, however, upon the group's arrival at an isolated house, where a violent confrontation ends with the crazed owner (producer/screenwriter/cinematographer Curtis Krick) dead, one of the group wounded and all of them stranded. Their troubles are far from over, however, as night brings a hungry denizen of the desert that feeds on flesh and blood. Like the bigger-budgeted *Reeker* films, *The Craving* utilizes a smell-driven gimmick to drive its belabored yet admittedly original story, and in some ways, handles its premise more creatively. There's also a not-so-subtle commentary on the perils of addiction amidst the tits and gore, and the film is at least attractively cast and decently acted (particularly by female leads Wallis Herst and Lesley Patterson, who carry the second half of the film). Director/producer/editor Sean Dillon summons up an effectively desolate atmosphere through some well-chosen locations (the film was shot in the modern-day ghost town of Desert Center, California) and wisely limits our glimpses of its creature to a few brief close-ups, relying more on sound effects and performances to drive the tale. If a bit overlong at 100 minutes, *The Craving* delivers some decent third-act shocks and surprises to reward the patient viewer, and has an overall seriousness of purpose (and genuine sense of fun) missing from many similar self-funded enterprises.

Continuing the "olfactory horror" trend begun by *Reeker* and *The Craving* is the awkwardly titled follow-up *No Man's Land: The Rise of Reeker* (2008). Once again, a motley group of souls come together at an out-of-the-way desert outpost (in this case, the Six Corners Travel Stop, a location previously seen in *The Devil's Rejects* as the Kahiki Palms) to face off against—to quote one character—"a smelly-ass Grim Reaper lookin' thing." A 1978 prologue reveals the Reeker's original human incarnation as the Death Valley Drifter (Michael Robert Brandon), a traveling salesman and Nam vet with a penchant for torture and murder who, after death, is reborn as the Reeker. In the present day, the bored denizens of a desert-bound motel/cafe—including retiring sheriff (Robert Pine), his estranged son/successor, Harris (Michael Muhney) and new waitress Maya (Mircea Monroe)—are shocked out of their daily routine by the sudden arrival of a trio of Vegas casino robbers: British ringleader Binky (Desmond Askew, *The Hills Have Eyes 2006*), badly wounded Carlos (Wilmer Calderon), and Alex (Stephen Martines), who also happens to be Maya's ex-boyfriend. A shootout-triggered explosion leads to a quake-like rippling effect, followed by an "invisible wall" that prevents escape beyond the premises.

As in the original film, characters pair off and try and make sense of their increasingly bizarre situation while creepy, apparently random images materialize out of nowhere: an elderly hospital patient staggers through the desert, blood gushing from an open chest wound; a pair of disembodied legs (an homage to the original film's "half trucker"?) race out of a motel room; and Native American Eaglesmith (Gil Birmingham) rants about "being trapped between light and dark, night and day." Father/son reunions and ex-lovers' reconciliations are interrupted by sudden attacks by the Reeker, whose methods of killing (save a scorching flamethrower attack) haven't changed much since the first movie. More disgusting than any of the film's murders is the film's emphasis on toilet humor, with scenes of characters reaching into the john, swimming through raw sewage, and—in a cinematic first—using the flammable vapors from a septic tank to destroy the "ghost with a hygiene problem."

To distinguish it from its parent, Payne and returning director of photography Mike Mickens set most of *No Man's Land* in the daytime, and its bright, naturalistic look is a considerable improvement over the previous film's murky nighttime palette. It also has a somewhat larger scope, with the action extending to the surrounding desert environs this time around. The characters, many of whom are locals with personal connections to the area and each other, also register more strongly than the original's group of generic rave-bound teens. Monroe brings a winning combination of looks and talent to her admittedly limited role, much of which is spent (of course) in the restroom. All this accumulated visual detail and backstory, unfortunately, is still in service to a "twist" ending, which feels more reverse-engineered than *Reeker*'s denouement and dispatches its characters with the callousness of the *Final Destination* films. Bearing more similarities than differences with its predecessor, *No Man's Land* also suffers from many of the same faults.

Despite an opening disclaimer stating that it was inspired by true events, the misleadingly-titled *Death Valley* (2008) feels more inspired by other desert terror movies, though not so much 1982's same-named death driver flick as the last few years of rave-set road thrillers like *Detour* and *Reeker*. The film starts in a similar fashion to its contemporaries, as four male friends—privileged Daniel (Rider Strong), ladies' man Anthony (Bumper Robinson), philosophical Brick (Wayne Young) and birthday boy Josh (Eric Christian Olsen)—escape their office-drone existences in Los Angeles to blow off some steam at a massive party deep in the desert. There, the naïve quartet of city kids lose themselves in the hedonistic atmosphere through a long night of mescaline-fueled hallucinations and hookups before waking the next morning to find the other celebrants gone—and their van robbed of its battery. Along with Anthony's new squeeze Amber (Genevieve Cortese), the group quickly finds themselves at the mercy of a violent gang of motorbike-riding tweakers led by the zonked-out Dom (Dash Mihok), whose plans switch from extortion to murderous revenge following the accidental death of one of his cohorts.

While much of the slickly-produced *Death Valley* feels overly familiar—from its *Hills Have Eyes*–type setup to action scenes that recall '80s outings like *Survival Run* and *Raw Courage*—the film distinguishes itself with naturalistic performances and a raw, realistic tone. Its script holds few true surprises, but at least offers a more adult approach to its subject matter, rejecting the dumbed-down slasher clichés and labored finales of many of its contemporaries. Similarly, co-directors David Kebo and Rudi Liden adopt a more low-key style that emphasizes the details of the group's increasingly dire situation over cartoonish violence and histrionics. At times, *Death Valley* feels almost too subdued for its own good; two key scenes, the attempted rape of Amber by two of Dom's goons and Dom's violent act of retribution against Daniel, are defined more by off-screen action than graphic nudity or bloodletting; a willingness to dwell just a bit more on the ugliness

Filmed under the title *Mojave*, *Death Valley* (2008) received a title change and appropriately subtle artwork for its video release.

of these moments would have added substantially to their dramatic impact. If loathe to indulge in *Devil's Rejects*–style gore, the film is merciless in its treatment of its four protagonists, few of whom make it back from their fateful trip.

Along the way, *Death Valley* pays lip service to the genre's civilization versus savagery themes and conflicts ("Take this trip. Learn something about yourself. Don't come back the same," Brick insists prophetically on the ride out of L.A.) while adding some vague racial undertones to the proceedings ("Nigers Die" is scrawled on a dumpster, and hotheaded African American Anthony seems to be the gang's most obvious target). Instead of exploring this notion to add extra layers of depth or intensity, the film consigns it to the background in favor of a series of a well-mounted but predictable series of confrontations between the guys and Dom, who, in addition to being introduced a bit too late in the game, lacks the intensity or charisma of the best desert terror heavies. *Death Valley*'s muted, less exploitative tone may account for its relative obscurity; though completed in 2004 (under the original title *Mojave*), it didn't debut on home video until four years later. Ironically, the film was shot in neither Mojave nor Death Valley, but in the flattened desert landscapes of Albuquerque, New Mexico.

Rounding out the decade's DIY efforts, the microbudget *Feeding Grounds* (2009) dispatches yet another group of hard-partying, twenty-something Angelenos into the desert for a cut-rate alien invasion that emphasizes emoting, paranoia, and vacuous "style" over old-fashioned scares, gore, or atmosphere. A trail of abandoned vehicles and a sign reading "Doom Desert" do nothing to dissuade the group from continuing their drug-fueled odyssey while strange sounds (most of which sound like a growling stomach, suggesting tardy caterers more than extraterrestrial life forms) gurgle on the soundtrack. The discovery of a Lynchian severed ear is casually dismissed with the comment: "Don't be so intense about it. People get killed out here all the time. It's the friggin' desert for chrissakes." As the road becomes an endless loop and the friends succumb to a mysterious illness, vegan Mary (Kiralee Hiyashi) tunes into the invisible creatures' vibe: "The more you fight, the quicker they'll come."

Once again fashioned by a few key collaborators wearing several hats (lead actor Alex Ballar also executive produced and co-wrote the screenplay), *Feeding Grounds* is a dull and pretentious would-be creature feature that, rather than attempt to visualize its otherworldly beasties, adopts an obtuse "psychological" style that allows the already shaky storyline to degenerate into a blur of badly improvising non-actors and editorial horseplay. Like an even more impoverished replay of the 2003 *Detour* (which it resembles in many ways, down to its lesbian double-murder prologue), *Feeding Grounds* tests the viewer's patience with its obnoxious characters and lack of action and does absolutely nothing new with its desert setting. Along with *Delirium* and *The Craving*, the film is commonly found in a budget-priced DVD multipack titled *Highways to Hell*, which also includes the superior *Hell's Highway*. Aside from the last title, none are essential viewing for desert terror fans, but the set stands as an accurate representation of the genre's microcinema output during the aughts.

One of the genre's most fruitful decades closed with a group of films that invoked past desert terrors while returning to more adult themes and subject matter. The first of these, the dark melodrama *Hurt* (2009), strands its talented cast of veterans and newcomers in a *Sadist*-like junkyard setting, along with a soapy screenplay and one vengeful little girl. Following her husband's death in a car accident, Helen (Melora Walters) and her teenage kids Lenore (Johanna Braddy) and Conrad (Jackson Rathbone) are forced to move in with Helen's foster brother Daryl (William Mapother), who still lives in their parents' home and continues to operate the family business: a massive scrapyard. Easygoing Conrad occupies his time welding sculptures out of spare parts, but bitter Lenore can only count the days until an insurance settlement delivers them from their high-strung uncle, who still harbors affections for Helen. With tensions already building between Daryl and her two children, Helen makes the kindly but ill-fated decision to foster ten-year-old Sarah (Sofia Vassilieva), a withdrawn orphan whose parents also died tragically. The eerie parallels to Helen's own situation are gradually revealed as more than coincidence, as Sarah pits Helen's family against each other in an increasingly deadly series of manipulations.

A different kind of stranded scenario, *Hurt* begins promisingly, driven by understated performances, atmospheric setting, and slow-burn plotting. Ample conflict is wrung out of the hothouse environment before Sarah's arrival, which happens through somewhat muddled circumstances and feels frankly unbelievable given Helen's already compromised situation. Co-writer/director Barbara Stepansky is mostly successful at keeping Sarah's machinations—which encompass voyeurism, subterfuge, and even murder—grounded in reality, but eventually they begin to feel less connected to the main narrative and more akin to the devious plotting of the femme fatales in "cuckoo in the nest" thrillers like *The Hand That Rocks the Cradle* or *Poison Ivy* (both 1992). The final explanation for Sarah's behavior is far-fetched and only serves to destroy any sense of realism achieved by the earlier, more dramatic material.

Despite its convoluted screenplay, the film sustains interest thanks to its well-written characters and equally fine ensemble acting from the small cast led by the consistently underappreciated Walters and Mapother. The absence of a defined central protagonist is more of an asset than a liability, as the more balanced approach both keeps the story flowing in an unpredictable manner and allows a deeper understanding of each character. Both the scrapyard and Daryl's dwelling are treated with a similar attention to detail, picking out visual and aural elements (Helen's handmade jewelry, a metal door banging in the wind) that, like the best desert terrors, combine to create a separate world that is at once borderless and maddeningly claustrophobic. Additionally, the screenplay confronts family issues—sibling bonds, effects of child abuse, the challenges of foster parenting—seldom explored in the genre, and even rarely with such depth or sensitivity. If *Hurt* ultimately surrenders to more commercial impulses, its commendably earthy, character-driven storytelling approach gives it an edge over many of its effects-oriented contemporaries.

A welcome return to the biker-themed desert terror, writer/director Julian Higgins' *Poker Run* (2009) strives for a more commercial sensibility while keeping one leather boot firmly set in the grindhouse golden age. After a gory prologue set "somewhere tonight in the dark, dirty Mojave Desert," the film introduces buddies Allen (J.D. Rudometkin) and Robert (Bertie Higgins), a couple of "RUBs" (short for Rich Urban Biker) itching to ditch their high-paying but dull corporate gigs for a weekend "poker run," a road trip that starts in Victorville, California, and ends in Las Vegas, with plenty of beer stops along the way. After convincing their wives Cheri (Jasmine Waltz) and Susan (Debra Hopkins) to come along for the ride, Allen and Robert purchase a pair of used motorcycles from smooth-talking biker Ray (Robert Thorne) and his tweaker associate Billy (Jay Wisell), and they're off and running.

During their first break at a Mojave bar, Allen and Robert have a not-so-chance meeting with Ray and Billy, who show a more than passing interest in the guys' attractive spouses. Soon, the party of four grows to six, with Ray guiding the group away from the established "poker run" route and into the uncharted wilds of the desert. The group ends up at the Four Aces motel, where further trouble ensues; Robert and Susan argue over her wish to start a family, while hot-to-trot Cheri leaves her snoozing hubby for hot, bondage-style sex with Ray. Unsurprisingly, both women end up captives of the bikers, who leave a few arcane clues for their husbands before disappearing into the night. For the next few excruciating days, the two RUBs are forced to carry out a series of nightmarish demands as they desperately try and locate their significant others.

Mercilessly paced and unafraid to get its hands dirty (or bloody), *Poker Run* contains many classic desert terror tropes: a road-tripping storyline, grimy middle-of-nowhere locations, marital tensions that explode into sex and violence, and—perhaps most importantly—a unique spin on the time-honored theme of civilization vs. savagery. At the same time, its plot and visual style feel more recycled from the recent *Joy Ride* films and TV shows like *Breaking Bad* and *Sons of Anarchy* than inspired by the desert terrors of the '70s and '80s. Part of the problem is the lightning-fast pacing and choppy editing which strive for unnecessary speed; the casualties are atmospheric detail, character nuance, and any semblance of suspense. It's a shame, too, as the central character relationships between Allen and Robert, and the men and their wives, are genuinely compelling. A third-act parting of the ways between the two surprises in several ways, not the least of which is Robert's unexpected (and graphic) demise. Allen and Cheri's crumbling union isn't as well explored, but her infidelity leaves several questions that the film fails to answer.

The characters of Ray and Billy are not quite as well drawn. Introduced as a giggling meth-lab caricature, Billy eventually gains additional depth as he tries to impose his warped need for family on the terrified Susan. Ray, despite his speechifying, fails to invoke the kind of oddball charisma or over-the-top nastiness necessary for a desert terror heavy. His fast-money schemes—whether selling stolen bikes or pawning off women into third-world prostitution—seem pitifully small-time and lack motivation; when Cheri barks, "Why do you do this?" Ray's disappointing answer (which oddly recalls *The Sadist*'s Charlie Tibbs) is, "You know what I really want? Pie." Similarly, Ray's trail of clues (left with a playing card, of course) feel increasingly convoluted, as more and more locals seem to be in on the game, while Allen descends into a hell of one murder after another. While this type of paranoid plotting worked to a certain degree in desert terrors like *Dying Room Only* and *Breakdown*, here it verges on ridiculous.

Appropriately, Ray and Allen's final showdown takes place at a movie-set ghost town, where the film makes glib references to the genre's western heritage ("Ghost town. Empty streets. Damsel in distress … perfect.") without further exploring the idea. *Poker Run*'s high noon is fought with words, not bullets, as Ray asks Alan: "Are you ready to kill again for that cheatin' whore of a wife?" Although Allen wins the match, the biker still maintains the upper hand, whispering, "You'll never be free" as he dies. Like *The Hitcher*, *Nature of the Beast*, or *The Pass*, *Poker Run* is really a struggle between two men; however motivational to the plot, the women remain definitively on the sidelines. And like those films, the "victorious" protagonist assumes some of his adversary's personality, as Allen pockets Ray's skull totem before riding his motorcycle into the sunset. A tacked-on "surprise" ending, which ruins whatever muddled poetry these images achieve, is typical of the film's unsure, hurried technique. *Poker Run* is never dull, and sometimes even shocking, but many of its more interesting, and disturbing, ideas remain frustratingly undeveloped.

Damaged relationships also surface in *Blood River* (2009), a more serious desert terror tale which, like earlier New Minimalist efforts, fashions its potent, religious-themed drama around just one primary location and three main characters. Elevated by stylish photography and a fearless cast, British co-writer/director Adam Mason's sophisticated supernatural horror film is a welcome return to more dramatic stranded scenarios like *The Sadist* and *When You Comin' Back, Red Ryder?*. A young, attractive Los Angeles couple, Clark (Ian Duncan) and his recently pregnant wife Summer (Tess Panzer), drive through the broiling desert, on a road trip to visit her parents. They pass a drifter (Andrew Howard) dressed in western garb, commenting on the "crazy bastard" without slowing down. Checking into a motel room, they fail to notice the same drifter at the bar, flirting with the attractive innkeeper (Sarah Essex). The next morning, as the couple drives away, the drifter watches stoically as his now-apparently hypnotized lover slices her wrists.

After their car blows a tire, Summer and Clark find themselves stranded in the middle of the Nevada desert, with their only hope a town five miles away named "Blood River." Upon arrival, they realize the place is a literal ghost town, a broken-down outpost filled with junked cars and animal carcasses ... and devoid of any human life. When the drifter, who calls himself "Joseph," arrives, Summer immediately takes a liking to him, despite his odd behavior and inexplicable knowledge of her pregnancy. Clark has a distinctly opposite reaction, and a competitive tension soon forms between the two men. Joseph volunteers to help Clark with his car, but not until the following morning; that night, the trio share an awkward campfire dialog. Summer shows Joseph a photo of Ben, her son from a previous relationship, while the hitchhiker needles white-collar Clark about "working for the man." While Summer excuses Joseph as an eccentric free spirit, Clark fears that there is a more sinister side to the drifter's anti-authority tirades and religious platitudes.

The following day, Joseph leaves Summer with a pistol before he and her husband head out on the five-mile trek to the car. During the walk, Joseph insists that he "knows" Clark, challenging his ivory tower outlook: "Get paid real nice. Wear a suit and tie to make you feel important. Pretty wife, baby on the way, big house. I bet you got two cars, don't you?" Back at Blood River, Summer enters an empty house after hearing a litany of religious babble coming from an old record player. Joseph's accusatory monologue reaches a fever pitch, insisting that "everyone has a secret" as they reach the car. As Clark opens the trunk to find a dead body inside, Summer finds Ben's photo tacked to the wall, eyes scratched out. Events take a surreal turn as Joseph suddenly appears next to Summer, telling her Blood River is "where the sinful come to die." The gun is useless, empty of bullets. "This is my child now," the drifter says as he etches a cross into Summer's forehead. Clark returns just in time, attacking Joseph and beating him unconscious.

The third, most grueling, act finds Summer caught between Clark, who reveals a shockingly animalistic side, and Joseph, who assumes an ever more godlike role as the film races to its hellish conclusion. "You can't kill me, man! You have created this monster!" Joseph cackles as Clark maims and mutilates his adversary. Wavering between fear and anger, Summer is unsure who to trust or believe—and neither are we, even after the last drops of blood have been shed. An apocalyptic finale, set in a cemetery teeming with the graves of the damned, poses the question at the film's center—how well do we really know those that we love? When Summer screams "Who are you?" to her husband, he has no response. Her final act doesn't bring her any closer to the truth, nor does she escape Joseph's judgment. "Your sin was apathy. You knew what he was, but did nothing," he says before leaving her alone to deal with this new, terrible knowledge.

Defined by its three-hander cast, stark setting, and unexpected lashings of violence, *Blood River* comes as close as any recent desert terror film to resurrecting the rugged, unpredictable spirit of *The Sadist*. Aesthetically, the dusty, junk-strewn ghost town of Blood River recalls that film's lonely auto yard, as does the story arc, with helpless out-of-towners pitted against a predatory drifter with murder (and possibly worse) in mind. Also like *The Sadist* (and many other desert terrors from *The Hills Have Eyes* to *Poker Run*), *Blood River* critiques the complacent (upper) middle class, who must ultimately resort to savagery to survive the attacks from a vicious "outsider." Mason's film differs from its model(s) in several significant ways, however, the most obvious of which is its treatment of antagonist Joseph, who, over the course of the film, transforms from dangerous, Tibbs-like societal outcast to an avenging angel with time and space-bending abilities to rival *The Hitcher*'s John Ryder (he even heals himself at one point). In a film that thrives on ambiguities, the story leaves little doubt that Joseph's meeting with Clark and Summer was no random incident, but preordained.

Though part of a long tradition of desert terror films that examine marital discord, *Blood River* is the first to incorporate overtly religious material into its narrative. Mason's film does so with a straight-faced seriousness of purpose that echoes Joseph's fire-and-brimstone tirades, as the director uses swooping overhead shots to suggest an omniscient point of view. Crucially, the film's metaphysical elements never overwhelm the human drama at its core, as Clark and Summer's deep-seated conflict blossoms long before Joseph intrudes into their lives, with an auto breakdown leading to one bitter exchange to another. Like the best desert terrors, the film utilizes the isolating effect of its uninhabited location to tease out the secret fears and desires of its characters. While Mason sometimes goes stylistically overboard with an unrelentingly earthy palette of browns and greys, Stuart Brereton's deft photography aptly conveys the heat, discomfort, and maddening psychological effect of being stranded in the forgotten, crumbling town.

In crafting such an ambitious tale, Mason and co-writer Simon Boyes inevitably fumble a few story elements. For example: if Clark is a murderer, why would he hide the body in his trunk before starting a cross-country odyssey with his wife? Joseph's targeting of the motel also feels a bit arbitrary, given his "fateful" meeting with Clark and Summer the very next day. And Joseph's keen interested in Summer's pregnancy, or what his true intentions are for her child, is never really explained. While these and a few other questions are left hanging, the film remains buoyed by a trio of strong lead performances (in a first for the genre, all three actors were born outside the United States), fresh ideas, and a plethora of arresting images. A mesmerizing balancing act of realism and the spiritual, *Blood River* charts its own course into the dark heart of existential horror.

Like the most important indie desert terrors of the aughts—*Gerry*, *Twentynine Palms*, *Blood River*—*The Canyon* (2009) rests on the shoulders of just a few players and one visually striking location. Boasting strong performances, slick production values, and the most relentlessly grim survival narrative since *The Oasis*, Richard Harrah's feature debut carves out its own gritty yet uniquely humanistic take on the genre. Likable young newlyweds Nick (Eion Bailey) and Laurie Conway (Yvonne Strahovski) drive straight from their Las Vegas elopement to the Grand Canyon, where Nick plans on taking a guided mule ride into the park. Arriving too late to secure a permit, the couple's prayers

One of the best desert terror films of the last ten years, *The Canyon* (2009) benefits tremendously from a strong lead performance by Yvonne Strahovski.

are answered when crusty, eccentric "guide extraordinaire" Henry Pritchard (character actor great Will Patton) offers his services. More inclined to "stay in bed all day" and wary of Henry's reliability, Laurie is finally convinced by Nick's question, "What if we never get another chance at this? What if there are no more trips?" His words will assume an eerily prophetic quality over the next few days.

The trio's journey into "The Canyon" begins on a playful note, as Henry regales the couple with Davy Crockett–like tall tales in between sips from a flask. Laurie's inherent skepticism is replaced with hope for the future as she and Nick romantically explore an enormous cavern together. When Henry suggests leaving the established trail to check out some ancient petroglyphs, Nick once again persuades his doubtful bride to go along with it. The decision turns out to be ill-fated, however, when Henry's mule is attacked by a rattlesnake, which bites him both in the arm and (in a cringe-worthy moment) the face. In the fracas, most of the group's animals gallop away, including their supply mule, leaving them stranded with little more than a matchbook, a hunting knife and a few sticks of gum. Laurie's attempts to use her cell phone are, of course, useless ("Sometimes them things work up here, and sometimes they don't," is Henry's calm reaction), forcing them to camp for the night. Far-off howls prompt the ailing Henry to groan, "They're just looking to survive, just like you and me."

Survival, indeed, becomes a serious concern over the next few days, as the couple retrace their steps while Henry becomes sicker and less coherent by the hour. The vast, unending landscape of rocky hills and mountains quickly turns from awe-inspiring to ominous as Laurie realizes they are lost in the canyon—and utterly alone. Henry's death, followed by Nick's leg injury forces the previously deferential Laurie to make a series of tough decisions for them both. In a grueling series of literal trials by fire, Laurie takes agonizingly slow steps toward freedom while fending off repeated, and increasingly deadly, attacks from indigenous wildlife. Far from the gentler pace established earlier, these sequences play out in relentlessly real time, often inducing exhaustion (if not outright sickness) in the viewer as Laurie resorts to savage methods to survive against increasingly difficult circumstances. Worn down by the heat, their injuries, and desert predators, the beleaguered pair struggle to make their final stand against their pursuers. The finale is both heart-rending and sadly believable, as Laurie's herculean efforts are ultimately no match for the unforgiving world of the canyon.

The few desert terrors exploring "man versus nature" often add human antagonists to create additional conflict; *The Canyon* stands apart from these films by embracing the theme in an undiluted way, as Laurie and Nick are not at war with anyone (even their arguments are relatively brief) except the harsh environment of the canyon itself. Even while rooting for the couple to make it out alive, the film refuses to demonize its environment or its native wildlife. Henry's final words—"It ain't that Mother nature's cruel. She don't care one way or another about it. But make no mistake, she will have her day."— summarize the film's neutral attitude; if anything, Harrah passes judgment on the careless humans who've infringed on the natural landscape over the years. "We've encroached on their territory for so long … nothin' left for them to eat," is Henry's accurate description of the wolves, and it's hard to argue with him, even as we can't help sympathizing with "intruders" Laurie and Nick.

The Canyon also distinguishes itself with its distinctively strong, resourceful, and consistently relatable female lead. From its inception, desert terror has typically been a male-dominated genre, with leading women's roles usually limited to the terrified victim

(*Night Terror*, *Leatherface*), the partner of a tougher male (*Kingdom of the Spiders*, *Nightwing*), or a psychotic bitch (*The Velvet Vampire*, *Prey of the Chameleon*, *U-Turn*). Heroic female leads (such as *Dying Room Only*'s Jean Mitchell or Joan White in *White of the Eye*), on the other hand, are a rarity. Aussie actress Strahovski, who displays charm, intelligence and great chemistry with co-lead Bailey, not only joins that short list, but automatically moves to its upper echelon. Through her tour-de-force performance, Laurie's gradual transformation from sheltered suburbanite to primal survivalist is refreshingly believable, with self-doubt and exhaustion repeatedly overshadowing her hard-earned triumphs. Bailey is equally good, perhaps shining brightest in the film's grueling last third. Nick and Laurie's relationship, which has barely entered a new phase before being strained to the breaking point, achieves a genuine emotional pull that never becomes maudlin thanks to the combined talents of the two performers. Even the toughest situations are tempered with a strain of black humor, which gives both the characters and the audience a chance to breathe. Unlike other desert terrors of the period, which explore the violent dissolution of male/female relationships (*Twentynine Palms*, *Dreamland*, *Poker Run*, *Blood River*), *The Canyon* focuses on a couple's unified fight to survive. Far from corny or traditionalist, it lends the film an edge over its more distanced contemporaries, and creates a level of viewer engagement rarely experienced in the genre.

Alongside its impressive performances (including Patton, who steals nearly every scene he's in) and straightforward, well-paced script, Harrah's muscular direction gives an edge to the action sequences while smartly allowing the emotional beats room to breathe. Nelson Cragg's Utah location photography is among the best of the new millennium, with the titular location presented in a dynamic yet naturalistic way. Like the best desert terror films, the location easily counts as an additional character, with Harrah successfully conveying both the staggering beauty and terrifying loneliness of the Grand Canyon's massive grounds. Crisp editing, an atmospheric score, and some subtle but effective makeup effects also contribute to the film's success, as it smartly resists the urge for excessive stylization and rightly concentrates on its characters' horrifying predicament. Emotionally stirring but never melodramatic, *The Canyon* is one of the most engaging, visceral and uncompromising entries of the New Minimalist era and a worthy finale to one of desert terror's most fiercely individualistic decades.

12

New Blood

"Now, I could kill you right here, and that would be one end. But this started in the desert. And it's gonna end there, brother, you understand?"— Jack, *Mojave*

The aughts, a troubled yet fascinating period which yielded some of the most obscure and widest-release desert terrors of all time, ultimately saw the independents forge ahead with numerous innovative efforts as the studios retreated to safer, more predictable, waters. While 2009 marked one of the most prolific and distinguished years for the genre, independent filmmakers were ultimately not able to sustain such high levels of production. As a result, the first few years of the so-called "twenties" (2010–the present) were relatively quiet, as both studios and indies alike limited their desert terror output to the lowest levels of production in the genre's fifty-year history. Out of these lean years, the modern desert terror film emerged. These "new era" desert terrors bear both studio and indie qualities, with slicker production values and big-name talent (James Franco, Michael Douglas, Kurt Russell) combined with the lingering traits of New Minimalism: off-kilter storylines, reduced casts, and atmospheric, more naturalistic location shooting.

Recent desert terror films have tended to be higher-profile than the past decade's crop, thanks to the prestige talent involved and the rise in popularity of film festivals and theatrical venues (like Austin's indie-friendly Alamo Drafthouse, since expanded into a national chain) that cater to an increasing interest in alternative programming. *Dark Blood*, for example, gained recognition solely from festival screenings while the more commercial entries that followed—*Bone Tomahawk*, *Beyond the Reach*, and *Mojave*—all enjoyed (limited) theatrical exposure in advance of widespread Blu-Ray and VOD debuts. Perhaps what all these films indicate, aside from their stars' and creators' interest in pursuing more challenging projects that fall outside studio guidelines, is the modern audience's willingness to take the genre seriously again, perhaps for the first time since the Tarantino/Rodriguez–dominated '90s.

The major studios' contributions to the current era, if not as innovative (or consistent), at least demonstrate a willingness to support the desert terror genre after a long period of inactivity. The first significant desert terror film of the decade, Danny Boyle's *127 Hours*, was released by studio indie division Fox Searchlight and perfectly embodies the new model: a minimalist, single-character narrative supported by an Oscar-winning director, an A-list movie star, and a studio (indie division) release. More recently, the star-driven, minimalist films of Jason Blum's horror-centric production company Blumhouse also blur the lines between independent and studio content. The company's first desert terror effort, *Curve*, is more than just a vehicle for its dancer/singer/ actress star, while *The Darkness* employs even bigger name talent to resurrect the Native American horror film after many years of dormancy. Blum's interest in desert terror also extends to the recently proposed *Tremors* reboot, which, according to a 2015 Hollywood Reporter article, would include the participation of original *Tremors* star (and *The Darkness* headliner) Bacon. Whether others beyond Blum will take up the cause remains to be seen, but hardly matters; the independents remain, as always, the most vital, and consistent, creators of desert terror.

After a sporadic series of uneven (and underseen) offerings throughout the last few years of the aughts, studio-supported desert terror returned in a major way with *127 Hours* (2010), a slickly-produced, stylishly-directed "man against nature" tale that follows closely in the footsteps of the previous year's *The Canyon*. Like Gus Van Sant's minimalist *Gerry*, the film is based on a true story, in this case Aron Ralston's 2005 bestseller *A Rock and a Hard Place*, the grueling account of the author's struggle to survive after becoming trapped in a crevasse while hiking through Colorado's Blue John Canyon in 2003. Little time is wasted in the hyperkinetic opening, which follows loner Ralston (James Franco) as he quickly packs for the trip, then drives through the night to his destination. Mountain biking frantically through the desert the next morning, Ralston meets a pair of attractive female hikers (Kate Mara and Amber Tamblyn), who provide temporary company as the trio frolic in a stunning underground lake. Despite his promises to attend the girls' party, the obsessively driven Ralston won't make it; while traversing a crevasse, he falls between two rock walls, his left arm pinned by an immovable boulder.

For the remainder of *127 Hours*, we're trapped with Ralston as he battles fatigue, hunger, freezing temperatures, inclement weather and his own fears and insecurities while trying to devise some way to extract himself from an increasingly dire situation. At first, he's surprisingly sanguine about his predicament, carefully laying out all the tools at his disposal and examining various possibilities for escape (while cursing himself for forgetting an essential pocket knife). Like his protagonist, Boyle uses every cinematic device imaginable to draw us into Ralston's cramped physical space while simultaneously expanding the somewhat limited narrative through a variety of memories, dreams, and hallucinations. One of the director's most effective techniques is drawn directly from life; throughout the film, Ralston records himself with a MiniDV camera, narrating his trials and tribulations with a mixture of self-awareness, pathos and wry humor. Thanks to Franco's generous performance, these sequences achieve a degree of intimacy, growing increasingly uncomfortable as Ralston slides into self-pity and dementia.

Anyone who has even a passing knowledge of Ralston's experience (which is verbally and visually referenced in *The Canyon*) knows how the film must end, and here, Boyle dispenses with all photographic gimmickry or ironic music interludes and returns to the bracing reality of MiniDV to present the graphic process by which, after exhausting all other options, the hiker must sever his own arm to live. Shown mostly through the lens of Ralston's own handycam, the film accurately conveys the gory details of the drawn-out process in what is easily its most disturbing sequence. If technically well-accomplished, the key to its effectiveness remains Franco's selfless portrayal, equally agonized and liberated as he violently insures his freedom. The film doesn't stop there, either, following Ralston as he drags himself through the desert before finally securing help. An uplifting, if a bit sappy, finale brings the real Ralston (and his family) into the narrative.

Despite its focus on physical extremes, *127 Hours* features a psychological depth consistent with the genre's best efforts. Its use of a singular protagonist—the smallest cast yet for a desert terror film—is more than incidental; in the hands of Boyle and screenwriter Simon Beaufoy, Ralston's dilemma becomes as much about coming to terms with his own personality flaws as it does with freeing himself from his rocky prison. Spectral flashes of failed or undernourished relationships (an ex-girlfriend, his sister) float in and out of the narrative unexpectedly, pushing Ralston toward a greater self-understanding alongside his more pressing life-or-death struggle. Through Ralston's ordeal, Boyle posits not just the standard man versus nature debate familiar to the genre, but also uses the desert as a source of introspection about human relationships in the modern age. "This rock has been waiting for me my entire life," sighs Ralston in a Zen-like moment before severing his own limb. The film's existential leanings, however, never lessen the film's moments of creeping dread and abject terror, which register as strongly as any other desert terror film.

Anchored by Franco's engaging lead performance, the film is as visually and aurally impressive as any of Boyle's varied credits. If its playful visions and use of music recall the cinematic highs of *Trainspotting* (1996), *127 Hours* is even more influenced by Boyle's more recent *Slumdog Millionaire* (2008), which earned Oscars for both Best Picture and Best Director. This was Boyle's immediate follow-up project, and several *Slumdog* alums—Danish director of photography Anthony Dod Mantle (sharing credit with Enrique Chediak), Indian composer A.R. Rahman, and British co-writer Beaufoy—contribute their distinctive international flavors to enrich and expand Ralston's internalized narrative. Mantle's nimble videography, which brings the rough, technically minimalist Dogme conventions to big-budget desert terror for the first time, is especially noteworthy. An upmarket, more obviously dramatic addition to the survival subgenre pioneered by films like *The Oasis* and *The Canyon*, *127 Hours* remains the most ambitious studio contribution to the genre in the current decade.

The straight-to-video efforts following *127 Hours* continued the aughts' New Minimalism stylings. The first of these, the arty thriller *Drifter* (2010), occupies a shaky middle ground between *Bone Dry*'s flashback-fueled narrative and the *Reeker* films' anything-goes atmosphere. In a landscape of infinite dunes, investment banker Martin (Cameron Daddo) wakes up with a still-fresh scar stitched across his back. Urban legends of organ theft circulate as Martin meets up with three more stranded souls, including wiseass Jake (Ryan Alosio) and photographer Grace (Darcy Halsey), who also woke up in the desert without a clue as to how they got there. Mistrust and conflicts soon break out, though Martin takes a more philosophical view of their surreal plight, insisting, "Somehow we're connected.... I've seen you all before." After their first night in the desert (which introduces the first of Martin's many flashbacks to his "former" work and private life), things get grisly: Jake tears away his stitches and pulls a ring (?!) from inside his body cavity while a thirsty Martin laps up blood from Grace's wound.

Instead of explaining these *Saw*-like grotesqueries, Dutch co-writer/director Roel Reine (who also produced, photographed and co-edited) pulls the action out of the desert, transporting the foursome from one scenic environment after another (a canyon lake, lush tropics, downtown Los Angeles) as they try to unravel the meaning behind their increasingly nightmarish (and nonsensical) predicament. "We're being tested," Martin keeps repeating, and the audience will likely feel the same way; *Drifter* suffers from the same frustratingly jumbled plotting as several of its contemporaries, with reality and fantasy bumping randomly against one another before a last-minute revelation provides an "a-ha" moment for the frazzled audience. The film's story weaknesses might matter less if the characters were more likable, but "hero" Martin is an unpleasant, materialistic prick who fails to elicit the necessary viewer sympathy, and his companions are thinly drawn at best. Slickly made and often visually appealing (especially in the first half hour, which takes place entirely at California's picturesque Algodones Dunes), *Drifter* ultimately becomes mired in the sands of its own pseudo-existential narrative.

The similarly ambitious—and even loopier—*Life Blood* (2010) finds lesbian vampires stalking the desert for the first time since *The Velvet Vampire*. A 1969 prologue finds attractive young Sapphic lovers Brooke (Sophie Monk) and Rhea (Anya Lahiri) making out at a Hollywood pad during a New Year's Eve party. The celebration turns decidedly un-groovy when man-hating Brooke stabs an abusive actor (Justin Shilton) to death after he sexually attacks a young fan (Scout Taylor-Compton). Riding through the desert along Pearblossom Highway, Brooke's confession of murder leads to a cataclysmic cycle of events, climaxing with her being whisked away into the sky (?!), while sweet-natured Rhea is visited by a glowing, naked female Goddess (Angela Lindvall), who gives Rhea "the gift of eternal life" through a passionate kiss in a scene that awkwardly intertwines sexual and religious imagery. Before departing, the Goddess agrees to resurrect murderess Brooke, warning Rhea that "You shall kill to survive ... the truly wicked are the ones you must destroy."

Things get even weirder in 2009, as Brooke and Rhea crawl out of *Body Snatchers*-like cocoons (both still smoking hot, and wearing the clingiest of nighties) after a forty-year nap. "We're more alive than ever. Time is now eternal," Rhea sighs dreamily before laying out the rules of their new, vampiric/angelic existence. Brooke is more concerned with finding her next meal, which appears in the form of a motorist and his hitchhiker pal ("If I'd known this is what it'd be like, I'd have killed forever ago," Brooke snorts, in one of the film's many grammatically-challenged lines). As the sun rises, the undying duo seek shelter at the strangely-named "Murder World" gas station, where Brooke sexually torments clerk Dan (Patrick Renna)–and the audience—with lines like "You want to play with me the way I'd like to play with you?" in between bickering with her goody two-shoes girlfriend. Brooke racks up a minor body count ("I *am* Murder World," she scoffs) before heading back to the desert, where a head-scratching finale finds the two ex-lovers once again locked in supernatural conflict.

Poised uncomfortably between male-gaze lesbian fantasy and humorless religious hokum, *Life Blood* (which was shot under the less commercial title *Pearblossom*) is an unbalanced concoction to say the least. Unlike previous desert terror vampire outings like *Near Dark* or *The Forsaken*, the film generates surprisingly little sexual heat, does even less with its desert location and makes no attempt at social commentary. The intriguing opening, with its femme fatale couple and lost highway lunacy, flirts with a pseudo–Lynchian atmosphere before dissolving in a fizz of (literal) angel dust, and the claustrophobic, stagy Murder World scenes drain the narrative of any remaining energy it has left. Co-leads Monk and Lahiri are certainly easy on the eyes, but their light-and-dark act gets old fast, with Rhea's new-age nattering ("In the face of the Lord, I will rid this world of evil.... I am your soldier!") contrasting sharply with hyper-sexualized Brooke, whose plumped lips, fake breasts and over the top performance ("I'm going to kill you and kill you and kill you!"), plays like an unwitting parody of a typical B-movie seductress.

Swerving from high camp to deadly seriousness, writer-director Ron Carlson

Lesbian vampires Brooke (Sophie Monk, left) and Rhea (Anya Lahiri) hunt the desert for fresh victims in *Life Blood* (2010).

demonstrates consistence only in a commitment to pulling his punches in the sex and violence departments. Brooke and Rhea share just a few smooches, and a smattering of half-hearted nudity is provided solely by Lindvall (in two brief appearances) and a few extras during the opening party scenes. The film's vampire action is handled in a similarly restrained fashion, with Brooke spilling just a few drops of blood over several murders. The various supernatural manifestations rely on goofy visual effects or even sillier dialogue ("Your knowledge is your power") that often confuses rather than illuminates. Even worse are the film's attempts at humor, which consist of the local sheriff (Charles Napier, in a welcome return to the genre after his memorable lead in the short film "China Lake") guffawing at an inane T&A show called "Chics Chasing Chickens" while his dwarf deputy (Danny Woodburn) drives around town trying to solve the mystery.

Like *Death Valley*, *Route 666* and *Dreamland*, *Life Blood* grounds its action in a real place (the desert community of Pearblossom is about eighty miles northeast of Los Angeles); unfortunately, it lacks the specific environmental details needed to bring its location to life on screen. The introductory nighttime scenes are severely underlit, effectively eliminating any much-needed background atmospherics. The later, daytime desert material is minimal and similarly uninspired. In an effort to distract from the film's visual deficiencies, Carlson populates his cast with newly minted semi-stars like Monk (*The Hills Run Red*), Taylor-Compton (Rob Zombie's *Halloween*) and Electra Avellan (*Machete*) in a misguided effort to lend the project some kind of exploitation cred. An unpalatable combination of the sacred and the profane, *Life Blood* is a much more anemic affair than its title would suggest.

One of the most significant desert terror films of the current decade was shot over twenty years ago, and that's only one of the many mysteries and contradictions surrounding George Sluizer's *Dark Blood* (2012). In 1993, the film had completed its location shooting Utah and was still shooting on Los Angeles soundstages when, on Halloween night, its star River Phoenix died of a drug overdose at the notorious Viper Room on Sunset Boulevard. Though nearly completed, the financial entities involved opted to pull the plug on the project and archive the footage, leaving the film in limbo until 2011, when director Sluizer, who was himself in poor health, edited together an incomplete but releasable version. It is this cut, which Sluizer himself termed "a chair with three legs," which screened at film festivals around the world throughout 2012 and 2013, allowing audiences a long-awaited look at the final screen credit of both Phoenix and Sluizer, director of the excellent *The Vanishing* (1989), who passed away in 2014. The resulting work, which incorporates occasional voice-over passages in place of missing scenes, is far from perfect, but much more coherent and involving than one might expect.

Middle-aged Hollywood couple Harry (Jonathan Pryce) and his alcoholic wife Buffy (Judy Davis) drive through the New Mexico desert in an absurdly incongruous Bentley, arguing their way through a second honeymoon before returning to Los Angeles. Their stay at a motel is blighted by the odd behavior of the proprietor (Karen Black), who wistfully recalls the days of "actual nuclear tests" which generated "wall to wall tourists." "You could hear the big bang from here," she sighs before pointing out the "bad moon" in the night sky. The next morning, Harry's car breaks down in the middle of a desolate canyon, with not a filling station (or other car) in sight. The couple's bitter repartee, which feels like an endless game with no clear winner, reaches a fever pitch as they blame each other for the situation. "We're going to let it all hang out, are we? I'll scream, you'll shout. We'll have some tears, kiss and make up. I'll give you a quick one in the back seat," Harry sighs, suggesting this is far from the first time this has happened. That night, Buffy follows a distant light to the isolated dwelling of Boy (River Phoenix), a young man of mixed descent ("I'm one-eighth Hopi Indian—got dark blood in my veins") who lives alone in the desert. Strangely charmed by Buffy, Boy takes her and Harry in for the night.

Over the next few days, Harry's plans to have his car repaired are consistently thwarted by Boy, who, aided by the local Indian community, continues to delay or complicate to the work involved. At first, Boy seems eccentric but genuinely sympathetic, with his "full-blooded Navajo" wife lost to cancer and a close association with the local tribe, who were moved off their native lands by the government's nuclear tests. His sexual interest in Buffy, however, is clearly felt as he shows her his retreat, a cave decorated with candles and hand-carved totems that is half religious sanctuary, half bomb shelter. "You don't get something you want because you're lucky. You get it because you will it," he says while stroking her hair. "You're a very disturbing young man," she replies, sounding more intrigued than scared. Boy's intentions become even clearer once she finds a photo of her former self, cut from the pages of an old Playboy and pinned to the wall.

Harry's mounting frustration at being marooned in Boy's middle-of-nowhere shack is exacerbated by their host's increasingly obvious advances on Buffy. A tense hunting trip taken by the two men ends with Boy's angry disappearance, forcing Harry to find his own way back. After several foiled escape attempts, Boy imprisons Harry in a shed while, in exchange for her and her husband's freedom, Buffy agrees to make love with their obsessed captor. A final confrontation between Harry and Boy results in an accidental, but fatal, injury that, like many scenes in the film, pairs sex and death in a disturbing way. As Boy dies in Buffy's arms, leaving a smear of dark blood on her bosom, one can't help but think of Phoenix's own untimely passing during the shooting of this troubled, and troubling, would-be masterpiece.

Dark Blood's journey from its interrupted production (which is well documented in Gavin Edwards' book *Last Night at the Viper Room*) to festival screenings has been a long and difficult one, but the more-or-less completed film works surprisingly well. The first two-thirds of the film move along relatively smoothly; in fact, Sluizer's voice-over interruptions sometimes do more harm than good, often pulling the viewer out of the developing story instead of filling in the blanks. The third act, which focuses primarily on Buffy and Boy's deepening connection, is the most disjointed, as several intimate scenes between the two (including their crucial lovemaking scene, which, due to lack of interior footage, is witnessed solely through a window) are simply missing. The loss of those scenes is a real shame, as while all three performances are top notch, the connection between Boy and Buffy really forms the heart of the movie, and the scenes featuring Phoenix and Davis—such as Boy's sharing of his cave shelter with Buffy—reveal a genuine chemistry. Thankfully, enough key moments—such as their final scene together—are retained, with the actors' performances often conveying more with a simple gesture than any words could express.

Despite having been filmed in the early '90s, *Dark Blood* doesn't feel dated at all; if anything, the film's environmental and cultural observations are more pertinent now than ever. Ironically, its three-hander dramatics, pared-down plot and intense focus on its natural environment place the film more comfortably within contemporary New Minimalist trends than its own production period. Like its contemporaries *Twentynine Palms*, *Blood River* and *The Canyon*, *Dark Blood* fuses classic desert terror elements (stranded

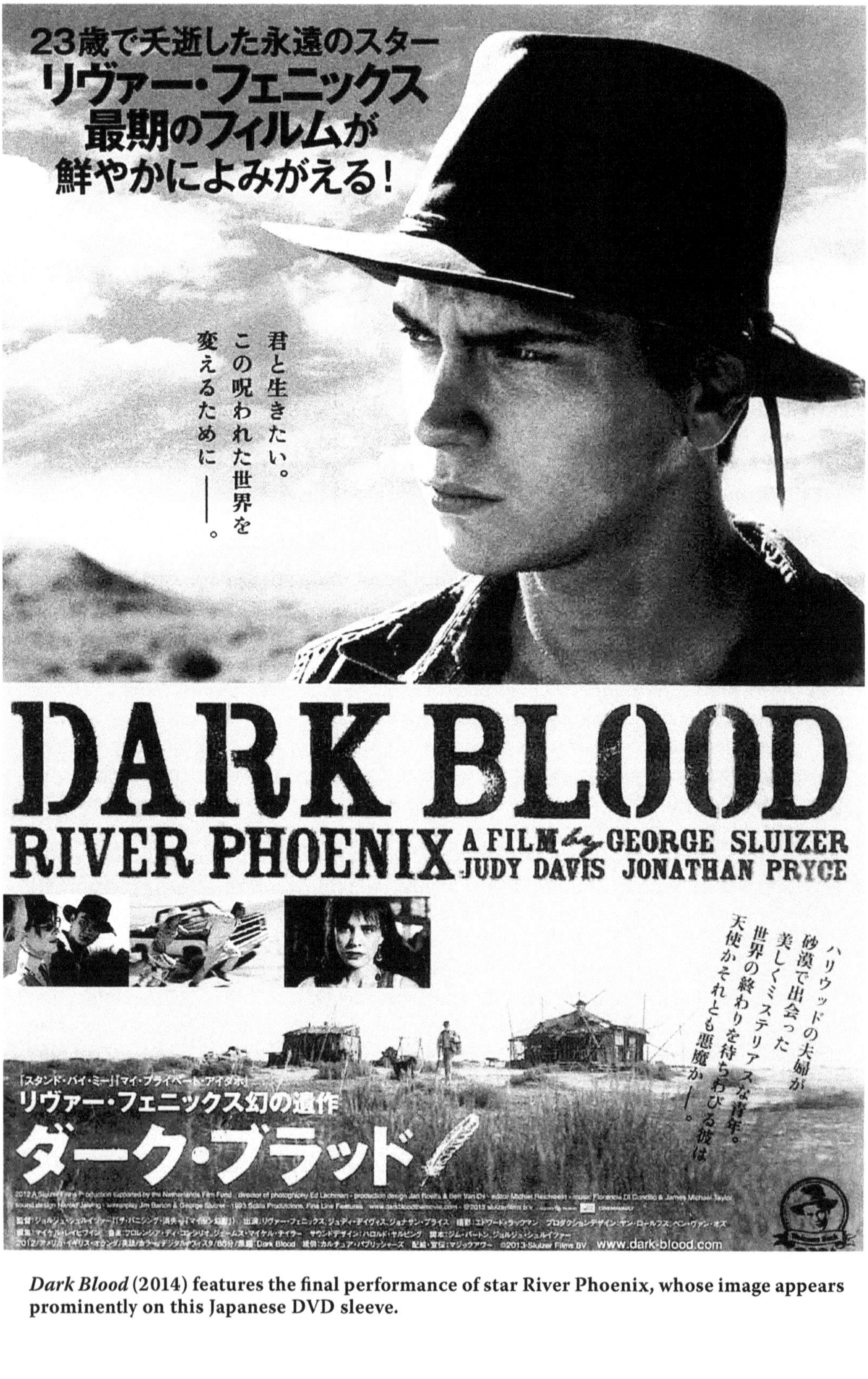

Dark Blood (2014) features the final performance of star River Phoenix, whose image appears prominently on this Japanese DVD sleeve.

travelers, man against nature) with new twists and themes to breathe new life into many of the genre. From the first shots of the primal Boy howling at the moon, followed by a drunken Buffy carrying on amidst the remains of Native American civilization (now a tourist destination), the film contrasts city dwellers' behavior with that of the locals upon whose lands they have intruded. It's a theme familiar to many classic desert terrors, from *The Sadist* to *Kalifornia*, but *Dark Blood* challenges typical viewer assumptions further by making Harry and Buffy equally unpleasant from the beginning and treating the deranged Boy with notable empathy. As the roles reverse and Boy's sinister intentions are revealed, the viewer must rethink their opinion of all parties involved. The final scenes, which paints the mentally disturbed Boy as strangely noble, and makes Harry a murdering coward, refuses to give easy answers.

Through Boy's part–Hopi character, *Dark Blood* stands as the first desert terror film—and likely one of the first Hollywood productions—to seriously address current Native American issues within a dramatic context. Put into production years before Johnny Depp's ill-fated passion project *The Brave* (with which it shares more than a few similarities), Sluizer's thriller delves directly into the fate of the Native American population, with the radiation-related death of Boy's wife a singular tragedy that symbolizes an entire community uprooted—and poisoned—by postwar nuclear testing in the area. "It was all theirs once … now a Chicago bank owns it," Boy says ruefully as he gazes out on a breathtaking canyon. "They used to have a better place in this valley … then the tests started. They were down wind, so the army moved 'em out." At the same time, the film is unafraid to show how such values can be twisted by one's own personal psychology, as Boy's end-of-the-world shelter (which he plans to "share" with Buffy) adopts spiritual motifs and symbolism in the service of his own weirdly apocalyptic prophecies. Ironically, the only "end" Boy achieves through his possessive, violent actions is his own.

Just as Jim Barton's script utilizes Boy's isolation to comment on the treatment of indigenous peoples, it also employs Buffy and Harry's broken relationship to take shots at Hollywood. Instead of embodying the usual showbiz clichés, the pair are far from the glamorous stereotypes one would expect, with Buffy's "Bunny" period long since passed, and "working actor" Harry's desperation to return to Los Angeles based primarily on losing a part in an admittedly lousy project ("I haven't worked in a year," he confides to Boy). The couple's "romantic weekend" (per Sluizer's description) becomes more like an extended therapy session, as Buffy is forced to finally act on years of flirtatious behavior, while Harry finally calls her out, and fights to protect them. Though undeniably cathartic, the lingering effects of their encounter with Boy are left intentionally ambiguous. The film's final shot, which brings the entire narrative full circle, watches stoically from the back seat as Harry and Buffy drive away from Boy's burning residence. "Are you okay?" Harry asks after some time has passed. Her measured response, which receives no answer, is, "No. Are you?"

If everything had gone according to plan, *Dark Blood* would likely have been released in 1994 or 1995, which would likely have seen it eclipsed by the likes of *Natural Born Killers* and *From Dusk Till Dawn*, as the desert terror genre moved away from smaller-scale, morally ambiguous thrillers in favor of a "more is more" approach that featured bigger, louder visions of cartoonish violence decorated with marquee names. Much like Richard Stanley's 1992 desert thriller *Dust Devil* (which features the same producers, and a similar visual aesthetic, as Sluizer's film), *Dark Blood* would be "lost" for years before a filmmaker-sponsored reconstruction led to its long-awaited appraisal by curious cinema fans. While impossible to ignore its missing sections, the reconstituted *Dark Blood*'s strengths—its three central performances, Ed Lachman's gorgeous photography, a strong screenplay—far outnumber its weaknesses. At the 2014 Cannes Film Festival, Lionsgate announced plans to acquire and distribute the film on VOD, but, nearly three years later, any kind of Stateside release has yet to occur. *Dark Blood* remains commercially available only in Japan, where a DVD was released in 2014.

In the absence of studio or major independent releases, smaller, straight to video efforts continued to dot the landscape. Shot in the deserts just north of Los Angeles, *Venom* (2013) and *Reservation* (2014) usher the micro-budget desert terror film into the current era. The former, and more appealing of the two, references earlier creature features like *Rattlers* while providing some of the genre's best reptile action since *Curse II*. Gary Breslin's modest survival thriller may never reach that film's lunatic heights, but its central conceit—that a snake would seek revenge for one of its own, to the extent of pursuing its victims over miles of open desert—is still pretty loopy. Trying to detox from her booze-and-dug fueled existence in Los Angeles, Helen (Jessica Morris) takes her worldly teenage daughter Lilly (Oliviah Crawford) on a reparative road trip to a horse ranch deep in the outlying desert. Mom (who Lilly insists on calling "Helen") and daughter don't get along too well, and Helen's accidental killing of a snake (which ends up wrapped around her front tire) only adds to the tension. Soon afterward, another serpent shows up in the front seat, biting Helen on the arm before slithering away. But it's not the last time they'll see this particular snake, as it, along with a growing army of its cold-blooded cousins, returns to menace them again, and again, and again.

Most of the time, *Venom* (not to be confused with the superior 1981 Oliver Reed/Klaus Kinski thriller or 2005's lame swamp-slasher) plays as a minimalist, and unusually female-oriented, update of the revenge of nature films of the '70s. Helen does some pretty stupid things (like tossing away an all-important cell phone early in the game) and has zero sense of direction, but Lilly makes up for it with knowledge gleaned from her iPad and general street smarts. The pair also benefit from the advice of a wizened old desert rat (Chuck Kelley) who explains that the snakes aren't simply following the scent of the female Helen ran over, but seeking to avenge her death. "The whole desert's after you—there's no stopping that," he insists before falling victim to a bite on the neck while asleep (why the snakes didn't bite Helen or Lilly is never brought up).

Unfortunately, the mother/daughter survival quest is constantly interrupted, and ultimately overshadowed, by a dumb subplot about various thugs scouring the desert for stolen drug money. These scenes, which emphasize action over horror, feel more like filler to pad out a skimpy screenplay, but nevertheless provide a few amusing moments. In one, crafty Lilly stuffs a snake into a man's canteen, only to bite him in the mouth when he drinks. A later scene finds main baddie Viggo (Roberto Sanchez) attacked by a bunch of the slimy critters when he gets coated with the scent. Like most of *Venom*, these scenes don't deliver the, ahem, bite that one would hope for; even the snakes—despite a constant rattling sound effect—are some of the least-threatening invertebrates ever to slither across the screen. An abrupt—and decidedly non-empowering—ending fails to provide a strong enough antidote to the previous eighty minutes of well-meaning but defanged filmmaking.

If *Venom* fails to completely capitalize on its poisonous title, *Reservation* might just be the perfect moniker for writer-director Michael McGowan's lifeless and unscary debut, which lacks the occasional scrappy inventiveness of most DIY entries. In an unpromising

Striking artwork for the snakes-meets-smugglers thriller *Venom* (2013).

setup, eight of the most unlikely campers ever (led by rapper-turned-actor Vyshon "Silkk The Shocker" Miller) drive out to the desert for a weekend getaway, where they have the bad luck to pitch their tents on an ancient Indian burial ground. In the middle of a campfire party, malevolent spirits appear (via some bad CGI) to separate the group and kill them off one by one while Richard (Ian Chidlaw, also credited with the hackneyed screenplay) flips through an *Evil Dead*–type book to understand what the hell is happening.

Nearly thirty years after such quirky outings as *Scalps* and *Haunted*, *Reservation* represents the genre's return to Native American horror, but its slipshod technique and lack of ideas only makes one appreciate the originality of those rough-edged, yet more engaging, outings. The film's more ethnically diverse cast, while refreshing, is mostly squandered as none of the characters are significantly developed beyond outmoded—and denigrating—"bros and hos" clichés. The jerky camerawork and choppy editing squander the vast desert locations, and the film's second half is literally unwatchable, with scenes lit solely by lighters and flashlights. Miller's presence, as well as the incessant rap/hip-hop soundtrack, leads one to feel that the film was reverse-engineered around the music, all of which was produced by the film's financier/distributor. "I seen too many scary movies to know how this shit end up," opines Miller, and he's not the only one; caught somewhere between a ghostly chiller and nu-slasher, *Reservation* will satisfy neither audience.

Like the creature feature and Native American horror film, the weird western had also endured somewhat of a dry spell since 2008's muted *The Burrowers*. S. Craig Zahler's *Bone Tomahawk* (2015) is a welcome return to the form and represents a mid-decade turning point in the types of budgets and stars that would be afforded future desert terror films. This seriocomic tale of cowboys and cannibals opens in the 1890s, as outlaws Purvis and Buddy (desert terror vets David Arquette and Sid Haig) are attacked by a barely seen "savage" while poking around a skull-strewn burial ground. Days later, Purvis arrives in the town of Bright Hope, where he is shot while scuffling with local Sheriff Franklin Hunt (Kurt Russell, in a welcome return to the genre after *Breakdown*). The next morning, a stable boy is found gutted, and Purvis, along with Deputy Nick (Evan Jonigkeit) and physician Samantha O' Dwyer (Lili Simmons), is gone. After the abductors are identified as a tribe of inbred cave dwellers who "rape and eat their own mothers," Hunt selects an oddball crew of volunteers including Samantha's wounded husband Arthur (Patrick Wilson), backup deputy Chicory (Richard Jenkins) and cold-blooded hired gun Brooder (Matthew Fox) to set out on a doomed rescue mission.

The pace slows considerably during the group's arduous three-day journey, as the script focuses on scuffles between the men (Brooder seems to bring out the worst in everyone he meets), an encounter with horse thieves (which forces them to make the last part of their journey on foot) and the progressive worsening of Arthur's injuries. Things get more interesting—and a lot bloodier—once Hunt and company reach the Valley of the Starving Men, where a tribe of "troglodytes" hold Samantha and Nick prisoner in a nearly inaccessible cave (which recalls *Riders of the Whistling Skull*'s spooky central location). In a series of increasingly violent, sometimes blackly humorous, confrontations, Hunt and his companions face off against the freakish clan of flesh-eaters. As with much of the film, nothing goes exactly as expected, with Arthur as the group's only hope for survival.

Boasting a unique concept and skillfully balancing western and horror elements, *Bone Tomahawk* also suffers from a frustratingly slow pace and overly austere direction. In his quest to convey the brutality and ennui of frontier life, Zahler leaves in a few too many non-essential "character" scenes that should have been shortened or eliminated (particularly during the film's middle section). Similarly, the director's visual approach tends toward wide framing and long takes, with some of the most static compositions since the silent era. The minimalist production design and monochromatic cinematography are rarely more than functional and suggest lack of funds rather than verisimilitude. Of the film's few desert locations, only the gulch, burial ground and cave scenes summon up an appropriately dark mood.

These artistic and storytelling deficits are mostly redeemed, however, by some spot-on casting, a wicked sense of humor ("It's got to taste better than people," Chicory remarks when one of the clan sips opium from Hunt's flask) and the cannibalistic trogs, who, with their white body paint and haunting screeches, make a much stronger impression than *The Burrowers*' barely-glimpsed creatures. Gore fans will enjoy the last half hour, which is chock full of graphic eviscerations, dismemberments, and decapitations as the title weapon is put to good use. Between this film and *The Hateful Eight*, 2015 was clearly The Year of the Bloody Kurt Russell Western, and fans of the actor's dependably cranky anti-heroes from his John Carpenter collaborations will undoubtedly enjoy seeing him spit out dialogue like, "You mention horses again, I'll slap you red." If more a cult curiosity than modern classic, *Bone Tomahawk* still ranks as the best weird western since *Silent Tongue*.

The Michael Douglas vehicle *Beyond the Reach* (2015) also applies Hollywood star power to its minimalist narrative, along with more polished production values. The first desert terror remake not based on a successful exploitation movie, *Reach* is the second film adaptation of the novel *Deathwatch*, first dramatized in 1974 as the TV movie *Savages*. With nearly forty years, a substantially larger budget, and a more permissive R rating separating the two films, it's surprising how closely *Reach* mirrors its predecessor while still tweaking and developing the material in several interesting ways. As in *Savages*, the story begins with Madec (Douglas, who also produced) hiring young tracker Ben (Jeremy Irvine) to accompany him on a Mojave Desert hunting trip. The film's amped-up aesthetic is immediately felt, as Madec is now a Trump-like billionaire who drives a Mercedes 6 × 6 truck and is in the middle of a $120 million deal. Local boy Ben is both less eccentric this time around and better developed, with a family who died in a desert sojourn and a devoted Native American girlfriend Laina (Hanna Mangan Lawrence). As the two men begin off-roading through the uninhabitable "reach," Madec intones, "Beyond this point, there will be monsters."

The film's only monster, of course, turns out to be Madec himself. After accidentally killing a local hermit (Martin Palmer) with an ill-timed shot, Madec goes into crisis-management mode. After Ben refuses his offer of hush money, Madec forces him at gunpoint to strip down to his underwear and reveals his intentions: "I'm not killing you, Ben. I'm just gonna watch you wander around for a while." Madec's "hunt" for Ben adds a few pleasing diversions, such as Ben's discovery of the hermit's subterranean camp, while preserving memorable moments—like Madec's martini—from the earlier film. As in *Savages*, Ben slips free of his tormentor into secret tunnels or taps hidden supply stashes time and again before enduring painful defeats. Throughout the ordeal, memories of Laina drive Ben onward, till he finally gathers enough energy to face off against Madec for an explosive final standoff, which pits slingshot against dynamite.

Like *Savages*, *Beyond the Reach* goes a bit limp in its third act, which jettisons the first film's lengthy interrogations (which follow the original novel) for a preposterous detour into slasher-style antics as Madec returns to further torment Ben and Laina. Until then, the film is at least as good if not better than its predecessor, anchored by a pair of strong lead performances and some jaw-droppingly beautiful cinematography by Russell

Beyond the Reach (2015) successfully updates Robb White's novel *Deathwatch* with bigger stars—like Michael Douglas—and slicker production values.

Carpenter (*Titanic*), whose stunning night sequences recall Australian outback classics like *Wake in Fright* and *Razorback*. The script by Stephen Susco (*The Grudge* 2004) supplies just enough character detail while upping the ante considerably in the chase/action/suspense sequences. Douglas, who plays Madec like a more psychotic version of his iconic Gordon Gekko character, has all the best lines ("Fool me once, shame on you.

Fool me twice, you die!"), but relative unknown Irvine proves a worthy adversary, with an expressive physical performance that allows us to feel the stinging heat, freezing cold, and every other painful sensation in between. Director Jean-Baptiste Leonetti, in his first American film, keeps the narrative moving while never neglecting the accompanying emotional content

Along with preserving the novel's inversion of typical desert terror tropes, Leonetti's film amplifies some of the themes inherent in its source material, with Madec's ceaseless quest for financial gain superseding morality gaining a chilling immediacy. Douglas' Madec is not only more unscrupulous and sadistic than Griffith's portrayal, he's far richer and more flamboyant, as well as a more experienced outdoorsman. Aside from making he and Ben more evenly matched, it allows their conflict to play out in more obvious terms of a class struggle, with poor and primitive battling high-tech wealth. The film's rugged New Mexico locations provide the perfect battleground for Madec and Ben's private war, with the desert by turns beautiful and deadly. Regardless of its implausible ending, *Reach* is still more satisfying than any of the studio desert terror remakes, and one that successfully updates its subject matter while making good use of its superior technical and budgetary resources.

The same year *Bone Tomahawk* and *Beyond the Reach* played in limited release, Universal returned to desert terror's most enduring series with *Tremors 5: Bloodlines* (2015). Like Miramax's *From Dusk Till Dawn* sequels, this fifth chapter in the studio's long-running horror/comedy franchise was shot in South Africa. The story also takes place there as well, resulting in a new spin on the usual Southwestern desert landscapes and the introduction of several new species of monsters. Series stalwart Burt Gummer (Michael Gross) returns once again, now a wannabe reality star paired with obnoxious videographer Travis (a puffy-looking Jamie Kennedy) to hunt down more advanced graboids and ass-blasters ("It's Africa. Everything's bigger," boasts a local as Burt surveys the bloody aftermath of a monster attack) in the wilds of Africa. Assisted by "smoking hot" scientist Nandi (Pearl Thusi) and undermined by shady profiteer Van Wyk (Daniel Janks), the ill-matched Burt and Travis combat giant worms and flying beasties—and each other—in a splattery series of standoffs in between bizarre non-sequiturs (Burt bathes in and drinks his own urine while trapped in a cage) and topical jokes (mostly supplied by Kennedy) that mostly fall flat.

The first *Tremors* film produced without the involvement of original scripters (and directors of the subsequent sequels) Brent Maddock and S.S. Wilson, *Bloodlines* is a somewhat schizophrenic outing that tries hard to entertain, but fails to unify its numerous plot threads (the script is credited to three writers, one of whom wrote *Tremors 3*) or strike a consistent tone. Actor-turned-director Don Michael Paul delivers plenty of monsters and gore (despite bearing a PG-13 rating, this is by far the most violent of the *Tremors* films) in a series of hyperkinetic action scenes, but leaves out much of the laid-back humor (and political asides) that previously defined the franchise. Though one can't take a film that features lines like "those fart-flaming sons of bitches have crossed your DMZ!" too seriously, there is an overall darker tone to the enterprise, with Burt more irritable than usual and often prone to angry outbursts at Kennedy, who calls his associate "Gummy Bears" and generally gets on everyone's nerves before finally saving the day.

Many of the film's best features are derived from its new locale, with Johannesburg's Cradle of Humankind wildlife preserve providing the perfect base of operations for various monster hunts, and its colorful locals—particularly strong and sexy Nandi, who's got quite a way with a flaming arrow—exhibiting more personality than usual as they clash with the American interlopers. While not exactly culturally probing, *Bloodline* is certainly an improvement over *Tremors 2: Aftershocks*, whose Mexican (by way of Southern California) setting and characters felt interchangeable with U.S.-set installments. Unsurprisingly, the graboids and other creatures are mostly rendered in CGI this time around and, while suitably fearsome, lack the handmade charm of the miniatures and puppetry associated with earlier films in the series. *Tremors 5* won't alienate hardcore *Tremors* fans, but it's unlikely to inspire new converts.

The following year, Blumhouse released its first desert terror film, *Curve* (2016) which, true to its title, frequently diverges from audience expectations. Chief among them is a strong lead performance by dancer-turned-actress Julianne Hough as young bride-to-be Mallory, who we first meet driving her fiancée's Bronco to Denver through a mountainous landscape. Reluctant to commit and annoyed with her beau's last-minute cancellation of their honeymoon, Mallory opts to take the scenic route. Soon afterward, her vehicle stalls in the middle of a canyon pass, leaving her stranded with no cell service. The appearance of hunky hitchhiker Christian (Teddy Sears) saves the day, however, as he fixes her engine before humbly accepting a ride to the next town. "You seem nice enough," she says, flirting with the idea of shacking up with a stranger. "You don't know me that well yet," is his bemused reply. Over the next few days, Mallory will find out many things about her new passenger—and even more about herself.

For a time, *Curve* follows the hitcher-killer template before suddenly switching gears, as Mallory's attempt to force the knife-wielding Christian out of her car results in a deadly off-road crash that ends with the vehicle landing at the bottom of a ravine. Christian emerges relatively unscathed, but Mallory is trapped inside the upside-down car with a serious leg injury. "You're on your own now," Christian says as he leaves her screaming for help, but in fact, he returns daily to check on her "progress," taunt her with food, or chat about her sex life. Most of the time, though, Mallory is utterly alone, and the film's best scenes—which play like a female take on *127 Hours*—follow her solo survival efforts in surprisingly grim detail. In one desperate moment, a starving Mallory kills a rat (by stabbing it with her car keys!), grills and eats it; in another, she drinks her own urine. Among survival-themed stranded scenarios, *Curve* might not rival *The Oasis*, or even *The Canyon*; but for a slicker, studio-funded production, it's grittier and more realistic than expected.

The film's disappointing third act abandons both road and survival genres for a more commonplace "thriller" ending that finds Mallory dodging slasher clichés (corpses wearing party hats, a body crucified to the wall) before taking on Christian one final time in a *Straw Dogs*–inspired finale that, if not totally believable, at least gives her a great parting line ("Maybe you just got in the wrong fucking car!"). The strange dynamic between Mallory and Christian lacks the mystical edge felt in *The Hitcher*'s Halsey/Ryder relationship, with a sexual undercurrent that goes nowhere and a trite explanation for Christian's psychotic behavior (his name is a clue) tossed off so casually it barely registers. *Curve* works best during Mallory's private moments, as when she burns her wedding dress for warmth while contemplating her fate. Director Iain Softley finds plenty of creative ways to frame the potentially repetitive (and claustrophobic) car interior sequences, and the opening driving scenes sport a bigger look than most Blumhouse films. Unfortunately, audiences did not have the chance to assess *Curve*'s attributes on the big screen, as (like many recent desert terror sequels) it was released straight to video by parent company Universal.

Blumhouse's sophomore stab at desert terror, *The Darkness* (2016) trades *Curve*'s road games for a suburban take on Native American horror. During a family camping trip to the Grand Canyon, autistic youth Mikey Taylor (David Mazouz) stumbles onto five "ritual stones" inside an underground cavern, which he secretly brings home to Los Angeles. The strange disturbances that follow—bad smells, thuds in the attic, sinister black handprints—are ignored or downplayed by the family, most of whom are too caught up in their own personal dramas: their father, architect Peter (Kevin Bacon) spends all his time at the office, while Mikey's big sister Steph (Lucy Fry) is a secret bulimic. Only the boy's mother, photographer Bronny (Radha Mitchell) takes the spooky phenomena seriously, especially after an unexplained fire breaks out on her son's bedroom. Convinced that "there's something else in this house," Bronny conducts her own online investigation, resulting in the discovery an ancient group of five spirits known as "The Dark Ones," who once plagued the Anasazi Indians before being trapped within a group of ceremonial rocks. Faced with the reality of what their son has brought into their lives, the Taylors must band together—as well as confronting their own personal demons—to combat "The Darkness."

Despite its bigger-name cast, genre-friendly director Greg McLean (*Wolf Creek*) and expansive Grand Canyon opening, *The Darkness* is, in many ways, the lesser of producer Jason Blum's pair of contributions to the desert terror genre. Its desert material is minimal (the opening canyon/cave scenes total less than ten minutes), preferring to remain in a suburban enclave for most of the story. In this way, the film less resembles earlier works like *The Returning* (with which it shares an almost identical first act) than equally house-bound Blumhouse horrors like *Insidious* (2010) and *Sinister* (2012). While there are passing references to Native American folklore and imagery, much of it feels half-baked, and, in many instances, disappointingly old-fashioned. The film's relentless focus on the faceless Dark Ones and their powers veers dangerously into the "evil Indian" territory that was first questioned and subsequently dispelled throughout the '70s. Potentially even more offensive—and ridiculous—is the film's suggestion that autistic children are more likely to possess paranormal abilities. The film goes even further, treating Mikey less like an innocent and more as a willing conduit for evil ("You never talk about the creepy stuff he does," Steph complains early on) as he attacks his grandmother's cat, drones on about "The Sky People," and opens a hellish portal in his bedroom wall. His sudden transformation into a hero toward the end feels not only corny, but noticeably out of line with previous actions.

The film's most intriguing suggestion is that the Taylor family's own dysfunctional past makes them more susceptible to the spirits' attacks. Between Peter's infidelity, Bronny's alcoholism, and Steph's body issues, this family has plenty of "darkness" of its own to contend with before any supernatural assault takes place. More than just turning on water faucets or leaving dirty handprints, the Dark Ones and their manifestations force the Taylors to confront hidden problems (as in Steph's example) or settle long-unresolved conflicts (Peter and Bronny's past transgressions). When Bronny suggests that the phenomena might be "karmic," Peter half-jokingly exclaims, "For what, bad things that we've done?" Perhaps, but rather than skillfully balancing character conflict with ghostly encounters, the film slides further into trite haunted-house clichés, particularly in the excruciating final act, which references everything from *The Amityville Horror* (1979) to *Poltergeist* as the family enlists a pair of spiritual cleansers whose actions lead to a busy yet unconvincing CGI climax. More comfortable in suburbia than the desert, *The Darkness* remains as banal and forgettable as its title.

In 2016, the independents definitively reclaimed the desert terror genre, beginning with one of the most personal, self-reflexive efforts of the new era. "You go out to the desert to find out what you want, what you are," muses burnt-out movie star Tom (Garrett Hedlund), whose crumbling marriage and dead-end business relationships cause him to abruptly leave Los Angeles behind for the untamed deserts of *Mojave* (2016). Tom's self-destructive retreat is interrupted one night by the arrival of chatty but slightly sinister drifter Jack (Oscar Isaac), who dresses like *Dust Devil*'s titular killer and carries a hunting rifle with six notches in the stock. He asks the suspicious Tom a series of probing questions, referring to him as "brother" before going on to ridicule middle-class values and invoking Jesus' temptation by Satan ("Look at where the world is because of solitary dudes going mental in the desert."). When Tom finally asks Jack what he does, Jack's oblique yet ominous response ("I fall upon travelers") presages a violent scuffle, during which Tom knocks his assailant unconscious and takes off with the weapon.

The next day, Tom's predicament worsens considerably when he accidentally shoots and kills a park ranger, a crime witnessed by Jack. After unsuccessfully attempting to eliminate the drifter, Tom arranges the crime scene to frame him for the murder. Upon returning to L.A., Tom attempts to reassume the idle existence which he had tried to escape: a drug and booze-fueled merry-go-round of loveless sex with French actress Milly (Louise Bourgoin), contentious meetings with former coke dealer turned producing partner Norman (Mark Wahlberg, overacting wildly) and shuffling from one vacant residence to another. Jack, himself responsible for a series of murders in Mojave, arrives in Los Angeles and begins stalking Tom and his associates, ostensibly to force the actor to pay for his actions back in the desert. "Do you know which one of us is the bad guy yet?" Jack asks Tom mockingly, but he might as well be asking the audience, and the question hangs in the air even after its violent, discomfiting conclusion.

Like *The Drifter* or *The Returning*, *Mojave* concentrates on the lingering psychic aftereffects of a brief but fateful desert encounter which continue to plague the protagonist upon their return to civilization. The film differs from those earlier thrillers, however, with its even-handed treatment of the two central characters (neither of whom, the film stresses, is necessarily worse than the other), along with its more existential approach to both its desert and city (in this case, Hollywood) material. Though the Mojave Desert lies just an hour north of Los Angeles, the physical proximity between the two places is rarely explored onscreen. *Mojave*'s Oscar-winning writer-director, William Monahan (*The Departed*), however, repeatedly blurs the boundaries separating the twin worlds of Hollywood and The Desert visually and thematically through the crisscrossing paths of the ethically-challenged Tom and Jack, whose shared artistic aspirations—and ability to shrug off cold-blooded murder—make them more similar than different.

Though bookended by desert sequences, the bulk of *Mojave* takes place in Los Angeles, which Monahan depicts, rather than a vibrant, bustling contrast to the desert, as a ghostly netherworld full of empty houses and dying dreams. While the desert terror genre has commented on the entertainment industry since its inception (most recently, in *Twentynine Palms*), none of these films dissect the movie business as thoroughly as *Mojave*, from its deadpan dialog ("You wanna talk, you don't wanna talk, I get fifteen percent all day long," sniffs Tom's alcoholic agent, Walton Goggins) to its grimly amusing details (an eviction notice tacked to the front door of "big shot" Norman's McMansion). Tom is haunted by his own too-early success and fractured family life, with his lack of decent human connections ("Are you still in touch with anybody not useful?" Jack asks

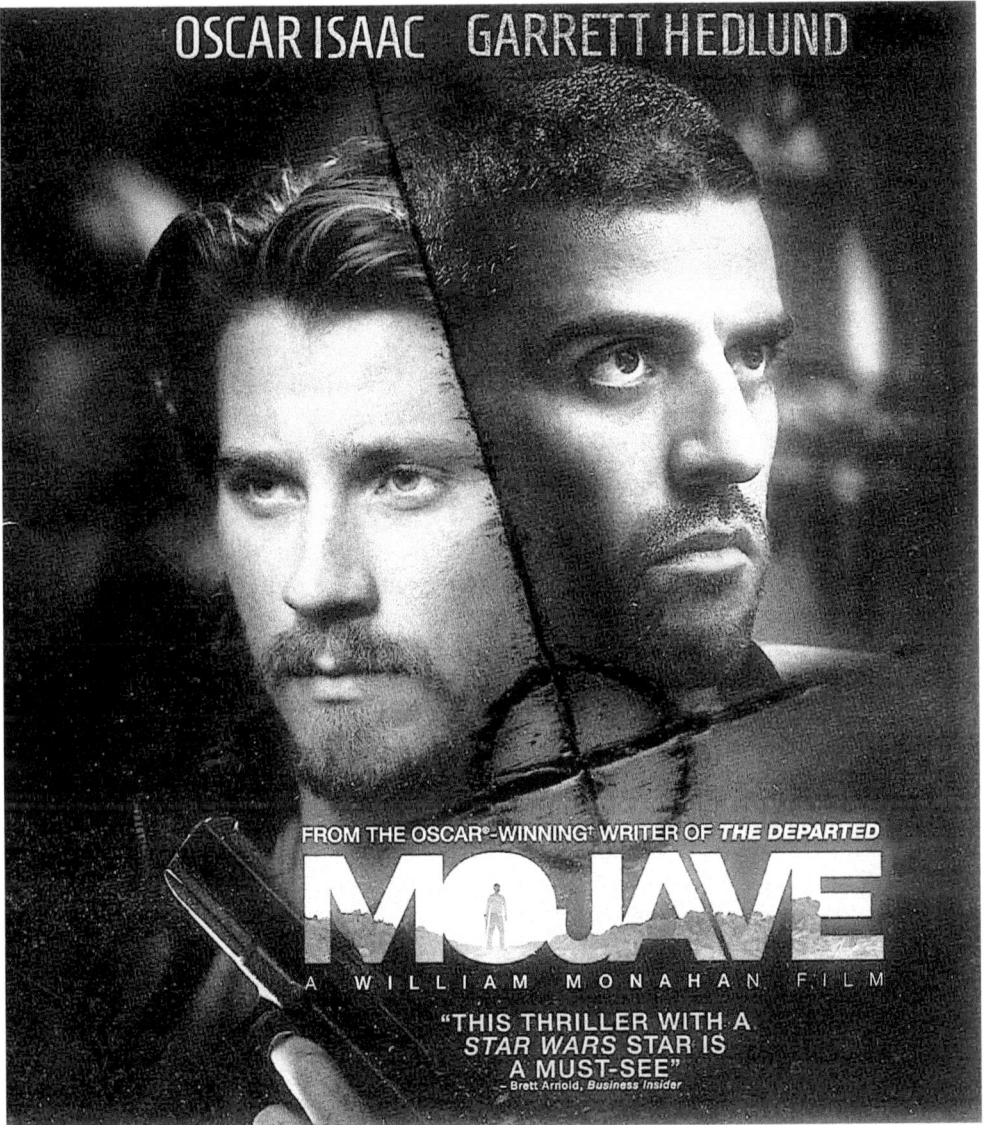

Tom (Garrett Hedlund, left) and Jack (Oscar Isaac) face off in *Mojave* (2016), a modern noir inspired by writer/director William Monahan's personal frustrations with the movie industry.

during their first Hollywood meeting) matched only by his own inability to communicate; when Milly asks what happened in Mojave, Tom merely offers: "There was a situation. I survived. Someone else didn't."

Despite the film's primary emphasis on Tom's L.A. lifestyle, the desert material showcases its strongest visuals and most powerfully dramatic scenes. The Mojave sequences, such as Tom's drunken trek into the desert and, later, his pursuit by Jack, are conveyed in elegantly wordless passages via a succession of starkly beautiful images. The climactic return to the desert adds further layers of detail, as Jack brings Tom to his camp, anchored by an airstream trailer stuffed with books, instruments—and the occasional human skull.

Echoing the manmade junk-worlds of *Far from Home*, *Sonny Boy*, *The Brave* and so many other desert terrors, Jack's habitat is a physical representation of his twisted inner psychology; yet its secondhand clutter, if dripping with menace, still achieves a depth and warmth missing from Tom's gorgeous, but depressingly vacant, Hollywood Hills home. The appropriately hellish finale, which sees Jack's miniature world engulfed in flames, adds an unexpected layer of empathy to the self-destructive themes found throughout the genre, from *The Hitcher* to *White of the Eye* to *Dark Blood*.

Monahan stresses Tom and Jack's duality as his two protagonists travel freely between savagery and civilization, adopting whatever guise or untruth is necessary at the moment. Absurdly rich Tom staggers through the desert like a vagabond, while "ninety-nine percenter" Jack slips into a dead man's designer threads and comfortably plays producer upon his move to L.A. Despite their staggering difference in financial status, the two are ultimately portrayed as two sides of the same coin (appropriately, it's a coin toss that finally settles Jack and Tom's dispute). While it's an interesting idea, the film stumbles a bit when suggesting that a mere twist of fate separates Tom's superstardom from Jack's obscurity. Neither character is fully developed enough for us to know, or even guess, their backstory, with Tom remaining a cipher from beginning till the end, while Jack's assertions about his own dark past are either vague (he attributes his current status to "women and the weather") or untrustworthy ("My mother was a whore"). Most of the time, however, the characters' lack of depth is overcome through Hedlund and Isaac's performances or Monahan's stagy yet strangely compelling dialogue, which makes more direct references to the desert than any other desert terror film in the genre's history.

If overreaching at times (Monahan's script runs heavy on literary allusions, name-checking everyone from Shakespeare to Shaw) and a bit light on action and suspense, *Mojave* is still a better-than-average stab at desert terror noir. Its earnest, pared-down narrative clearly places it in the company of later entries like *Bone Dry* and *Blood River*, while its deadened Hollywood atmosphere and relentless show business satire is not only mordantly funny (when Tom tells Milly he has a stalker, she snaps back, "I have twenty-seven, not counting the ones in jail."), but blends surprising well with the more traditional desert material. In one amusing if improbable moment, Tom watches the legendary desert climax of Von Stroheim's silent masterpiece (and ultimate desert terror progenitor) *Greed* on television. It's a smart reminder that, over sixty years after its humble beginnings, the genre not only hasn't forgotten its roots, but still retains the ability to both honor and transcend them in new and exciting ways.

Afterword: The Road Ahead

"It's fun to kill people. You should try it sometime."—Ray Marcus, *Nocturnal Animals*

The desert terror film has journeyed a long way, down a multitude of occasionally intertwining paths, since its humble grindhouse beginnings in 1963. Over six decades, the genre has weathered shifting public tastes, cinematic trends, studio adoption (and abandonment), and industry upheaval while continuing to adapt and grow in a variety of exciting and unpredictable ways. Along the way, it has generated a number of recognized cult classics (*The Sadist, The Hills Have Eyes, The Hitcher*), successful mainstream franchises (*Tremors, From Dusk Till Dawn, Joy Ride*) and controversial works from major filmmakers (*Natural Born Killers, Lost Highway*). The genre has also provided an artistic playground for first-time directors (*The Drifter, Kalifornia, The Brave*), future Oscar winners (*Duel, Near Dark, Highway to Hell*) and established auteurs looking for fresh ways to engage their audiences (*Gerry, Vampires, 127 Hours*). Perhaps most importantly, it has provided a voice to many unheralded, yet equally significant, talents, whose inspired use of the desert and its denizens has given us brilliant, idiosyncratic American masterpieces like *When You Comin' Back, Red Ryder?, The Oasis, White of the Eye* and *Sonny Boy*. These films, and many others, remain as essential to desert terror's development—and American cinema as a whole—as the better-known, more popular works of Tarantino and Rodriguez.

Desert terror's ability to assimilate such an incredible diversity of tones, storylines, and genres insures that the genre will never become stale or stagnant. If anything, more recent entries over the past year utilize an increasingly personal approach and even more pronounced rejection of genre models and norms. The well-received *Carnage Park* (2016) finds a gorily entertaining spin on the stranded scenario; the existential horror film *Deserted* (2016), which features desert terror vets Lance Henriksen and Jake Busey, takes a more dramatic approach; the desert terror anthology *Southbound* (2016) features a variety of approaches to the genre; Rob Zombie returned to the desert for more bloody mayhem in *31* (2016); and the Alfonso Cuaron–produced *Desierto* (2016) incorporates political elements into its minimalist tale of survival horror at the U.S./Mexico border. Perhaps most intriguing of all are the micro-budget *Desert Cathedral* (2016), an arthouse thriller that mixes genuine found footage recorded in 1992 with dramatic recreations for its disturbing missing-person tale; and Tom Ford's ambitious, Golden Globe–winning *Nocturnal Animals* (2016), which enlists A-list stars (Amy Adams, Jake Gyllenhaal) and stunning imagery to realize another genre first: a desert terror film within a film. Such a wide

Afterword

John Ryder (Rutger Hauer) threatens Jim Halsey (C. Thomas Howell) in the legendary first scene of *The Hitcher* (1986).

range of styles and subject matter prove that the genre, far from being established and repetitive in its patterns, has only begun to scratch the surface of its infinite possibilities.

As new desert terrors arrive in theatres or on video, the genre's complex cinematic legacy continues to be recognized. During the writing of this book, several key titles formerly languishing in VHS limbo—*Sonny Boy*, *Highway to Hell*, *White of the Eye*—received special edition Blu-Ray releases through boutique labels. This is good news for desert terror fans, but many more films (*When You Comin' Back, Red Ryder?*, *The Oasis*, *Raw Courage*, *Blood Frenzy*, *The China Lake Murders*—to name just a few of the more worthy selections) have yet to receive any kind of digital upgrade, while lost films like *Mirage*, *The Brave*, and *Dark Blood* still await a legitimate U.S. release. I hope this book will, at the very least, inspire the reader to unearth those elusive films that spark their interest, and perhaps encourage some enterprising indie labels to grant some of these obscure but deserving movies a legitimate DVD or Blu-Ray release in the future.

Meanwhile, my own dialogue with the desert persists. A few years prior to starting work on *Terror in the Desert*, I returned to the Mojave Desert to direct a segment titled "The Scout" for the horror anthology film *Hi-8: Horror Independent Eight* (2013). Many of the familiar locations I had used on previous films no longer existed, vast junkyards replaced by housing developments and fields of Joshua trees now blighted by massive wind turbines. However, we soon discovered new, even more suitable locations, which only the desert can provide, and the script was subsequently rewritten around these unique, often hidden spots. As happens so often in desert terror films, the awe-inspiring environment took center stage—and brought with it a picturesque yet palpably hostile

Madison (Alexis Codding) and Adrian (Mark Sadr) explore some desert ruins in "The Scout," a segment from the anthology *Hi-8: Horror Independent Eight* (2013).

atmosphere that can't be found anywhere else on earth. No doubt future desert terror filmmakers will be inspired, as I have been, by the desert's menacing beauty.

Now, our cinematic journey comes to an end—or does it? The complex, violent history of the desert terror genre is, in many ways, the history of America; both are still being written. Just as a historian continually uncovers new information which forces them to reevaluate their views, my own (initially limited) perception of the desert terror genre has been consistently challenged and broadened by the many films I've discovered during the process of composing this text. Writing this book has been as much road trip as treasure hunt, with plenty of pit stops along the way to unearth those cinematic "diamonds in the rough." While I've dug up and examined many of these obscure yet significant films, no doubt many more still await discovery off the less-traveled routes of desert terror. Along with those hidden gems, this uniquely mutable and personal genre promises even more challenging works for the next sixty years. For as long as the deserts of the American Southwest exist to inspire, challenge, entrance and terrify audiences and filmmakers, there will be desert terror films.

Appendix: Filmography

Barn of the Naked Dead (1974, Twin World)
Director: Alan Rudolph; Producers: Gerald Cormier, Alan Rudolph; Writer: Roman Valenti, Gerald Cormier; Cast: Andrew Prine (Andre), Manuela Thiess (Simone), Sherry Alberoni (Sheri), Gyl Roland (Corinne)

Bats (1999, Sony)
Director: Louis Morneau; Producers: Brad Jenkel, Louise Rosner; Writer: John Logan; Cast: Lou Diamond Philips (Sheriff Emmett Kimsey), Dina Meyer (Dr. Sheila Casper), Bob Gunton (Dr. Alexander McCabe), Leon (Jimmy Sands)

Beyond the Reach (2015, Roadside Attractions)
Director: Jean-Baptiste Leonetti; Producers: Michael Douglas, Robert Mitas; Writer: Stephen Susco (based on the novel *Deathwatch* by Robb White); Cast: Michael Douglas (John Madec), Jeremy Irvine (Ben), Hanna Mangan Lawrence (Laina), Ronny Cox (Sheriff Robb)

Black Noon (1971, CBS)
Director: Bernard L. Kowalski; Producer: Andrew J. Fenady; Writer: Andrew J. Fenady; Cast: Roy Thinnes (the Rev. John Keyes), Yvette Mimieux (Deliverance), Ray Milland (Caleb Hobbs), Lynn Loring (Lorna)

Blood Frenzy (1987, Hollywood Family Entertainment)
Director: Hal Freeman; Producer: Hal Freeman; Writer: Ted Newsom; Cast: Wendy McDonald (Dr. Barbara Shelley), Tony Montero (Rick Carlson), Lisa Loring (Dory), Lisa Savage (Cassie), Hank Garrett (Dave Ash)

Blood River (2009, Epic Pictures)
Director: Adam Mason; Producers: Timothy Patrick Cavanaugh, Mary Church, Patrick Ewald, Lee Librado, Adam Mason; Writers: Adam Mason, Simon Boyes; Cast: Andrew Howard (Joseph), Tess Panzer (Summer), Ian Duncan (Clark), Sarah Essex (Inn Keeper)

Blood Shack (1971, Shriek Show)
Director: Ray Dennis Steckler; Producers: Carolyn Brandt, Ray Dennis Steckler; Writer: Ron Haydock, Ray Dennis Steckler; Cast: Carolyn Brandt (Carol), Ron Haydock (Tim), Jason Wayne (Daniel), Laurel Spring (Connie)

Bone Dry (2008, Allumination)
Director: Brett A. Hart; Producers: Brett A. Hart, Greg Hughs, John Nolan; Writers: Brett A. Hart, Jeff O'Brien; Cast: Luke Goss (Eddie), Lance Henriksen (Jimmy), Dee Wallace (Joanne), Tommy "Tiny" Lister (Mitch)

Bone Tomahawk (2015, RLJ Entertainment)
Director: S. Craig Zahler; Producers: Jack Heller, Dallas Sonnier; Writer: S. Craig Zahler; Cast: Kurt Russell (Sheriff Hunt), Patrick Wilson (Arthur), Matthew Fox (Brooder), Richard Jenkins (Chicory), Lili Simmons (Samantha)

The Brave (1997, Majestic Film International)
Director: Johnny Depp; Producers: Charles Evans, Jr., Carroll Kemp; Writers: Paul McCudden, Johnny Depp, D.P. Depp (based on novel by Gregory McDonald); Cast: Johnny Depp (Raphael), Elpidia Carrillo (Rita), Marlon Brando (McCarthy), Luis Guzman (Luis), Marshall Bell (Larry)

Breakdown (1997, Paramount)
Director: Jonathan Mostow; Producers: Dino de Laurentiis, Martha de Laurentiis; Writer: Jonathan Mostow, Sam Montgomery; Cast: Kurt Russell (Jeff Taylor), Kathleen Quinlan (Amy Taylor), JT Walsh (Red Barr), M.C. Gainey (Earl), Jack Noseworthy (Billy)

The Burrowers (2008, Lionsgate)
Director: JT Petty; Producers: William Sherak, Jason Shuman; Writer: JT Petty; Cast: William Mapother (Will Parcher), Sean Patrick Thomas, Dough Hutchison (Victor), Karl Geary (Coffey), Clancy Brown (John Clay)

The Canyon (2009, Magnolia)
Director: Richard Harrah; Producer: Mark Williams; Writer: Steve Allrich; Cast: Yvonne Strahovski (Lori Conway), Eion Bailey (Nick Conway), Will Patton (Henry)

The Car (1977, Universal)
Director: Elliot Silverstein; Producers: Elliot Silverstein, Marvin Birdt; Writers: Dennis Shyrack, Michael Butler, Lane Slate; Cast: James Brolin (Wade Parent), Kathleen Lloyd (Lauren), R.G. Armstrong (Amos), John Marley (Everett)

Carnage Road (2000, Brain Damage Films)
Director: Massimiliano Cerchi; Producer: Massimiliano Cerchi; Writers: Massimiliano Cerchi, John Polonia; Cast: Dean Paul (Robert), Molinee Dawn (Linda), Sean Wing (Mike), Melissa Brown (Amy)

China Lake (1983, Kinowelt)
Director: Robert Harmon; Producers: Robert Harmon, Beth Tate; Writer: Robert Harmon; Cast: Charles Napier (Donnelly), William Sanderson (Little Germ), Gilmer McCormick (Helene)

The China Lake Murders (1991, Universal)
Director: Alan Metzger; Producer: William Beaudine, Jr.; Writer: Nevin Schreiner; Cast: Tom Skerritt (Sheriff Sam Brodie), Michael Parks (Officer Donnelly), Nancy Everhard (Cindy), Bill McKinney (Capt. Finney)

Chopper Chicks in Zombietown (1989, Troma)
Director: Dan Hoskins; Producers: Nancy Paloian, Maria Snyder; Writer: Dan Hoskins; Cast: Jamie Rose (Dede), Catherine Carlin (Rox), Don Calfa (Ralph Willum), Billy Bob Thornton (Donny)

The Craving (2008, Brain Damage Films)
Director: Sean Dillon; Producers: Sean Dillon, Jason Kehler, Curtis Krick; Writer: Curtis Krick; Cast: Grayson Berry (Brian), Jesse C. Boyd (Scotty), Wallis Hearst (Diane), Lesley Patterson (Jeannie)

Creepshow 2 (1987, New World Pictures)
Director: Michael Gornick; Producer: David Ball; Writers: George A. Romero, Stephen King (stories); Cast: George Kennedy (Ray Spruce), Dorothy Lamour (Martha Spruce), Frank Salsedo (Ben Whitemoon), Holt McCalleny (Sam Whitemoon), Don Harvey (Andy)

Curse of the Undead (1959, Universal)
Director: Edward Dein; Producer: Joseph Gershenson; Writers: Edward Dein, Mildred Dein; Cast: Eric Fleming (Preacher Dan Young), Michael Pate (Drake Robey/Don Drago Robles), Kathleen Crowley (Dolores Carter)

Curse II: The Bite (1988, Trans World)
Director: Fred Goodwin (Frederico Prosperi); Producer: Ovidio G. Assonitis; Writers: Susan Zalouf, Frederico Prosperi; Cast: Jill Schoelen (Lisa); J. Eddie Peck (Clark), Jamie Farr (Harry Morton), Bo Svenson (Sheriff), Sydney Lassick (George)

Curve (2016, Universal)
Director: Iain Softley; Producers: Jason Blum, Jaume Collet-Serra, Juan Sola, Julie Yorn; Writers: Kimberly Lofstrom Johnson, Lee Patterson; Cast: Julianne Hough (Mallory Rutledge), Teddy Sears (Christian Laughton), Drew Rausch (Deputy)

The Danger Zone (1987, Charter Entertainment)
Director: Henry Vernon; Producers: Tom Friedman, Jason Williams; Writers: Tom Friedman, Karen Levitt, Jason Williams; Cast: Michael Wayne (Moss), Jason Williams (Wade Olson), Robert Canada (Reaper), Suzanne Tara (Heather), Jamie Ferreira (Janice)

Dark Blood (2012, Lionsgate)
Director: George Sluizer; Producer: JoAnne Sellar; Writer: Jim Barton; Cast: River Phoenix (Boy), Jonathan Pryce (Harry Fletcher), Judy Davis (Buffy Fletcher), Karen Black (Motel Woman)

Dark Country (2009, Sony)
Director: Thomas Jane; Producers: Patrick Aiello, Ashok Armitraj; Writer: Tab Murphy;

Cast: Thomas Jane (Dick/Bloodyface), Gina (Lauren German), Ron Perlman (Highway Patrolman)

The Darkness (2016, Universal)
Director: Greg McLean; Producers: Jason Blum, Matthew Kaplan, Bianca Martino; Writers: Greg McLean, Shayne Armstrong, S.P. Krause; Cast: Kevin Bacon (Peter Taylor), Radha Mitchell (Bronny Taylor), David Mazouz (Michael Taylor), Lucy Fry (Stephanie Taylor)

The Day Time Ended (1979, Compass International/Manson)
Director: John "Bud" Cardos; Producer: Steve Neill, Wayne Schmidt; Writers: Wayne Schmidt, J. Larry Carroll, David Schmoeller; Cast: Jim Davis (Grant), Christopher Mitchum (Richard), Dorothy Malone (Ana), Marcy Lafferty (Beth)

Death Valley (1982, Universal)
Director: Dick Richards; Producer: Elliot Kastner; Writer: Richard Rothstein; Cast: Peter Billingsley (Billy), Paul Le Mat (Mike), Catherine Hicks (Sally), Stephen McHattie (Hal), Wilford Brimley (Sheriff)

Death Valley (2008, Allumination)
Directors: Rudi Liden, David Kebo; Producers: Mark Borman, David E. Allen; Writers: Rudi Liden, David Kebo; Cast: Eric Christian Olsen (Josh), Rider Strong (Daniel), Genevieve Cortese (Amber), Bumper Robinson (Anthony), Dash Mihok (Dom)

Delirium (2007, York Entertainment)
Director: Mark Allen; Producers: Fiona Finlayson, Mark Allen; Writer: Mark Allen; Cast: Mike Burnell (Sheriff Speakman), Tallia Cuellar (Lucy), Louie Del Monaco (Kirk), Wren Napier (Reyna)

Desperation (2006, Lionsgate)
Director: Mick Garris; Producer: Kelly Van Horn; Writer: Stephen King (based on his novel); Cast: Tom Skerritt (John Edward Marinville), Steven Weber (Steve Ames), Matt Frewer (Matt Carver), Annabeth Gish (Mary Jackson), Ron Perlman (Collie Entragian)

Detour (1945, PRC)
Director: Edgar G. Ulmer; Producer: Leon Fromkess; Writer: Martin Goldsmith; Cast: Tom Neal (Al Roberts), Ann Savage (Vera), Edmund McDonald (Charles Haskell, Jr.)

Detour (2003, The Asylum)
Director: S. Lee Taylor; Producers: Susan Wright, Steven Grabowsky; Writers: Steven Grabowsky, S. Lee Taylor; Cast: Ashley Elizabeth (Tara), Aaron Buer (Loopz), Danna Brady (Harmony), Brent Taylor (Neil)

The Devil Thumbs a Ride (1947, RKO)
Director: Felix Feist; Producer: Herman Schlom; Writer: Felix Feist (based on the novel by Robert C. DuSoe); Cast: Lawrence Tierney (Steve Morgan), Ted North (Jimmy Ferguson), Nan Leslie (Beulah), Betty Lawford (Agnes)

The Devil's Rejects (2005, Lionsgate)
Director: Rob Zombie; Producers: Mike Elliot, Andy Gould, Marco Mehlitz, Michael Ohoven, Rob Zombie; Writer: Rob Zombie; Cast: Sid Haig (Captain Spaulding), Bill Moseley (Otis), Sherri Moon Zombie (Baby), William Forsythe (Sheriff Wydell) Ken Foree (Charlie Altamont)

Dreamland (2006, Image)
Director: James Lay; Producers: Kenny Saylors, Kyle Saylors; Writer: James Lay; Cast: Jackie Kreisler Megan), Shane Elliott (Dylan), Jonathan Breck (Blake)

The Drifter (1988, Concorde)
Director: Larry Brand; Producer: Ken Stein; Writer: Larry Brand; Cast: Kim Delaney (Julia Robbins), Miles O'Keefe (Trey), Timothy Bottoms (Arthur), Al Shannon (Kriger), Larry Brand (Morrison)

Drifter (2010, Osiris)
Director: Roel Reine; Producer: Roel Reine; Writers: Roel Reine, Michael Rauch; Cast: Cameron Daddo (Martin), Jake (Ryan Alosio), Grace (Darcy Halsey), Gabrielle Dennis (Miranda)

Driven to Kill (1991, PM Entertainment)
Director: John Gazarian; Producer: John Gazarian; Writer: Frank Norwood; Cast: Jake Jacobs (Harry), Michele K. McNeil (Vivian), Chip Campbell (J.R.), Darlene Landau (Mary)

Duel (1971, Universal)
Director: Steven Spielberg; Producer: George Eckstein; Writer: Richard Matheson (based on his short story); Cast: Dennis Weaver (David Mann), Eddie Firestone (Café Owner), Carey Loftin (The Truck Driver)

Dying Room Only (1973, ABC)
Director: Philip Leacock; Producer: Allen

S. Epstein; Writer: Richard Matheson (based on his short story); Cast: Cloris Leachman (Jean Mitchell), Ross Martin (Jim Cutler), Ned Beatty (Tom King), Dabney Coleman (Bob Mitchell)

Eight Legged Freaks (2002, Warner Bros.)
Director: Ellory Elkayem; Producers: Bruce Berman, Dean Devlin; Writers: Ellory Elkayem, Jesse Alexander; Cast: David Arquette (Chris McCormick), Kari Wuhrer (Sheriff Samantha Parker), Scarlett Johansen (Ashley Parker), Doug E. Doug (Harlan Griffith)

Evil Sister II: Bound by Blood (2001, LEO Films)
Director: Brad Sykes; Producer: David Sterling; Writer: Brad Sykes; Cast: Heather Branch (Tam/Lorna), Joseph Haggerty (Frank), Jarrod Robbins (Widow), Jeff Loughridge (Jake), Susannah Devereux (June)

Eye of the Storm (1991, Columbia TriStar)
Director: Yuri Zeltser; Producers: Oliver Eberle, Carsten H.W. Lorenz; Writers: Michael Stewart, Yuri Zeltser, Cast: Craig Sheffer (Ray), Bradley Gregg (Steven), Lara Flynn Boyle (Sandra Gladstone), Dennis Hopper (Marvin Gladstone)

Far from Home (1989, Vestron Pictures)
Director: Meiert Avis; Producer: Donald P. Borchers; Writer: Tommy Lee Wallace; Cast: Drew Barrymore (Joleen Cox), Matt Frewer (Charlie Cox), Richard Masur (Duckett), Andras Jones (Jimmy Reed). Anthony Rapp (Pinky Sears)

Feeding Grounds (2009, Brain Damage Films)
Director: Junior Bonner; Producer: Jamie Gannon; Writers: Alex Ballar, Jamie Gannon; Cast: Alex Ballar (Stephano), Chic Daniel (Rob), Jamie Gannon (Marcus), Kiralee Hayashi (Mary)

Fleshburn (1984, Crown International)
Director: George Gage; Producer: Beth Gage; Writers: George Gage, Beth Gage (based on novel by Brian Garfield); Cast: Steve Kanaly (Dr. Sam McKenzie), Karen Carlson (Shirley Pinter), Malcolm McCalman (Earl), Robert Chimento (Jay), Sonny Landham (Calvin Duggai)

The Forsaken (2001, Sony)
Director: J.S. Cardone; Producers: Scott Einbinder, Carol Kottenbrook; Writer: J.S. Cardone; Cast: Kerr Smith (Sean), Brendan Fehr (Nick), Izabella Miko (Megan), Johnathan Schaech (Kit), Simon Rex (Pen)

From Dusk Till Dawn (1996, Miramax)
Director: Robert Rodriguez; Producers: Gianni Nunnari, Meir Teper; Writer: Quentin Tarantino, from a story by Robert Kurtzman; Cast: George Clooney (Seth Gecko), Quentin Tarantino (Richard Gecko), Harvey Keitel (Jacob Fuller), Juliette Lewis (Kate Fuller), Ernest Liu (Scott Fuller)

From Dusk Till Dawn 2: Texas Blood Money (1999, Dimension)
Director: Scott Spiegel; Producers: Gianni Nunnari, Meir Teper, Michael S. Murphey; Writers: Scott Spiegel, Duane Whitaker; Cast: Robert Patrick (Buck), Bo Hopkins (Sheriff Otis Lawson), Duane Whitaker (Luther), Muse Watson (Niles), Brett Harrelson (Ray Bob)

From Dusk Till Dawn 3: The Hangman's Daughter (2000, Dimension)
Director: P.J. Pesce; Producers: Gianni Nunnari, Meir Teper, Michael S. Murphey; Writers: Alvaro Rodriguez, Robert Rodriguez; Cast: Marco Leonardi (Johnny Madrid), Michael Parks (Ambrose Bierce), Temuera Morrison (The Hangman), Ara Celi (Esmerelda), Sonia Braga (Quixtla)

Gargoyles (1972, CBS)
Director: B.W.L. Norton; Producers: Robert W. Christiansen, Rick Rosenberg; Writers: Steven Karpf, Elinor Karpf; Cast: Cornel Wilde (Dr. Mercer Boley), Jennifer Salt (Diana Boley), Bernie Casey (The Gargoyle), Scott Glenn (James Reeger), Woody Chambliss (Uncle Willie)

Gerry (2003, Miramax)
Director: Gus Van Sant; Producer: Dany Wolf; Writers: Casey Affleck, Matt Damon, Gus Van Sant; Cast: Matt Damon (Gerry), Casey Affleck (Gerry)

The Ghost Dance (1982, Trans World)
Director: Peter F. Buffa; Producer: Robert Sutton; Writer: Peter F. Buffa, Robert Sutton; Cast: Julie Amato (Dr. Kay Foster), Victor Mohica (Tom Eagle), Henry Bal (Nahalla/Aranjo), Frank Salsedo (Ocacio)

Ghost Gunfighter (1995, Mill Creek)
Director: Scott Gulbrandsen; Producers: Chuck Williams, William Burr; Writers: Judy Mathai, Chuck Williams; Cast: Stacie Randall (Heather/Mary/Jessica), Chuck Williams (Shane), Jeff Burr (Pete), Dena Rae Hayess (Marcie)

Ghost Town (1988, New World Home Video)
Director: Richard Governor; Producer: J. Larry Carroll; Writer: Duke Sandefur; Cast: Franc Luz (Langley), Catherine Hickland (Kate), Jimmie F. Skaggs (Devlin), Penelope Windust (Grace), Bruce Glover (Dealer)

Ghosts That Still Walk (1977, VCI Home Video)
Director: James T. Flocker; Producer: Lynn S. Raynor; Writer: James T. Flocker; Cast: Ann Nelson (Alice Douglas), Matt Boston (Mark Douglas), Jerry Jensen (Harold Douglas), Caroline Howe (Ruth Douglas), Dr. Sills (Rita Crafts)

Greed (1924, MGM)
Director: Erich Von Stroheim; Producer: Irving Thalberg; Writers: June Mathis, Erich Von Stroheim (based on the novel McTeague by Frank Norris); Cast: Gibson Gowland (McTeague), Jean Hersholt (Marcus), ZaSu Pitts (Trina)

Grim Prairie Tales (1990, Academy Entertainment)
Director: Wayne Coe; Producer: Richard Hahn; Writer: Wayne Coe; Cast: James Earl Jones (Morrison), Brad Dourif (Farley), William Athertone (Arthur), Lisa Eichhorn (Maureen), Scott Paulin (Martin)

Haunted (1977, VCII Home Entertainment)
Director: Michael A. DeGaetano; Producer: Michael A. DeGaetano, Nicholas P. Nizich; Writer: Michael A. DeGaetano; Cast: Aldo Ray (Andrew McCloan), Virginia Mayo (Michelle), Ann Michele (Abanaki/Jennifer Baines), Jim Negele (Patrick), Brad Rearden (Russell)

Haunted Gold (1932, Warner Bros.)
Director: Mack Wright; Producer: Leon Schlesinger; Writer: Adele Buffington; Cast: John Wayne (John Mason), Joe Ryan (Harry Woods), Sheila Terry (Janet Carter)

Hell's Highway (2002, Brain Damage Films)
Director: Jeff Leroy; Producer: David Sterling; Writer: Jeff Leroy; Cast: Phoebe Dollar (Lucinda), Mark Overholt (Eric), Brittany James (Sarah), Beverly Lynne (Monique), Joseph Haggerty (Preacher)

Hex (1973, Fox)
Director: Leo Garen; Producer: Clark Paylow; Writers: Leo Garen, Stephen Katz; Cast: Keith Carradine (Whizzer), Cristina Raines (Oriole, as Tina Herazo), Scott Glenn (Jimbang), Hilarie Thompson (Acacia), Gary Busey (Giblets)

High Desert (1993, Mill Creek)
Director: Charles T. Lang; Producer: Howard Allen; Writers: Jerry Carroll, Ron Jason; Cast: Edward Glinski (Frank), Alice Davidson (Pam), Ron Jason (Joe), Carla Marrero (Suede)

High Desert Kill (1989, Universal)
Director: Harry Falk; Producers: T.S. Cook, John Epstein; Writer: T.S. Cook; Cast: Anthony Geary (Dr. Jim Cole), Marc Singer (Brad Mueller), Micah Grant (Ray Bettencamp), Chuck Connors (Stan Brown)

Highway to Hell (1991, Hemdale)
Director: Ate de Jong; Producers: John Byers, Mary Ann Page; Writer: Brian Helgeland; Cast: Chad Lowe (Charlie Sykes), Kristy Swanson (Rachel), Patrick Bergin (Beezle), Adam Storke (Royce), Jarrett Lennon (Adam)

The Hills Have Eyes (1977, Vanguard)
Director: Wes Craven; Producer: Peter Locke; Writer: Wes Craven; Cast: Robert Houston (Bobby), Susan Lanier (Brenda Carter), Michael Berryman (Pluto), Martin Speer (Doug Wood), Janus Blythe (Ruby)

The Hills Have Eyes (2006, Fox)
Director: Alexandre Aja; Producers: Wes Craven, Peter Locke, Marianne Maddalena; Writers: Alexandre Aja, Gregory Levasseur; Cast: Ted Levine (Big Bob Carter), Kathleen Quinlan (Ethel Carter), Vinessa Shaw (Linn Carter), Emilie de Ravin (Brenda Carter), Robert Joy (Lizard)

The Hills Have Eyes Part II (1984, Castle Hill)
Director: Wes Craven; Producers: Peter Locke, Barry Cahn; Writer: Wes Craven; Cast: Tamara Stafford (Cass), Kevin Blair (Roy), Janus Blythe (Rachel/Ruby), Michael Berryman (Pluto), John Bloom (The Reaper)

The Hills Have Eyes II (2007, Fox)
Director: Martin Weisz; Producers: Wes Craven, Peter Locke, Marianne Maddalena; Writers: Wes Craven, Jonathan Craven; Cast: Jessica Stroup (Amber), Jacob Vargas (Crank). Michael McMillian (Napoleon), Michael Bailey Smith (Papa Hades)

The Hitch-Hiker (1953, RKO)
Director: Ida Lupino; Producer: Collier Young; Writers: Collier Young, Ida Lupino; Cast: Edmond O'Brien (Roy Collins), Frank Lovejoy (Gilbert Bowen), William Talman (Emmett Myers)

The Hitcher (1986, TriStar)
Director: Robert Harmon; Producers: Kip Ohman, David Bombyk; Writer: Eric Red; Cast: Rutger Hauer (John Ryder), C. Thomas Howell (Jim Halsey), Jennifer Jason Leigh (Nash) Jeffrey DeMunn (Capt. Esteridge)

The Hitcher (2007, Universal)
Director: Dave Meyers; Producers: Michael Bay, Andrew Form, Brad Fuller, Alfred Haber, Charles R. Meeker; Writers: Eric Red, Jake Wade Wall, Eric Bernt; Cast: Sean Bean (John Ryder), Sophia Bush (Grace), Zachary Knighton (Jim Halsey), Neal McDonough (Lt. Esteridge)

The Hitcher II: I've Been Waiting (2002, Universal)
Director: Louis Morneau; Producers: Charles R. Meeker, Kevin M. Kallberg, Alfred Haber, Oliver G. Hess; Writers: Molly Meeker, Charles R. Meeker, Leslie Scharf; Cast: Jake Busey (Jack), Kari Wuhrer (Maggie), C. Thomas Howell (Jim Halsey), Shaun Johnston (Sheriff Castillo)

Hurt (2009, Monterey Media)
Director: Barbara Stepansky; Producers: Eduardo Levy, James Martin; Writers: Alison Lea Bingeman, Barbara Stepansky; Cast: Melora Walters (Helen), William Mapother (Darryl), Johanna Braddy (Lenore), Jackson Rathbone (Conrad), Ava Gaudet (Elise)

Into the Badlands (1991, Universal)
Director: Sam Pillsbury; Producer: Harvey Frand; Writers: Dick Beebe, Marjorie David, Gordon Dawson; Cast: Bruce Dern (T.L. Barston), Mariel Hemingway (Alma Huesser), Helen Hunt (Blossom), Dylan McDermott (McComas), Lisa Pelikan (Sarah Carstairs)

It Came from Outer Space (1953, Universal)
Director: Jack Arnold; Producer: William Alland; Writers: Harry Essex, Ray Bradbury; Cast: Richard Carlson (John Putnam), Barbara Rush (Ellen Fields), Charles Drake (Sheriff Matt Warren), Joe Sawyer (Frank Daylon)

Joy Ride (2001, Fox)
Director: John Dahl; Producers: J.J. Abrams, Chris Moore; Writers: J.J. Abrams, Clay Tarver; Cast: Steve Zahn (Fuller), Paul Walker (Lewis), Leelee Sobieski (Venna), Jessica Bowman (Charlotte)

Joy Ride 2: Dead Ahead (2008, Fox)
Director: Louis Morneau; Producer: Connie Dolphin; Writers: James Robert Johnston, Bennett Yellin; Cast: Nicki Aycox (Melissa), Nick Zano (Bobby), Laura Jordan (Kayla), Kyle Schmid (Nik)

Kalifornia (1993, Gramercy)
Director: Dominic Sena; Producers: Steve Golin, Sigurjon Sighvatsson, Aristides McGarry; Writer: Tim Metcalfe; Cast: Brad Pitt (Early Grayce), Juliette Lewis (Adele Corners), David Duchovny (Brian Kessler), Michelle Forbes (Carrie Laughlin)

Kingdom of the Spiders (1977, Dimension Pictures)
Director: John "Bud" Cardos; Producers: Igo Kantor, Jeffrey M. Sneller; Writers: Richard Robinson, Allen Caillou; Cast: William Shatner (Rack Hansen), Tiffany Bolling (Diane Ashley), Woody Strode (Walter), David McLean (Gene)

Laserblast (1978, The Irwin Yablans Company)
Director: Michael Rae; Producers: Charles Band, J. Larry Carroll; Writers: Franne Schact, Frank Ray Perilli; Cast: Kim Milford (Billy), Cheryl "Rainbeaux" Smith (Kathy), Roddy McDowall (Dr. Mellon), Eddie Deezen (Froggy)

Leatherface: The Texas Chainsaw Massacre III (1990, New Line Cinema)
Director: Jeff Burr; Producer: Robert Engelman; Writer: David J. Schow; Cast: Kate Hodge (Michelle), Ken Foree (Benny), Viggo Mortensen (Tex), Joe Unger (Tinker), R.A. Mihailoff (Leatherface)

Legend of the Phantom Rider (2003, MTI Home Video)
Director: Alex Erkiletian; Producers: Alek

Erkiletian, Hans Rodionoff, Tod Swindell; Writer: Robert McRay; Cast: Denise Crosby (Sarah Jenkins), Robert McRay (Blade/Pelgidium), Stefan Gierasch (Nathan), Angus Scrimm (Preacher)

Life Blood (2010, Lionsgate)
Director: Ron Carlson; Producers: Rachel North, Ron Carlson; Writer: Ron Carlson; Cast: Sophie Monk (Brooke), Anya Lahiri (Rhea), Dan (Patrick Renna), Angela Lindvall (Goddess), Charles Napier (Sheriff)

Lost Highway (1997, October Films)
Director: David Lynch; Producers: Mary Sweeney, Deepak Nayar, Tom Sternberg; Writers: David Lynch, Barry Gifford; Cast: Bill Pullman (Fred Madison), Patricia Arquette (Renee Madison/Alice Wakefield), Balthazar Getty (Pete Dayton), Robert Loggia (Mr. Eddy/Dick Laurent), Robert Blake (Mystery Man)

Mad at the Moon (1994, Republic Pictures)
Director: Martin Donovan; Producers: Matt Devlen, Cassian Elwes, Michael Kastenbaum; Writer: Martin Donovan, Richard Pelusi; Cast: Mary Stuart Masterson (Jenny Hill), Hart Bochner (Miller Brown), Stephen Blake (James Miller), Fionnula Flanagan (Mrs. Hill)

Mad Jack (2001, Vista Street)
Director: Brad Sykes; Producers: Brad Sykes, Jack Wareing; Writer: Brad Sykes; Cast: Jack Wareing (Jack), Angela Ford (Angel), Christopher Rydman (Peter), Mark Overholt (Driver)

Marked Men (aka *Desert Escape*, 1940, PRC)
Director: Sam Newfield; Producer: Sigmund Neufeld; Writer: George Bricker; Cast: Warren Hull (Bill Carver), Isabel Jewell (Linda Harkness), John Dilson (Dr. Harkness), Paul Byar (Joe Mellon)

Mirage (1990, New World Home Video)
Director: Bill Crain; Producers: Bill Crain, Michael Crain; Writers: Bill Crain, Michael Crain, Chuck Hughes; Cast: Jennifer McAllister (Chris), Todd Schaefer (Kyle), Kevin McParland (Trip), B.G. Steers (Villain)

Mojave (2016, A24)
Director: William Monahan; Producers: Aaron L. Ginsburg, William Green, Justin Jones, William Monahan; Writer: William Monahan; Cast: Garrett Hedlund (Tom), Oscar Isaac (Jack), Louise Bourgoin (Milly), Mark Wahlberg (Norman), Walton Goggins (Jim)

The Mummy an' the Armadillo (aka *The Scare Hole*, 2004, Hart Sharp)
Director: J.S. Cardone; Producers: Scott Einbinder, Carol Kottenbrook; Writer: J.S. Cardone (based on his play); Cast: Betty Buckley (Let), Lori Heuring (Billy), Clare Kramer (Sarah), Johnathan Schaech (Jesse), Brad Renfro (Wyatte)

Natas: The Reflection (1986, Avid Home Video)
Director: Jack Dunlap; Producers: Jack Dunlap, Peggy Dunlap; Writer: Jack Dunlap; Cast: Randy Mulkey (Steve), Pat Bolt (Terry), Craig Hensley (Jay), Kelli Kuhn (Angie), Fred Perry (Spec)

Natural Born Killers (1994, Warner Bros.)
Director: Oliver Stone; Producers: Don Murphy, Jane Hamsher, Clayton Townsend; Writers: Quentin Tarantino (story), David Veloz, Richard Rutowski, Oliver Stone (screenplay); Cast: Woody Harrelson (Mickey Knox), Juliette Lewis (Mallory Knox), Tommy Lee Jones (Warden Dwight McClusky), Robert Downey, Jr. (Wayne Gale), Tom Sizemore (Det. Jack Scagnetti)

Nature of the Beast (1995, New Line Cinema)
Director: Victor Salva; Producers: Daniel Grodnik, Robert Snukal, John Tarnoff; Writer: Victor Salva; Cast: Lance Henriksen (Jack Powell), Eric Roberts (Adrian), Brion James (Sheriff Gordon), Eliza Roberts (Patsy)

Near Dark (1987, DEG)
Director: Kathryn Bigelow; Producer: Steven-Charles Jaffe; Writers: Kathryn Bigelow, Eric Red; Cast: Adrian Pasdar (Caleb Colton), Jenny Wright (Mae), Lance Henriksen (Jesse Hooker), Bill Paxton (Severen), Jenette Goldstein (Diamondback)

Night Terror (1977, NBC)
Director: E.W. Swackhamer; Producers: Joel Glickman, Daniel Selznick; Writers: Richard Deneut, Carl Gabler; Cast: Valerie Harper (Carol Turner), Richard Romanus (The Killer), Michael Tolan (Walter Turner)

Nightmares (1984, Universal)
Director: Joseph Sargent; Producer: Chris-

topher Crowe; Writer: Christopher Crowe; Cast: Cristina Raines (Lisa), William Sanderson (Gas station attendant), Lance Henriksen (Macleod), Tony Plana (Father Del Amo), Timothy Scott (Sheriff)

Nightwing (1979, Columbia)
Director: Arthur Hiller; Producer: Martin Ransohoff; Writers: Steve Shagan, Bud Shrake, Martin Cruz Smith (based on the novel *Nightwing* by Smith); Cast: Nick Mancuso (Youngman Duran), David Warner (Philip Payne), Kathryn Harrold (Anne Dillon), Stephen Macht (Walker Chee)

No Man's Land: The Rise of Reeker (2008, Lionsgate)
Director: Dave Payne; Producers: Tina Payne, Dave Payne, Don Dunn; Writer: Dave Payne; Cast: Michael Muhney (Harris), Mircea Monroe (Maya), Desmond Askew (Binky), Stephen Martines (Alex)

The Oasis (aka *A Savage Hunger*, 1984, CBS)
Director: Sparky Greene; Producers: Sparky Greene, Myron Meisel; Writer: Tom Klassen; Cast: Chris Makepeace (Matt), Suzanne Snyder (Jennifer), Scott Hylands (Jake), Richard Cox (Paul), Dori Brenner (Jill)

127 Hours (2010, Fox)
Director: Danny Boyle; Producers: Danny Boyle, Christian Colson, Michael Maker, John Smithson; Writers: Danny Boyle, Simon Beaufoy, based on the book by Aron Ralston; Cast: James Franco (Aron Ralston) Kate Mara (Kristi), Amber Tamblyn (Megan), Treat Williams (Aron's Dad), Clemence Poesy (Rana)

Parasite (1982, Embassy)
Director: Charles Band; Producers: Charles Band, Irwin Yablans; Writers: Alan J. Adler, Paul Shoob, Frank Levering; Cast: Demi Moore (Patricia Welles), Robert Glaudini (Dr. Paul Dean), Luca Bercovici (Ricus), Cherie Currie (Dana), Tom Villard (Zeke)

The Pass (aka *Highway Hitcher*, 1998, York Entertainment)
Director: Kurt Voss; Producers: Ehud Bleiberg, Yitzhak Ginsberg, Samuel Benedict; Writer: Kurt Voss; Cast: William Forsythe (Charles Duprey), James Le Gros (Hunter), Elizabeth Pena (Zeena), Michael McKean (Willie L.), Nancy Allen (Shirely Duprey)

The Petrified Forest (1936, Warner Bros.)
Director: Archie Mayo; Producer: Hal B. Wallis; Writers: Charles Kenyon, Delmer Daves; Cast: Leslie Howard (Alan Squier), Bette Davis (Gabrielle Maple), Humphrey Bogart (Duke Mantee), Charley Grapewin (Gramp Maple), Paul Harvey (Mr. Chisholm)

Phantasm IV: Oblivion (1998, Orion Home Video)
Director: Don Coscarelli; Producer: Don Coscarelli; Writer: Don Coscarelli; Cast: A. Michael Baldwin (Mike), Reggie Bannister (Reggie), Angus Scrimm (The Tall Man/Dr. Jebediah Morningside) Bill Thornbury (Jody)

Phase IV (1974, Paramount)
Director: Saul Bass; Producer: Paul B. Radin; Writer: Mayo Simon; Cast: Nigel Davenport (Dr. Ernest Hubbs), Michael Murphy (James Lesko), Lynne Frederick (Kendra Eldridge), Alan Gifford (Mr. Eldridge)

Poker Run (2009, Phase 4)
Director: Julian Higgins; Producer: Bertie Higgins; Writers: Larry Madill, Bertie Higgins, Julian Higgins; Cast: J.D. Rudometkin (Allen), Bertie Higgins (Robert), Jasmine Waltz (Cheri), Susan (Debra Hopkins), Robert Thorne (Ray)

Prey of the Chameleon (1992, Prism)
Director: Fleming B. Fuller; Producers: Patrick Peach, Ron Rothstein; Writer: Fleming B. Fuller, April Campbell Jones; Cast: Daphne Zuniga (Patricia/Elizabeth Burrows), James Wilder (J.D.), Alexandra Paul (Carrie), Don Harvey (Resnick)

Quicksilver Highway (1997, Fox)
Director: Mick Garris; Producers: Mick Garris, Ron Mitchell; Writer: Mick Garris (based on story by Stephen King); Cast: Raphael Sbarge (Bill Hogan), Silas Mitchell (Bryan Adams)

Rattlers (1976, Boxoffice International)
Director: John McCauley; Producer: John McCauley; Writers: Jerry Golding, John McCauley; Cast: Sam Chew (Dr. Tom Parkinson), Elisabeth Chauvet (Ann Bradley), Dan Priest (Col. Stroud), Ron Gold (Capt. Delaney)

Raw Courage (1984, New World)
Director: Robert L. Rosen; Producer: Ronny Cox; Writer: Mary Cox, Ronny Cox; Cast: Ronny Cox (Pete Canfield), Art Hindle

(Roger), M. Emmet Walsh (Col. Crouse), Tim Maier (Craig)

The Rawhide Terror (1934, Superior)
Directors: Bruce Mitchell, Jack Nelson; Producer: Writer: Jack Nelson Cast: William Barrymore (Jim Brent), Frances Morris (Betty Blake), Tommy Bupp (Jimmy Brent)

Reeker (2007, Paramount Home Video)
Director: Dave Payne; Producers: Dave Payne, Tina Illman, Amanda Klein; Writer: Dave Payne; Cast: Devon Gummersall (Jack), Derek Richardson (Nelson), Tina Illman (Gretchen), Michael Ironside (Henry), Eric Mabius (Radford)

Reservation (2013, Sedona Studios)
Director: Michael A. McGowan; Producer: Sacha Parisot, Kerry Rhodes, Kara Torsney-Weir; Writers: Michael A. McGowan, Kerry Rhodes; Cast: Vyshonn "Silkk The Shocker" Miller (Drez), Ian Chidlaw (Richard), Dylan Diehl (Cindy), Skye P. Marshall (Tawanna)

Riders of the Whistling Skull (1937, Republic)
Director: Mack Wright; Producer: Nat Levine; Writers: Oliver Drake, John Rathmell; Cast: Robert Livingston (Stony Brooke), Ray Corrigan (Tucson Smith), Max Terhune (Lullaby Johnson), Mary Russell (Betty Marsh)

The Road Killers (1994, Artisan)
Director: Deran Serafian; Producers: John Flock, Lance Hool; Writer: Tedi Serafian; Cast: Christopher Lambert (Jack), Craig Sheffer (Cliff), David Arquette (Bobby), Josh Brolin (Tom), Adrienne Shelley (Red)

Route 666 (2001, Lionsgate)
Director: William Wesley; Producers: William Wesley, Terrence M. O'Keefe; Writers: Scott Fivelson, Thomas Weber, William Wesley; Cast: Lou Diamond Philips (Jack La Rocca), Lori Petty (Steph), Steven Williams (Rabbit), Dale Midkiff (P.T.), LQ Jones (Sheriff Conaway)

The Sadist (1963, Fairway International)
Director: James Landis; Producer: L. Steven Snyder; Writer: James Landis; Cast: Arch Hall, Jr. (Charles A. "Charlie" Tibbs), Richard Alden (Ed Styles), Marilyn Manning (Judy Bradshaw), Helen Hovey (Doris Page), Don Russell (Carl Oliver)

Sands of Oblivion (2007, Syfy)
Director: David Flores; Producers: Karen Bailey, Kevin VanHook; Writers: Jeff Coatney, Kevin VanHook; Cast: Morena Baccarin (Alice Carter), Adam Baldwin (Jesse Carter), Victor Webster (Mark), George Kennedy (John Tevis)

Savages (1974, ABC)
Director: Lee H. Katzin; Producers Leonard Goldberg, Aaron Spelling; Writer: William Wood, based on the novel "Deathwatch" by Robb White; Cast: Andy Griffith (Horton Madec), Sam Bottoms (Ben), James Best (Sheriff Hamilton)

Scalps (1983, 21st Century Film Corporation)
Director: Fred Olen Ray; Producer: T.L. Lankford; Writer: Fred Olen Ray; Cast: Jo Ann Robinson (D.J.), Richard Hench (Randy/Black Claw), Roger Maycock (Kershaw), Frank McDonald (Ben)

Seduced by Evil (1994, USA Network)
Director: Tony Wharmby; Producer: Bob Roe; Writer: Bill Svanoe, based on the novel *Brujo* by Jann Arrington Wolcott; Cast: Suzanne Somers (Leigh Lindsay), James B. Sikking (Nick Lindsay), John Vargas (Cerio), Julie Carmen (Rayna)

Silent Tongue (1993, Trimark Pictures)
Director: Sam Shepard; Producers: Ludi Boeken, Carolyn Pfeiffer; Writer: Sam Shepard; Cast: Alan Bates (Eamon McCree), Richard Harris (Prescott Roe), River Phoenix (Talbot Roe), Dermot Mulrony (Reeves McCree), Sheila Tousey (Awbonnie/Ghost)

666: The Demon Child (2006, Silver Nitrate)
Director: Carey Howe; Producer: Cary Howe; Writer: Carey Howe; Cast: Jennifer L. Jackson (Karen), Jose Rosete (Steve), Jennie Epstein (Jackie), David Carchidi (Daryl)

Sonny Boy (1989, Trans World)
Director: Robert Martin Carroll; Producer: Ovidio G. Assonitis; Writer: Graeme Whifler; Cast: David Carradine (Pearl), Paul L. Smith (Slue), Brad Dourif (Weasel), Michael Griffin (Sonny Boy), Sydney Lassick (Charlie P.)

South of Reno (1987, Castle Hill)
Director: Mark Rezyka; Producer: Robert Tinnell; Writers: T.L. Lankford, Mark Rezyka; Cast: Jeffrey Osterhage (Martin Clark), Lisa

Blount (Anette Clark), Joe Estevez (Hector), Lewis Van Bergen (Willard), Bert Remsen (Howard Stone)

Sundown (1989, Vestron Pictures)
Director: Anthony Hickox; Producer: Jefferson Richard; Writers: John Burgess, Anthony Hickox; Cast: David Carradine (Mardulak), Jim Metzler (David), Morgan Brittany (Sarah), Bruce Campbell (Van Helsing), Maxwell Caulfield (Shane)

Survival Run (1979, Film Ventures International)
Director: Larry Spiegel; Producer: Lance Hool; Writers: G.M. Cahill, Frederic Shore, Larry Spiegel; Cast: Peter Graves (Kandaris), Ray Milland (Professor), Vincent Van Patten (Chip), Cosi Costa (Al), Susan Pratt O'Hanlon (Stephanie)

Tarantula (1955, Universal)
Director: Jack Arnold; Producer: William Alland; Writers: Robert M. Fresco, Martin Berkeley; Cast: John Agar (Dr. Matt Hastings), Mara Corday (Stephanie Clayton), Leo G. Carroll (Prof. Gerald Deemer). Nestor Paiva (Sheriff Andrews)

The Terror Within (1989, Concorde Pictures)
Director: Thierry Notz; Producer: Roger Corman; Writer: Thomas M. Cleaver; Cast: Andrew Stevens (David), George Kennedy (Hal), Starr Andreeff (Sue), Terri Treas (Linda)

Them! (1954, Warner Bros.)
Director: Gordon Douglas; Producer: David Weisbart; Writer: Ted Sherdeman, Russell Hughes; Cast: James Whitmore (Sgt. Ben Peterson), Edmund Gwenn (Dr. Harold Medford), Joan Weldon (Dr. Patricia Medford), James Arness (Robert Graham)

Tombstone Canyon (1932, Sono-Art Worldwide)
Director: Alan James; Producers: Samuel Bischoff, Burt Kelly, William Saal; Writer: Claude Rister; Cast: Ken Maynard (Ken), Cecilia Parker (Jenny Lee), Frank Brownlee (Alf Sykes)

Track of the Moon Beast (1976, Cinema Shares)
Director: Dick Ashe; Producer: Ralph Desiderio; Writers: William Finger, Charles Sinclair; Cast: Chase Cordell (Paul Carlson), Donna Leigh Drake (Kathy Nolan), Gregorio Sala (Prof. Salinas), Patrick Wright (Police Captain McCabe)

Tremors (1990, Universal)
Director: Ron Underwood; Producers: Brent Maddock, S.S. Wilson; Writers: S.S. Wilson, Brent Maddock; Cast: Kevin Bacon (Valentine McKee), Fred Ward (Earl Bass), Finn Carter (Rhonda LeBeck), Michael Gross (Burt Gummer), Reba McEntire (Heather Gummer)

Tremors II: Aftershocks (1996, Universal)
Director: S.S. Wilson; Producers: Nancy Roberts, Christopher DeFaria; Writers: Brent Maddock, S.S. Wilson; Cast: Fred Ward (Earl Bass), Helen Shaver (Kate Reilly), Chris Gartin (Grady), Michael Gross (Burt Gummer)

Tremors 3: Back to Perfection (2001, Universal)
Director: Brent Maddock; Producer: Nancy Roberts; Writer: John Whelpley; Cast: Michael Gross (Burt Gummer), Shawn Christian (Desert Jack Sawyer), Susan Chuang (Jodi Chang), Tony Genaro (Miguel)

Tremors 4: The Legend Begins (2004, Universal)
Director: S.S. Wilson; Producer: Nancy Roberts; Writer: Scott Buck; Cast: Michael Gross (Hiram Gummer), Sara Botsford (Christine Lord), Billy Drago (Black Hand Kelly), J.E. Freeman (Old Fred)

Tremors 5: Bloodlines (201, Universal)
Director: Don Michael Paul; Producer: Ogden Gavanski; Writers: Woodrow Truesmith, M.A. Deuce, John Whelpley; Cast: Michael Gross (Burt Gummer), Jamie Kennedy (Travis Welker), Pearl Thusi (Dr. Nandi Montabu), Danile Janks (Erich Van Wyk)

Trip with the Teacher (1972, Crown International)
Director: Earl Barton; Producer: Earl Barton; Writer: Earl Barton; Cast: Zalman King (Al), Brenda Fogarty (Miss Tenny), Cathy Worthington (Julie), Dina Ousley (Bobbie), Robert Gribbin (Jay)

Twentynine Palms (2003, Wellspring)
Director: Bruno Dumont; Producers: Rachid Bouchareb, Jean Brehat; Writer: Bruno

Dumont; Cast: Yekaterina Golubeva (Katia), David Wissak (David)

U-Turn (1997, Tristar)
Director: Oliver Stone; Producers: Dan Halsted, Clayton Townsend; Writer: John Ridley (based on his novel *Stray Dogs*) Cast: Sean Penn (Bobby Cooper), Jennifer Lopez (Grace McKenna), Nick Nolte (Jake McKenna), Billy Bob Thornton (Darrell), Powers Boothe (Sheriff Potter)

Ultraviolet (1992, New Concorde)
Director: Mark Griffiths; Producer: Catherine Cyran; Writer: Gordon Cassidy; Cast: Esai Morales (Nicholas Walker), Patricia Healey (Kristin Halsey), Stephen Meadows (Sam Halsey)

Vampires (1998, Columbia Pictures)
Director: John Carpenter; Producer: Sandy King; Writer: Don Jakoby (based on the novel *Vampire$* by John Steakley); Cast: James Woods (Jack Crow), Daniel Baldwin (Anthony Montoya), Sheryl Lee (Katrina), Thomas Ian Griffith (Jan Valek), Tim Guinee (Father Adam Guiteau)

Vampires: Los Muertos (2002, Sony)
Director: Tommy Lee Wallace; Producer: Jack Lorenz; Writer: Tommy Lee Wallace; Cast: Jon Bon Jovi (Derek Bliss), Cristian de la Fuente (Father Rodrigo), Natasha Wagner (Zoey), Arly Jover (Una), Diego Luna (Sancho)

The Velvet Vampire (1971, New World Pictures)
Director: Stephanie Rothman; Producer: Charles S. Swartz; Writers: Maurice Jules, Charles S. Swartz, Stephanie Rothman; Cast: Michael Blodgett (Lee Ritter), Sherry Miles (Susan Ritter), Celeste Yarnall (Diane LeFanu), Gene Shane (Carl Stoker)

Venom (2013, Vision Films)
Director: Gary Breslin; Producer: Wolf Schmidt; Writer: Joan Canning Boris; Cast: Jessica Morris (Helen Pace), Oliviah Crawford (Lilly), Roberto Sanchez (Viggo)

Victims! (1985, Simitar Video)
Director: Jeff Hathcock; Producer: Jeff Hathcock; Writer: John O'Hara; Cast: Robert Axelrod (Serial Killer #1), Lonny Withers (Serial Killer #2), Phil DeCarlo (Sheriff)

Werewolves on Wheels (1971, The Fanfare Corporation)
Director: Michel Levesque; Producer: Paul Lewis; Writers: David Kaufman, Michel Levesque; Cast: Stephen Oliver (Adam), D.J. Anderson (Helen), Gene Shane (Tarot), Severn Darden (One)

Wheels of Terror (1990, USA Network)
Director: Christopher Cain; Producer: Richard Learman; Writer: Alan B. McElroy; Cast: Joanna Cassidy (Laura), Marcie Leeds (Stephanie), Arlen Dean Snyder (Detective Drummond), Kimberly Duncan (Kimberly)

When You Comin' Back, Red Ryder? (1979, Columbia Pictures)
Director: Milton Katselas; Producer: Marjoe Gortner, Melvin Simon; Writer: Mark Medoff (based on his play); Cast: Marjoe Gortner (Teddy), Candy Clark (Cheryl), Peter Firth (Stephen Ryder), Lee Grant (Clarisse Etheridge), Hal Linden (Richard Etheridge)

Whispers from a Shallow Grave (2006, Tempe Video)
Director: Ted Newsom; Producer: Trudi Keck, Ted Newsom; Writer: Ted Newsom; Cast: Trudi Keck (Linda Sobek), Charles Rathbun (Gerald Brodin), Gewn Bronson (Trudi's Roommate), Michelle Bauer (Rape Victim)

White of the Eye (1988, Palisades Entertainment Group)
Director: Donald Cammell; Producers: Sue Baden-Powell, Cassian Elwes, Brad Wyman, Elliot Kastner; Writers: Donald Cammell, China Cammell, from the novel *Mrs. White* by Andrew and Laurence Klavan; Cast: David Keith (Paul White), Cathy Moriarty (Joan White), Alan Rosenberg (Mike Desantos), Art Evans (Det. Charles Mendoza), Alberta Watson (Ann Mason)

The Wraith (1986, New Century Vista)
Director: Mike Marvin; Producer: John Kemeny; Writer: Mike Marvin; Cast: Charlie Sheen (Jake Kesey/The Wraith), Sherilyn Fenn (Keri), Nick Cassavettes (Packard), Randy Quaid (Sheriff Loomis)

Bibliography

Bauer, Jorg (Dir.). *The Hitcher: How Do These Movies Get Made?* (38 min., color). Germany: Kinowelt Entertainment, 2003.

Bear, Liza. "Bruno Dumont's Lust in the Dust; Talking About 'Twentynine Palms.'" *Indiewire*, April 9, 2004.

Bouzereau, Laurent (Dir.). *Duel: A Conversation with Steven Spielberg* (36 min, color). USA: Universal Studios, 2001.

Edwards, Gavin. *Last Night at the Viper Room: River Phoenix and the Hollywood He Left Behind*. New York: HarperCollins, 2013.

Gettrell, Oliver. "River Phoenix's Final Film to Get U.S. Release After 21-Year Limbo." *Los Angeles Times*, May 16, 2014.

Goldberg, Lesley. "Kevin Bacon to Star in 'Tremors' TV Reboot from Jason Blum." *Hollywood Reporter*, November 24, 2015.

Green, Jack. "The Lost City: Recycling the Past, Regaining the Present." Los Angeles: Hammer Museum, 2016, pp. 1–5. Essay from the exhibition catalog for *Made in L.A.* (June 12 through August 28, 2016).

Hamsher, Jane. *Killer Instinct*. New York: Broadway, 1997.

Isenberg, Noah. *Edgar G. Ulmer: A Filmmaker at the Margins*. Berkeley: University of California Press, 2014.

Jaworzyn, Stefan. *The Texas Chain Saw Massacre Companion*. London: Titan Books, 2003.

Lynch, David, and Barry Gifford. *Lost Highway*. London: Faber & Faber, 1997.

Martin, Perry (Dir.). *Looking Back on the Hills Have Eyes* (55 min., color). USA: Anchor Bay, 2003.

Matheson, Richard. "Duel." In *Duel and Other Horror Stories of the Road*, edited by William Patrick. London: W.H. Allen, 1987.

McDonald, Gregory. *The Brave*. New York: Barricade Books, 1991.

Murphy, Don. "A Murderer in Their Midst." Online: http://www.donmurphy.net/bad5_thebrave.html.

Newman, Kim. *Nightmare Movies*. New York: Harmony Books, 1988.

Norton, B.W.L. Audio commentary for *Gargoyles* DVD. Hen's Tooth, 2000.

Prine, Andrew. On-camera interview for *Barn of the Naked Dead* DVD supplements. Legend House, 2008.

Sargeant, Jack, and Stephanie Watson (Editors). *Lost Highways: An Illustrated History of Road Movies*. London: Creation Books, 1999.

Smith, Martin Cruz. *Nightwing*. New York: W.W. Norton, 1977.

Steakley, John. *Vampires*. New York: Roc Books, 1990.

Steckler, Ray Dennis. On-camera interview for *Blood Shack* DVD supplements. Shriek Show, 2008.

Thrower, Stephen. *Nightmare USA: The Untold Story of the Exploitation Independents*. Surrey, UK: FAB Press, 2007.

U-Turn, DVD liner notes. Sony, 1998.

Umland, Rebecca A., and Samuel J. Umland. *Donald Cammell: A Life on the Wild Side*. Surrey, UK: FAB Press, 2006.

White, Robb. *Deathwatch*. New York: Bantam, 1972.

Williams, Mark. *Road Movies*. New York: Proteus, 1982.

Index

Abrams, J.J. 202
Adams, Amy 279
Adamson, Barry 72
Affleck, Casey 236–238
After Hours 74
After Sundown 235
Agar, John 13–14
Ahlberg, Mac 143, 168
Aja, Alexandre 212, 216–218
Alden, Richard 21, 24
Alexander, Alexis 184
Alias 202
Alien 168
Alien 3 174
Alien Arsenal 166
Aliens 174
Allen, David 166–167
Allen, Heck 145
Allied Artists 20
Alonso, Danielle 219
Alosio, Ryan 261
Altman, Robert 35
Alyn, Kirk 136
Amato, Julie 135–136
The Amazing Colossal Man 14
American International Pictures 20
American Perfekt 69
The Amityville Horror (1979) 275
The Amityville Horror (2005) 219
Anders, Allison 113
Anders, Donna 159
Andreeff, Starr 168
Anguish 60
Anton, Nicole 83
Antonioni, Michelangelo 127, 239
Apacheland Movie Ranch 132–133
Argento, Dario 60
The Argument (short film) 61
Arizona 8, 16, 22, 28, 32, 44, 57–58, 61, 73–74, 80, 109, 122, 132, 140, 143, 152–153, 162–163, 175, 187, 204, 206, 208–209, 215, 228, 231, 233, 236, 243, 248
Arizona Dream 156
Armendariz, Pedro, Jr. 44
Armstrong, Vaughn 170
Arnold, Jack 12, 14, 168
Arnold, Victor 137
Arquette, David 94–95, 208, 270
Arquette, Patricia 69–72

Arredondo, Jeri 150–151
Askew, Desmond 217, 248
Assonitis, Ovidio 65, 169–170
The Asylum 226, 233–235
Attack of the Giant Leeches 127
Avellan, Electra 264
Avis, Meiert 63
Aycox, Nicki 222

Baccarin, Morena 221
Backtrack 68
Bacon, Kevin 172–174, 260, 275
Bad Dreams 68
Badalamenti, Angelo 72
Badlands 109
Bagley, Paul 89
Bailey, Eion 255, 258
Baise-Moi 239
Baja 69, 114
Bal, Henry 135
Baldwin, A. Michael 178
Baldwin, Adam 221
Baldwin, Daniel 193–194
Ballar, Alex 251
Ballen, Tony 163
Band, Charles 106, 143–144, 165–168
Bannister, Reggie 178
Barn of the Naked Dead 2, 28, 31–32, 35, 82, 156, 159, 212, 241
Barnes, Priscilla 212
Barrow, Clyde 23, 136
Barrymore, Drew 61–63, 68
Barton, Earl 36–37
Barton, Jim 267
Basic Instinct 105
Bass, Saul 160–163
Bates, Alan 148, 151
Bats 180–181, 210
Bats: Human Harvest 181
Bauer, Michelle 241
Bay, Michael 219
Bazelli, Bojan 110
Bean, Sean 220–221
The Beast of Yucca Flats 14
Beatty, Ned 32
Beaufoy, Simon 261
Beauty and the Beast 41
Bell, Marshall 153
Benny and Joon 156
Bercovici, Luca 167

Bergin, Patrick 175, 177
Berryman, Michael 3, 39, 41, 50–51, 213
Beyond the Reach 34, 259, 271–273
Bierce, Ambrose 199, 201
Bigelow, Kathryn 103, 185, 184–185, 187
Billingsley, Peter 80–81
Birdsong, Lori 172
Birmingham, Gil 249
Black, Karen 212, 264
Black Day, Blue Night 69, 204
Black Noon 31, 125, 127, 128, 152
Blair, Kevin 50
Blake, Robert 69, 72
Blake, Stephen 148
Blodgett, Michael 183
Blood and Black Lace 60
Blood Feast 20
Blood Frenzy 3, 53–55, 85, 241, 244, 280
Blood River (1991) 193
Blood River (2009) 29, 227, 254–255, 258, 265, 278
Blood Shack 3, 28, 31, 125–127, 133, 137, 157, 159, 192, 206, 212, 221, 227, 231, 243
The Blood-Spattered Bride 183
Bloom, John 52
Blount, Lisa 55
Blue Desert 68–69
Blue Steel 187
Blue Velvet 72
Blum, Jason/Blumhouse 259–260, 274–275
Blythe, Janus 38–39, 50
Bochner, Hart 148
Bogart, Humphrey 14–15
Bogdanovich, Peter 26
Bolling, Tiffany 163, 165
Bolt, Pat 140
Bon Jovi, Jon 206–207
Bone Dry 226, 246–248, 261, 278
Bone Tomahawk 1, 259, 270–271, 273
Bonnie and Clyde 212
Boone, Mark, Jr. 194
Boothe, Powers 73
Border Radio 113
Boston, Matt 131
Botsford, Sara 211

295

Bottoms, Sam 33
Bottoms, Timothy 104
Bourgoin, Louise 276
The Bourne Identity 138
Bower, Tom 216
Bowie, David 69
Boyes, Simon 255
Boyle, Danny 259–261
Boyle, Lara Flynn 68
Boys Don't Cry 105
Bradbury, Ray 12
Braddy, Joanna 251
Braga, Sonia 199
Brain Damage Films 226, 231
Bram Stoker's Dracula 189, 206
Branch, Heather 230–231
Brand, Larry 103
Brando, Marlon 154, 156
Brandon, Michael Robert 248
Brandt, Carolyn 126
The Brave 3, 28, 126, 153–157, 267, 279–280
Breakdown 2, 29, 79, 96–98, 198, 222, 253, 270
Breaking Bad 253
Breathless 28
Breck, Jonathan 245
Brenner, Dori 48
Brenner, Jules 48
Breslin, Gary 268
Brimley, Wilford 81
Bring Me the Head of Alfredo Garcia 147
Brittany, Morgan 188
Brodin, Gerald 241
Brolin, James 119, 165
Brolin, Josh 94
Brown, Clancy 223
Brownrigg, S.F. 241
Brujo 152
Bryar, Paul 16
Buck, Scott 211
Buckley, Betty 240
Buechler, John 143
Buer, Aaron 235
Bundy, Ted 110
Burgess, John 189
Burning Man Festival 159, 194, 248
Burns, Robert 41
Burr, Jeff 66–67, 152
Burr, William 152
The Burrowers 199, 222–225, 270–271
Burum, Stephen 81
Busey, Gary 71, 128
Busey, Jake 209–210, 221, 279
Bush, Sophia 220
Butler, Lucy 71
Butler, William 66
Byrd, Dan 216

Cabin Fever 212
Cain, Christopher 123
Calderon, Wilmer 248
Calfa, Don 170
Calico Ghost Town 132
California 8, 20–21, 28, 32–33, 38, 41–42, 44, 66–67, 73–74, 83, 96, 105, 108–110, 115, 128, 132, 137, 157, 159, 163, 169, 178, 180, 183, 221–222, 231, 248, 252, 262, 274
Cameron, James 187
Cammell, Donald 57, 59–61
Campbell, Bruce 188–189, 196
Campbell, Chip 87
Canada 197–198, 210, 221–223
Canada, Robert 52
The Candy Snatchers 165
Cannes Film Festival 156, 268
The Canyon 2, 28, 227, 255–258, 260–261, 265, 274
Cape Fear 92
The Car 115, 119–123, 165
Carchidi, David 243
Cardone, J.S. 68–69, 76, 168, 204–206, 240–241
Cardos, John "Bud" 165–166
Carillo, Elpidia 153
Carlisle, Steve 64
Carlsbad Caverns 160
Carlson, Karen 140
Carlson, Richard 11
Carlson, Ron 262, 264
Carmen, Julie 152
Carmilla 183
Carnage Park 279
Carnage Road 227–228, 231, 236, 244
Carnival of Souls 20–21
Carpenter, John 192–196, 206, 271
Carpenter, Russell 272
Carradine, David 64–65, 188–189
Carradine, Keith 128
Carroll, Robert Martin 65
Cartel, Michael 184
Carter, Finn 173–174
Carter, James L. 67, 96
Casey, Bernie 160
Cassavettes, Nick 122
Cassidy, Gordon 106
Cassidy, Joanna 123
Castellaneta, Dan 221
Caulfield, Maxwell 188
Celi, Ara 199
Cerchi, Massimiliano 227
Chambliss, Woody 160
Chauvet, Elisabeth 163
Checa, Maria 196
Chediak, Enrique 261
Cherry 2000 177
Chew, Sam 163
Chidlaw, Ian 269
Children Shouldn't Play with Dead Things 142
Chiles, Lois 82
Chimento, Robert 140
China Lake (short film) 85–86, 101, 121, 264
The China Lake Murders 3, 29, 47, 78, 80, 85–87, 172, 190, 280
Choose Me 35
Chopper Chicks in Zombietown 170–171
The Choppers 20
Christian, Shawn 201
Chuang, Susan 201
The Cisco Kid 142
Clark, Candy 44–45
Clark, John 53
Clay Pigeons 77
A Climate for Killing 68
Clooney, George 190–192
Close Encounters of the Third Kind 28, 119, 122, 166
Clownhouse 112
Clutesi, George 134
Cochise, Nino 140
Codding, Alexis 281
Cohen, Leonard 90
Cole, Renee Madison 233
Coleman, Dabney 32
Columbia Pictures 134, 180
Combs, Mike 128
Connell, Anthony 235
Connors, Chuck 170, 172
Convoy 121
Cooder, Ry 156
Cook, Billy 18
Cook, Doria 128
Coppola, Francis Ford 30, 206
Corday, Maria 13–14
Cordell, Chase 131
Cordio, Carlo Maria 65
Corman, Roger 103, 105–106, 168–169, 180, 182, 244
Cormier, Gerald 35
The Corpse Grinders 28
Cortese, Genevieve 249
Coscarelli, Don 178, 180
Costa, Cosie 42
Coughlin, David 237
Cox, Richard 48
Cox, Ronny 81–82
Crafts, Rita 131
Cragg, Nelson 258
The Cramps 185
Crash and Burn 168
Craven, Jonathan 218
Craven, Wes 37–41, 51–52, 209, 216–219
The Craving 248, 251
Crawford, Oliviah 268
Creature from the Black Lagoon 12
Creepshow 142
Creepshow 2 142, 225
Criswell 166
Crockett, Davey 257
Crosby, Denise 235–236
Crowley, Kathleen 10
Crown International 42
Cruz, Raymond 196
Cuaron, Alfonso 279
Currie, Cherie 167–168
The Curse 169
Curse of the Undead 10–11, 143, 188
Curse II: The Bite 65, 169–170, 268
Curve 260, 274–275
Cushing, Peter 112

Daddo, Cameron 261
Dahl, John 68–69, 202–204, 222
Damon, Matt 236–237
Danes, Claire 73
The Danger Zone 52–54
Dangerfield, Rodney 90

Daniels, Jerry 183
Dante, Joe 27
Darden, Severn 159
Dark Blood 3, 28, 152, 259, 264–268, 278, 280
Dark Country 198–199, 224–225
The Dark Half (novel) 216
Dark Harvest 89, 177
Dark Shadows (TV series) 189
The Darkness 260, 275
Daughters of Darkness 183
Davenport, Nigel 162
Davidson, Alice 89
Davidson, Curtis 233
Davidson, James 167
Davis, Bette 14–15
Davis, Jim 166
Davis, Judy 264–265
Dawn of the Dead (2004) 213
Day, Kim 152
The Day Time Ended 143, 158, 166–167
Deadly Weapon 166
Dearden, Brad 132
Death Becomes Her 148
Death Proof 124
Death Valley 8, 30, 50, 80–81 105–106, 178, 184, 227, 237, 246, 248
Death Valley (1982) 42, 78, 80–81, 85, 172, 198, 264
Death Valley (2008) 249–251
Death Valley: The Legend of Bloody Bill 235
Death Wish (novel) 138–139
Deathwatch 33–34, 271–272
Debney, John 148
The Deer Hunter 28
Deezen, Eddie 165
DEG (DeLaurentiis Entertainment Group) 189
DeGaetano, Michael A. 133
De Jong, Ate 175–176
De la Fuente, Cristian 206–207
Delaney, Kim 103
Delirium 243–244, 251
Deliverance 28
Delusion 68
DeMille, Cecil B. 8, 221
Deming, Peter 72
The Departed 276
Depp, D.P. 154
Depp, Johnny 153–157, 267
De Ravin, Emilie 216
Dern, Bruce 145–147
The Descent 219
Desert Cathedral 279
Desert Saints 77
Deserted 279
Desierto 279
Desperation 112, 213–216, 225
Detour (1945) 16–17, 68, 224, 233–234
Detour (2003) 233–235, 236, 244, 249, 251
The Devil Thumbs a Ride 17, 19, 99
The Devil Thumbs a Ride (book) 72
Devil's Den 67

The Devil's Rejects 29, 69, 192, 198–199, 212–213, 223, 233, 248, 251
Devlin, Dean 208–209
El Diablo 192
Dillinger 17
Dillinger, John 15
Dillon, Sean 248
Dimension Films 190, 197
Django 128
Doe, John 114
Dohler, Don 131
Dollar, Phoebe 231, 233
Don Juan DeMarco 156
Donner Party 123, 231
Donovan, Martin 148
Don't Be Afraid of the Dark 160
Don't Go in the House 138
The Doors 48, 101
The Doors (1990 film) 69
Double Indemnity 68
Doug, Doug E. 209
Douglas, Michael 259, 271–273
Dourif, Brad 64–65, 145
Downey, Robert, Jr. 91
Dracula (1931) 133
Drago, Billy 211, 217
Drake, Donna Leigh 130
Dreamland 227, 245–246, 258, 264
Drifter 261–262
The Drifter 99, 103–104, 110, 231, 276, 279
Driven to Kill 87–89
Drop Dead Fred 175
Duchovny, David 108, 110
Duel (1971 film) 29, 31–33, 78, 80, 96, 103, 115–119, 121, 123–124, 127, 159–160, 172, 192, 198, 202, 222, 246, 279
Duel (short story) 115, 117, 119
Dumont, Bruno 236, 238–240
Duncan, Ian 254
Dune 69
Dunlap, Jack 140
Durning, Charles 214
Dust Devil 267, 276
Dying Room Only 3, 29, 31–33, 55, 96, 127, 241, 253, 258

Easterbrook, Leslie 212
Eastwood, Clint 122
Easy Rider 30, 239
EC Comics 142
Edmo, Alexandra 223
Edwards, Gavin 265
Eegah 20, 22
Eight Legged Freaks 198, 208–209
Elcar, Dana 32
Elders, Mickey 52
Elephant 237
Elkayem, Ellory 208
Elliott, Shane 245
Elvira, Mistress of the Dark 141
Emmerich, Roland 208–209
Empire Pictures 143
Engel, Roy 165
Eraserhead 72
Erkiletian, Alex 236
Essex, Sarah 254

Estevez, Joe 55
E.T. 135
Evans, Art 58
Everett, Tom 66–67, 202
Everhard, Nancy 85
The Evil Dead 270
Evil Dead 2 196
Evil Sister II: Bound by Blood 226, 228, 230
Excessive Force 194
Eye of the Storm 2, 28, 31, 68–69

Fade to Black 130
Falk, Harry 172
Fann, Al 169
Far from Home 2, 29, 31, 32, 61–63, 206, 228, 278
Faracy, Stephanie 44
Farnsworth, Richard 175
Farr, Jamie 169
Fat Girl 239
Fatal Attraction 103
Fear in a Handful of Dust 138
Feeding Grounds 251
Fehr, Brendan 204–205
Feist, Felix 17
Feldman, Edward 186
Female Vampire 231
Fenn, Rick 57
Fenn, Sherilyn 122
Filac, Vilko 156
Final Destination 249
Firth, Peter 44
Flanagan, Fionnula 148
Fleming, Eric 10
Fleshburn 28, 125, 138–140
Fletch (novel) 153
The Fog (2005) 217
Fogarty, Brenda 36
Food of the Gods 160
Fool for Love 151
Forbes, Michelle 69, 94, 108, 110
Forbidden World 168
Ford, Angela 230, 232
Ford, Lita 175
Ford, Tom 279
Foree, Ken 66–67, 212
Foreman, Deborah 189
The Forsaken 168, 198, 204–206, 240–241
Forster, Robert 69
Forsythe, William 113–114, 212–213
48 HRS. 140
Fosse, Bob 241
Fox, Matthew 270
Franco, James 259–261
Franco, Jess 231
Frankenstein (1931) 133
Frederick, Lynn 162
Freeman, Hal 53
French, Ed 170
Frewer, Matt 61, 215
Friday the 13th 50, 136, 138, 227
Friday the 13th Part III in 3D 201
Friday the 13th Part VI: Jason Lives 175
Frogs 160
From a Whisper to a Scream 66
From Dusk Till Dawn 1–2, 5, 67,

93, 106, 182, 189–196, 198–199, 201, 204, 206, 212–13, 219, 225, 228, 231, 237, 267, 279
From Dusk Till Dawn (TV series) 192
From Dusk Till Dawn 2: Texas Blood Money 192, 196–197, 201, 228, 273
From Dusk Till Dawn 3: The Hangman's Daughter 192, 197–201, 210–211, 273
Fry, Lucy 275
Fugate, Caril Ann 22, 110
Fulci, Lucio 60, 143, 193

Gage, George 140
Gainey, M.C. 96
Galaxy of Terror 169
Gale, Ed 170
Gammons, John A., III 153
Garfield, Brian 138
Gargoyles 31, 127, 158, 160, 166–167, 169, 182
Garrett, Hank 53
Garris, Mick 112, 213, 215–216
Gartin, Chris 178
Gayheart, Rebecca 199–200
Geary, Anthony 170
Geary, Karl 223
Gein, Ed 110
Genaro, Tony 201
German, Lauren 224
Gerry 227, 236–238, 240, 255, 260, 279
Gersak, Savina 65
Getty, Balthazar 69, 91
Ghazal, Aziz 157
The Ghost Dance 125, 135–137, 152
Ghost Gunfighter 3, 152–153, 227
Ghost Town 2, 125, 143–145, 153, 166, 168
Ghosts That Still Walk 125, 131–132, 142
The Giant Spider Invasion 209
Gidley, Pamela 175
Gifford, Barry 71–73
Gillis, Alec 174, 178
Gish, Annabeth 214
Gladiator 180
Glaudini, Robert 167
Glenn, Scott 160
Glinksi, Edward 89
Glover, Bruce 143
Godard, Jean-Luc 237
Goggins, Walton 276
Goldstein, Jenette 185, 187
Golubeva, Yekaterina 238
The Good, the Bad, and the Ugly 47
Gordon, Lance 39
Gorky Park 134
Gornick, Michael 142
Gortner, Marjoe 44–46
Goss, Luke 246–247
Gottfried, Gilbert 175
Gowland, Gibson 8–9
Graham, C.J. 175–177
The Grand Canyon 227, 255, 258, 275

Grant, Lee 44, 46
Grant, Micah 170
Graves, Peter 42
Greed 4, 8–9, 16–17, 278
Greenberg, Adam 186–187
Greenberg, Sarah 230
Greene, Sparky 49–50
Gregg, Bradley 68
Gribbin, Robert 36
Grieve, Russ 38
Griffin, Michael 64
Griffith, Andy 33
Griffith, Thomas Ian 5, 193–195
Griffiths, Mark 106
Grim Prairie Tales 125–126, 145
Gross, Jerry 26
Gross, Michael 172, 178–179, 201, 211, 273
The Grudge (2004) 272
Gruszynski, Alexander 50, 174
Guadalupe Dunes 8, 221–222
Guinee, Tim 193–194
Gulbrandsen, Scott 152
Gummersall, Devon 244
Gun Crazy 68
Gunton, Bob 180
Guzman, Luis 154, 156
Gyllenhaal, Jake 279

Haboucha, Shane 214
Haggerty, Dan 130
Haggerty, Joe 230–231
Haig, Sid 212, 270
Hail, Mack 227
Hair, Stephen 209
Hall, Arch, Jr. 20–23, 25–27
Hall, Arch, Sr. 20–21, 26, 126
Halloween (1978) 53, 68, 135
Halloween (2007) 264
Halloween III: Season of the Witch 63, 201
Halloween 4 123
Halsey, Darcy 261
Hammer Films 189
Hamsher, Jane 93
The Hand That Rocks the Cradle 252
Hardware 67
Hare, Jim 145
Harmon, Robert 85, 86, 101, 103, 187, 210, 221, 233
Harper, Valerie 80
Harrah, Richard 255, 257–258
Harrelson, Brett 196
Harrelson, Woody 90, 92
Harris, Richard 148–149, 151
Harrold, Kathryn 134
Harryhausen, Ray 166
Hart, Brett A. 246, 248
Harvey, Don 104
The Hateful Eight 271
Hathcock, Jeff 83, 293
Hauer, Rutger 2, 100, 102–103, 210, 220–221, 280
Haunted 125, 132–134, 136, 206, 241, 243, 270
Haunted Gold 8–10, 28, 126
Haunted Ranch 9
Hawkes, John 190

Haydock, Ron 126
Hayek, Salma 190, 192, 199
Hayess, Dena Rae 152
Healy, Patricia 105
Heavy Metal 176
Hedlund, Garrett 276–278
Helgeland, Brian 175
Hell House 115
Hellman, Monte 151
Hellraiser 177
Hell's Highway 2, 226, 231, 233, 251
The Hellstrom Chronicle 162
Hemingway, Mariel 146–147
Hench, Richard 137
Henriksen, Lance 110–111, 121–122, 185, 187–188, 246–247, 279
Henry: Portrait of a Serial Killer 67
Hensley, Craig 142
Hersholt, Jean 8, 9
Herst, Wallis 248
Heschong, Gregg 106
Heuring, Lori 240
Hex 2, 31, 76, 121, 125, 128–130, 134, 151, 157, 198, 223
Hi-8: Horror Independent Eight 280–281
Hickland, Catherine 143
Hickox, Anthony 188–189
Hickox, Douglas 189
Hicks, Catherine 80–81
Higgins, Bertie 252
Higgins, Julian 252
High Desert 3, 80, 89, 227
High Desert Kill 158, 170, 172
High Plains Drifter 122
High Tension 216
Highway to Hell 2, 158, 175–178
Hill, Grady 243
Hill, Jack 184
Hiller, Arthur 134–135, 180
The Hills Have Eyes (1977) 1–3, 28, 31–32, 36–42, 48, 50, 53, 65–66, 78, 106, 109, 177, 192, 198–199, 212–213, 227, 233, 239, 241, 246, 248–249, 255, 279
The Hills Have Eyes (2006) 5, 216–218, 220–221, 225, 233, 248
The Hills Have Eyes II (2007) 218–219, 222
The Hills Have Eyes Part II (1984) 31, 50–52, 66, 138, 209, 219
The Hills Run Red 264
Hillside Cannibals 235
Hindle, Art 81
Hingle, Pat 44
Hiroyuki-Tagawa, Cary 194
Hirschfield, Gerald 121
Hitch-Hike 230
Hitchcock, Alfred 160
The Hitcher 1–2, 6, 29, 32, 35, 47, 50, 55, 78, 85, 87, 92, 99–103, 109, 112, 185–189, 192, 198, 199, 204, 206, 231, 233, 239, 246, 253, 255, 274, 278–280
The Hitcher (2007 remake) 219–221
The Hitcher II 209–210, 220–221
The Hitch-Hiker 9, 17–20, 22, 24, 28, 68, 78, 99, 125, 224, 242

The Hitchhiker (2007) 235
Hitler, Adolf 246
Hiyashi, Kiralee 251
Hodge, Kate 66
Hoffman, Henner 208
Hollywood 17, 21, 72, 93, 106, 127, 132, 133, 142, 153, 157, 178, 198, 221, 262, 264, 267, 271, 276–278
Hollywood Chainsaw Hookers 137
Hooper, Tobe 66–67
Hopkins, Bo 73, 196
Hopkins, Debra 252
Hopper, Dennis 30, 68–69, 133
Hostel 222
Hough, Julianne 274
House of 1,000 Corpses 212
Houston, Robert 38, 50
Hovey, Helen 21
Howard, Andrew 254
Howard, Leslie 14–15
Howe, Cary 243
Howell, C. Thomas 2, 6, 100, 102–103, 209–210, 220, 280
Howell, Caroline 131
Hull, Warren 16
Humanoids from the Deep 169
Hunt, Helen 145–146
Hurt 28, 251–252
The Hurt Locker 185
Hutchison, Doug 223
Hutchison, Galen 223
Hylands, Scott 48

I Am Legend (novel) 115
I Spit on Your Grave 26
Idol, Billy 122
Illman, Tina 244
In Cold Blood 45, 69, 110
In the Mouth of Madness 193
The Incredibly Strange Creatures Who Stopped Living and became Mixed-up Zombies 28
Independence Day 208
Inland Empire 73
Insidious 275
Interview with the Vampire 189
Into the Badlands 28, 126, 145–148, 152, 223
Invaders from Mars 193
Ireland, John 188
Ironside, Michael 244
Irreversible 239
Irvine, Jeremy 271
Isaac, Oscar 276–278
Isham, Mark 100
It Came from Outer Space 7, 11–12, 33, 168, 172
Ivy, Bob 178

Jackson, Jennifer L. 243
Jacobs, Jake 87
Jakoby, Don 193
James, Brittany 233
Jane, Thomas 224–225
Janis, Conrad 64
Janks, Daniel 273
Jason, Ron 89
Jaworzyn, Stefan 66
Jaws 119, 135, 163

Jayne, Robert 201
Jeepers Creepers 112
Jenkins, Richard 270
Jensen, Jerry 131
Jerry Springer (TV show) 239
Jerry's Video Rerun 3
Jesse James Meets Frankenstein's Daughter 158
Jewell, Isabel 16
Jobim, Antonio Carlos 72
Johannson, Scarlett 209
Johnson, Kenneth 83
Johnson, Tor 14
Jones, Andras 61–62
Jones, James Earl 145
Jones, L.Q. 228
Jones, Tommy Lee 91
Jonigkeit, Evan 270
Jordan, Laura 222
Jover, Arly 206–207
Joy, Robert 216
Joy Ride 198, 202–204, 225, 253, 279
Joy Ride 2: Dead Ahead 222–223
Joy Ride 3: Road Kill 223
Jur, Jeff 204

Kalifornia 2, 29, 32, 48, 55, 90, 92, 94, 99, 106, 108–110, 213, 243, 267, 279
Kaminski, Janusz 145
Kanaly, Steve 140
Kaproff, Dana 81, 172
Katselas, Milton 44, 48
Katzin, Lee 33
Kaufman, David 159
Kebo, David 249
Keck, Trudi 241–243
The Keep 221
Keitel, Harvey 190, 192
Keith, David 57, 58
Kelegian, Sylvia 214
Kelley, Chuck 268
Kennedy, George 142, 221
Kennedy, Jamie 114, 273
Kibbe, Gary 193
Kidder, Margot 160
Kieslowski, Krzysztof 148
Kill Me Again 68
Killer Instinct 93
Killer Klowns from Outer Space 50
King, B.B. 44
King, Stephen 112, 142, 213–216
King, Zalman 36
King of New York 110
The Kingdom of the Spiders 29, 158, 163–166, 180, 198, 258
Klassen, Tom 49–50
Klavan, Andrew 61
Klavan, Laurence 61
Klimovsky, Leon 128
Kljakovic, Miljen Kreka 156
KNB EFX 181, 189–190, 194, 208, 211, 216
Knighton, Zach 220
Knife in the Water 28, 230
Kodikian, Raffi 237
Kolden, Scott 166
Koontz, Dean 216

Kowalksi, Bernard 127
Kramer, Clare 240
Kreisler, Jackie 245–246
Krick, Curtis 248
Kuhn, Kelli 142
Kurtzman, Robert 189

L.A. Confidential 175
Lachman, Ed 268
Lafferty, Marcy 166
Lahiri, Anya 262–263
Lambert, Christopher 94
Lamour, Dorothy 142
Landham, Sonny 140
Landis, James 20–22, 26, 28–30
Lang, Charles T. 89
Lanier, Susan 38
Lankford, T.L. 55
Las Vegas 26, 52, 90, 224, 255
Laserblast 143, 158, 165–167
Lassick, Sidney 64–65, 169
Last Days 237
The Last Horror Film 49
The Last House on the Left 37, 39
The Last Movie 133
Last Night at the Viper Room 265
LaVey, Anton 119
Lawford, Betty 17
Lawrence, Hannah Mangan 271
Lay, James P. 246
Leachman, Cloris 32
Leatherface: Texas Chainsaw Massacre III 32, 52, 66–67, 96, 152, 202, 258
Lee, Alexandra 94
Lee, Philip 228
Lee, Sheryl 193–195
Leeds, Marcie 123, 186
LeFanu, J. Sheridan 183
Legend, Johnny 26–27
Legend of the Phantom Rider 235
Legros, James 113–114
Leigh, Jennifer Jason 101
Le Mat, Paul 80–81
The Lemon Grove Kids Meet the Monsters 126
Lennon, Jarrett 175
Lenny 241
Leon 180
Leonardi, Marco 199–200
Leone, Sergio 233
Leonetti, Jean-Baptiste 273
Leroy, Jeff 231, 233
Leslie, Nan 17
Letts, Tracy 241
Levasseur, Gregory 217
Levesque, Michel 159
Levine, Ted 202, 216, 222
Levitt, Joseph Gordon 94
Lewis, Geoffrey 212
Lewis, Juliette 90, 92, 108–110, 190, 192
Lewis & Clark & George 69
Liden, Rudi 249
Lieber, Mimi 58
Life Blood 262–264
Lifeforce 193
Lightning, Cody 153
Linden, Hal 44, 46

Lindenlaub, Karl Walter 69
Lionsgate 213, 223, 268
Liotta, Ray 77
Lisa and the Devil 132
Little House on the Prairie 145
Liu, Ernest 190
Live Evil 235
Lloyd, Kathleen 121
Lo, Ming 211
Locke, Peter 52, 216
Lockhart, Anne 48
Loftin, Lennie 199, 201
Logan, John 180
Loggia, Robert 71–72
The Lone Ranger 156
Lopez, Jennifer 4, 73, 75–76, 293
Loring, Lisa 53
Loring, Lyn 127–128
Los Angeles 2, 12, 16–17, 20, 32, 35–36, 38, 41, 49, 53, 61, 65, 71–72, 85, 87, 103–104, 106, 116, 121, 123, 127, 137, 160, 166–167, 183–184, 204, 228, 233, 238, 244–245, 249, 254, 261, 264, 267–268, 275–276
Lost Highway 1–2, 32, 69–74, 76, 180, 198, 279
Loughridge, Jeff 230
Lovecraft, H.P. 169
Lovejoy, Frank 17–18
The Loveless 187
Lowe, Chad 175, 177
Lucas, George 165
Lucas, Henry Lee 110
Lucretius 246
Luna, Bigas 60
Luna, Diego 206–207
Lupino, Ida 17–19, 22
Luz, Franc 143
Lynch, David 69–73, 225, 251, 262
Lynne, Beverly 231
Lynyrd Skynyrd 212

Macabre 132
MacDonald, Wendy 53
Machete 264
Macht, Stephen 134
Mad at the Moon 148–149, 223
Mad Jack 228, 230, 232
Mad Max 168, 190
Mad Max: Fury Road 102
Maddock, Brent 178, 202, 273
Maier, Tim 82
Makepeace, Chris 48
Malick, Terence 109
Malone, Dorothy 166
The Man Who Cried 156
Mancera, Nicole 153
Mancuso, Nick 134
Manfredini, Harry 50, 138
Manning, Marilyn 22–23
Manson, Charles 91, 159, 172, 184
Manson, Marilyn 72
Mansy, Deborah Anne 172
Mantle, Anthony Dod 261
Mapother, William 223, 252
Mara, Kate 260
El Mariachi 106
Marin, Cheech 190, 192

Marked Men 16, 19
Marley, John 119
Marnhout, Heidi 178
Marrero, Carla 89
Mars Attacks! 209
Marta, Jack 118
Martin, Ross 32
Martin, Strother 135
Martines, Stephen 248
Mason, Adam 254–255
Mason, Nick 57
Massacre Time 143
Masterson, Mary Stuart 148
Masur, Richard 63
Matheson, Richard 32–33, 96, 115–119
Maycock, Roger 137
Maynard, Ken 9
Mayo, Archie 15
Mayo, Virginia 132–133
Mazouz, David 275
McAllister, Jennifer 83
McCabe and Mrs. Miller 28
McCallany, Holt 142
McCalman, Macon 140
McCauley, John 163
McCrary, Darius 206–207
McCudden, Paul 157
McCurdy, Sam 219
McDermott, Dylan 145
McDonald, Christopher 94
McDonald, Gregory 153
McElroy, Alan 123
McEntire, Reba 172
McGowan, Michael 268
McGrory, Matthew 212
McLean, Greg 275
McMilian, Michael 219
McNeil, Michele 87
McParland, Kevin 83
McRyan, Robert 235
McTeague 8
Meadows, Stephen 105
Means, Russell 91
Medoff, Mark 44
Meeker, Charles 186, 209–210
Meryl, Randi 42
Metcalfe, Tim 109
Metzger, Alan 85
Metzger, Michael J. 147
Metzler, Jim 188
Mexico 18, 44, 48, 53, 152, 156, 178, 190, 196, 199, 201, 206, 208, 274, 279
Meyer, Dina 180
Meyer, Russ 170
Meyers, Dave 219–221
Michele, Ann 132
Mickens, Mike 249
Midnight Cowboy 65
Midnight Express 65
Mihailoff, R.A. 52, 66–67
Mihok, Dash 249
Mikels, Ted V. 28
Miko, Izabella 204–205
Miles, Sherry 183
Milford, Kim 165–166
Milland, Ray 42, 127–128
Miller, Dick 63, 228

Miller, Joshua 185–186
Miller, Vyshon 269–270
Mimic 3 223
Mimieux, Yvette 127–128
Mind Ripper 219
Miner's Massacre 235
Mirage 78, 83, 85, 244, 246, 280
Miramax Films 190, 237, 273
Mirror, Mirror 68
Misery (novel) 216
Mr. Ice Cream Man 227
Mitchell, Radha 275
Mitchell, Silas Weir 112
Mitchum, Chris 166
Mohica, Victor 136
Mojave 28, 259, 276–278
Mojave Desert 2, 17, 33, 163, 168, 227, 230, 251–252, 271, 276–277, 280
Monahan, William 276–278
Monk, Sophie 262–264
The Monk and the Hangman's Daughter 199
The Monolith Monsters 14
Monroe, Mircea 248–249
Montero, Tony 53
Monument Valley 30, 91
Moore, Demi 167
Moore, Freddy 167
Morales, Esai 105–106
Moriarty, Cathy 57
Morneau, Louis 180–181, 210, 220, 222
Morocco 197, 218–219, 227
Morricone, Ennio 47, 73, 76
Morris, Jessica 268
Morrison, Temuera 199–201
Mortensen, Viggo 66
Moseley, Bill 212
Mostow, Jonathan 96, 98
Motley Crue 122
Mrs. Parker and the Vicious Circle 35
Muhney, Michael 248
Mulholland Dr. 73
Mulkey, Randy 140
Muller, Marcia 147
Mulroney, Dermot 149–150
The Mummy an' the Armadillo 226, 240–241
Murawski, Bob 231
Murphy, Don 156
Murphy, Michael 162
Musuraca, Nicholas 9, 19

Nance, Jack 72
Napier, Charles 264
Naschy, Paul 128
Natas: The Reflection 125, 140–143, 153, 243
Natural Born Killers 1–2, 29, 48, 69, 72–73, 75, 78, 89–93, 106, 156–157, 192, 198, 208, 212–213, 237, 267, 279
Nature of the Beast 2, 47, 99, 110–112, 114, 253
Neal, Tom 16
Near Dark 2, 29, 103, 182, 185–189, 198, 206, 208, 262, 279

Negele, Jim 132
Nelson, Ann 131
Nevada 1, 11, 28, 35, 55–57, 61, 87, 94, 109–110, 113, 126–127, 172, 201, 211, 215, 227, 245, 254
New Line Cinema 66–67
New Mexico 5, 44, 48, 65, 81–82, 121, 130, 148, 160, 169, 170, 172, 193, 216, 218, 221, 223, 225, 251, 264, 273
Newsom, Ted 53, 241–243
Nicholson, James I. 177
Night of the Living Dead 20–21, 26, 165
Night Terror 78–81, 83, 121, 258
A Nightmare on Elm Street Part 4: The Dream Master 175
Nightmares 115, 121–123, 130, 225
Nightwing 125, 134–135, 180, 198, 258
Niles, Chuck 35
Nine Inch Nails 221
Nitzche, Jack 48
No Man's Land: The Rise of Reeker 69, 248–249
Nocturnal Animals 4, 279
Nolte, Nick 73, 76
Noonan, Tom 208
Norby, Kate 212
Norris, Frank 8
North, Ted 17
Norton, B.W.L. 160
Noseworthy, Jack 96
Nowhere to Run 103

The Oasis 3, 28, 31, 48–50, 174, 246, 255, 261, 274, 279–280
Oates, Joyce Carol 102
O'Bannon, Dan 170
The Objective 219
Oblivion 145
Oblivion 2: Backlash 145
O'Brien, Declan 223
O'Brien, Edmond 18
Occurrence at Owl Creek Bridge, An 199
Ocean's Eleven 236
O'Hanlon, Susan Pratt 42
O'Keefe, Jodi Lynn 241
O'Keefe, Miles 103
Old Tucson Studios 140, 143, 153
Oliver, Stephen 159
Olsen, Eric Christian 249
One Flew Over the Cuckoo's Nest 65
127 Hours 259–261, 274, 279
O'Neal, Griffin 122
Opera 60
Ortiz, Laura 217
Oruche, Phina 204–205
Oshley, Mostea 137
Osterhage, Jeffrey 55
Ousley, Dina 36
Out of the Past 9
Outside Ozona 76, 206
Overholt, Mark 233
Overton, Kelly 214

Palmer, Robert 122
Panzer, Tess 254

Parasite 143, 158, 167–169
Paris, Texas 151
Parker, David 152
Parks, Michael 85, 190, 192, 199–201
Parmet, Phil 223
Pasdar, Adrian 185
The Pass 99, 113–114, 253
The Passenger 239
Pate, Michael 10
Patrick, Robert 196
Patterson, Lesley 248
Patton, Will 257–258
Paul, Alexandra 104
Paul, Dean 227
Paul, Don Michael 273
Paulie, Mike 227
Paulin, Scott 145
Paxton, Bill 185, 187
Payne, Dave 244–245, 249
Peake, Don 52
Peck, J. Eddie 169
Peckinpah, Sam 64, 75
Peeping Tom 58
Pelikan, Lisa 147
Pena, Elizabeth 113
Penn, Sean 4, 36, 73–74, 76
Pepin, Rick 53
Performance 57
Perlman, Ron 214–215, 225
Perry, Fred 142
Pesce, P.J. 201, 211
The Petrified Forest 14–15, 28, 46, 125
Petticoat Planet 145
Petty, JT 223
Petty, Lori 228
Phantasm 178
Phantasm III: Lord of the Dead 178
Phantasm IV: Oblivion 158, 178, 180, 236
Phantasm V: Ravager 180
The Phantom City 9
Phantom of the Range 9
Phantom Town 145
Phase IV 31, 158, 160–162
Philips, Alex, Jr. 44
Philips, Drew 152
Philips, Lou Diamond 180, 228–229
Phoenix 77
Phoenix, Joaquin 73, 75–76
Phoenix, River 148–149, 151–152, 264–266
Piazzoli, Robert D'Ettore 65
Pieces 65
Pilgrim 77
Pillsbury, Sam 148
Pine, Robert 248
Pink Floyd 57, 93
Pirates of the Caribbean 156
Pitt, Brad 106, 108–110
Platinum Dunes 219
Pleasence, Donald 135
PM Entertainment 53, 88
Podell, Rick 48
Poelman, Brian 137
Poison Ivy 252

Poker Run 252–255, 258
Polanski, Roman 230
Poltergeist 167, 275
Pop, Iggy 156
Porter, Robert 36
The Postman Always Rings Twice 68, 87
Powers, Alexandra 64
PRC (Producers Releasing Corporation) 16
Predator 140
Prey of the Chameleon 99, 104–105, 148
Priest, Dan 163
Prince of Darkness 194, 221
Prine, Andrew 35–36
Prutow, Jon 231
Pryce, Jonathan 264
Psycho (1960) 19, 26, 160
Psycho (1998) 236
Pullman, Bill 69–70, 72
Pulp Fiction 148
Pumpkinhead 110
Pyper-Ferguson, John 95

Quaid, Randy 122
Quick 69
The Quick and the Undead 235
Quicksilver Highway 112–113
Quinlan, Kathleen 96–97, 216

Radioactive Dreams 177
Rae, Michael 166
Rahman, A.R. 261
Railsback, Steve 209, 213
Raines, Cristina 121, 123, 128, 130
Ralston, Aron 260–261
Rambaldi, Carlo 135
Rammstein 72
Randall, George 136
Randall, Stacie 152–153
Rapp, Anthony 63
Rashomon 241
Rathbone, Jackson 251
Rathbun, Charles 241, 243
Rattlers 158, 163, 165, 180, 268
Raw Courage 29, 81–82, 169, 249, 280
The Rawhide Terror 9
Ray, Aldo 132–133
Ray, Fred Olen 137
Razorback 272
Re-Animator 143
Rebane, William 209
Rebel Without a Cause 123
Red, Eric 101, 103, 185–187, 220
Red Lights 89
Red River 188
Red Rock West 68, 202
Red Ryder (serial) 45, 47
Red Sands 219
Red Shoe Diaries 36
Reeker 2, 227, 244–246, 248–249, 261
Reine, Roel 261
Remsen, Bert 55
Renfro, Brad 240
Renna, Patrick 262
Republic Pictures 56

Reservation 268–270
Reservoir Dogs 93, 106
The Return of the Living Dead 48, 170
Return of the Living Dead, Part II 50
The Returning 125, 137–138, 152, 275–276
Reznor, Trent 72
Rezyka, Mark 55
Richard III 246
Richards, Dick 81
Richards, Kim 121
Richards, Kyle 121
Richardson, Robert 75, 92
The Riders of the Whistling Skull 10–11, 270
Ridley, John 73, 75–76
RKO Studios 19
The Road Killers 29, 48, 67, 69, 80, 93–96
Roam, Brent 211
Robbins, Jarrod 230–231
Roberts, Eric 110–111
Roberts, Tyleen 89
Robinson, Andrew 145
Robinson, Bumper 249
Robinson, Jo-Ann 136
Robocop 102
A Rock and a Hard Place 260
Rodriguez, Alvaro 199
Rodriguez, Robert 106, 180, 189–190, 192, 196, 199, 201, 212–213, 223, 226, 259, 279
Rollin, Jean 127, 184, 231
Romanus, Richard 80
Romero, George A. 142, 170
Rosales, Thomas, Jr. 194
Rose, Jamie 170
Rosen, Robert 82
Rosenberg, Alan 58
Rosher, Charles 130, 134
Roth, Eli 212
Rothman, Stephanie 183
Route 666 228–229, 264
Route 66 99, 228
Rudolph, Alan 35–36
Rudometkin, J.D. 252
Runaway Nightmare 184
Rush, Barbara 11
Russ, William 82
Russell, Don 21
Russell, Kurt 96–97, 195, 259, 270–271
Russo, Gino 166
Ryan, Natasha 166
Rydman, Christopher 230, 232

Saa, Yvonne 168
Saarinen, Eric 41
The Sadist 1, 4, 20, 21–33, 35–36, 44, 46, 50, 61, 68, 78, 80, 83, 92, 99–100, 106, 109, 119, 126, 158, 163, 189, 192, 198, 212, 239, 242, 251, 253–255, 267, 279; cast 21–22; effect on desert terror genre 28–30; production 20–21; release and reception 26–28
Sadr, Mark 281

Sagan, Carl 166
Sala, Gregorio 131
Salsedo, Frank 136
Salt, Jennifer 160
Salva, Victor 112
San Fernando Valley 8, 42, 52, 71
Sanchez, Roberto 268
Sand Trap 77
Sanderson, William 121, 123
Sands of Oblivion 221–222
Santa Clara Pueblo (NM) 172
Sarafian, Deran 95
Sarafian, Richard 95
Sargent, Joseph 122
Sauvage, Marianne 44
Savage, Ann 16
Savage, Lisa 53
Savages 28, 32–35, 271
Savini, Tom 190, 192
Saw 212, 222, 247
Sbarge, Raphael 112
Scalps 55, 125, 136–137, 269
Schaech, Johnathon 204–205, 240–241
Schell, Maximillian 193
Schmid, Kyle 222
Schmoeller, David 143, 166
Schoelen, Jill 169
Schow, David J. 66
Schreiner, N.D. 85
Scorpion Spring 69
Scorsese, Martin 30
Screaming Mad George 169
Scrimm, Angus 178, 236
The Sea of Trees 237
Seale, John 102
Sears, Teddy 274
Seduced by Evil 152
The Sentinel 130
Shadowzone 168, 206
Shakespeare, William 246, 278
Shane, Gene 159–160
Shannon, Al 104
Shatner, William 163, 165
Shaver, Helen 178
Shaw, Vinessa 216
Sheen, Charlie 122
Sheffer, Craig 68–69, 94
The Sheik 8
Shelley, Adrienne 94–95
Shepard, Sam 148–151
Shepis, Tiffany 233
Sherwood, Robert Emmet 14
The Shooting 151
Shyamalan, M. Night 244
The Silence of the Lambs 91
Silent Night, Deadly Night 145
Silent Tongue 28, 126, 148–152, 157, 271
Silva, Henry 127–128
Silveria, Monica 53
Silverstein, Elliott 119
Simenon, Georges 89
Simmons, Lili 270
Simon, Mayo 162
Simpson, O.J. 92
Sin City 225
Singer, Marc 170, 172
Sinister 275

Sisters 160
666: The Demon Child 226, 243–244
The Sixth Sense 245
Sizemore, Tom 91
Skaggs, Jimmie F. 143
Skerritt, Tom 85, 214
Skotak, Robert 174
Slow Burn 77
Sluizer, George 264–265, 267
Slumdog Millionaire 261
Smith, Cheryl "Rainbeaux" 166, 168
Smith, David 231
Smith, Kerr 204
Smith, Martin Cruz 134–135
Smith, Michael Bailey 216, 219
Smith, Paul L. 64–65
Smokey and the Bandit 121
Snyder, Suzanne 48, 50
Sobek, Linda 241–243
Sobieski, Leelee 202
Softley, Iain 274
Soles, P.J. 213
Somers, Suzanne 152
Son of the Sheik 8
Sonny Boy 2, 5, 28, 64–66, 156, 169, 241, 278–280
Sons of Anarchy 253
Sony 206, 208, 225
South Africa 197–199, 227, 244, 273
South of Reno 28, 31, 55–57, 63, 154
Southbound 279
Spahn Ranch 184
Speer, Martin 38
Spiegel, Larry 42
Spiegel, Scott 196
Spielberg, Steven 28, 115, 118–119, 145, 167
Spiro, Jordana 199
Spring, Laurel 126
Squirm 160
The Stand 216
Stanford, Aaron 216
Stanley, Richard 267
Star 80 110, 241
Star Trek (TV show) 169
Star Wars 165
Starkweather, Charles 22, 46, 109–110
Steadman, John 38
Steakley, John 192
Steckler, Ray Dennis 26, 106, 126–127, 192
Steers, B.G. 83
Stepansky, Barbara 252
Stevens, Andrew 168–169
Stevens, William 160
Stewart, Charlotte 201
Stone, Oliver 4, 69, 73–74, 78, 89, 90, 92–93, 157
Storke, Adam 175
Strahovski, Yvonne 255–256, 258
Strasberg, Susan 137
Stratten, Dorothy 241
Straw Dogs 44, 274
Stray Dogs 73

Strong, Rider 249
Stroup, Jessica 219
The Sugarland Express 119
Sundown 182, 188–189, 243
Survival Run 32, 42–44, 48, 52–53, 82, 89, 249
Susco, Stephen 272
Svenson, Bo 169
Swanson, Kristy 175
Syfy (channel) 160, 181, 210, 221
Sykes, Brad 232

Talman, William 18
Tamblyn, Amber 260
Tangerine Dream 162, 186
Tarantino, Quentin 89, 92–93, 106, 124, 180, 189–192, 196, 201, 212, 223, 226, 239, 259, 279
Tarantula 13–14, 158, 160, 168, 172
Targets 26
Tarver, Clay 204
Taylor, Steve 233
Taylor-Compton, Scout 262, 264
Temple, Lew 212
The Ten Commandments 8, 221
Terminal Island 183
The Terminator 187
Terminator 2: Judgment Day 187
The Terror Within 158, 168–169
Terror Within 2 145, 169
The Texas Chainsaw Massacre (1974) 6, 41–42, 65–67, 212–13, 217, 227
The Texas Chainsaw Massacre (2003) 213, 220
The Texas Chainsaw Massacre Companion 66
The Texas Chainsaw Massacre: The Beginning 219
Theater of Blood 189
Thelma and Louise 75
Them! 11–12, 36, 158, 160, 208
They Live 195
Thiess, Manuela 35
Things Behind the Sun 113
Thinnes, Roy 127–128
31 279
This Mortal Coil 71
Thomas, Henry 214
Thomas, Jeremy 156
Thomerson, Tim 185, 235
Thompson, Elizabeth 121
Thompson, Hilary 128
Thornbury, Bill 180
Thorne, Robert 252
Thornton, Billy Bob 73, 76, 170–171
Thorpe, Alexis 204
3-D process 12, 168, 225
The Thrill Killers 26, 126
Thusi, Pearl 273
Tierney, Lawrence 17
Tilly, Jennifer 63
Titanic 272
Tolan, Michael 80
Tombstone Canyon 9, 11
Too Young to Die 110
El Topo 125, 147
Tourist Trap 6, 41, 143

Tousey, Sheila 148, 151
Track of the Moon Beast 125, 130–131, 157, 243
Trainspotting 261
Trejo, Danny 190, 192, 196, 199–200
Tremors 1, 29, 50, 158, 172–175, 177–178, 198, 201–202, 209, 211, 223, 260, 279
Tremors (2004 TV series) 210–211
Tremors 2: Aftershocks 177–179, 211, 222, 274
Tremors 3: Back to Perfection 198, 201–202, 211, 273
Tremors 4: The Legend Begins 211–212, 223
Tremors 5: Bloodlines 273–274
Trip with the Teacher 36–37, 53, 82, 89
Troma Ent. 170, 206
True Romance 89, 106
20th Century Fox 216, 202, 222–223, 225, 259
Twentynine Palms 227, 236, 238–240, 255, 258, 265, 276
29 Palms 239
The Twilight Zone 74, 116, 244
Twin Peaks 72, 194
Twin Peaks: Fire Walk with Me 72
Two-Lane Blacktop 151
2001: A Space Odyssey 162–163
Tyrell, Susan 61

U-Turn 1–2, 4, 29, 32, 69, 73–76, 93, 198, 215, 258
Ulmer, Edgar G. 16–17, 233
Ultraviolet 2, 99, 105–107
Underwood, Ron 211
Unger, Joe 67
Universal Pictures 9–10, 12–14, 19, 115, 118–119, 121, 133, 172, 188–189, 210–212, 273–274
Urioste, Frank J. 102
Urrea, Luis Alberto 156
Utah 20, 28, 61, 120–121, 137–138, 189, 258, 264

Valetta, Al 184
The Valley of Gwangi 158
Vampire$ (novel) 192
Vampires (1998 film) 5, 182, 192–196, 204, 206, 208, 219, 225, 228, 233, 279
Vampires: Los Muertos 63, 198, 206–208
Vampires: The Turning 208
Van Bergen, Lewis 55
Vandenberg, Sijtske 184
The Vanishing 264
Vanishing Point 95
Van Patten, Vincent 42
Van Sant, Gus 236–238, 260
Vargas, Jacob 219
Vargas, John 152
Vasquez Rocks 137, 169
Vassilieva, Sonia 252
The Velvet Vampire 2, 31, 159, 182–184, 198, 258, 262
Venom (2013) 268–269

Vestron Pictures 189
Victims! 78, 82–84, 137, 239
Vidgeon, Robin 177
Vietnam conflict 44, 48, 53, 83, 248
Villa, Pancho 199
Villard, Tom 167
Vincent, Virginia 38
The Viper Room 264
The Visitor 65
Voight, Jill 36
Voight, John 73
Von Stroheim, Erich 8, 17, 278
Voss, Kurt 113

Wagner, Natasha 71, 206–207
Wahlberg, Mark 276
Wake in Fright 272
Walker, Paul 202
Wallace, Dee 38, 246
Wallace, Tommy Lee 63, 206
Walsh, Gabriel 137
Walsh, J.T. 96–97
Walsh, M. Emmett 82, 189
Walters, Melora 251–252
Walton, Bryce 147
Waltz, Jasmine 252
Wan, James 212
War of the Colossal Beast 14
Ward, Fred 172–174, 178–179
Wareing, Jack 230
Waring, Katie 57
Warner, David 135
Warner Brothers 12, 208–209
Watson, Alberta 58
Watson, Muse 196
Way of the Gun 77
Wayne, Jason 126
Wayne, John 8–9, 48
Weaver, Dennis 116, 118–119
Weaver, Robby 42
Weber, Steven 214
Webster, Victor 221
Werewolves on Wheels 3, 31, 53, 89, 158–160, 182, 198, 221
Wesley, William 228
Wheels of Terror 115, 123–124
When a Stranger Calls (2006) 217
When You Comin' Back, Red Ryder? 29, 31–32, 44–48, 50, 55, 78, 90, 169, 240–241, 254, 279–280
Whifler, Graeme 65
Whispers from a Shallow Grave 226, 241–243
Whitaker, Duane 196
White, Robb 33–34, 272
White of the Eye 2, 29, 31, 32, 57–61, 87, 258, 278–280
White Sands 68
White Zombie (band) 212
Whitesnake 122
Whitworth, James 39
Whyte, Tom 153
Wicar, Tom 153
The Wicker Man 128
Wild at Heart 71–72
The Wild Bunch 125
Wild Guitar 20, 26

Wilder, Cornel 160
Wilder, James 104
Williams, Chuck 152
Williams, Clarence, III 154, 156
Williams, Jason 52
Williams, Steven 228
Williams, Wade 240
Williamson, Fred 190, 192
Wilson, Patrick 270
Wilson, S.S. 178, 202, 211, 273
Winston, Stan 160, 167
Wisell, Jay 252
Wissak, David 238
Wolcott, Jann Arrington 152
Wolf Creek 275
The Wolf Man 131
Wong, Victor 172
Wood, Edward D., Jr. 14
Wood, Oliver 138
Woodburn, Danny 264
Woodruff, Tom 174, 178
Woods, Harry 9
Woods, James 193–195
World Gone Wild 33
Worthington, Cathy 36
The Wraith 115, 122–124, 172
Wright, Jenny 185
Wright, Mack 10
Wrong Turn 223
Wuhrer, Kari 208–210
Wynette, Tammy 45

X 113

Yarnall, Celeste 183
Young, Lee Thompson 219
Young, Wayne 249
Young Guns 123

Zabriskie Point 180, 239
Zahler, S. Craig 270
Zahn, Steve 202
Zandalee 148
Zano, Nick 222
Zeltser, Yuri 68
Zimmerman, Vernon 130
Zombie 193
Zombie, Rob 192, 198, 212–213, 216, 226, 264, 279
Zombie, Sheri Moon 212
Zombie High 157
Zsigmond, Vilmos 22, 25–26, 28, 30, 61, 119, 126
Zuniga, Daphne 104, 148